VOLTAIRE'S REVOLUTION

VOLTAIRE'S REVOLUTION

Writings from His Campaign to
Free Laws from Religion

Edited, Translated, and with an Introduction by

G. K. NOYER

 Prometheus Books

59 John Glenn Drive
Amherst, New York 14228

Published 2015 by Prometheus Books

Cover design by Grace M. Conti-Zilsberger
Cover images © Corbis / Bigstock

Inquiries should be addressed to
Prometheus Books
59 John Glenn Drive
Amherst, New York 14228
VOICE: 716–691–0133
FAX: 716–691–0137
WWW.PROMETHEUSBOOKS.COM

19 18 17 16 15   5 4 3 2 1

Library of Congress Cataloging-in-Publication Data

Voltaire, 1694-1778.
   [Works. Selections. English]
   Voltaire's revolution : writings from his campaign to free laws from religion / edited, translated, and with an introduction by G.K. Noyer/
      pages cm
   Includes bibliographical references and index.
   ISBN 978-1-63388-038-2 (paperback) — ISBN 978-1-63388-039-9 (e-book)
   1. Religion and law. 2. Religion and politics. 3. Religion--Controversial literature. 4. Religious tolerance. 5. Deism. I. Noyer, G. K. (Gail K.), 1953- editor, translator, writer of introduction. II. Title.

B2172.E5 2015
194—dc23

                        2015003741

Printed in the United States of America

For Guy, Gilles, and Clare, with love—
and Karen Henry, for a lifetime of support

CONTENTS

ACKNOWLEDGMENTS

I would like to give my heartfelt thanks to all the real experts who have allowed me to consult them over the years. They include Christiane Mervaud, Patrick Nieirtz, Graham Gargett, Guillaume Metayer, Christine Guyot-Clément, but first and foremost, Bertram E. Schwarzbach, and Professor Emeritus Sylvain Menant, whose kind patience, comments, and suggestions for exploring various topics have been priceless.

INTRODUCTION

René Pomeau, one of the great twentieth-century experts on Voltaire, named the final volume of his biography on him, *On a voulu l'enterrer*— They wanted to bury him.[1] Pomeau was referring to the refusal of the Church to allow burial for Voltaire,[2] but it is a perfect heading for an essay on Voltaire and his legacy in America. Yes, outstanding efforts have been made to bury Voltaire. Why does it matter?

For the past generation or two, when we hear of Voltaire at all in America, it is generally as the author of *Candide*, invariably hailed as his masterpiece. All the rest is *dépassé*, outdated, we are assured, besides perhaps a few other short stories. But much of the civilized world from his day to our own would vehemently disagree. What mattered most about Voltaire is what he wrote in his powerful, and worse, successful, *écrasez-l'infâme* campaign to "crush the infamous" monsters of intolerance and superstition: a tidal wave of books and pamphlets he unleashed to persuade the eighteenth century it was high time to unseat the clergy and religion as the ultimate authorities in everything. This "flood of books and pamphlets," as French Enlightenment philosopher Condorcet, his younger contemporary, called it, was the only way to finally put an end to ten centuries of bloodshed and persecutions over religion. And it did: it ushered in the modern era.

This campaign swept the Western world from America to Budapest,[3] and readers of this selection (or of a very few others still available in English)[4] can now judge for themselves whether they are outdated or not. They would not be alone in finding them as pertinent as every generation has when newly threatened with the forces of tyranny and fanaticism. But even if one's interest is purely historical, these texts and others like them are the reason the era is called the Age of Voltaire, not *Candide*. Considering that important eras had previously been named after emperors like Alexander or Augustus, it would have been very odd indeed to name one after a commoner for the very first time in history thanks to a novella. And just as interesting for Americans, no doubt, will be the point to which well-known quotations from the founding fathers on religion echo certain passages in these texts. They were largely echoed both in their day and ever since, thanks to Voltaire's knack for framing ideas in such a highly memorable way. Once read, they never leave your mind, in the words of the Great Agnostic, Robert Ingersoll.[5]

Our schoolbooks used to note the influence of the French Enlightenment writers on the founding of our nation and our revolutionary new laws, but the names of Voltaire and Montesquieu have nearly vanished in recent years, along with the very word *Enlightenment*. Where it subsists, the word "French," automatically joined to it for two centuries, has completely vanished. We sometimes see an "Enlightenment" evoking only the safer names of Benjamin Franklin, English philosopher John Locke, or Sir Isaac Newton. The battle against the Bible as a basis for law and science never happened, despite thousands of books on the subject throughout the world.[6] The result is that, although many the world over have called America the first embodiment of the Enlightenment's principles,[7] a great many Americans don't know it. And naturally, the total incomprehension of those rights and principles and of our real history has contributed greatly to America's violent polarization over religion—a situation practically unique to our country in the Western hemisphere.

"Christian nation" crusaders have clearly had a hand in these revisions. They make no secret of their determination to do so in myriad books and articles.[8] More amazingly though, even a number of biographies on Voltaire published in America omit any mention of this huge crusade, despite its impact and despite the fact that it consumed the last quarter of his life; rather as though it were feared that any knowledge of the subject might increase the crime rate.

The facts are explained plainly enough, however, in countries where the crime rate is a quarter of ours, at most. "The term Enlightenment underlines the aspiration of these eighteenth-century thinkers to free their contemporaries from superstitions," a tenth-grade French history textbook tells us. "These philosophers, key to the eighteenth century, fought for liberty, tolerance and progress. . . . Voltaire is the symbol through his combat for tolerance."[9] Or as even the *Dictionnaire de Théologie catholique* (the French Dictionary of Catholic Theology) put it: "it was principally through the efforts of Voltaire that the modern world came into being . . . in which the state, *freed from the church* and purely laic, guarantees each citizen the freedom of his person, of thought, of speech, of the press, of *conscience and religion*" (my italics).[10] This phrase, incidentally, sums up the First Amendment to the US Constitution practically verbatim.

"Freedom of his person" meant that we would no longer be tortured, burned, or imprisoned because of our religious beliefs, or lack of them, as we had been throughout the previous ten centuries. This was not only a critical chapter in our own history but a stupendous revolution in thought throughout the Western world. The erasure of that chapter from our school books is, at best, foreboding.[11]

Like many of the key founders in America (despite their being consigned to various churches by conservatives nowadays),[12] Voltaire was a deist. In fact, a huge wave of deism emerged in America during the years of his campaign (roughly 1760 until his death in 1778), which guided the reforms of the next half-century at least. "[D]eism . . . is a dominant note in that interesting epoch," American historian Howard Mumford Jones wrote, "[I]n the future republic, the story of religious and political thought in the eighteenth century is the story of the rising tide of deism. . . . Toleration and rationalism go hand in hand." The error in the popular conception of Puritans, etc., fleeing persecution to set up a new religious order, he added, is that in fact, they came reluctantly, then persecuted others themselves.[13]

To say our founders were all Christians is true, but it omits some very significant details. Birth certificates did not exist, only baptismal records. No marriages were performed, or burials, without the consent of a pastor or a priest; and excommunication deprived you of those rights. So how likely was it that you wouldn't be a Christian? You didn't officially exist otherwise. We only have a civil status—an identity outside the control of a church—today thanks to Enlightenment reforms.

Through Thomas Jefferson's struggles to change these laws, we learn that a person raised a Christian who denied its divine authority lost his civil rights, custody of his children, and could be imprisoned for life in America. Obstinate refusal to recant could earn the death penalty. Quakers had been hanged under the heresy laws, he adds, and church attendance was required every Sunday, barring "lawful excuse of absence."[14] In rural areas especially, education was long impeded by the fact that each sect insisted on having its own school.[15]

As the eminent American Voltairian Norman Torrey put it, Voltaire (and everyone else) was forced to deal with religion every moment of their lives.[16] Automatically born a Catholic in France, Voltaire had to obtain permission from the reigning Calvinists in Geneva to acquire a home there in 1755.[17]

These facts may help us grasp why deism won so many converts. Though often labelled atheists, deists or theists believe in God, just not in religion. Deists consider all sacred books to have been written by fallible human beings not "God," or what they more usually call a "supreme intelligence." This Supreme Being or creator is the reason for the world's existence, but governs it through natural and universal laws, discernible everywhere. Deism especially rejects the notion of any "chosen people" or spokesmen for god on earth.

"A catechist announces god to children and Newton demonstrates him to the wise," Voltaire wrote in the *Philosophical Dictionary* ("Atheist"), adding that there seemed to be fewer atheists than ever in his day, thanks to the growing discoveries of these universal laws in science. In "Theist" he explains that the theist does not flatter himself that he knows how god acts or punishes, but perceives that he does act in all places and all times. All religions contradict each other, he adds, but theism, the simple worship of one god, is the most ancient and widespread belief. Its only rule is to treat others as we would wish to be treated, as Confucius wrote five hundred years before Christ. The very words *theology*—"knowledge of god"—and *metaphysics*—"above nature"—expose the presumption and charlatanism of all antiquity. How can man know what God thinks, or what he is? How can we know anything "above nature?" Voltaire asks in *Dieu et les hommes* ("God and Human Beings"). Religions manifest the secret voice of God, which speaks to all humanity. They should unite and not divide us: hence any religion that belongs to only one people is false.[18] Whether we read Confucius, Jesus, Mahomet, or Cicero, good morals are conveyed everywhere by men who calmly use their reason. "Morals, everywhere the same, come from God. Theology, everywhere different and ridiculous, comes from men. Whoever dares say 'God spoke to me' is a criminal in the eyes of God and men. If God had orders, he would give them to the entire earth"—not in books prone to copying and translation errors.[19]

Author of close to sixty plays, many of them historical, and of another dozen history books, besides countless essays and polemical works, Voltaire spent most of his eighty-four years researching history, philosophy, and religion. He had of course learned the Greek and Roman classics in school, like all those educated in his era, and borrowings from them and from the older Egyptian, Babylonian, and Phoenician nations among whom the biblical Jews lived became apparent while poring through the ancient texts and church fathers. Borrowings from Plato on later Christian dogmas such as "The Word" and the Trinity became evident. The earliest version we have of the New Testament was written in Greek. To paraphrase what Voltaire has a disciple of Confucius tell a holy man, "People have more sense today than you think. Many laugh at your miracles and superstitions, and by making religion ridiculous or immoral, you become guilty of all the vices into which they plunge." (In the *Dictionary* entry "Fraud: Should Pious Frauds be Practiced on the People?")

Atheists dismiss Voltaire for belief in any creator at all, and others charge him with having deprived people of a "personal God." If a personal God can only be the biblical god, perhaps a little self-analysis is in order. Nineteenth century French writer Stendhal voiced the crux of the matter in his classic novel, *The Red and the Black*. His hero, Julien Sorel, is not consoled in prison by "the God of the Bible, a petty despot, cruel and filled with a thirst for vengeance," but by "Voltaire's God: just, good, and infinite." At heart a moralist seeking better morals, the brotherhood of man and our interconnectedness was what Voltaire discovered and promulgated more powerfully than anyone.

He was also hailed as the first "real historian" for his *Essay on Universal History*[20] in 1756—the first world history "liberated from the straitjacket of theology" in the words of Theodore Besterman, founder of the Voltaire Foundation at Oxford.[21] A comparison with its illustrious predecessor, Bossuet's *Histoire Universelle*, demonstrates the point. Bishop Bossuet based his "universal history" primarily on the Bible and on his own visions of God's will, which clearly intended to impose the Catholic faith.[22] With elegant, understated purpose, Voltaire's world history actually includes the rest of the world, not just Christendom. As American historian of philosophy Will Durant wrote, it enraged by taking views of Rome later developed by British historian Edward Gibbon in his *History of the Decline and Fall of the Roman Empire* and by giving China, India, Persia, and their religions "the dimensions geography had given them . . . with the impartiality of a Martian. A vast and novel world was revealed, and every dogma faded into relativity."[23] The conception of modern history dates from that book, wrote British historian John Cruickshank and others.[24]

Though obviously no one causes a revolution of such magnitude alone, Voltaire made himself the most compelling voice of a world grown weary—at last, if not unanimously—of Crusades, Inquisitions, religious wars and massacres, heretic and witch burnings, book burnings, and persecutions. He became "the greatest mental fighter of his age, perhaps of any age" according to free-thought historian, J. M. Robertson, "a 'power-house' not to be matched in human history."[25] The Thirty Years War alone, a clash between Catholic and Protestant states in the previous century that engulfed all Europe from Spain to Sweden, had reached a death toll some estimate at twelve million, razing entire regions and half the male population. Another twelve million "heathens" had been annihilated on the American continent. To drive home the novel concept that heresy is only "the crime of disagreeing with us," as Voltaire did, was crucial.

And he was far from alone. Protests against this state of affairs had been evolving since the Renaissance, as he reminds us in *Letters on Rabelais and Other Writers Accused of Writing against the Christian Religion.* The Protestants had already rejected a certain number of superstitions. Other untenable Judeo-Christian beliefs had been probed most notably by French Protestant philosopher Pierre Bayle, and Jewish Dutch philosopher Baruch Spinoza. A whole wave of English Deists, many of them clergymen, had contested the miracles, prophecies, revelation, and morality of the book said to be the Word of God, a half century before Voltaire launched this all-out campaign. But nothing had changed, as Condorcet explains in his eyewitness account of Voltaire's battle and its effect (included in the Appendix).

As Voltaire lived in England from 1726 to 1729, many have assumed he became a deist there. But he had already been denounced to the French police for a deistic poem written in 1722.[26] Handmade copies of the poem circulated anonymously for fifty years, not only in French, but translated into English, German, Latin, Russian, and Italian, before Voltaire dared include it in his printed works.[27] Entitled *Epître à Uranie* or *Le Pour et Le Contre* (For and Against), it sums up the emotions that obviously inspired the decades of research that followed.

In it, he says that he wishes to penetrate mysteries concerning "the God they announce and the one hidden from us," not as a libertine would but respectfully, for "I want to love God; I seek in him a father, and we are shown a tyrant we should hate." The God they portray, he continues, created us to love pleasure only the better to torment us, in this life and the next. Scarcely has he created us, than he repents and commands the sea to drown us all. To create a purer race? No—a race of brigands and cruel tyrants more wicked than the first, among whom he sends his only son to preach three years, then die in agony to save us. But in vain! We are not saved. So he plunges a hundred nations as far away as America into hell forever, for never having known that a carpenter's son expired on a cross in Syria. Voltaire is unable to recognize the God we should adore in this unworthy image. "I would insult him if I did," he concludes, for he is the creator of *all* men. He ends addressing the creator directly: "If I am not a Christian, it is to love you more."

Voltaire's contemporaries saw him as the era's leading poet, playwright, historian, and *philosophe*. *Candide* was just a footnote. Something akin to 80 percent of his massive output (comprising some ninety volumes, currently being expanded by Oxford) aimed at spreading this broader, less tribal view of "God." The strategy included making the findings of scientists accessible to a broader public, for what Voltaire did learn about in England was Sir Francis Bacon, Newton (from Newton's friend, Dr. Samuel Clarke, no less), and John Locke.

Voltaire was pivotal in spreading understanding of Bacon's empirical method, applied by Newton, throughout Europe by explaining it in French—the international language of the day. The clarity of those works, much more accessible than Newton had been, spurred translations into other languages as well, including English. Voltaire's *Lettres philosophiques* in 1734, usually translated as *Letters on England*, followed by his *Elements of Newton* in 1738, hugely expanded acceptance of Newton's theory of gravity. John Locke's *Essay on Understanding*, another cornerstone of empirical thinking Voltaire made far more widely known, and the relative tolerance he found in England, became his model for years.

Locke had written a *Treatise on Toleration* in the wake of Cromwell and the Thirty Years War, arguing for tolerance in England, but only among Protestant sects toward each other. Catholics and unbelievers were best not tolerated, he felt. Though purportedly attacked by an anti-Catholic mob himself in London,

Voltaire praised what had struck him about English tolerance in slightly different terms. In *Letter* 6, he famously observed that, with one religion, there is danger of despotism; with two, they cut each other's throats; but with thirty or more, they all live in peace. Jews, Muslims, Quakers, and Anglicans all traded peaceably together at the London Stock Exchange, he reported, calling only those who went bankrupt infidels. Decades later, James Madison, the "Father of the American Constitution," liked to cite this passage to illustrate the concept of freedom of beliefs (which didn't save him from having to explain it over and over throughout his time in office).[28]

Letters on England was burned in France as impious and seditious. Voltaire had to flee arrest,[29] but it was a huge international success. Multiple listings of *Voltaire's Letters* in American library and bookseller catalogues probably are referring to *Letters on England*, and in France it set off a veritable vogue for all things English. In his 1914 essay on "Voltaire and England," British writer Lytton Strachey credited the book with planting the first seed of friendship that flourished mightily between France and England after centuries of hostility, and two years after Voltaire's *Letters* appeared, the twenty-four-year-old heir to the Prussian throne began sending fan letters to the forty-two-year-old *philosophe*, initiating what would become a forty-two year correspondence. Frederick the Great, as the young German ruler was later known, declared Voltaire his master in everything, to the astonishment of Europe. When he acceded to the throne in 1740, he immediately abolished torture and censure, granting freedom of beliefs with a line straight out of Voltaire's *Letters on England*: "Here, everyone is free to go to heaven in his own way."[30]

The alliance of Frederick with Voltaire made a big impact in the days of the divine rights of kings. Thanks in part to the highly efficient postal spies of the Old Régime, some of their letters were read aloud in salons and reprinted in gazettes as far away as America. In an attack on American founding father John Adams, Alexander Hamilton called him an ordinary man who dreams himself a Frederick. When Adams came to Paris in 1777 to help Benjamin Franklin obtain military aid for the American Revolution, he was amazed to discover that Franklin was as famous there as Frederick and Voltaire.[31] Frederick dabbled in composing poetry and music, and we find some of America's budding poets writing verses they attributed to Voltaire or Frederick, in imitation of those they sent each other. Frederick became the archetype of the "enlightened monarch" thanks to Voltaire, later imitated by other monarchs such as Catherine the Great of Russia or King Christian VII of Denmark.[32]

But as to be expected, the perennial foes of these reforms have also been prolific in myths and malicious tales about Voltaire and his "royal pupil" over the ages. What mattered to the eighteenth century about them has been well-nigh lost in a "welter of anecdotes"[33] over various clashes they had. Their conflicts were mostly related to Frederick's wars and to Voltaire's refusal to make a permanent move to Berlin for fifteen years because it would have meant abandoning Madame du Châtelet, a brilliant Newtonian and the love of his life. After her unexpected death at the age of forty-three, he finally did move to Berlin in 1750, but resentments and misunderstandings slowly built to a spectacular blowout over a satire Voltaire wrote on the president of Frederick's academy, lampooning some of the president's machinations against colleagues and himself. Frederick ordered a public burning of the satire and had Voltaire arrested—again, to the astonishment of all Europe.

A complex story to begin with, the rise of nationalism in the nineteenth century spilled oceans of ink seeking to blame only the Frenchman or the German for everything that went wrong between them. Most of the tales were based on gossip gleaned from servants or diplomats not privy to the facts, as contemporary historian Christiane Mervaud's masterly study illustrated.[34] Some bitter *Memoirs* Voltaire later burned and a rewriting of some letters to his niece with an epistolary novel in mind (in the vein of De Laclos' *Dangerous Liaisons* or Richardson's *Pamela*) were conserved by his niece and passed into his real correspondence for two centuries, adding to the confusion. André Magnan only disentangled Voltaire's real letters from those intended for the novel in 1986,[35] along with a wealth of other fascinating unknown incidents still strangely not incorporated in recent biographies.

And yet, what really mattered about these two was not lost on the eighteenth century. Two things rise to the fore.

The status of writers, and common men, was one of them, for Frederick's ill treatment of Voltaire was not as universally applauded as an autocrat might have expected at the time. Invitations poured in for Voltaire from other German rulers offering protection, and from the Empress of Russia a few years later. Writers, when not aristocrats themselves like a Lord Bolingbroke or a Baron Montesquieu, had previously been viewed as little more than servants. They survived chiefly on pensions awarded by wealthy patrons. This had been the case of Molière and Racine under the previous French king. Copyright did not exist. Book piracies were rampant. Performances of their plays at courts engendered no ticket sales to live on, and it was mostly a losing battle to obtain one's fair share of the profits from both the regular theaters and publishers. Voltaire made himself financially independent early on through astute investments, to avoid the poverty and toadying all this guaranteed. But Frederick's moving letters extolling Voltaire's genius, talents, and humanity as of far greater worth than birth and rank had also had their effect. It inspired and emboldened a great many.

Their joined forces against the stranglehold of religion also mattered greatly, as we have seen, and they both knew it. It was Voltaire's principal reproach to Frederick after their blowout in Berlin.[36] What to do about religious tyranny is a constant in their letters from the start, and the deepest bond they shared until the very end. Frederick's *Eulogy of Voltaire* in the Appendix ends on this note. And though omitted from numerous biographies, it has been well known since at least the early nineteenth century that Voltaire began his *Philosophical Dictionary* in Berlin with king's collusion. His *Defense of Milord Bolingbroke* was issued there. The deadlier *Sermon of the Fifty* first appeared there too, and may have germinated with Frederick's discovery of an isolated community of deists during one of his battles. It was even Fredrick's banter about *l'infâme* that evolved into Voltaire's *écrasez-l'infâme* slogan in 1759,[37] for even if their biographers did not reconcile, they eventually did.

Not all these details were known to the public, but their stance most certainly was. American founding father John Adams often linked their names together on the subject. It is primarily the burying or ignoring of these great religious issues that reduced them both to caricatures in so many later works. Voltaire becomes a "vain and greedy courtier," for why else would he have gone to Berlin?[38]

If royal pensions and the ego-boost of hobnobbing with royalty were what interested Voltaire, however, he certainly had lots of options when he left Berlin. Instead, he hunted for a safer harbor, to get straight back to work. And soon after he settled, first in Geneva, then in Ferney on the French-Swiss border in 1759, the *ecr l'inf* pamphlets—as he called them in abbreviation—began appearing in increasing levels of militancy as continuing persecutions came to light, as did books: the *Treatise on Tolerance* in 1763; the *Philosophical Dictionary* in 1764; *Lord Bolingbroke's Important Examination* in 1767 (the most ferocious); and *God and Human Beings (Dieu et les hommes)* in 1769.

Voltaire had gone to Berlin in 1750 for protection and the freedom to work in peace at last. He told Frederick as early as 1739 that he feared losing his freedom or his life every week thanks to anonymous letters denouncing him, defamatory libels and scandalous writings penned by enemies who then attributed them to him.[39] This was no feverish imagining on his part, as some have claimed. Not only was he himself imprisoned twice, exiled, forced to flee then recant, long lists of other victims have been compiled, from Bishop Warburton in England to the French "Father of Natural History" Buffon, for his theories on geology. Writers didn't even sign cookbooks for fear of saying something untoward. A simple glance through original eighteenth-century printings shows most of them unsigned.[40]

And protection was what Frederick had proposed from the very beginning without being asked, and what he promised repeatedly. Twentieth-century French philosopher Roland Barthes called Voltaire "The Last Happy Writer" because the time was ripe, he said, for what he accomplished and there were men in power who supported him. There were indeed, along with many who were not in power, but depictions of Voltaire battling imaginary foes like a Don Quixote are ill informed at best.[41] Beyond the many victims Voltaire championed himself, such as nineteen-year-old Chevalier de La Barre, tortured and beheaded for failing to doff his hat before a religious procession, police archives show that commoners had their tongues torn out for "blasphemy" or a hand chopped off for the "sacrilege" of stealing a church candle. Meanwhile a wealthy bishop might feed communion to a roasted pig at a libertine orgy. Voltaire provides many such examples in his works. In Great Britain, a few deists had been imprisoned but only an eighteen-year-old boy, who was not a lord or bishop, seems to have been hanged for openly professing deism.[42]

Voltaire's younger contemporary Louis-Sébastien Mercier also tells us that "the poor are nothing and the rich are everything." The rich literally got away with murder. Mercier complains of the horrid *daily* accidents in which they ran over the penniless in their carriages while racing to the theaters. The streets near theaters in Paris were dyed in blood, he says. The wealth of the clergy is said to belong to the poor, he adds, before proceeding to describe the charity hospitals they ran and dared to call the "mercy houses of God." These contained up to six in a bed, lying in each other's excrement and breathing in the infections all around them.[43] A police archivist shared details of hangings "too numerous to count," for the theft of a shirt or a napkin. Unlike depictions in most movies, these gruesome hangings were an agonizing asphyxiation that left the victim convulsed for hours or even days before he or she expired. Beheadings, more merciful, were reserved to nobles. And despite affirmations to the contrary, archives show that people were still burned alive for a variety of crimes, some in iron cages, right up to the eve of the French Revolution. Commoners were burned for parricide, poisoning, arson, sodomy, and sacrilege, and not just before the *Place de Grève* (Town Hall) but all over Paris.[44]

Far from exaggerating, Voltaire was rather not graphic enough for readers of our day, but for those of his own, he clearly felt no need to describe scenes that were only too familiar. His late-life purchase of two chateaux, one in Ferney and another in nearby Lausanne, Switzerland, with their associated seigniorial titles, has been much mocked and jeered. In his own day, Baron d'Holbach and Baron von Grimm portrayed it as a sign of foolish vanity. One hears far less of this from non-aristocratic contemporaries, however, who knew exactly what it meant to be a *seigneur*, a land-owning lord, in terms of prevailing police attitudes.

And despite Voltaire's late-life titles, his age, and his fame, contemporary French Enlightenment writer Denis Diderot reports that French *Parlement* debated burning Voltaire, not just his books, in 1768. Madame Suard relates more threats in our Appendix.[45] It was, after all, the law. Heresy, apostasy, and sacrilege were all punishable with death by fire together with the confiscation of all goods (to leave your family destitute), and generally, only after torture had been applied. French journalist Élie Fréron had no compunction about printing his fervent desire to see the king "exterminate Philosophy," presumably by applying these laws to Voltaire.[46] The laws prescribed no right to a trial or even to a hearing in most countries, nor did they limit prison terms. As in present-day Guantanamo Bay, you simply rotted there "until it pleased the king to release you," as the writs of the era put it. Nor is rot an overstatement given the pestilential conditions of most prisons. It was in the punishment of crimes, however trivial, that the unholy alliance of church and state did its worst, while a confessor consoled you by evoking the agonies of Christ. Voltaire denounced it all vividly in his *Commentary on Beccaria*, his second most popular book in the American colonies.[47]

The problem with mere tolerance, Voltaire came to realize, is that it implies that someone knows "the truth" and is only putting up with "errors." The beast of human vanity is only sleeping. History showed that senseless wars and persecutions over "the real meaning" of the Bible, which no one had ever agreed upon, had spilled oceans of blood ever since Christianity had come to power. Locke had argued for tolerance using passages from the Bible. This surely explains why he has replaced Voltaire in American schoolbooks, but it was also highly problematic, since so many other passages call for slaughter in God's name. And these passages, often used by the clergy, were highly familiar to the public. Voltaire makes the point in his entry on "War" (Guerre) in the *Philosophical Dictionary*:

> What is marvellous about this infernal undertaking is that each chief of murderers has his banners blessed and solemnly invokes god before he sets off to exterminate his neighbours. . . . [O]rators are everywhere paid to celebrate [by speaking] of what was done of old in Palestine. The rest of the year, these people declaim against vices. They prove . . . that ladies who lightly spread a little rouge on their fresh cheeks will be the eternal objects of eternal vengeance . . . and speak ceaselessly against love, which is mankind's only consolation and the only way of perpetuating it.[48]

In *God and Human Beings* (*Dieu et les hommes*), he again reminds us that all the religious murders in England, Ireland, Scotland, France, Germany, Spain, Holland, and Flanders, including the assassinations of kings for being of the wrong religion, were justified by the examples of Phinehas, Ehud, Jael, Judith, and all the murders with which the Holy Scriptures abound.[49] Religiously motivated assassination attempts were made on the kings of France and Portugal during Voltaire's lifetime.[50] The Puritans also frequently justified their slaughter of Native American Indian women and children in their memoirs with what they considered equivalent slaughter of unchosen people in the Bible.

The highly vocal groups working to prove America "a Christian nation," or make it one, have largely replaced the Enlightenment in our schoolbooks with the Methodist- and Baptist-led "Great Awakening" Christian revival movement. The revision makes the evangelists responsible for the secular laws they now want overturned. It does not, however, correspond to perceptions at the time, nor to the Christian laws already in force in all countries. The Baptists, Presbyterians, and other sects did indeed demand liberty of conscience and the disestablishment of other churches, but "awakened" Baptists also petitioned Thomas Jefferson to not extend tolerance to other dissenters.[51] And in 1817, long after the Bill of Rights, guaranteeing religious freedom, had passed in 1791, John Adams said this to Jefferson about the Methodist Great Awakening leader George Whitefield:

> Oh Lord! Do you think Protestant Popedom is annihilated in America? Have you ever attended to the ecclesiastical strifes in Maryland, Pennsylvania, New York, and every part of New England? What a mercy it is that these people cannot whip and crop, and pillory, and roast! If they could, they would. . . . Quakers, Anabaptists, Moravians, Swedenborgians, Methodists, Unitarians . . . are employing underhand means to propagate their sectarian system in these States. . . . [L]et a George Whitefield arise, with a military cast, like Mahomet . . . and what will become of all the other sects?[52]

Inclusion of the Quakers here surprises. Voltaire had been using them as a model of tolerance since his *Letters on England*. But Benjamin Franklin, citing Voltaire's *Treatise on Tolerance* (in the original French, soon after it appeared), which again praises Quaker tolerance in Franklin's home state of Pennsylvania, also wrote to a friend, "while we sit for our Picture to that able Painter, 'tis no small advantage to us, that he views us at a favourable Distance."[53] And forty years later, Thomas Paine, born a Quaker, was refused burial by them for having written what Adams called his "plagiary of Voltaire," *The Age of Reason*.[54]

Our recent schoolbook revisions are not even supported by what the Methodist leaders said themselves. The first visit of Methodist-founder John Wesley to America in 1736 was a failure, ending in flight. English missionaries sent in 1771 fared no better. Francis Asbury, later an American Methodist bishop, reports in his own journal that he found himself before a deistical audience in Annapolis, Maryland, in 1777, where "many openly deny the Holy Scripture."[55]

Three months later, no house would let him preach in it. He called New Haven, Connecticut, "a seat of science and sin" and reported "a great dearth of religion in the South." "The patriots looked upon the Methodists as enemies to the cause of liberty," Mumford Jones wrote. "The storm was so great . . . Asbury went into hiding in Delaware." A biographer of first Methodist bishop, Dr. Thomas Coke, also noted that anti-Methodist feeling was so strong Asbury was forced to preach in the open air. Native preachers had to take an oath of allegiance to the new nation or suffer fine and imprisonment.

Meanwhile, the above situation was being blamed on Voltaire. Harriet Beecher Stowe's father, Lyman Beecher, wrote that when he attended Yale in the 1790s, the college "was in a most ungodly state. . . . Most of the class before me . . . called each other Voltaire, Rousseau, D'Alembert, etc." The president of Yale, Reverend Timothy Dwight, dedicated a poem, *The Triumph of Infidelity*, to Voltaire—for to whom could it be dedicated with more propriety, he asked. Yet only ten years earlier, Dwight himself had been singing the praises of the rights of man and rule by law.[56] And a historian who contests this picture as false offers as proof a study that tells us, on the contrary, that there was a rise of deism both at Yale and in the country at large "to a degree never known before."

These remarks read in such startling contrast to what we read today that some background is in order. First, we should note that those who want the "Christian nation intentions" of America's founders taught cite the Mayflower Compact of 1620 and the Fundamental Orders of Connecticut in proof.[57] These were the Puritan laws that made heresy punishable by burning and made it a penal offence to refuse to have your children baptized.[58] Their authors indeed refer to themselves as "saints" who have come to spread the Kingdom of God. However, these are also the very laws the builders of the new United States wanted abolished one hundred and fifty years later. Jefferson was crystal-clear about their intentions in his *Autobiography*. He authored the first bill for religious freedom ever written, in 1778. This fact was surely behind the effort to erase him from our schoolbooks in 2010—although, amazingly, this cogent detail was not even mentioned in most newspaper accounts of the endeavor.[59] The bill was adopted by his home state of Virginia in 1784, largely through the efforts of James Madison. It was a historical first that Jefferson was very justly proud of, and here is what he himself wrote about its passage:

The bill for establishing religious freedom . . . still met with opposition but, with some mutilations . . . it was finally passed. . . . An amendment was proposed [adding that] "coercion is a departure from the plan of Jesus Christ, the holy author of our religion"; the insertion was rejected by a great majority, in proof that they meant to comprehend within the mantle of its protection, the Jew, the Gentile, the Christian and Mahometan, the Hindoo and Infidel of every denomination.[60]

Adding Jesus was rejected by a great majority? To protect other religions— and infidels? Apparently so, since a great many pressed for a Bill of Rights, guaranteeing similar protection in all states. Every landowner (white and male, of course) had the right to vote, and in some states it sufficed to be a taxpayer: the vast *majority*, as eminent historian of early America Edmund S. Morgan explained.[61] This was not a question of an elite imposing unwelcome laws on humbler citizens, and renowned American historian Bernard Bailyn has widely documented the intense participation in debates of citizens from all walks of life.[62] Voices had been raised decades earlier decrying the famous sermons of Puritan preacher, Jonathan Edwards, for example, as shocking, not only for consigning "abominable creatures wallowing like swine in the mire of their sins" to eternal damnation but for describing the exaltation and "lively relish" the sight of it will give "saints" like himself.[63]

Nor did the similarity of such doctrines to "the rule of tyrants" go unnoticed. A king high above his people, who nevertheless decides the most minute affairs, privileging only a pre-selected elite while the rest could not be saved by either prayers or good actions, was the living image of Calvinist pre-destination. These "reverend drones," said Boston minister Jonathan Mayhew, "who preach the divine right of titles and . . . sinecures are not ministers of God but pirates and highwaymen." William Livingston, later signatory to the Declaration of Independence and Governor of New Jersey, huffed over the senility of such bombast: "No virtue more Christian . . . than a passive submission."[64]

These voices mark the change from the Calvinistic/Puritan view to the deistic rational one, American historian Woodbridge Riley explained, adding that Locke was merely the former in disguise. It was a positive change, not a negative one, from passive Calvinist predestination and pessimism to freedom, optimism, and activity.[65] The Jansenists, seventeenth-century French philosopher Pascal's beloved sect that Voltaire refers to often, shared similar views on predestination and human depravity, though French Catholics, and they predominated in the *Parlement* of Paris.

Poor Puritans fleeing religious persecution is a given in America today. But unlike us, our eighteenth-century ancestors had not forgotten that Cromwell's Puritans reigned in Britain in the mid-1600s. Churchill called it the most hated regime of spying and prying in English history.[66] Their massacre of half a million Catholics still haunts Irish memory. And in the 1700s, British Anglicans were accusing the Methodists, Quakers, and most Dissenters of resembling Cromwell's Puritans.[67] Rhode Island was founded to escape their persecutions.[68] Eminent Enlightenment scholar, Peter Gay, reproduced "a remarkably modern diagnosis" of them written in 1621 by Oxford scholar Robert Burton. The emotional displays of Puritans, Burton said, are symptoms of a desire for notoriety. Politicians and priests ruthlessly exploit this, playing upon fear, pride, stupidity, jealousy, and frustration.[69]

In her history of American secularism, *Freethinkers*, Susan Jacoby notes that during these past two decades conservatives have been relegating all Enlightenment heroes to "the kook's corner" or "the memory hole" of American history, or denigrating them as an elitist minority. The brainwashing began much earlier, as we will see, for Jacoby herself understandably hesitates to infer much from two astonishing items she mentions: an eighteenth-century study that estimated that only five percent of Americans had formal ties with a church or synagogue in 1790, and a complaint from Samuel Mather, whose ancestor Cotton had stoked the Salem witchcraft trials, that only one in six of his fellow Bostonians could be counted on to attend church regularly in 1780.[70] Five percent? One in six? Is this the best-kept secret in America? Samuel Mather was far from alone in these perceptions, as we have seen, and historians of a century ago or more say outright that during the last decades of the eighteenth century half-belief or unbelief prevailed.[71] Even well into the 1800s, Jefferson believed that Americans had shown themselves too enlightened to return to rule by "priestcraft" and would remain a beacon of light, inspiring others to adopt her freedoms.[72]

In any case, the terms infidel and atheist should be viewed with caution. Not only were these epithets hurled at deists, such as Voltaire or Jefferson, various sects also hurled them at each other. Methodist founder John Wesley was charged with "blasphemy, impiety, and atheism" by a foe, and he himself proclaimed all other religions, including Protestant ones, "Godless" save his own.[73] That said, and whatever the ratio of irregular or non-churchgoers was, the cover-ups and blatant falsifications regarding Voltaire are both extraordinary and massive.

For just a few examples, we see an American translator who wants to prove Voltaire an atheist strike his famous deistic "Prayer to God" from the *Treatise on Toleration*. (It is included in this book for that reason.)[74] The editor of a selection of letters between John Adams and Thomas Jefferson strikes Voltaire from a list of writers Adams "rejoices over" because they have done more for religious freedom than "Calvin or Luther or even Locke."[75] Voltaire and Priestley topped the list. Many underline the late dates of first American editions of Voltaire to show that no American read him before the American Revolution. Studies show, however, that the vast majority of books in the colonies were imported then, and principally from England and France. Due to the scarcity of paper and local printers, both resources were employed almost entirely on local periodicals and government tracts[76]

Studies researching which French books were imported and reacted to in America have also been published. They vary widely in results, from Mary-Margaret Barr's *Voltaire in America: 1744 -1800*, which seems to be the fullest on his subject, to another claiming that only Voltaire's short story "Micromegas" could be found.[77]

The much-cited American historian Carl Becker tells us outright "it has sometimes been thought that Jefferson and his American contemporaries must have borrowed their ideas from French writers, must have been 'influenced' by them, for example by Rousseau. But it does not appear that Jefferson, or any American, read many French books."[78] And if we turn to the complete correspondence of Thomas Jefferson and John Adams, the index shows only three references to Voltaire. Those pages lead to two apparent denigrations of Voltaire by Adams, inspired by Baron Grimm's tart portrayals of Voltaire (and almost everyone else, as Adams noted) and one in which Adams simply says he is reading the "controversies" of Voltaire and Nonotte, a Jesuit who "scourged" Voltaire and was scourged back, as Adams put it.

But there are fourteen other references to Voltaire that go unlisted in the index. Moreover, if one keeps track of the index, it turns out that well over seventy references to French Enlightenment writers have been similarly "overlooked."[79] Just as strikingly, of three comments Adams made on George White-field, Methodist leader of the "Great Awakening," the one cited above, in which Adams says that Whitefield and his followers would destroy all the other sects if they could, will not be found by looking up Whitefield in the index either.[80]

In America, even authors who do grant Voltaire a big effect remain curiously mum on his subject, or attribute his popularity to other causes. In his book on *The Ideological Origins of the American Revolution*, Bernard Bailyn tells us that, despite efforts to discount their influence, Voltaire, Rousseau, and Montesquieu "were quoted everywhere in the colonies, by everyone," not just by Franklin, Adams, or Jefferson, and specifies that Voltaire was especially quoted "on the evils of clerical oppression." After which, Voltaire disappears.[81] In *The Enlightenment in America*, Henry May makes dozens of references to Voltaire, much read before the Revolution, with increasing popularity after it, he says, "partly because much of his work was either inoffensive or pretended to be." And yet May also confusingly refers to him elsewhere as the leading infidel or skeptic.[82] In his book on the founders' faiths (mostly deistic he agrees), American religious specialist David Holmes tells us that deism was personified in England, France, and America by "such controversial figures as Anthony Collins, Voltaire and Thomas Paine."[83] The keen-witted Voltaire satirized systems, argued for common sense, and spread Locke's ideas on tolerance, we're told. "Perhaps no writer has attacked dogmatic Christianity more effectively," he ends—to say no more about it, except that Voltaire had derided organized religion, but Paine "went further," claiming that the Almighty never communicated anything to man by any mode or means.

Woodbridge Riley agreed with John Adams that Paine's *Age of Reason*, was essentially a plagiary of Voltaire, among others, although, unaware of it, admiring editors take him for a Prometheus. Like "the belated deism of [Edward] Gibbon,"[84] Paine simply repeats old arguments, he says. In any case, Paine's *Reason* came too late (1794) to be the cause of what had already occurred: the total abolition of obligatory beliefs, as Paine says himself on the very first page.[85] But to be fair, the bulk and range of Voltaire's works, not to mention the thousands of writings about him, are undoubtedly terrifying, as Theodore Besterman remarked,[86] himself responsible for tripling the size of Voltaire's known correspondence in the twentieth century. One book on the subject by Thomas Paine is assuredly more manageable.

Paul M. Spurlin's book, *The French Enlightenment in America*, satisfyingly disproves the claim that French books were little read. Just among the key founders, those able to read French included Benjamin Franklin, Thomas Jefferson, John Adams, John Paul Jones, John Jay, James Madison, Alexander Hamilton, Benjamin Rush, Aaron Burr, Governor Morris, James Monroe, and John Quincy Adams. George Washington read Voltaire in translation he told his revolutionary co-commander, French General Lafayette.[87]

A great many of Voltaire's works were available in English too,[88] even though the international language in his day was French, and as Benjamin Franklin said in a letter to Noah Webster, "even those who don't speak it know it well enough to read it." Franklin mused that it was perhaps because Voltaire's *Traité sur la tolérance* (*Treatise on Tolerance*) was in French that "it has had so sudden and great an Effect on the Bigotry of Europe as almost entirely to disarm it." He also rightly *guessed* that its unsigned author was Voltaire because "it is full of the good sense and sound reasoning mix'd with those Pleasantries that mark the Author as strongly as if he had affixed his name."[89]

Spurlin also concedes that "Voltaire, archapostle of reason and 'genius of mockery,' was an awakener of consciences"—and that the change was swift.[90] The majority in France thought like their bishops, then suddenly "began to think like Voltaire: it was a revolution." And though Voltaire and Rousseau both stirred men to end authority based on divine rights, he adds, the writings of Voltaire were more widely advertised and disseminated in America than those of any other French Enlightenment writer.

In the rest of the book, however, he primarily gives citations reviling Voltaire (most of them from the "erudite, discerning" Presbyterian clergyman Samuel Miller) or insisting that Voltaire was only known as a historian in America. Two of the highest eighteenth-century American praises of Voltaire he cites—on his "beautiful character" and "extraordinary genius"—are tucked away in a chapter on French natural scientist, Buffon.[91] His chapter on Voltaire, conversely, focuses only on the South. It opens intriguingly with a "tidal wave of infidelity" that hit the University of North Carolina and cites a preacher growling that the writings of Voltaire "were in the hands of almost all" out of gratitude to the French, poisoning the public—then says no more on the subject. From that point on, Spurlin's citations repeatedly assure us that Voltaire was "best-known" or "only known" as a historian. *Candide* was "surprisingly" little-read. After a fleeting mention or two of the *Philosophical Dictionary*, he concludes that he "can say no more," though confident that a methodical study would reveal much more. "Opinions of Voltaire . . . uncovered are all too few" to permit generalizations, he says, but "I have been struck by the apparent lack of abuse of the French writer in the South."

His regret is palpable and yet his referring us to Mary-Margaret Barr to "bear out" the fact that Voltaire was best known as a historian[92] is also enigmatic, as she does quite the contrary.

Barr reports that a London translation of Voltaire's *History of Charles XII*, the king who defended Sweden against Peter the Great, was acquired in 1744 by the first public library in Philadelphia, founded by Franklin. This is the earliest listing she found, so it no doubt defined her title: *Voltaire in America: 1744–1800*.[93] The mass of information she gathered is sometimes unwieldy and her page on this work does indeed say that "Voltaire's histories were his most popular works." But a few pages further, we discover she meant that *Charles XII*, being the oldest work found, simply had the most listings, for the explosion of interest in Voltaire in America came later. His *Commentary on Beccaria* on law reforms and his *Philosophical Dictionary* were his second and third most popular books, she then informs us, followed by his world history, *Essai sur les mœurs*.[94] *Beccaria* and the *Dictionary* both had at least twice as many listings as the *Age of Louis XIV*, which Spurlin highlights repeatedly along with *Charles XII*.

Both Spurlin and Barr report that the influence of newspapers and magazines was huge. Periodicals were far cheaper and more widely available than books. But in Spurlin's account they are "a minor source of information" about Voltaire, whereas in Barr's they kept Voltaire "constantly before the public's eye." Anecdotes about him even served as frequent filler material[95] and her wealth of excerpts from newspapers and magazines bears it out, but, unlike many, she provides the enthusiastic reactions as well as the hostile ones. Among many others, the *Massachusetts Gazette* shares a British opinion in 1786 reporting that "Voltaire, though occasionally licentious, has by his writing, eminently contributed to diffuse liberality of sentiment through most of the European states. He excited a spirit of free inquiry, and with success attacked the strongholds of superstition. The rage of religious disputation and a fiery zeal have subsided."[96] Adrian Jaffe's research confirms Barr's: over half the magazines in eighteenth-century America had material on Voltaire, who was "without question the most frequently discussed . . . and reprinted," and many of the reprints are from the *Philosophical Dictionary*.[97]

Many writers besides Spurlin cull mainly the hostile reactions to Voltaire, but Barr, Mumford Jones, Riley, Jaffe, and others tell us that these gained the upper hand only after the Reign of Terror in France. At the start of the French Revolution in 1789 it was hoped that a constitutional monarchy like the one in England could be formed, but the French king and queen made a foiled attempt to join waiting troops and were thereafter viewed as dangerous traitors. French Revolutionary Maximilien de Robespierre then launched a paranoid series of guillotinings for the next ten months, now called the Reign of Terror. The king and queen were beheaded in 1793, just as King Charles I had been in England the previous century by Cromwell and his Puritans.

Two false notions often seem to infuse American polemics over the Enlightenment; one being that it was a battle between the clergy and unbelievers, and the other stemming from a long tradition of Protestant English bias. The victors always write the history books as they say, but some of our schoolbooks have been correcting long-oversimplified notions of America's English origins. A glance at maps of America in 1650 shows us not only a New England, but a New Sweden, a New France, and a New Spain (Florida).[98] New York was originally New Amsterdam, and as late 1760 half the city was Dutch.[99] So was much of Pennsylvania.

Another quarter of New York was French. French Protestants, called Huguenots, had large pockets of settlements throughout the colonies. John Jay, Alexander Hamilton, and Paul Revere had Huguenot origins, among other notable figures. And there were so many Germans in 1751 that Benjamin Franklin feared the colonies would become "Germanized."[100] A German visitor saw lots of tavern signs bearing the head of Frederick the Great in 1783. The Scotch-Irish, the Portuguese, Jews from Brazil, and others entered the mix. By the 1750s, eighteen languages could be heard in the streets of New York.[101] Thomas Paine likewise tells us in his famous pamphlet, *Common Sense*—usually credited with spurring the fight for independence—that less than one third of the colonialists were English; therefore the English had no business dictating. "Europe, and not England, is the parent country of America," he wrote.[102]

Among the arguments frequently used to assure us that no American colonial read Voltaire, or any French writer generally, we are told of anti-French sentiment sparked by the French-Indian War of 1754–1763.[103] The defeat of the French gave control of territories east of the Mississippi to Britain, but only thirteen years before our War of Independence. Some historians also point to founders who couldn't speak French or portray the French as "hated Catholics." But this overlooks the fact that "John" Calvin was actually "Jean"—born in France.

The anti-French tradition has been greatly exaggerated Mumford Jones tells us, furnishing not only several pages worth of French place names in America but long lists of French works "in great demand" and widely found early in the 1600s. They include not only Calvin but French authors Fénelon, Descartes, Gassendi, Malebranche, Pascal, and a great many lesser-known philosophers and theologians.[104] Novels were frowned upon. Americans reading Voltaire in the eighteenth century had far less need of footnotes than we do today, and he can hardly be accused of an offending papist bias. His battles on behalf of Jean Calas and other persecuted French Protestants were the subject of his *Treatise on Tolerance*, frequently excerpted in America periodicals and heralded the world over.[105] In *Catechism of the Honest Man* he says that, if forced to become a Christian, he'd probably choose a Protestant sect. He certainly reproached the Catholics with many of the same dogmas Protestants did: the "infallibility" of popes, the worship of relics, transubstantiation, and allowing "two masters in one state," kings and popes, for example. His real hope, however, was that a Protestant nation, having got rid of twenty superstitions, might be first to get rid of the rest.[106]

Nor was the Enlightenment a clear-cut battle between the clergy and "infidels" by any means. Many of the earlier English Deists had been clergymen. Countless clergymen joined the Enlightenment's demands for reforms in France, Germany, America, and elsewhere. Before the Enlightenment, universities only produced theologians, or "divinities" as Americans called them: it was the purpose of their founding. Scientists and lawyers had to find their training elsewhere, and it was not all that rare after the Age of Discovery for study of the Bible to lead to doubt or disbelief. Most of the "new worlds" discovered were uncounted for in Scripture. Among the favorable reactions to Voltaire in America we see a Boston clergyman write a friend that, although he could not agree with what appeared to be Voltaire's designs—the entire subversion of revelation—he had read his *Phi-*

losophy of History and his *Philosophical Dictionary* "with high delight, as containing much useful learning, many fine observations . . . and written in such an entertaining & masterly way . . . that I would not be long without them for twice their value." A satire of Rousseau's *New Heloise* novel in the *New York Magazine*, said to be written by Voltaire, turned out to have been written by a clergyman's daughter, in excellent imitation of his style.[107] The Prince de Broglie, who fought with the Americans during their War of Independence, mentions hearing a preacher cite Voltaire and Rousseau from the pulpit.[108]

Many historians concur that when the French sent forty-six thousand troops to help us fight for our independence, enthusiasm for all things French became well-nigh universal. French soldiers outnumbered Americans two to one at Yorktown.[109] Puritan preachers, "formerly praying for the fall of the pope, were praying for the health of the Catholic King of France," notes Mumford Jones, and countless engravings in American parlors showed Voltaire and Benjamin Franklin embracing[110]—as they did indeed at the demand of a crowd in the Academy of Science in Paris in 1778 while Franklin was there—to the joy of both sides of the Atlantic, it appears.[111] John Adams, also there, described the event in his *Diary*.

Exchanges between the two countries in this era were so great, Garry Wills wondered whether Patrick Henry's famous cry, "Give me liberty or give me death!" didn't originate with Voltaire's "Dieux! Donnez-nous la mort plutôt que l'esclavage!" from his play *Brutus*, which also became a rallying cry in France.[112] And when the French stormed the Bastille in 1789, heralding their own revolution just five years after our own was won, "the people of no importance"—in Hamilton's famous phrase—went wild with joy throughout America, dancing and toasting in the streets and taverns, church bells ringing. Even the simplest citizens knew that *liberté, égalité, fraternité* meant democracy and were moved to the depths, wrote Mumford Jones. Every major event of the French Revolution, along with the speeches of Mirabeau, Robespierre, and other French revolutionaries, filled American papers. A dozen holidays were created to commemorate our battles and alliances with the French.[113]

As often remarked, the early stages of the French Revolution were very Voltairian. Both the *cahiers de doléance* (list of grievances) presented to the States-General and the French *Declaration of the Rights of Man* "contain a remarkably close similarity to Voltaire's programme of reform," notes Enlightenment historian Haydn Mason: liberty of speech, press, and religion; equality before the law; secular laws as the highest authority; the right to property and security; equitable taxation; and reform in criminal procedures abolishing torture, unnecessary punishment, and arrest without due process.[114] The French *Declaration* was often reprinted in American periodicals, and another high point of this period was also reported: the return of Voltaire's remains to Paris. They had been refused burial by the authorities at his death in 1778 and secretly transported out of Paris. In 1791 they were returned and literally enshrined in the Panthéon, a newly created mausoleum "To the Great Men to Whom the Country is Grateful," converted from a new church the king was having built for the patron saint of Paris, St. Geneviève.

The size of the crowds attending Voltaire's reinterment varies in estimate from one hundred thousand to six hundred thousand. We will suppose the latter exaggerates, since it would have comprised the entire population of Paris, although thousands of foreigners also poured in to watch and numerous towns feted the casket on its four-day journey to Paris.[115]

Barr provides a detailed account from a Boston paper enthusiastically describing the crowds proclaiming "Fanaticism is expiring!" and calling the event, without exaggeration, a "cavalcade unequalled at the funeral of any Monarch upon earth." And when Ben Franklin died in 1790, Americans were gratified to learn that the French revolutionaries declared three days of national mourning. The French National Assembly and the market draped themselves in black to hear a host of speeches given by Lafayette, Condorcet, Mirabeau, and others in Franklin's honor.[116]

But the people of importance—the "commercial princes" and some of the once all-powerful clergy—were far less enthusiastic. John Adams reported that England, our most important trading partner traditionally, meant to crush the colonies commercially after losing the war. When the guillotinings began in France, American opinions were not all as shocked as usually said, but pro-British Tory papers ridiculed the French and dwelt unceasingly on the massacres and bloodshed caused, it was often said, by the "irreligion of Voltaire." And few, noted one observer, made more efforts than president of Yale, Rev. Timothy Dwight, grandson of the famous preacher Jonathan Edwards, to "slay the dreadful M. de Voltaire." Dwight crops up often indeed, relating Satan's exultation at his many converts thanks to Voltaire, or snarling over the "dissolute French soldiers" who had flooded America, all disciples of Voltaire. These men "know intuitively . . . that moral obligation is a chimera; that animal pleasure is the only good." The common people were never honored by Voltaire with any higher title than rabble, he claims, but were taken in by offers of help from such men until "[h]appily it was discovered that France [had only] changed tyrannies; and that man, unrestrained by . . . religion, is a mere beast of prey."[117] Dwight was far from alone, however.

In one gazette after another, Voltaire and Frederick are now among those held chiefly responsible for the bloodshed in France and the spread of "infidelity." Jefferson "reeks of French garlic in his noxious admiration of Voltaire," says one journalist. Voltaire's every page is defiled with gross indecencies, disgusting ribaldry, rails another, paying no respect to the Deity, religion, virtue, or morals. Others meanwhile continued to hail "the judicious Voltaire."[118] On Jefferson's return from France, where he had replaced Franklin, he was shocked to see some openly expressing a preference for kings. John Adams, now Washington's vice president, watched in terror as a throng of ten thousand marched upon them demanding they send aid to the French. The country split in two over the French Revolution in a seething mass of excitement, with Jefferson's "pro-French" Republicans battling Hamilton's "pro-British" Federalists. Riley opined that the latter showed themselves in a very bad light, having been willing enough to take French gold just a few years earlier.[119]

Outrageous deathbed tales added to the uproar, for "the devout know how the impious die," as René Pomeau remarked.[120] Like Tom Paine or Scottish *philosophe* David Hume, Voltaire was said to have died in the most atrocious agonies, "desperate and frantic." He saw flaming pits full of demons open at his feet. He ate his excrement. "One would think the compilers had gone mad to meet their private ends," said Riley. Yet these ludicrous tales were retailed for over a century. Voltaire apparently died from stomach cancer and his own doctor, Tronchin, attributed the suffering to his impiety; that is, until he saw the pious Swiss scientist von Haller die in similar pain. And according to everyone present (unlike his doctor), Voltaire slept peacefully the last four days. The popularity of deism in America was defeated by neurotic reactions, according

to Riley, the majority "drawn off by an emotional substitute for thought"—
with the result that it was not the common but the uncommon people who
profited by it.[121]

Certainly in France, just as the battle had been greater, the orthodox
clergy, despite repeated "victories," never did manage to herd so many back
into the fold as they did in America. When Pope Pius VI declared the reforms
of the French Revolution and the *Declaration of the Rights of Man* sacrilegious,
Napoleon marched on Rome and imprisoned *him*. "Many assumed that the
destruction of the Holy See at last had been accomplished," writes religious historian J. N. D. Kelly. Napoleon's idol was Frederick and he had learned from
Voltaire's world history all the harm a pope can do an emperor—so it was "a
little bit Voltaire's fault," wrote René Pomeau.[122] Of course, with the demise
of Napoleon in 1815, Pope Leo XII reinstated the Index of Prohibited Books,[123]
intolerance, feudal aristocracy, and ecclesiastic courts, threw the Jews back
into their ghettos, and announced a holy war for the year of Our Lord 1825.
He died "profoundly unpopular," Kelly notes.[124]

After the fall of Napoleon and throughout the nineteenth century, France
became the sort of battleground Victor Hugo depicted in *Les Misérables*, with
the Church-backed monarchists repeatedly restoring themselves to power and
the republicans battling to restore rights won by the Revolution. Every restora-
tion of church and king, not incidentally, returned control of education to the
clergy. The "tyrants of beliefs," as the eighteenth century called them, always
exert their greatest efforts on indoctrinating children. But in France a main
weapon of the opposition was, also not incidentally, Voltaire.

For one example, seven years after Louis XVIII (brother of the guillotined
French king, Louis XVI) became the first king restored to the throne, the Minister of the Interior received a report: some 1,598,000 volumes of Voltaire
had since flooded the market. They were "infesting every class of society, from
the lowest to the highest." One priest growled that he had seen "even the most
rustic of peasants lay down their plows to read Voltaire." A million and half
brochures were released, or screamed from the pulpits, to stop the Voltaire
torrent. One inspector wondered what the point of so many new editions was,
given that three million others were still in circulation.[125]

Voltaire had once told a scoffer that "there are more philosophers among the peasants than you think," but these figures are nevertheless stunning in a population of only some thirty million. Robert Darnton's estimates of the best-selling books of the eighteenth century did not surpass a few thousand, and the literacy rate in England is estimated at only roughly eighty thousand in a population of six million in the same period.[126] These constant reversals in nineteenth-century France ended under the Third Republic with the rallying cry, "Clericalism is the enemy!" and the educational reforms of 1881, which made primary schools free, laic, and obligatory from the ages of six to thirteen.[127]

In America, evangelizing desires make the reversals more difficult to pinpoint. Some claim that the French Revolution provoked the decisive antideist change, pointing to all the abuse heaped upon Jefferson during his presidential campaign of 1800. This seems a bit early for the religious right to cry victory, however, since, after all, he was elected. Moreover, his closest collaborator, James Madison, was elected as his successor, succeeded by their other close collaborator, James Monroe: all deists. Thirty-five years later, testimonies abound that even Abraham Lincoln was a deist who read and thought like Voltaire and Thomas Paine.[128]

Uncommon men indeed, but still winning the majority of votes. Mark Twain's favorite tourist in America, English novelist Frances Trollope, also attests to startling declarations of "disbelief" from women at tea parties in 1830, despite the religious revivals sweeping the country in which "every tinker and tailor" seemed to be creating an endless variety of sects, and the despite the fact that women were allowed no other pastime than church events. Trollope was shocked by the behavior of preachers during these midnight revival frenzies and felt that it was so suggestive Englishmen would have punished them for it. She also reports in great surprise that applause drowned out the booing at a lecture she attended when the speaker declared that George Washington was not a Christian.[129]

Susan Jacoby remarked on how difficult it is to decode the true religious opinions of the founders. It is "like searching for the real Jesus in the conflicting passages of the Scriptures," she writes.[130] Franklin, Jefferson, and Adams leap to mind, not only as the three most famous founders but also as the three most often labeled deists, though indeed often with too little proof offered, as those who contest it argue.

Franklin is the easiest to confirm, as he tells us himself in his *Autobiography* that he became "a thorough deist" at age fifteen. Some books against deism were put into his hands, he says, which had "the opposite effect intended." And he reconfirmed his deism just before he died in a letter to the former president of Yale, Ezra Stiles. In it, Franklin says he believed that Jesus' morals were excellent *as he left them*, but that he "apprehended" they had undergone "various corrupting Changes" and with "most of the present Dissenters," he had doubts as to his Divinity.[131]

Regarding French books, Franklin also reports that he began studying French in 1733 and was soon "able to read the books with ease." He published remarks on Voltaire's *Temple of Taste* in his *Pennsylvania Gazette* that same year, and we have already seen several approving remarks on Voltaire from his letters. A scientist, Franklin and his Philosophical Society had more exchanges with French scientists than with Voltaire, but they read each other's works, in fact.[132] Shortly before he died, Voltaire let Franklin make him an honorary Freemason in Paris in a sort of mutual tribute, despite the fact that he privately considered secret societies somewhat silly.[133]

After the death of Franklin, Thomas Jefferson became the most abused man in America for his supposed Voltairianism. Yet in his correspondence with John Adams it is Adams who evokes Voltaire and the *philosophes* over and over, reviewing their lives in retirement, while Jefferson remains curiously silent on the subject, although he says how much he enjoys the reminiscences.[134] The abuse he had suffered may be the reason for the silence, on top of the fact that his letters to Unitarian Church cofounder, Joseph Priestley, had just been published without his permission, containing some acid remarks about the "bigots."[135] And another man soon enraged him by offering to print his exchanges with Adams as well, tipped off by the post office, he presumed.[136]

It would be odd, to say the least, to see Adams chatter on at such length about a subject that did not interest Jefferson—over seventy unindexed references, as we saw earlier—but his silence naturally lends itself to the claim. One of the most frequently cited experts who made it is Gilbert Chinard, renowned editor and biographer of Jefferson. Chinard tells us that Jefferson's correspondence reveals no interest in Voltaire, no mind paid to his ideas even, except to Voltaire's "ridiculous theory on fossils."[137] So before attempting to decipher chatty Adams, we will attempt to decipher "the American Sphinx," Thomas Jefferson.

Jefferson's remarks on Voltaire's fossil theory are in his *Notes on the State of Virginia*, Query XI. Jefferson does indeed contest Voltaire's theory here, although he took it seriously enough to hurry when he reached France to consult a scientist in Touraine Voltaire had cited.[138] However, in reading Jefferson's *Notes*, we might also discover two other remarks he made on Voltaire in Query VI.

Query VI addresses claims made by Buffon and Abbé Raynal that living in America caused biological degeneration to men, plants, and animals—a silly but popular theory at the time. Franklin was so irritated by it that he printed a tale of whales leaping up Niagara Falls in a single bound. Jefferson, equally annoyed but more diplomatic, says in Query VI that when America has existed "as long as the Greeks did before they produced a Homer, the Romans a Virgil, the French a Racine and Voltaire"—then we will worry. The remark sets Voltaire among the world classics, and further on we find another compliment, but couched in terms that further the controversy. Jefferson says "we are but just becoming acquainted" with France, which so far gives us "high ideas of the genius of her inhabitants. It would be injuring too many of them to name particularly a Voltaire, a Buffon, the . . . Encyclopedists and Abbé Raynal himself, etc."[139]

The remark is used to prove that Jefferson was unfamiliar with any of them before he reached Paris in 1784. He published his *Notes on Virginia* there the following year. He wrote the first draft in 1781, however, and if Jefferson was only just discovering Voltaire in Paris, another often-cited remark he made on his arrival must be explained. Shocked by the conditions of the poor in Paris, he wrote, "the truth of Voltaire's observation offers itself perpetually, that every man here must be either the hammer or the anvil."[140] This line is in Voltaire's *Philosophical Dictionary* ("Tyranny"). We might also note that Jefferson bought the seventy-volume clandestine Kehl edition of Voltaire's complete works while in Paris, as well as a bust of the writer from the famous sculptor Houdon, later set prominently in his "gallery of worthies" at home in Monticello.[141] His secretary, William Short, who stayed behind, sent him several gazettes relating the return of the remains of "the great man" to Paris in 1791.[142] These details would be odd regarding a man who had no interest in Voltaire.

Jefferson's letter to his brother-in-law Robert Skipwith recommending

Voltaire's histories in 1771 is what is usually cited to prove some interest.[143] He also recommended them to two of his nephews, however, and lists of books in French he ordered for his nephew, Peter Carr, also include Voltaire's *Oeuvres complètes* (Complete Works). Jefferson not only tells Carr that he must learn French, as their books on sciences, mathematics, and history are better than the English ones, he also encourages him to "shake off fears and servile prejudices" in examining the Bible.[144]

The invectives over Jefferson's Voltairianism during his presidential election resumed when the government bought his library to replace the original Library of Congress, lost in a fire during the War of 1812. By this date, Voltaire had become the apostle of the French Revolution's Reign of Terror with his "irreligious" books, to some minds, and those decrying the purchase just *assumed* the library was full of books by Voltaire from things Jefferson had said or written. Paul Spurlin confirms, however, that "Jefferson did indeed have many books by and on Voltaire" and lists some in his endnotes.[145] Query XVII in *Notes on Virginia* contained so many echoes of Voltaire, in any case, that Jefferson may have thought it unnecessary to name him. A few have been pointed out in the notes to *Catechism of the Honest Man* and *Dinner at Count de Boulainvilliers'*. Cases might be made for other lines as well.[146]

The strangest indications of early interest bring us back to Professor Chinard, however. Spurlin and Mary-Margaret Barr both cite extracts from Voltaire that Jefferson copied into his *Commonplace Book*, a sort of notebook students kept for copying passages of special interest from their readings. Chinard was the editor of two separate editions of it. Barr and Spurlin both give exact page numbers for the extracts in his 1926 edition.[147] However, Chinard brought out a second edition just two years later, from which the excerpts from Voltaire have vanished. And it is in the preface to this second edition that Chinard tells us Jefferson took no interest in Voltaire. Spurlin juxtaposes the two facts in his footnotes. A new "improved" edition of Jefferson's *Commonplace Book* released in 1989 contains no Voltaire extracts either.[148]

Does Voltaire shock to that extent? Examples like the above can hardly be ascribed to "oversights." Whatever the motivations behind this incessant burying of Voltaire, we read a rare confession of it in what amounts to yet another example in 1976. That year, the *American Quarterly* magazine celebrated the bicentennial of "The American Enlightenment" in a special summer edition. In one article, D. H. Meyer informs us that the French Revolution showed that the Enlightenment "had to be stripped of it impieties."[149] His article opens citing a sermon given in 1788 by an American preacher who feared that people were getting "laughed out of religion." Despite all the absurdities exposed, despite the great humanitarian work these *philosophes* had accomplished, the reverend says, we must not abandon our Christian faith. Meyer then explains that saving Protestantism—now the basis of American identity, he further claims—"sanctified" the Enlightenment with supernatural revelation. But the grave threat, he says, was David Hume. Voltaire has vanished yet again. His name is never even mentioned, although getting people "laughed out of religion" seems an odd reproach to make of David Hume. Nor was he particularly famous for great humanitarian deeds, as Voltaire was.

In any case, it is nothing less than stupefying to read such views in a respectable magazine as late as 1976. Even French author Chateaubriand, who believed Christianity destroyed in 1802 thanks to "Voltaire's impieties" and wrote his *Genius of Christianity* to rescue it, later realized that the excesses of the Revolution were due to the horrible oppression in France, not to Voltaire. In fact, he liked to quote Voltaire to unbelievers—"to prove the truth of religion," he added perplexingly. (His contemporary, literary critic Sainte-Beuve replied that, in any case, Christianity was more likely to recover from Voltaire's blows than from the return to old fables in the *Genius of Christianity*.)[150]

On the subject of Voltaire, however, one can hardly be more perplexing than John Adams. And even though Jefferson never names Voltaire in their exchanges, it is patently clear that he and Adams are both keenly interested in "the frauds and corruptions" of Christianity, and that they echo Voltaire's views on nearly every point. Their refrains—from Plato's "foggy mind" and its effects on "artificial Christianity," to the "laboriousness of German scholars," to the vanity of insects such as ourselves in daring to explain the Creator, to the universality of basic morals, to deistic declarations of faith in the governor of the universe and in doing good to all his creatures, *period*—are Voltaire's refrains. They even refer to their "machines" when discussing their health.[151] After his stay in Frederic's Berlin court, which also included La Mettrie, the atheist author of "Man, the Machine," it became a running gag for Voltaire to speak of his "machine" running down, getting old, or feeling better, etc., in his letters, as Adams and Jefferson do in theirs.

This wealth of coincidences can hardly be explained by the fact that Jefferson and Adams both also read the English deist, Bolingbroke; the only deistic influence some allow them. A former keeper of the John Adams collection, Zoltán Haraszti, wrote that, of the three thousand books remaining of Adams' library, more than a hundred had marginal notes—and that most of these were in books by Bolingbroke, Voltaire, Rousseau, and a dozen others. Nearly two hundred of Adams marginal notes were in collections of Frederick's correspondence with Voltaire and D'Alembert; and these were made during a mysterious seven-month leave of absence Adams took during his presidency to withdraw to his farm in 1799. Haraszti extracted some fifty lines or snippets to give a sampling of Adams comments. Chinard did the same for a dozen of Adams' comments on works by Voltaire. One finds a majority of negative remarks in both samplings.[152] But Adams' complete correspondence with Jefferson may well present a fuller picture of his views. And they swing maddeningly back and forth!

Voltaire is "the greatest literary genius," the greatest wit along with Jonathan Swift, even "the greatest genius of them all," and Adams rejoices that Voltaire lived because of all he did for religious liberty. In other moods, or sometimes in the very same breath, he was also a "vain, extravagant animal," "incapable of governing mankind," and "the greatest Coward . . . at his death."[153]

It is hard to believe that Adams, who constantly bemoans his own martyrdom as a public figure,[154] believed the deathbed tales, but his delight in finding chinks in everyone else's armor, as Haraszti put it, surely accounts for some of these incongruities, as does his forgivable vanity for having argued some excellent checks and balances into the US Constitution. Jefferson's first impression of Adams was that he seemed to dislike everyone equally, but he later told James Madison that he would love Adams if he got to know him. Adams was vain, irritable, and a "bad calculator" of men's motives, he said, but amiable, profound, and totally impartial. The description seems to fit, but a few of Adams' outbursts can be contextualized, while others, seemingly never mentioned are far more interesting.

Lines from Adams showing disapproval of the "gross ideology" of the French *philosophes* are often brought to our attention. He first uses the term on July 13, 1813, and, here and elsewhere, he clarifies what he means by it: the mistake of not incorporating checks and balances into the new government in France and the "madness" of trying to establish a republic in a country where twenty-four and a half million of twenty-five million "could neither read nor write." In the first context, he specifically criticizes Turgot, Rochefaucault, Condorcet, Benjamin Franklin, and Jefferson himself: "Checks and Ballances, Jefferson, however you and Party may have ridiculed them, are our only Security."[155]

Reminding Jefferson that the first time they ever differed was over the French Revolution, he also specifies *whose* ideology he means: "I have never read reasoning more absurd than . . . the subtle labours of [French *philosophes*] Helvétius and Rousseau to demonstrate the natural Equality of Mankind." God has made us all so unequal in ability that no policy can change it, he continues. Justice for all and "do as you would be done by is all the Equality that can be defended by common sense." Not only does Adams—correctly—not include Voltaire in this reproach, in his *Discourses on Davila*, written to denounce these errors as he reminds Jefferson, he cites Voltaire in several chapter headings. And in 1814, he added a note saying that with Napoleon now in exile, we should reread Voltaire's *Candide* and *Zadig* "and see if there is anything extravagant in them."

Voltaire made the same distinction as Adams: we will never be equal in intelligence, physical strength, or abilities, but we can and should be equal before the law. It is the greatest liberty possible, for that very reason.[156] Both men have been accused of being monarchists at heart, and the debate has spilled a great deal of ink. In Voltaire's case, the form of government was not the crucial issue. He had lived under a constitutional monarchy in England, absolute monarchs in France and Prussia, a "republic" in Geneva and had known a great many monarchs, ministers, and republicans. What mattered to Voltaire were good laws, applicable to all, including kings or presidents, humanely enforced, as he had been saying since his *Letters on England* in 1734. Only this can free us from the whims of those in power. To a man defending monarchy as the best form, Voltaire replied, "That is true only if Marcus Aurelius is the monarch; for otherwise, what does it matter to a poor wretch whether he is devoured by one lion or a hundred rats?" Republics are not necessarily "virtuous" as some were claiming.[157]

Part of the polemic stems from the fact that Voltaire's friendships with Frederick and Catherine (both the Great) suddenly became a problem for the French revolutionaries while they were lopping off crowned heads. Tracts denouncing Voltaire's "shameful weakness" in "cajoling Frederick" or "in seeking the favors of the great" inundated Paris.[158] Thomas Paine, who had gone to join the French Revolutionaries, echoes these views in his *Rights of Man*. A few years earlier, in Paine's *Pennsylvania Magazine*, Voltaire had been "judicious and humane," but later, in *Rights*, Voltaire only deserves our thanks rather than our esteem for ending superstitions because of his "impure principles as a flatterer of despots." Soon, however, poor Tom was nearly guillotined for voting against beheading the French king.[159]

In any case, Voltaire had not sought "the favors of the great," as Adams knew, having read his correspondence with Frederick. Frederick and Catherine both initiated their correspondences with Voltaire, and he unsurprisingly welcomed their support. While battling persecutions sanctioned by divine rights, "one should always have a few crowned heads up one's sleeve," he quipped.[160] But as Peter Gay demonstrated, the supposed preference for enlightened despots so frequently attributed to Voltaire makes "an unwarranted leap" from acceptance of the Old Régime he lived in to a "theoretical preference for it." And his early enthusiasm for Frederick was just as justified as his later disappointment. A realist, Voltaire didn't expect monarchs to give up their jobs. Enlightening them to the benefits of tolerance and education was what he strove for and, amazingly, obtained. However, "his most strongly held convictions, the rule of law and free expression, directly contradict authoritarianism in any form," Gay points out, even the Prussian philosophical version.[161] Humane reform was what was urgent.

Lines about church frauds are extracted by atheists to show John Adams on their side. Fifty gospels destroyed! Among other records destroyed or forged by priests and despots, Adams exclaimed, again echoing Voltaire.[162] "The question before the human race," he tells Jefferson on June 20, 1815, "is Whether the God of nature shall govern the World by his own laws, or Whether Priests and Kings shall rule it by fictitious Miracles?" But who shall take God's side? Brachmans? Mandarins? Frederick? Voltaire? Rousseau? he asks. "These Phylosophers have shewn themselves as incapable of governing mankind, as the

[French kings]," he scolds. Adams is fuming in this letter because Condorcet "confessed" in his history of the progress of the human mind[163] that "the Phylosophers" adopted some of the priests' own wiles to overthrow them. When will honesty or veracity ever be found in any sect or party? Adams wails, regretting that he has "only an English translation." Whether he later read the original text we don't hear, but two months later he made one of the most remarkable mentions of Voltaire of all, in quite a different frame of mind.

On August 24, 1815, he muses over a book he thinks might "ecraser le miserable" in the language of Frederick, Voltaire, etc.,[164] then segues into musings on the American Revolution. "What do We Mean by the Revolution? The War?" he asks. War was only the consequence. "The Revolution was in the Minds of the People, and this was effected from 1760 to 1775. . . . The Records . . . Pamphlets, Newspapers . . . ought to be consulted . . . The Congress of 1774 resembled in some respects . . . the Counsell of Nice in Ecclesiastic History. It assembled the Priests from the East and the West the North and the South who compared Notes, engaged in . . . debates and formed Results . . . which went out to the world as unanimous." Adams' misspelling refers to the Council of Nicaea, which chose our four gospels from the fifty-odd circulating in 325 CE—and which deified Jesus. This last decision brought protests from two thousand priests, Voltaire tells us in the *Philosophical Dictionary* ("Councils"), and from three-quarters of the empire, according to his *Sermon of Rabbi Akib*. The years 1760 to 1775 also happen to be when Voltaire's *écraser l'infâme* campaign was in full swing.

Coincidence? These lines are often discussed but with Nicea, the Priests, Voltaire, etc., left out; and regrettably, Adams never tells us. His editor Lester J. Cappon promptly intervenes, however, to inform us that Adams rejected Voltaire's atheism.[165] He cites as proof Adams' letter of March 2, 1816: "No man is more Sensible than I am of the Services to Science and Letters, Humanity Fraternity and Liberty that would have been rendered By . . . Voltaire, Dalembert [*sic*], Buffon, Diderot, Rouseau [*sic*] . . . Frederick and Catherine, if they had possessed common sense." They seemed to think whole nations had been converted from Christianity by their opinions "almost as suddenly as Catholicks and Calving[is]ts believe in instantaneous Conversion," he says, adding, "And what was their Phylosophy? Atheism; pure unadulterated Atheism." Adams immediately follows this, however, with, "Diderot, D'Alembert, Frederick . . . and Grimm were indubitable Atheists." Adams is surely correcting himself here for inadvertently including Voltaire because in this letter, he is recounting Grimm's "impartial . . . lashing" of Voltaire and all the French writers—and Grimm often mocked Voltaire for *not* being an atheist like himself.[166] Moreover, several more letters follow discussing Grimm, and Voltaire is never included among atheists again. It was, after all, his main point of contention with the atheistic circle of Barons Grimm and d'Holbach and with Diderot, co-editor of the *Encyclopédie* with the famous mathematician, Jean le Rond d'Alembert. However, despite Adams' relish of Grimm's "History of their Quarrels," the relations of Voltaire with Diderot, and d'Alembert especially, also contained a great deal of respect and mutual admiration.[167]

This letter is doubly interesting however because it provokes Jefferson to name some of the *philosophes* in response—for the first and only time in their letters. Adams' tirade continues for three pages, till he catches himself enough to ask, "This Grimm must've been in Paris when you were there. Did you know or hear of him?" Jefferson replies, "Yes, most intimately." Grimm was "pleasant, conversible, but a man of irony, cunning and egoism. No heart, not much science . . ." And yes, Grimm probably was "of the school of . . . d'Holbach's system of atheism." Rousseau left "biting anecdotes of Grimm" and d'Holbach's circle in his *Confessions*, he ends suavely.

Had Adams hit a nerve? Grimm was hardly impartial[168] and Adams' delight in malicious gossip is a tad unpleasant. He evidently took it as a reproach himself, for a month later he writes that he has finished all fifteen volumes of Grimm: "Hold your tongue."[169] Twice more he badgers Jefferson to read Grimm, "the most entertaining work I ever read." Jefferson finally replies four months later that perhaps he will read these anecdotes before he dies, by an acquaintance, the "traverses of whose mind I knew."

Lines are extracted from Adams, Jefferson, and Franklin in schoolbooks, biographies, and all over the internet to prove them Congregationalists, Unitarians, Anglicans, or some form of Christian, with every "Lord help us" put on display. Adams, however, claims to have been sincerely investigating the "corruptions of Christianity" all his life, and the breadth of his reading on the subject is impressive.[170]

There were of course other Dissenters besides deists who rejected, not Jesus *per se*, but that he was a god. Ever since Jesus was deified, as Voltaire wrote, people have quarreled over whether there are three gods (including the Holy Ghost)—or one. Anti-Trinitarians, Socinians, and Unitarians also refuse the doctrine of three gods, and some historians affirm that Jefferson and Adams were Unitarians. They were both fond of leading Unitarian Joseph Priestley, and knew him personally. Jefferson in fact tells Adams in a letter that Priestley's *Corruptions of Christianity* and his *Early Opinions of Jesus* were "the basis of my own faith."

Adams, however, then guesses that he hadn't read any other works by Priestley, and Jefferson admits it. Priestley rejected certain biblical stories while still believing in miracles and in the Apocalyptic Beast, Adams says. Priestley had written to both Adams and their mutual friend Dr. Benjamin Rush that Napoleon was prophesized in the Apocalypse and would cause the downfall of all states, represented by the ten horns of the fourth beast of Daniel, etc., etc.[171] "I could never be a Disciple of Priestley's," says Adams. "He is absurd, inconsistent, credulous and incomprehensible," although he was "a Phenomenon, a Comet . . . like Voltaire, Bolingbroke, and Hume. Had Bolingbroke or Voltaire taken him in hand, what would they have made of him and his Creed?" Which Gibbon was right to call "Scanty," he adds. Jefferson then confides that he had asked Priestley to finish a work on Jesus he had once hoped to write himself, but that the result had been so disappointing, he would not use it.[172]

Alfred Noyes and others have attempted to prove that Voltaire was a Christian reformer. Their main source is a dream Voltaire relates in *Questions on the Encyclopedia*, in the article "Religion II." In the dream, a guide leads him through a mystical realm to show him mountains of dead Jews, American Indians, and Christians, all slaughtered in the name of God, flanked by mountains of gold and silver, jeweled crosses and mitres. Voltaire weeps, then a man we recognize as Jesus arrives, who tells him he did not say he had come to bring the sword, not peace, as the Bible relates, and he is just as horrified by all these crimes committed in his name. Voltaire replies, "If that's the case, I take you for my only master." However, as noted Voltairians Torrey and Pomeau both point out, in this text Voltaire is rather saying that Jesus was a deist too.[173]

Jefferson eventually finished the work on Jesus he had confided to Priestley.

It became the famous *Jefferson Bible*. But that is not the name he gave it. Jefferson called it *The Life and Morals of Jesus of Nazareth*. Considering it impossible that Jesus could have contradicted his own sublime teachings, Jefferson purged the New Testament of what he believed Jesus' ignorant rascally followers must have added—to show that Jesus was a deist. Adams was highly enthused by the project.[174] Furthermore, *Questions on the Encyclopedia* is one of the texts Mary-Margaret Barr said Jefferson had extracted in his *Commonplace Book*; that's to say, as we have seen, one of those that disappeared from later editions.

In *Lies My Teacher Told Me*, a study of how pressure groups deform what we are taught, James W. Loewen tells of an editor exclaiming, "Are you going to tell kids that Thomas Jefferson didn't believe in Jesus? Not me!"[175] We must suppose that the editor meant as a god, since in actual fact, Jefferson, Franklin, and most of the founders extolled Jesus as one of humanity's greatest moral teachers. Even the Muslims include him—so why lie about it? Honesty works well in Europe, and it is deplorable to see even a publisher so misconstrue, not only deism, but the whole point of the Enlightenment. As Jefferson bemoaned, "They wish it to be believed that he can have no religion who advocates its freedom." But they want no belief besides Christianity even mentioned, Loewen discovered.[176]

Adams emphatically agreed with Jefferson. After all, who won our independence? They were Roman Catholics, Episcopalians, Presbyterians, Methodists, Lutherans, Arians, Socinians, Moravians, Anabaptists, Calvinists, Universalists, Deists, and Atheists—among others! he reminds us. "Could I recommend [only] the Catholics, the Quakers, the Methodists . . . or the Philosophers? No. Only GENERAL PRINCIPLES could unite that beautiful assembly. . . . In favor of these, I would fill sheets of quotations from Frederick of Prussia, Hume, Gibbon, Voltaire."[177] Is such a remark not plain enough to make not only students but textbook editors understand our laws and history? It would certainly find an even larger consensus in today's multicultural society.

And sooner or later lies do get exposed. Among the "uncommon" people who mention being affected by Voltaire's views on religion we might happen across Chateaubriand, Stendhal, or Flaubert. Diderot reported that two bishops told him there would be no religion in fifty years, thanks to Voltaire.[178] Victor Hugo argued that Voltaire had waged "Christ's war" far better than the church.[179] Robert Ingersoll extolled Voltaire, thanking him specifically "for the liberty I am enjoying at this moment."[180] British philosopher Bertrand Russell credited Voltaire for making him realize how moral fervor and doctrines lead to ferocity and abominable cruelty.[181] Queen Victoria's Prime Minister, Disraeli, "devoured all his volumes, roaring with laughter, wonder and indignation over all our centuries of misrule and imposture."[182] George Bernard Shaw tells us Voltaire did a great service to religion, and railed against the ignorance of Englishmen who still think of him as a "French infidel" instead of as the champion of secularism. In Shaw's *Adventures of the Black Girl in Her Search for God*, the heroine meets Jehovah, Mahomet, and Jesus in person to find, in the end, Voltaire.[183] International students paraded with signs reading "Voltaire! Help!" when Muslim extremists vowed death to British Indian novelist Salman Rushdie for his *Satanic Verses* in the 1980s.[184]

From William Blake's "Mock on, Voltaire" to Lord Byron's "gay grave wit who overthrew fools and shook thrones," we could fill pages with surprising remarks about a man who "only" wrote *Candide*. Despite all the burying, he seems to be repeatedly revived whenever our freedoms are gravely menaced.[185] In the wake of the terrorist assassinations in Paris in January 2015, he was cited all over the internet, from across the world. Under Nazi occupation, French philosopher Paul Valéry did the same, calling Voltaire "unendingly topical" for his power in denouncing crimes against humanity.[186] Much of Voltaire's huge output is directed against oppression in general and religious oppression especially.

And naturally, for that very same reason, few men have been more vilified. As Voltaire himself observed, a man riddled with bullets in a battle does not lose his temper, but refuse him assent over religion and he becomes implacable.[187] We read that his vile attack on religion was born of a seedy, greedy thirst for fame, an insane desire to destroy and desecrate. He was "Satan's secretary"— or worse, his son!—in a nineteenth-century account of Satan coupling with Voltaire's mother, then dancing for joy in hell at his son's accomplishment. "Some shock virtue; Voltaire shocks vice!" shrieked French writer and minister, Joseph de Maistre,[188] who, with legions of others, then set out to prove it.

Yet regarding the usual charges—that Voltaire was vain and greedy, that he despised the people, that he was a vile flatterer of despots or had no capacity for friendship—"could not withstand, even in the most prejudiced mind, a reading of any one volume of his correspondence," said Norman Torrey, much less the other forty-nine volumes. Friendship, for a man who lives dangerously, forever risking life or liberty, Torrey continues, "is at once more precarious and more precious." And given the number of Voltaire's correspondents (now estimated at eighteen hundred) most of us would appear friendless in comparison. He ruled over intellectual Europe, and never has such a humane cosmopolitan society flourished since, subduing so many prejudices, Torrey concludes. He adds, in his chapter relating Voltaire's friendships, "His record is remark-able. . . . He ranked friendship second only to love of justice."[189] It might be added that the despair felt at his death was palpable, even in Grimm's occasion-ally sarcastic newsletter, included in the Appendix.[190]

The fact that Voltaire's fifty-volume correspondence (now being expanded by Oxford) has never been translated is, of course, a handicap for English readers. Torrey's penetrating analysis of the man is probably the best place to get a feel for his "spirit," as his title proposes. A few editions of selected letters have appeared in English, but "selections" sometimes mask agendas. A few of Voltaire's "best-known" phrases illustrate the point.

The one most often seen is no doubt, "If God didn't exist, we would have to invent him." As Peter Gay remarked, it sounds like a cynical injunction to rulers to invent a divine policeman for their ignorant subjects. But the original line reads, "If the heavens, despoiled of his august stamp could ever cease to manifest him, if God didn't exist, we would have to invent him so that the wise could announce him and *monarchs* fear him."[191] Part of a response to d'Holbach, the line in full says the exact opposite of what the butchered phrase conveys. Another frequently misused line is, "When the populace begins to argue, all is lost," meant to illustrate Voltaire's contempt for the masses. This phrase came from a letter saying that although some may be incapable of science, no one is incapable of virtue, and we should not waste our time arguing over whether theologians like Athanasius or Zwingli were right. "I agree with those who would make good laborers of foundlings, rather than theologians. When the populace begins to argue, all is lost."[192] By populace, he meant foundlings turned into monks.

"The method [all of his enemies use] is very simple," Voltairian scholar

Jean Sareil notes. "It consists in multiplying citations of his works outside of all context . . . and after two centuries of controversy, an incredible number of clichés remain that still set off false judgments."[193] René Pomeau, a leading twentieth-century Voltairian, observed that most of those who hate Voltaire have never read him.[194] Their views are based on extracts. Voltaire's own words are disregarded even by scholars, he adds, listing in example all those who have debated Voltaire's "real beliefs" over the ages, even though he maintained hundreds of times throughout his life he was a deist.[195] And as Peter Gay wrote, faced with all the polemics and the magnitude of the corpus—one hundred and twenty-nine volumes, also being expanded by Oxford—it is obviously far easier to borrow the opinions of others and just assume that "objectivity consists of believing at least half the charges made."[196] Yet two-thirds of the twenty-six thousand letters now at our disposal were utterly unknown to historians before the 1970s. And they have spurred hundreds of new studies since.[197]

The charge that Voltaire was an anti-Semite, with extracts "illustrating" it all over the internet, is surely the commonest cause of hatred today. Even some of the best Voltairians, like Peter Gay, accept the charge, with mitigations. Bertram E. Schwarzbach, who explored Voltaire's personal dealings with Jewish people, disagreed:[198] Voltaire's *bête noire* was the Bible, not the Jews, and more particularly the "sordid absurdity" of holding up Old Testament massacres, blood feuds, murders, incests, and adulteries as lessons in morality. On these subjects, Voltaire can be scathing indeed, but it is with the goal of proving the Bible a product of superstitious, tribalistic priests rather than God.

The fact that some of the works in this book have been unavailable for so long no doubt lends itself to the misrepresentations. It was clearer to eighteenth-century readers of the *Sermon of Rabbi Akib* that the burning of Jews by Christians was just as abhorrent to Voltaire as the biblical massacres of unchosen people. In his chapter "On the Jews" in *Letters . . . on Rabelais*, we see him feigning to deplore a great many Jewish views of Christianity with which he heartily agreed, a tactic he had used regarding Protestantism in his *Letters on England*. In his *Treatise on Tolerance* he held the tolerance of the Jews up as a beautiful example that Christians ought to imitate. In *Zapata's Questions*, Zapata asks his "wise masters" of theology, "If God is the God of Abraham, why do you burn the children of Abraham? And recite their prayers while burning them?

Why do you kill them for obeying their book of law, while adoring their book of law?" He receives no response, so he teaches virtue instead, and is roasted by the Inquisition.

Peter Gay accredited the charge first launched by Abbé Guénée, who, pretending to be a Jew, claimed that Voltaire was persecuting them because he had been bankrupted by a Jew in London and had had a lawsuit with another in Berlin. But Voltaire's reply was categorical: he had never intended to insult the Jews of his day.[199] Both Gay and Fulbright scholar Pierre Aubery deemed that Voltaire's intentions were rather to bring the Jews into the community of humanity from which not only anti-Semites but the prophets sometimes tried to oust them.[200] It is also worth noting that Voltaire's shrillest attacks on Judeo-Christianity always seem to have come in the wake of new persecuting "barbarities" brought to his attention.[201]

Extracts are also paraded to prove Voltaire a misogynist, a Muslim-hater, or a racist. German philosopher Immanuel Kant found learned women so unattractive he felt that Madame du Châtelet, the brilliant scientist Voltaire loved and lived with, might as well have worn a beard. Voltaire, on the contrary, praised her genius as superior to his own in countless writings. Rousseau's descriptions in *Emile* of how women should be brought up led eighteenth-century feminist Catherine Sawbridge Macauley Graham to remark he seemed to want to prepare them for a harem.[202] Voltaire's remarks in *The Education of Daughters* or in the ironic *Wives, Submit to Your Husbands* read in startling contrast to these men—and to a great many other men throughout the next two centuries.

Voltaire's play *Mahomet* was written as an exposé of fanaticism and "priest-craft" in the only way a Catholic living in France in the 1740s could: obliquely. This dark portrayal of the prophet has since been banned, but he had scarcely finished it before the research made him write to a friend that he had been wrong to accept the clergy's view. And he made a point of correcting the portrayal in all later works, such as *Wives Submit*, *Catechism of the Honest Man* and *The Dinner at Count de Boulainvilliers'* herein.[203] Men are only enlightened by degrees, as he himself said.

He has also been accused of being "tepid" on the slave trade. *Candide* contains the era's most famous denunciations of it, but it should be noted that slavery was not yet a racial issue in Voltaire's generation. For him, the term slavery included French Protestants made galley slaves for life, the pockets of serfdom that still existed, and close to a million whites who had also been captured and enslaved by the Barbary pirates. Despite claims to the contrary, the fact that it was becoming a racial issue only toward the end of his life is the reason the *philosophes* twenty to forty years younger than Voltaire, such as Diderot, Raynal, or Condorcet, were more vocal on the subject than he was.[204]

As evidenced by excerpts in the Appendix, a great many contemporaries, and near contemporaries like nineteenth-century historian Edgar Quinet, would have contested another later trope: that Voltaire was "a destroyer, not a builder." But the truth is that the sheer mass of the defamations penned over the centuries have affected everyone to some degree, including some of Voltaire's most fervent admirers. One amusing discovery made in the twentieth century however revealed that the "revolting traits" endlessly ascribed to him were first born of a libel written in reaction to his *Letters on England* in 1734. This fairly moderate book leaves most people wondering today how it could have set off warrants for his arrest.

And yet the libel, translated as *Anonymous Character Sketch* in our Appendix, circulated internationally, coloring everyone's fantasies about him. In America it was often attributed to his royal pupil, Frederick the Great, after their feud.[205] The caricature it contains lives on, even on the internet today: thin, caustic, vain, shrewd, greedy, friendless, unpatriotic, superficial, and prone to follies. He was "unpatriotic, caustic, vain, prone to follies" in the original text because the book offended the French by praising the relative tolerance of England; "shrewd and greedy" because he had dispersed the book among several printers in an effort to outfox the censor.[206]

Voltaire never believed the probable author, an aspiring writer, guilty. "I've never even seen him!" he protested. But as Pomeau points out, the man had no doubt seen him in cafés or theaters, which accounts for the startling half-truths in his descriptions.[207] These slurs were repeated so extensively they became clichés, Sareil wrote, to the everlasting joy of all his enemies.[208] Oliver Goldsmith echoes them, though he admired Voltaire deeply. Montesquieu and David Hume, who never met him, were similarly affected, as was even Frederick the Great, who did know him but who maliciously echoed them to justify his own poor behavior at times.[209] Doubtless countless others, such as John Adams, could be added.

For further corroboration of Sareil's remark, we need only read *Voltaire's British Visitors*, a collection of a hundred and fifty other character sketches left by English visitors who went to gawk at Voltaire during his *écraser l'infâme* campaign in Ferney on the Swiss border of France.[210] Their remarks fall into two almost evenly divided groups. Group 1: Those astonished at Voltaire's generosity and kindness (Gibbon is amazed by a dinner and ball he spontaneously threw for a hundred people who had come to see one of his plays),[211] at his love of the English and their language, at the simple beauty of his house and gardens "in the English style," and at all the energy and money he spent helping the local peasants and victims of persecution. Group 2: Those who went in "curiosity and horror" to see "the wicked wit, Voltaire," who invariably find him skeletal, vain, greedy, shallow, his language blasphemous, and his house and gardens in wretched taste "which he imagines are in the English style." All of them are astonished that Voltaire could converse in English, a language he had learned thirty years earlier, but few samples of his "blasphemies" are given. "By G——, I do love the Ingles (the English), G——damn!" is one of them.

One wonders how he ever picked up such ghastly language from English lords and lettered men. But the famous traveler James Boswell informs us, "He swore bloodily, as was the fashion when he was in England."[212] One would be hard put to find expletives in the fifteen thousand letters found of those he wrote in French, but more interesting is the fact that few accounts from either group are not tinged with the clichés inspired by the *Anonymous Character Sketch*. A few remark in surprise, "He's not that thin." Some more helpfully note that "he looks just like the many prints we see of him," and many concur with Lady Harrowby who found him "very cheerful & entertaining [and] not at all offensive in expressing his very unbelieving Sentiments," sensibly adding that, after all, everyone knew his views and what he wrote. The famous author of *The Wealth of Nations*, economist Adam Smith, visited five or six times and was always vehement in his defense of Voltaire, according to his friends. But, of course, nothing is easier than to select descriptions only from our second group to show "the real Voltaire." The wonder is rather that he kindly wined and dined so many intruders for so long, visitor John Moore wrote, including the obvious bigots.[213] But crowds were literally hanging on his gate.

Another factor that should be borne in mind, Sareil explained, was quite simply jealousy. Nicholas Cronk, director of the Voltaire Foundation at Oxford, points out that Voltaire dominated his century "in virtually all literary genres": theater, poetry, history, philosophy, most prose forms, and even, briefly, science.[214] As Frederick said in his *Eulogy* in our Appendix, nothing like it had been seen since Cicero, and perhaps not even then. Goethe complained to fellow German writer Johann Peter Eckermann in 1830, "You have no idea of the significance of Voltaire and his great contemporaries in my youth, and how they dominated the whole civilized world. My biography does not make it clear enough what influence these men had . . . and how much it cost me to defend myself against them."[215] Even those great Enlightenment contemporaries were not always devoid of envy.[216]

There is also much truth in Oliver Goldsmith's suggestion in the Appendix that accounts of Voltaire are more glowing from those who actually knew him. Despite invitations, Rousseau never met him and Diderot barely did, just before he died. Condorcet, who visited him two or three times, idolized him, and D'Alembert, who, of Diderot's circle, knew him best, was a loyal friend. The eighteenth century Kehl editors of their correspondence were dumbfounded by the absence of vanity and petty quarrels in their letters, so common in the letters of Racine and other writers. "The history of letters has not yet offered such an honorable example," we are informed. French writer Marmontel, the famous actor Lekain, and many others testified that Voltaire generously shared connections, advice, and financial aid. The truth is he launched more careers than anyone in his century, said Sareil.[217] Nor do we discover a greedy snob who despised the rabble in the warm memoirs left by three of his secretaries.[218] Nor in the inscription on the statue the peasants of Ferney raised to him. It reads:

> To the Benefactor of Ferney
> Voltaire built more than a hundred houses. He gave the town
> a church, a school, a hospital, a reservoir and a fountain. He
> loaned money without interest to the neighboring communities,
> dried up the swamps, and established fairs and markets. He
> nourished the inhabitants during the famine of 1771.

He also set up silk works, tile works, and watchmaker shops to help them earn a living, defended them against the rapacity of tax collectors, and forced a local monastery to free the serfs he was horrified to learn they still had. The years he spent defending victims of religious persecution already mentioned, often footing the legal fees, was widely heralded.

That he despised humbler folk is an absurd claim whichever way you look at it, despite moments of exasperation. The very fact of making these important facts on religion and science accessible to the masses voids the argument. And that degree of clarity was not only his conscious goal; it is what has always most contributed to his "most hated" status. Voltaire sometimes printed the works of others alongside his own: those he deemed well written. Works that he considered tedious or obscure, he only cites—the much heralded Bolingbroke, for instance. Although he borrowed his name twice as a pseudonym (once Bolingbroke was deceased and out of harm's way), he privately considered Bolingbroke's own works diffuse: "a tree of many leaves but little fruit."[219] And were it not for Voltaire, as Lanson noted, these men would never have moved so vast an audience.[220] In any case, as Condorcet said in his biography of Voltaire (extracted in the Appendix), they certainly hadn't so far.

Didier Masseau illustrated that this very readability is what infuriated most. The *anti-philosophes* were less angered by the content than by seeing information known only to scholars given to "young people, women and the frivolous."[221] Casanova, the notorious libertine once imprisoned for atheism, told Voltaire that he should leave the people in the chains of their superstitions. They could never be happy without "the beast." "I later regretted" the remarks, he wrote, and "fear my very humble amends . . . will not be read."[222]

But the campaign was not launched unthinkingly, whatever Casanova supposed. Whether the masses, who rarely reason, need superstitions, as Tacitus had argued, is a question Voltaire long debated, especially with Frederick. Given the towering rates of illiteracy, they both thought so for years.[223] In his first letter, Voltaire merely begged Frederick to never lend state-backing to the wars of theologians. "[T]heir arrogant, inflammatory words, when neglected, are lost in the wind." Frederick could not have agreed more. Furthermore, his first edicts accorded freedom of beliefs fifty years before France or America did.[224] But fifteen years later in Berlin, Voltaire's private notebooks betray some changes in his thinking. "It is impossible to end the rage between sects just by ignoring it." "There is not a single theological quarrel that has not torn up states." "Religion is between men and God." The thirst to dominate must go, he wrote among similar thoughts.[225]

Voltaire was well aware that few read books: hence these pamphlets and short works, which, along with gazettes, had a far larger audience, not only due to attention spans but cost. As he told d'Alembert, co-editor of the *Encyclopedia*, their twenty volumes, which most could not afford, would never cause a revolution.[226] He nonetheless duly contributed forty-five entries himself, promising to make them "as uselessly dull" as necessary to pass the scrutiny of the censors. And the official suppression of the *Encyclopedia* in 1759, despite it all, was also one of the triggers for this pamphlet war.[227]

Exposing the "inconvenient truths" about our history, religion, and the Bible is the only thing that can be done to tide fanaticism. As Voltaire asked in the *Philosophical Dictionary* ("Fanaticism"), "How do you answer a man who says he would rather obey God than men, and who is sure of earning heaven if he cuts your throat?" The fanatic is sure he knows what he cannot know and does not need to know, wrote Peter Gay. His fanaticism turns vicious because it masks disturbing doubts. And after more than two centuries of ink spilled over whether what Voltaire did was good or bad, Gay adds, the debate is, in the end, irrelevant. It was inevitable.[228]

Voltaire would have liked to liberate science, too, from its myriad "systems" and "schools of thought." His deepest conviction was that mankind did not know enough to explain the universe, whether by systems Cartesian, Leibnizian, or religious. "Systems offend my reason," he said, yet he is still disparaged as a skeptic today and not a "real philosopher," for not having created one. For Voltaire, skepticism was a method, not a system. Doubt is the crucial first step in scientific thinking; the beginning of all wisdom. And, as Torrey asked, how can the terms "skeptic" or "cynic" be properly applied to a man who had such faith in reason and mankind, and who was so tremendously active, with such astonishing recuperative powers? It "gives lie to the charge that . . . skepticism . . . leads to hopelessness, inaction and stagnation," he wrote.[229] "I am so happy, I am ashamed of it," Voltaire said in old age, seeing some effect from all his efforts, though beset with a half dozen infirmities no one could cure. The empirical methods he championed all his life had not yet produced the remedies we have today.

There is one science attributed to him, however. Norman Torrey and Bertram Schwarzbach both noted that Voltaire's main line of attack in these writings has evolved into the modern science called biblical exegesis. Torrey quipped that the more modern theological schools had nearly caught up with Voltaire by 1938, minus the humor.[230] That bantering tone gets him decried as superficial, but Reader, Beware. As Schwarzbach observed, it is amusing to note that all the fallacies and contradictions Voltaire points out in the Bible had been exposed before him in the most unimpeachable sources—the classic Christian and Jewish commentators, all struggling to reconcile these same contradictions.[231]

In one of his dialogues, Voltaire had Diogenes, Moses, and Locke debate the necessity of superstitions for the masses. Locke asks, "But if men were told the truth, might they not believe it? If Rulers were bold and honest, perhaps the follies of the people would disappear. I'd be happy to try the experiment." A number of facts relentlessly buried suggest that this "experiment" once gave spectacular results in America, constantly qualified by visitors in the last third of the eighteenth century as "the most enlightened country in the world." But as John Adams lamented in 1815, arbitrary power, including in popular assemblies, has never failed to destroy all the records, memorials, and histories it did not like. "The Priests are at their Old Work again," he fretted, as priests of all sorts clearly are again today. But as Strachey famously said of Voltaire, "Consider that life and take courage."[232]

> Tyrants always think that an ignorant people is easier to enslave, but their ignorance always enslaves us in the end.
> —Voltaire

> If a nation expects to be ignorant and free, it expects what never was, and never will be.
> —Thomas Jefferson

> You who are listening, remember that you are above all men before being citizens of a certain town and a certain society, professing a certain religion. The time has come to enlarge our sphere of thought, to become citizens of the world.
> —Voltaire

> My country is the world, and my religion is to do good.
> —Thomas Paine[233]

NOTE ON THE TEXTS

Eighteenth-century writers almost never signed their books (and who can blame them?) but Voltaire entertained himself and the public by signing his: just never with his name. It is estimated that he invented approximately 169 pseudonyms, attributing these texts to notorious, but safely deceased, freethinkers such as Lord Bolingbroke and La Mettrie, or to people invented altogether such as Dr. Goodnatur'd Wellwisher, the Pope of Church St. Toleranski, or the Count and Countess of Hiss-Priestcraft. The often repeated remark, that "everyone knew who wrote them," may be true of the literati, but the pseudonyms were not as futile and childish as Grimm claimed, who often trumpeted the real author's name himself. A large number of copies recovered from the period contain the uncertain annotation, "Said to be by Voltaire" (perhaps thanks to Grimm!) and even a postal spy once famously noted, "This Mr. Ecrlinf writes pretty well"—referring to the abbreviation of *Ecrasez l'infâme* Voltaire sometimes put on his missives.[234]

These false attributions will be explained in introductory remarks. A glossary is available at the end of the book to explain the most recurrent terms and characters that may be unfamiliar to the general reader of today.

Translating Voltaire into English poses a dilemma. We have numerous letters and essays written by Voltaire in English, and his English was naturally the English of the eighteenth century. His French, however, was strikingly modern. Professor of French linguistics Jérôme Vérain points out that he literally created modern French syntax and modernized its spelling. Since the clarity, pithiness, and flow of his style forced admiration even from his most rabid enemies, it has been decided to attempt a translation better reflecting the sprightly style of Voltaire as it reads in his native tongue, and without "the proliferation of semicolons and colons" added by compositors that Theodore Besterman deplored in the Introduction to his excellent translation of *The Philosophical Dictionary*.

The Protestant form of Biblical names have also been used, despite the fact that Voltaire used the Catholic forms found in the Vulgate Bible, because today's readers, both Catholic and Protestant, tend to be more familiar with the spellings used in the NIV Bible.

A final remark must be made regarding Voltaire's citations of the Bible.

"Errors" are sometimes pointed out, contrasting what Voltaire "makes the Bible say" with what it actually says. These remarks are based on the assumption that "God's Word" is invariable, but this is far from the case. Bible translations vary to a surprising degree, especially in the shocking passages. The notorious passage on homosexuals in Leviticus 20:13 serves as an example. Translations vary from "God doesn't like it" in the *Good News Bible* to "it's an abomination. They must be put to death," etc., in the *King James* and the *New International Version* Bibles. As Besterman pointed out, Voltaire mainly used the Latin Vulgate Bible. What he says about Ezekiel or David, among other disputed passages, is exactly what the Vulgate says and often what the *King James Bible* says as well—two versions still in print that existed in his day. For disputes among biblical exegetes also reveal that certain passages of our modern Bibles (for example, the passage on David sawing prisoners in half in 2 Samuel 12:31) have been changed "since the Enlightenment."[235]

GRATEFUL THANKS TO A CHARITABLE MAN

1750

Montesquieu's *The Spirit of the Laws* had been denounced as impious and scandalous in several editions of the *Nouvelles ecclésiastiques* (Ecclesiastical News), a gazette run by the Jansenists. The paper's stated mission was to report on "important truths or questions that interest Christians," which seems to have frequently involved reporting miracles or warring with the Jesuits. One issue, for example, complains bitterly of a Jesuit bishop who had granted permission to eat eggs during Lent.[1] This is Voltaire's sardonic anonymous response to the paper's attack on Montesquieu. The reason for his odd fictitious claim that the text was written in Marseilles is revealed at the end, although the usual need to veil one's identity from the authorities also came into play.

Montesquieu himself intensely disliked Voltaire, but his publisher included this riposte in some editions of Montesquieu's own *Defense of "The Spirit of Laws."* Robert Shackleton called it "one of the most generous documents of the eighteenth century."[2]

From Marseilles, the 10th of May, 1750

You have rendered a great service to humanity by wisely unleashing your rage at works written to pervert it. You never cease to write against *The Spirit of the Laws*, and it would seem even by your style that you are the enemy of anything spirited. You notify us that you have preserved the world from the venom spread by Pope's *Essay on Man*, a book I never cease to reread to fully persuade myself of the force of your arguments and the importance of your services. You do not waste your time, Sir, in examining the core of this work on the laws, in verifying its citations, in discussing whether it is accurate, profound, full of clarity or wisdom; whether its chapters spring from each other naturally and whether they form a coherent whole; in short, whether this book, which should be useful, is not by misfortune a book that is pleasant to read.

You go straight to the point, and regarding M. de Montesquieu as a disciple of Pope, you regard them both as disciples of Spinoza. You reproach them, with marvelous zeal, of being atheists, because you have uncovered, you say, the principles of natural religion throughout their philosophies. Nothing is assuredly, Sir, more charitable or judicious than to conclude that a philosopher who postulates that God speaks to the hearts of all men, recognizes no God.

"An honest man is the noblest creation of God," says the famous philosopher poet.[3] You have raised yourself above the honest man. You confound these fatal maxims that say that the Divinity is the author and link between all beings, that all men are brothers, and that God is the father of them all. There must be no innovations in religion, no disturbing of the peace established by a wise monarch, no saying that one must tolerate the feelings of men as well as their faults. Continue, Sir, to crush this horrid libertinage, which is the ruin of society. It is already a lot that through your ecclesiastical gazettes, you have made holy endeavors to ridicule all the powers, and even though the grace of being amusing is lacking you, *volenti et conanti*,[4] you have nevertheless the merit of having made every effort to write invectives agreeably. You have sometimes wished to rejoice the saints, but you have often tried to arm the faithful in very Christian fashion against one another. You preach schism for the greater glory of God. All that is very edifying; but it is still not enough.

Your zeal will not have achieved half the goal if you do not succeed in getting all the books of Pope, of Locke, of Bayle, *The Spirit of the Laws*, etc., burnt at a stake lit with a bundle of the *Nouvelles ecclésiastiques*.

For indeed, Sir, what appalling evils have a dozen verses from this *Essay on Man* by this villainous Pope not done to the world, or five or six articles from this abominable Bayle's *Dictionary*, or one or two pages by the rogue, Locke, or other arsonists of the sort? It is true that these men led pure and innocent lives, that all honest people cherished and consulted them, but that's precisely why they're dangerous. One sees their supporters, arms in hand, disturbing king-doms and lighting the torches of civil wars everywhere. Montaigne, Charron, the President of Thou, Descartes, Gassendi, Rohault, Le Vayer, these horrid men who held the same principles, wreaked havoc throughout France. It is their philosophies that set off so many battles and caused the St. Bartholomew's Day Massacre.[5] It is their spirit of tolerantism[6] that is ruining the world, and your holy zeal that spreads peace and concord everywhere.

You teach us that all the partisans of natural religion are the enemies of the Christian faith. Truly, Sir, you have made there a handsome discovery! Therefore, as soon as I see a wise man whose philosophy recognizes a Supreme Being everywhere, who admires Providence in the infinitely large and the infi-nitely small, from the creation of worlds to that of insects, I shall conclude at once that this man is no Christian. You warn us that we must think the same of all philosophers today. Surely nothing more sensible and useful to Christianity could be said than to assure us that our religion is scorned throughout Europe by all those whose profession is to seek the truth. You may boast there of having had a thought whose consequences will be of great advantage to the public.

How I love too your anger against the author of *The Spirit of the Laws* when you reproach him for having praised the Solons, the Platos, the Socrates, the Aris-tides, the Ciceros, the Catos, the Epictetuses, the Anthonies, and the Trajans! One would think, from your devout furor against those people that they had all signed the *Formulaire*.[7] What monsters, Sir, all these great men of antiquity! Let us burn all that remains of their texts, along with those of Pope, Locke, and Montesquieu. Indeed, all of these ancient sages are your enemies, for they were all enlightened by natural religion. And yours, Sir, I say yours in particular, seems to be so utterly unnatural that it does not surprise me that you so sincerely detest all these illustrious reprobates who, I know not how, did so much good on earth. Do thank God you have nothing in common with their conduct or their writings.

Your holy ideas regarding political government are a consequence of your wisdom. One can see that you know all the kingdoms of earth just as well as all the kingdoms of heaven. You condemn, upon your private authority, the gains one may make on taking maritime risks. You probably don't know what money "à la grosse" is,[8] but you call it *usury*. It is a new obligation the king will have to you, for preventing his subjects from doing commerce with Cadiz. These works of Satan should be left to the English and the Dutch, already hopelessly damned. I wish you would tell us, Sir, how much the holy commerce of the *Nouvelles ecclésiastiques* brings you. I imagine that the blessing lavished by this work of art must amount at least to three hundred percent. There has never been a profane commerce that has reaped such yields.

The maritime commerce you condemn might be excused, perhaps, in favor of its public utility, in the boldness of sending one's goods into another hemisphere and at the risk of shipwrecks. Your little business has a more perceptible utility: it requires more courage and exposes one to greater risks.

What could be more useful indeed than to inform the universe, four times per month, of the adventures of a few tonsured clerics? What could be more courageous than to outrage your king and archbishop? And what greater risk, Sir, than the small humiliations you may endure on the public square? But, I am mistaken. There is a charm in suffering for the right cause. It is better to obey God than men, and you appear to me wholly made for martyrdom, which I wish for you most cordially, being your very humble and obedient servant.

Speaking of which, Sir, my compliments to Abbé Pluche, who so bravely continues to copy from other books in order to display *The Spectacle of Nature* and who has become the *charlatan of the ignorant*. One cannot be happier than I am to see an *evangelical preparation* and even an *evangelical demonstration* printed beside the correct manner of raising silkworms.[9]

It is very charming of him to make an excellent physicist of Moses and to bravely maintain, despite all the academies, that our light does not come from the sun or from other luminous bodies, and to advance that Negroes became black gradually in relation to their descent from Chus.[10] This Pluche has apparently never seen a dissected Negro. I also learn that he has found the place in the earthly paradise where Adam's rib has been conserved, and the skin of the serpent who spoke to his wife. I have heard tell that Balaam's ass is still alive and that he grazes in those regions. I have no doubt that Pluche will soon converse with him and give an account of it to Monsieur the Prior and to the Chevalier.[11]

I have one more little thing to tell you. I read in the eighth volume of this Pluche that Mahomet had traveled to the seven planets in one night. He cites this voyage as being in the Koran and as being an article of faith among the Turks. He takes this occasion to say that Mahomet is fatuous.

If ever Pluche goes to Constantinople, I advise him to be more polite. I encountered a Turk the other day at the port of Marseilles and asked him whether this supposed trip to the seven planets is indeed in the Koran. He told me it was not. I told him that Monsieur Pluche had rather flippantly called his prophet fatuous. My Turk, who is a very wise man, told me that when one lives in a house of glass, one should not throw stones at his neighbor's house.

EXTRACT FROM A DECREE BY THE SACRED CONGREGATION OF THE INQUISITION OF ROME OPPOSING A LIBEL ENTITLED: *LETTERS ON THE VINGTIEME*

1750

A ten-percent tax (*le Dixième*) had been levied on everyone except the clergy to help finance the War of the Austrian Succession. But with France hugely in debt at the end of the war, the government proposed to replace it with a new five-percent tax (*le Vingtième*) to be paid by everyone. The clergy owned a third of France but refused to pay it, so a lawyer for the government wrote a brochure to prove that they should. The common people were already overburdened with taxes, which they also paid to the clergy, and the "free donation" (*don gratuit*) that the clergy contributed every five years was usually used to reward the king for some concession: the suppression of Diderot's *Encyclopedia*, for example. This brochure is the work of the "Antichrist" Voltaire refers to, facetiously pretending to speak for the Holy Inquisitor of Rome. Amusingly, he beat the Vatican's own condemnation of the brochure by just a few months.[1]

How clear it is that the world is about to end and that the Antichrist has already come, said Antichrist having already sent several circular letters to the bishops of France in which he had the audacity to call them Frenchmen and subjects of the king. Satan has joined this man of iniquity to finish off the desolation of holy places with an abomination, since said Satan has composed and sold a rash, offensive, heretical book that smells of heresy, worthy of him. He endeavors to prove that the ecclesiastics are a part of the state instead of admitting they are its masters, as they had formerly taught. He advances that those who own a third of the revenues of the State should at least contribute a third of that, completely forgetting that our brothers were made to have everything and to contribute nothing. In addition, the above-mentioned book is full of impious maxims drawn from natural law, the rights of men, the fundamental laws of the kingdom, and other pernicious prejudices, cruelly tending to strengthen royal authority, to put more money into circulation in the kingdom of France, and to relieve the impoverished parish priests, who have been righteously oppressed by the rich ones until now.

For these reasons, it has seemed good to the Holy Spirit, and to us, to burn said book while awaiting the opportunity to do so to its publisher who has been, in this debate, the secretary of Satan. Let us also declare and instruct that our annuities be paid to us with particular care, that Satan be condemned to drink holy water for supper every Friday, and let us enjoin him to enter the bodies of all those who read his book.

Decreed in Rome at St. Mary's without Minerva[2] in the twenty-fifth hour on the 20th of May in the year 1750. Signed: Coglione-Coglionaccio, Chief Cardinal, and below this:

Cazzo-Culo, Secretary of the Holy Office.[3]

IN DEFENSE OF MILORD BOLINGBROKE

by Doctor Goodnatur'd Wellwisher,
Chaplain of Count Chesterfield

1752

When Henry St. John Bolingbroke died in November 1751, his *Letters on History* containing attacks on the authenticity of the Bible was released to the public. Samuel Formey, a French Protestant pastor King Frederick the Great had made the Perpetual Secretary of his academy in Berlin, seized the occasion to publish a violent attack on incredulity, adding that kings who neglected to punish authors of such works "ceased to represent God on earth."[1] Voltaire was then living at Frederick's court and one his earliest attacks on Christianity, *Sermon of the Fifty*,[2] was circulating. He had also begun collaborating with the king on his *Philosophical Dictionary*—in secret, he believed. Voltaire had known Lord Bolingbroke in the 1720s. He published this measured reply under a very obviously fake English name. Lord Chesterfield, whose chaplain he humorously pretends to be, was also an acquaintance and admirer. This piece provides glimpses of his familiarity with many eminent biblical scholars of the time (Richard Simon, Abbadie, Houtteville) well before his full-fledged *écrasez-l'infâme* campaign began in the 1760s.

I t is a duty to defend the memory of our illustrious dead. We shall therefore take up the cause of the late Lord Bolingbroke, insulted in a few gazettes on the occasion of the publishing of his excellent letters.

71

It is said in these journals that his name should have no authority in matters of religion and morals. As to morals, the man who furnished the admirable Alexander Pope with all the principles of his *Essay on Man* is doubtless the greatest master of wisdom and propriety that ever was. As to religion, he never spoke of it except as a man accomplished in history and philosophy. He had the modesty to limit himself to the historical aspects, submitted to the examination of all scholars; and one must suppose that if those who had written against him so bitterly had carefully examined what this illustrious Englishman said, and what he chose not to say, they would have treated his memory with more consideration.

Milord Bolingbroke did not enter into theological discussions regarding Moses. We shall follow his example here, in taking up his defense.

We shall content ourselves with remarking that faith is the surest argument of the Christians, and that it is through faith alone that one must believe the stories reported in the Pentateuch. If it were necessary to cite these books in the tribune of reason alone, how could one ever put an end to the disputes they have occasioned? Is reason not powerless to explain how it is that the snake used to speak, how he seduced the mother of mankind, how the she-ass of Balaam spoke to her master, and so many other things our feeble knowledge cannot fathom? Do not the prodigious numbers of miracles that rapidly succeed each other appall human reason? Can reason, abandoned to its own lights, understand that the priests of the Egyptian gods performed the same prodigies as Moses, sent by the true God; that they, for example, turned all the waters in Egypt into blood after Moses had effected this prodigious transformation? What law of physics, what philosophy, can explain how these Egyptian priests still managed to find water to turn into blood, once Moses had already done so?

Indeed, if the weak and trembling light of human reason were our only guide, there are few pages in the Pentateuch we would be able to admit, according to the rules established by men to judge of human things. Everyone admits that it is impossible to conciliate the confused chronology that reigns in this book. Everyone admits that its geography is inaccurate in many places on the names of the towns it gives, which were not called by those names till long after the time of Moses. This still causes great grief, despite all the torturous efforts made to explain such difficult passages.

When Milord Bolingbroke applied the rules of analysis to the Pentateuch, his aim was not to shake the foundations of religion, and it was in this view that he separated dogmas from history, with a circumspection that should earn great praise from those who have sought to decry him. This powerful genius anticipated his adversaries by separating faith from reason, the sole means of terminating all these disputes. Many scholars before him, and especially Father Simon,[3] have been of his opinion, saying it mattered little whether Moses himself had written Genesis and Exodus or whether priests had later gathered the traditional stories Moses had left behind. It is enough to believe in these books with a humble, submissive faith, without knowing precisely to which author God alone visibly inspired them to confound reason.

The adversaries of the great man whose defense we undertake here say, "it is as well proven that Moses is the author of the Pentateuch as it is that Homer wrote the Iliad." They will permit us to respond that the comparison is unjust. Homer does not cite a single fact in the Iliad that happened long after he was dead. Homer does not give names to towns and provinces that they did not have in his time. It is therefore clear that by applying the rules of unsacred analysis, we may safely presume that Homer is the author of the Iliad, but not that Moses is the author of the Pentateuch. Submission to religion alone can cut through all these difficulties and I do not see why Milord Bolingbroke, as submitted to this religion as any other, has been so violently attacked.

They affect to pity him for not having read Abbadie. To whom do they make this reproach? To a man who has read nearly all of it; to a man who cites him.[4] He scorned Abbadie quite a bit, I agree; but I also acknowledge that Abbadie was not a genius to be compared with the Viscount of Bolingbroke. He sometimes defended truth with lies. He held opinions on the Trinity that have been judged erroneous and, in the end, he died in dementia in Dublin.

Lord Bolingbroke is reproached for not having read the book by Abbé Houtteville, entitled *The Verity of the Christian Religion Proven by the Facts.* We were personally acquainted with Abbé Houtteville. He lived for a long time with a tax farmer who had a very lovely harem. He then became secretary to the famous Cardinal Dubois, who refused the sacraments throughout his life and whose libertinage was all too public. He dedicated his book to the Cardinal of Auvergne, the Abbé of Cluny, *propter Clunes.* This occasioned much laughter in Paris where I was at the time (in 1722), both of the book and of the dedication, for we know that the objections against the Christian religion in this book, being unfortunately much stronger than his responses, made a disastrous impression whose effects we see every day with pain.

Milord Bolingbroke claims that Christianity fell into decadence long ago. Do not his adversaries admit as much? Do they not complain of it every day? We take the liberty here of telling them, for the good of the common cause and for their own good, that invectives and speaking so despisingly, joined to such poor reasoning, will never bring the spirit back to those who have the misfortune of being unbelievers. Insults revolt everyone, and convince no one. Reproaches of debauchery and bad conduct are too swiftly and flippantly dealt to philosophers who should only be pitied for having been led astray in their opinions.

For example, the adversaries of Milord Bolingbroke call him a debauchee for having communicated his thoughts on history to Milord Cornsbury.

We do not see what relation this accusation could have with his book. A man who wrote in favor of concubines while living in a harem, a loan shark who wrote in favor of usury, an Apicius who wrote of gluttony, a tyrant or a rebel who wrote against the laws; men such as these would no doubt deserve to be accused of letting their morals dictate their writings. But a statesman such as Milord Bolingbroke, living in philosophical retirement and using his immense culture to cultivate the mind of a lord worthy of being instructed by him, certainly did not deserve to have men, who should pride themselves on decency, impute to past debaucheries works that are only the fruit of reason enlightened by profound study.

In what case is it permitted to reproach the disorders of his life to a man? It is in this case alone, perhaps: when his morals give lie to what he preaches. One might have compared the sermons of a famous preacher of our time with the larcenies he committed on Milord Galloway, and with his amorous intrigues. One might have compared the sermons of the famous parish priest of Les Invalides, and of Fantin, the parish priest of Versailles, with the lawsuits brought against them for having seduced and robbed their penitents. One might have compared the morals of so many popes and bishops with the religion they upheld by fire and sword. One might have considered their plundering, their bastards, their assassinations on the one hand, with their papal bulls and mandates on the other. On such occasions it is excusable to be lacking in the charity that demands we hide the faults of our brothers. But who told the detractor of Milord Boling-broke that he liked wine and girls? And even if he had, even if he had as many concubines as David or Salomon or the Grand Turk, would we know any more about who the true author of the Pentateuch is?

We agree that there are only too many deists. We groan to see that Europe is full of them. They are in the magistracy, in the armies, in the Church, near the throne, and on the throne itself. Literature is especially inundated with it; the academies, overflowing. Can we say that it is the spirit of debauchery, of license, of abandoning themselves to their passions that unites them? Dare we speak of them with such affected contempt? If we despised them that much, we would write against them with less venom. But we greatly fear that this venom, which is too real, and this air of contempt, which is so false, might have quite the con-trary effect to what a gentle and charitable zeal, supported by a healthy doctrine and true philosophy, could produce.

Why should we treat deists, who are not idolaters, more harshly than the papists we have so often reproached with idolatry? We would jeer at a Jesuit who said today that it was licentiousness that produced Protestants. We would laugh at a Protestant who said that it was depravity of morals that made people go to mass. What right then do we have to say to philosophic worshippers of God, who attend neither mass nor sermons, that they are men plunged in vice?

It sometimes happens that indecent invectives are used to attack people who, in truth, are unfortunate enough to be mistaken, but whose lives could serve as models to those who attack them. We have seen journalists carry imprudence so far as to injuriously designate the most respectable people of Europe, and the most powerful. Not long ago, in a public paper, a man carried away by an indiscreet zeal, or some other motive,[5] made a strange attack on those who think that "wise laws, military discipline, a just government, and virtuous examples can suffice to govern men, while leaving to God the care of governing consciences."

A very great man[6] was referred to in this journalistic piece in terms not very measured at all. He could have avenged himself as a man, or meted out punishment as a prince, but he responded like a philosopher, "These wretches must be fully persuaded of our virtue, and especially of our indulgence, since they slander us so fearlessly and with such brutality."

Such a reply should indeed confound this author, whoever he is,[7] for having used such odious weapons while combatting for the cause of Christianity. We entreat our brothers to make themselves loved if they wish to make our religion loved.

What indeed can a diligent prince think, or a magistrate bent under years of labor, or a philosopher who has spent his life in study—in a word, all those who have had the misfortune of embracing deism through the illusions of a deceived wisdom when they see so many writings calling them birdbrains, dandies, fops, or wits without any morals? Let us be wary that the scorn and indignation inspired by such writings do not fortify their feelings.

Let us add yet another motive to these considerations: it is that this mass of deists that covers all Europe is more likely to receive our truths than to adopt the dogmas of the Roman communion.[8] They all admit that our religion is more sensible than that of the papists. Let us not estrange them from us then; we who are alone capable of bringing them back. They adore a god, as we do. They teach virtue, as we do. They want men to obey the authorities, to all be treated like brothers, and we think the same and share these principles. Let us treat them then as relatives who hold the titles of our families in their hands and who show them to those who, descended from the same lines, know only that they a share a common father, but who do not hold the titles.

A deist is a man who is of the religion of Adam, of Shem,[9] and of Noah. Up to that point, he agrees with us. Say to him: You have only one step to take from the religion of Noah to the precepts given to Abraham. After Abraham, pass on to those of Moses, to those of the Messiah and, once you've seen that the religion of the Messiah has been corrupted, you can choose between Wycliffe, Luther, John Huss, Calvin, Melanchthon, Oecolampade, Zwingli, Storck, Parker, Servet, Socinus, George Fox, and other reformers. That way, you will find a thread to guide you through this great labyrinth, from the creation of the earth right up through the year 1752. If he replies that he has read all these great men, and that he prefers the religion of Socrates, Plato, Trajan, Marcus Aurelius, Cicero, Pliny, etc., we will pity him, we will pray that God illuminate him, and we will not cast slurs on him. We don't slur Muslims or the disciples of Confucius. We don't even cast slurs on the Jews, who made our god die by capital punishment. On the contrary, we began with them, so we will accord them the greatest privileges. We therefore have no reason to cry out in such furor against those who worship a god along with the Muslims, the Chinese, the Jews, and us, and who do not accept our theology any more than other nations do.

We understand perfectly that horrible screaming went on in a time when indulgences and benefices were being sold on one side, while on the other, bishops were being dispossessed and convent doors smashed in.[10] Bile flowed with the blood. It was all about conserving or destroying usurpations. But we do not see that Lord Bolingbroke, Lord Shaftsbury, nor the illustrious Alexander Pope, who immortalized the principles of both, wished to nab the pension of any minister of the Holy Scripture. Jurieu had Bayle's pension taken away, but never did the illustrious Bayle think of diminishing the appointments of Jurieu.[11] Let us then rest in peace. Let us preach morals as pure as those of the philosophers, worshippers of a God who, in agreement with us on this great principle, teach the same virtues that we do, which no one disputes, but who do not preach the same dogmas we have been disputing these past seventeen hundred years, and which we will continue to dispute.

DIALOGUE BETWEEN A BRAHMIN AND A JESUIT ON NECESSITY AND THE CHAIN OF EVENTS

1756

Voltaire and Frederick the Great—whose court Voltaire had left for good three years earlier—first debated their differences over the problem of predestination versus free will in 1738. Here, Voltaire's Brahmin humorously echoes the German philosopher Leibniz and his unbreakable chain of causal links, much in vogue in Berlin, to jolt a Jesuit priest and shake up how some of us view prayers.[1]

THE JESUIT

It's apparently through the prayers of St. Francis Xavier that you have reached such a happy old age? A hundred and eighty years! That's worthy of the biblical age of the patriarchs.

THE BRAHMIN

My master, Fonfouca, lived three hundred years. It's the average life span for us. I have great esteem for Francis Xavier, but his prayers could never have disturbed the order of the universe, and had he even had the gift of prolonging the life of a fly an instant more than the chain of fate had determined, this globe we are on would be completely different from what you see today.

THE JESUIT

You have a strange opinion of future contingencies. So you do not know that man has free will, and that our will accounts for everything that happens on this earth? I can assure you that the Jesuits, for their part alone, have made consider-able changes.

THE BRAHMIN

I do not doubt the knowledge and power of the reverend Jesuit fathers. They make up a highly estimable part of this world, but I do not believe them the sovereigns of it. Every man, every being, whether Jesuit or Brahmin, is a part of the universe. He obeys his destiny and does not command it. What accounts for Genghis Khan's conquest of Asia? To the hour his father awoke one day in sleeping with his wife, to something a Tartar said a few years earlier. I myself, for example, just as you see me, am one of the principle causes of the deplorable death of your good King Henri IV, and you see me still afflicted by it.

THE JESUIT

Your Reverence must be joking. You, the cause of the assassination of Henri IV!

THE BRAHMIN

Alas! Yes. It was in the year 983,000 of the revolution of Saturn, which comes to the year 1550 of your era. I was young and foolish. I took it into my head to start a little walk with my left foot rather than the right, along the Malabar Coast, and from that, evidently, followed the death of Henri IV.

THE JESUIT

How so, I beg you? Because we, who were accused of playing all sides in this affair, had no part in it.

THE BRAHMIN

Here is how destiny arranged the thing. In advancing with my left foot, as I had the honor of telling you, I unfortunately made my friend, Eriban, a Persian mer-chant, fall into the water, where he drowned. He had a very pretty wife who married an Armenian merchant. She had a daughter who married a Greek. The daughter of this Greek settled in France and married the father of Ravaillac. If all that hadn't happened, you can sense that the affairs of the houses of France and Austria would have turned out differently. The whole system of Europe would have changed.[2] The wars between Germany and Turkey would have had other results, and these results would have had a bearing on Persia, and Persia on India. So you see that all that depended on my left foot, which was linked to all the other events in the universe, past, present and future.

THE JESUIT

I will propose this argument to one of our father theologians, and I will bring you his solution.

THE BRAHMIN

While waiting, I will also tell you that the servant of the grandfather of the founder of the Order of the Feuillants (since I have read your histories) was also one of the necessary causes of the death of Henri IV, and of all the accidents this death triggered.

THE JESUIT

That servant was quite a woman.

THE BRAHMIN

Not at all. She was an idiot her master got with child. It made Mme. de La Barrière die of chagrin. The lady who succeeded her, as your chronicles tell it, was the grandmother of the blessed Jean de La Barrière, who founded the Order of the Feuillants. Ravaillac was a monk in their order. He absorbed certain doctrines there, very much in vogue, as you know. This doctrine persuaded him that it would be a holy deed to assassinate the best king in the world. The rest is history.

THE JESUIT

Despite your left foot and the servant of the grandfather of the founder of the Feuillants, I will still believe that the horrid act of Ravaillac was a future contingent that could easily not have happened because, after all, men have free will.

THE BRAHMIN

I don't know what you understand by free will. I attach no meaning to these words. To be free is to do as one wishes, and not to wish what one wishes.

All I know is that Ravaillac voluntarily committed the crime he was destined to commit by unchangeable laws. This crime was a link in the great chain of destinies.

THE JESUIT

You can talk as you like, the things of this world are not as linked together as you think. What importance, for example, do you attribute this useless conversation we are having together on the banks of the Indian Ocean?

THE BRAHMIN

What you and I are saying does not account for much, no doubt, but if you were not here, the entire machinery of the world would be something other from what it is.

THE JESUIT

Your Brahmin Reverence is now advancing one mighty paradox.

THE BRAHMIN

Your Ignacian Paternity will believe as he wishes. But certainly we would not be having this conversation if you had not come to India. You would not have made this voyage had your St. Ignatius de Loyola not been wounded in the Battle of Pamplona, and if a king of Portugal had not stubbornly persisted in getting the Cape of Good Hope circumnavigated. This King of Portugal, did he not, with the help of a compass, change the face of the world? But first, a Neapolitan had to invent the compass. And now tell me that everything is not eternally dependent on a steadfast order that unites everything that arises by invisible and indissoluble links; everything that acts, that suffers and dies on this globe.

THE JESUIT

Hey! Then what becomes of future contingents?

THE BRAHMIN

They will become whatever they can. But the order established by an eternal, all-powerful hand must subsist forever.

THE JESUIT

To hear you, one should then never pray to God?

THE BRAHMIN

One should worship him. But what do you mean by praying to him?

THE JESUIT

What everyone means by it. That he favor our desires and satisfy our needs.

THE BRAHMIN

I see. You would like to see a gardener obtain sunshine at the hour God had destined for rain from all eternity and that a navigator obtain an easterly wind when a westerly wind is necessary to refresh the earth and seas. Father, to pray is to submit oneself. Good evening. Destiny calls me to my lady Brahmin.

THE JESUIT

And my free will urges me to go give a lesson to a young pupil.

DIALOGUES BETWEEN LUCRETIUS AND POSIDONIUS

1756

In Berlin, in daily contact with La Mettrie, notorious atheist and author of *Man a Machine*, and with the growing atheism of the king himself, his former "pupil," Voltaire reviews his thoughts in a dialogue. He pits the materialist doctrines of Lucretius, a first century BCE Roman poet and philosopher, against his contemporary Posidonius, not well known in the eighteenth century, but who, as a Stoic, might feasibly adopt a deistic view. The growing adamancy of atheists was becoming a new concern,[1] and a topic Voltaire would return to repeatedly, for he felt, sometimes using the Roman Empire as an example, that atheism could be fatal to virtue, except among real philosophers—and especially among kings, or persons wielding great power.[2]

FIRST DISCUSSION

POSIDONIUS

Your poetry is sometimes admirable, but Epicurean physics seem very wrong to me.

LUCRETIUS

What! You don't want to admit that atoms arranged themselves in a way that produced the universe?

POSIDONIUS

We mathematicians can only admit things that are evidently proven by incontestable principles.

LUCRETIUS

My principles are

> *Ex nihilo nihil, in nihilum nil posse reverti;*
> *Tangere enim et tangi nisi corpus nulla potest res.*
> From nothing comes nothing, nothing returns to nothing;
> And one body is only touched by another body.

POSIDONIUS

Even if I accord you these principles, and even atoms and empty space, you will no more persuade me that the universe formed itself in the admirable order that we see than if you told the Romans that Posidonius' armillary sphere made itself.

LUCRETIUS

But who then made the world?

POSIDONIUS

An intelligent being, more superior to the world and to me than I am to the copper I composed my sphere with.

LUCRETIUS

You who only admit evident things, how can you recognize a principle of which you have no notion?

POSIDONIUS

Just as, before meeting you, I judged that your book was written by an intelligent man.

LUCRETIUS

You admit that matter is eternal, that it exists because it exists. Therefore, if it exists by its nature, why can it not form suns, planets, plants, animals and men by its nature?

POSIDONIUS

All the philosophers who came before us thought matter eternal, but they did not prove it. And if it were eternal, this does not prove that it could form objects in which such sublime design is so apparent. This rock can be as eternal as you like, you will not convince me that it can produce Homer's *Iliad*.

LUCRETIUS

No, a rock will not produce the *Iliad*, any more than it will a horse. But matter, organized over time and become a mix of bone and flesh and blood will produce a horse, and, organized more finely, will compose the *Iliad*.

POSIDONIUS

You suppose it with no proof, and I must admit nothing without proof. I will give you bones and blood and flesh already made. I'll let you and all the Epicureans in the world work on it. Would you agree to make a deal in which you will possess the Roman Empire if you manage to make a horse with these prepared ingredients, or be hanged if you can't?

LUCRETIUS

No. That surpasses my powers, but not those of nature. It takes millions of centuries for nature, after having passed through all possible forms, to arrive at the only one which can make living beings.

POSIDONIUS

You can shake all the materials of the earth in a barrel your entire life, you will not so much as pull one well-shaped object from it; you will make nothing. If the time of your entire life cannot produce so much as a mushroom, will the lifetime of another man suffice? Why could several centuries do what one century cannot? You would have to have seen humans and animals born from earth, or wheat without seeds, etc., etc., to dare confirm that matter alone can take on such forms. No one that I know has ever seen such a thing. Therefore, no one should believe it.

LUCRETIUS

All right then! Humans, animals, trees have always existed. All the philosophers agree that matter is eternal. They will agree that generations are as well. It is in the nature of matter that celestial bodies turn, that birds fly, that horses run and that men make *Iliads*.

POSIDONIUS

In this new assumption, you change your opinion, but you still suppose what is in question. You admit a thing of which you have not the slightest proof.

LUCRETIUS

I am allowed to think that what exists today existed yesterday, existed a century ago, a hundred centuries ago, and going back interminably. I am using your argument. No one saw the sun and other heavenly bodies begin their course, the first animals get formed and come to life. We may therefore think that everything has been as it is eternally.

POSIDONIUS

There is a big difference. I see an admirable design, and I am forced to think that an intelligent being formed this design.

LUCRETIUS

You should not admit a being you have no knowledge of.

POSIDONIUS

That is like telling me that I should not admit an architect built the Capitoline because I was unable to see this architect.

LUCRETIUS

Your comparison is not valid. You have seen houses built and you have seen architects. Therefore you should think that a man much like the architects today built the Capitoline. But things are different in this instance. The Capitoline does not exist by its nature, and matter does. It is impossible for matter not to have a given form. So why do you not want it to possess by its nature the form it has today? Is it not far easier to imagine nature modifying herself than to imagine an invisible being modifying it? In the first case, you have only one difficulty, which is to understand how nature acts. In the second, you have two, which are to understand this same nature and an unknown being that acts upon her.

POSIDONIUS

It's just the contrary. I not only see the difficulty, but the impossibility of understanding that matter can have infinite designs, and I see no difficulty in accepting an intelligent being who governs this matter through infinite designs and through an all-powerful will.

LUCRETIUS

What! It is because your mind cannot understand one thing that it presumes something else? So it is because you cannot seize the art and mainsprings necessary for nature to arrange itself in planets, the sun, and animals that you resort to another being?

POSIDONIUS

No. I do not resort to a God because I cannot understand nature, but I understand that nature manifestly needs a supreme intelligence, and that is the sole reason that would prove God to me, if I did not have other proofs on top of it.

LUCRETIUS

And if this matter had intelligence on its own?

POSIDONIUS

To me it is obvious that it does not.

LUCRETIUS

And to me it is obvious that it does, since I see bodies like you and me who reason.

POSIDONIUS

If matter possessed reason in and of itself, you would have to say that it possesses it necessarily. However if this attribute were necessary to it, it would have it at all times and in all places, because a *necessary* attribute can never be separate from it. A piece of mud, the most vile excrement would think. Yet you will surely not say that dung thinks. Thought is therefore not a necessary attribute of matter.

LUCRETIUS

Your reasoning is a sophism. I hold movement to be necessary to matter. Nevertheless, this pile of dung, this heap of mud, are not presently in movement. They will be, when pushed by some body. By the same token, thought will only be an attribute of this body when this body will be organized to think.

POSIDONIUS

Your error comes from the fact that you always suppose what is in question. You do not see that to organize a body, to make it a man, a thinking being, thought needs to exist already; it needs a design that has been decided. Yet you cannot admit designs before the sole beings who have designs here below have been formed. You cannot admit of thoughts before the beings which have thoughts exist. You suppose what is in question again when you say that movement is necessary to matter, since what is absolutely necessary exists always; like extent exists in every form of matter. Movement however does not always exist. The pyramids of Egypt are certainly not in movement. Even if some subtle matter passed between the stones of the pyramids of Egypt, the mass of the pyramid is immobile. Movement is therefore not absolutely necessary to matter. It comes from somewhere else, just as thought comes to human beings from elsewhere. There is therefore an intelligent, powerful being that gives movement, life, and thought.

LUCRETIUS

I can answer that by saying that there has always been movement and intelligence in the world. This movement and intelligence have been distributed throughout all time, following the laws of nature. Matter being eternal, it is impossible that it didn't exist in some kind of order. It could not be in any order without movement and thought. Intelligence and movement were therefore necessarily in it.

POSIDONIUS

Whichever way you look at it, you can only make suppositions. You suppose an order. Therefore some intelligence was needed to arrange this order. You suppose movement and thought before matter was in movement and before there were human beings and thoughts. You cannot deny that thought is not essential to matter, since you dare not say that a stone thinks. You can only oppose *perhapses* to the truth pressing in on you. You sense the powerlessness of matter, and you are forced to admit a supreme being, intelligent, all-powerful, who organized matter and thinking beings. The design of this superior intelligence bursts forth on all sides, and you must perceive it in a blade of grass as in the course of the stars. We see that everything is directed toward a certain end.

LUCRETIUS

Are you not taking for a design what is only a necessary existence? Are you not taking for a certain end what is only the use we make of things that exist? The Argonauts built a ship to go to Colchis. Will you say that trees were created for the Argonauts to build a ship and that the sea was made so that the Argonauts could undertake their journey? Men wear shoes. Will you say that legs were made by a Supreme Being to be shoed? No, undoubtedly. But the Argonauts, having seen wood, built a ship, and having known that water could carry this ship, they undertook their voyage. Likewise, after an infinity of forms and combinations that matter adopted, it happened that the humors and the transparent cornea that compose an eye, formerly separated in different parts of the human body, became united in the head, and animals began to see. The organs of generation, which were scattered, assembled and took the form they have. Then generations were produced with regularity. The matter of the sun, long spread out throughout space, conglobed and made the star that lights us. Is anything impossible in all that?

POSIDONIUS

In truth you cannot seriously resort to such a system. First of all, in adopting this hypothesis, you abandon the eternal generations you spoke of earlier. Secondly, you are mistaken regarding final causes. There are voluntary uses we make of the gifts of nature; and there are indispensable effects. The Argonauts might not have used trees of the forests to make a ship, but these trees were visibly destined to grow on earth and to produce fruit and leaves. We can perfectly well not shoe our legs, but the leg was visibly made to carry the body and to walk, eyes to see, ears to hear, reproductive organs to perpetuate the species. If you consider that from a star, placed four or five hundred million leagues away from us, come rays of light that make the same determined angle in the eyes of every animal, and all those animals instantaneously have the same sensation of light, you will admit to me that there is a mechanism, an admirable design there. Therefore is it not unreasonable to admit a mechanism without an artisan, a design without intelligence, and such designs without a Supreme Being?

LUCRETIUS

If I admit this Supreme Being, what form will he have? Is he in a place? Is he beyond all space? Is he in time, or outside of time? Does he fill all space, or not? Why would he have made this world? What is his goal? Why create sensitive and unhappy beings? Why does moral and physical pain exist? Whichever way I look, I see only the incomprehensible.

POSIDONIUS

It is precisely because this Supreme Being exists that his nature must be incomprehensible, because if he exists, there must be infinity between him and us. We must admit that he exists, without knowing what he is, and how he operates. Are you not forced to admit asymptotes in geometry, without understanding how these lines can approach each other eternally yet never meet? Are there not things just as incomprehensible yet demonstrated in the properties of a circle? Conceive the fact then that we must admit the incomprehensible when the existence of this incomprehensible thing is proven.

LUCRETIUS

What! I would have to renounce the dogmas of Epicurus?

POSIDONIUS

Better to renounce Epicurus than reason.

SECOND DISCUSSION

LUCRETIUS

I'm beginning to recognize a Supreme Being inaccessible to our senses and proven by our reason, who made the world and preserves it, but as to everything I said about the soul in my third book, admired by all the learned of Rome, I don't think you can oblige me to renounce it.

POSIDONIUS

You say first:

> *Idque situm media regione in pectoris hoeret.*
> The spirit is in the middle of the chest.

But when you composed your lovely verses, did you not make any effort with your head? When you spoke of the intelligence of Cicero or of the orator Mark Antony, did you not say he had a good head? And if you had said he had a good chest, would people not think you were speaking of his voice or his lungs?

LUCRETIUS

But do you not feel that it is around the heart that feelings of joy, of pain, and of fear are formed?

> *Hic exultat enim pavor ac metus; haec loca circum Laetitiae mulcent.*[3]

Do you not feel your heart expand or tighten at good or bad news? Are there not secret springs there that relax or take on elasticity? It is hence there the seat of the soul.

POSIDONIUS

There is a set of nerves that starts at the brain, passes by the stomach and the heart and descends into the reproductive parts, and which registers movements upon them. Will you say that human understanding resides in the reproductive parts?

LUCRETIUS

No, I wouldn't dare say that. But even if I place the soul in the head, instead of in the chest, my principles will remain: the soul will still be an infinitely loosened matter, similar to the elementary fire that animates the whole machine.

POSIDONIUS

And how do you conceive that a loosened matter can have thoughts and feelings by itself?

LUCRETIUS

Because I experience it, because every part of my body being touched feels it. Because this feeling is spread throughout my whole machine, because it cannot be spread there except by an extremely subtle, rapid matter. Because I am a body, because a body can only be agitated by another body, because the interior of my body can only be penetrated by very loose corpuscles, and because my soul can consequently only be an assemblage of these corpuscles.

POSIDONIUS

We already agreed in our first discussion that it doesn't appear that a rock could compose the *Iliad*. Would a sunray be more capable of it? Imagine this sunray a hundred thousand times more subtle and rapid. This clarity, this subtleness, would it form sentiments and thoughts?

LUCRETIUS

Perhaps it would if it were in organs prepared for it.

POSIDONIUS

There you go with your *perhapses* again. Fire can no more think for itself than ice can. If I were to suppose that it is fire that thinks in you, that feels, that has a will, you would then be forced to admit that it isn't by itself that fire has a will, feelings, and thoughts.

LUCRETIUS

No, it wouldn't be by itself, it would be by the joining of this fire and my organs.

POSIDONIUS

How can you imagine that two things that do not think when on their own produce thought when they are united?

LUCRETIUS

Much like a tree and soil, taken separately, do not bear fruit, and bear it when the tree has been put in the soil.

POSIDONIUS

The comparison only dazzles. This tree carries the seed of its fruit; you can see it in its buds. And the sap of the soil develops the substance of these fruits. Fire would therefore need to carry the germ of thought, and the body's organs would have to develop this seed.

LUCRETIUS

What do you see impossible about it?

POSIDONIUS

I find that fire, this quintessential matter, does not possess the right to thought any more than a rock does. Something produced should contain something similar to what produces it. Yet a thought, a desire, a feeling, have nothing in common to igneous matter.

LUCRETIUS

Two objects that collide produce movement, and yet movement has nothing in common with these two objects. It does not have three dimensions as they do. It has no shape. So a thing can have nothing similar to the thing which produces it. Therefore a thought can be born of the joining of two things that have no thought.

POSIDONIUS

This comparison is again more dazzling than accurate. I see only matter in two objects in movement. I only see objects moving from one place to another. But when we reason together, I can see no matter in your ideas nor in mine. I will tell you only that I no more conceive of how one object has the power to move another than I can conceive of how I have ideas. They are both things equally inexplicable to me, and both prove to me equally the existence and power of a Supreme Being, author of both movement and thought.

LUCRETIUS

If our soul is not a subtle fire, an ethereal quintessence, what then is it?

POSIDONIUS

You and I have no idea. I will gladly tell you what it is not, but I cannot tell you what it is. I see that it is a power that is within me, that I did not give myself this power, and that consequently it comes from a being superior to me.

LUCRETIUS

You did not give yourself life. You received it from your father. You received thought with life from him, just as he received it from his father, and so on, going back to infinity. You no more know at heart what the principle of life is than you know what the principle of thought is. This succession of living, thinking beings has existed from all time.

POSIDONIUS

I still see that you are forced to abandon the system of Epicurus, and that you no longer dare say that the declension of atoms produces thought. But I have already refuted the eternal succession of feeling, thinking beings at our last discussion. I told you that if material thinking beings existed on their own, thought would have to be a necessary attribute to all matter; that if matter thought necessarily by itself, all matter would have thought. But that is not the case. Therefore a succession of material beings thinking on their own is untenable.

LUCRETIUS

This reasoning you repeat does not prevent a father from passing a soul on to his son while forming his body. This soul and body grow together. They fortify each other, are subject to illness and to the infirmities of old age. Our judgment deteriorates with the decline of our physical strength. The effect finally ceases with the cause, and the soul dissolves like smoke in air.

> *Praeterea, gigni partier cum corpore, et una*
> *Crescere entimus, pariterque senescere mentem.*
> *Nam velut infirmo pueri teneroque vagantur*
> *Corpore; sic animi sequitur sententia tenuis*

Inde, ubi robustis adolevit viribus aetas,
Consilium quoque majus, et auctior est animis vis:
Post, ubi jam validis quassatum est viribus aevi
Corpus, et obtusis ceciderunt viribus artus,
Claudicat ingenium, delirat linguaque mensque;
Omnia deficiunt, atque uno tempore desunt.
Ergo dissolvi quoque convenit omnem animai
Naturam, ceu tumus in altas aeris auras:
Quandoquidem gigni pariter, pariterque videtur
Crescere; et, ut docui, simul aevo fessa fatiscit.

(Bk. III, v. 446)[4]

POSIDONIUS

Those are some fine verses, but do you teach me the nature of the soul with them?

LUCRETIUS

No, I relate its story to you, and I reason with a bit of verisimilitude.

POSIDONIUS

Where is the likelihood that a father transmits the faculty of thinking to his son?

LUCRETIUS

Do you not see every day that children have the inclinations of their fathers, just as they have their features?

POSIDONIUS

But does a father creating his son not act as a blind instrument? Did he intend to make a soul, to make thoughts, in climaxing with his wife? Do either one know how a child is formed in the womb? Must we not resort to some superior cause in all the other operations of nature we have examined? Do you not sense, if you are of good faith, that men give nothing to themselves and that they are all in the hands of an absolute master?

LUCRETIUS

If you know more than I do, tell me what a soul is then.

POSIDONIUS

I don't pretend to know more than you. Let us enlighten each other. Tell me first what vegetation is.

LUCRETIUS

It is an internal movement that carries the sustenance of the earth into a plant, makes it grow, develops its fruit, extends its leaves, etc.

POSIDONIUS

You don't think, undoubtedly, that there is a being called *vegetation* that works these marvels?

LUCRETIUS

Whoever did?

POSIDONIUS

You must conclude from our preceding discussion that the tree did not give itself vegetation.

LUCRETIUS

I am forced to agree.

POSIDONIUS

And life? You can tell me what it is?

LUCRETIUS

It's vegetation with feeling in an organized body.

POSIDONIUS

And there is not a being called *life* that gave this feeling to an organized body.

LUCRETIUS

Without a doubt. Vegetation and life are words that refer to things that vegetate and live.

POSIDONIUS

If the tree and animals cannot give themselves vegetation and life, can you give yourself thoughts?

LUCRETIUS

I think that I can, for I think what I want. My will was to speak to you of metaphysics, and I'm speaking of them to you.

POSIDONIUS

Do you think you are the master of your thoughts? You know then what thoughts you will have in an hour, or in a quarter of an hour?

LUCRETIUS

I confess that I have no idea.

POSIDONIUS

You often have ideas while sleeping. You compose verses in your dreams. Caesar takes towns. I resolve problems. Hunting dogs chase deer in their dreams. Ideas then come to us independently of our will. So they are given to us by a superior force.

LUCRETIUS

How do you imagine it? Do you claim that a Supreme Being is continually occupied with giving ideas, or that he creates incorporeal substances that then have ideas on their own, sometimes with the help of the senses, sometimes without? Do these substances form at the moment of the animal's conception? Are they formed beforehand, and do they wait for bodies to slip into? Or do they lodge in them only when the animal is ready to receive them? Or is it in the Supreme Being that every animated being sees the idea of things? What do you think?

POSIDONIUS

When you tell me how our will effects a movement in our bodies instantly, how your arm obeys your will, how we receive life, how our foods are digested, how wheat turns into blood, I will tell you how we get ideas. I confess my ignorance on all that. The world may shed new lights one day, but from Thales up to our day, we haven't any. All we can do is feel our powerlessness, recognize an all-powerful being, and beware of systems.

REFLECTIONS FOR FOOLS

1760

Flaubert said that Voltaire's "Ecrasez- l'infâme" writings had the effect of a cri de guerre on him.[1] After having laid low certain enemies of the philosophes with other pamphlets in 1759–60,[2] this text reads like the opening shots in a broader war about to begin. It is also a forceful summary of points already made in his *Letters on England* in 1734 and in his reply to Jean Racine in 1722. Heightened confidence in the intelligence of the masses is also in evidence.

I f the governed masses were composed of cattle, and the small number governing of cowherds, then the small number would do very well to maintain the masses in ignorance.

But such is not the case. Several nations that wore horns and ruminated for a very long time have begun to think.

And once the time for thinking has begun, it is impossible to rob minds of the force they have acquired. Thinking beings must be treated like thinking beings, just as brutes must be treated like brutes.

It would be impossible for the Knights of the Garter, assembled at London's City Hall, to make people believe today that their patron Saint George is watching them from heaven, lance in hand, mounted on his charger.

King William, Queen Anne, George I, and George II have never cured anyone of scrofula. Formerly, a king who refused to perform this holy service would have caused his nation to revolt. Today, a king who would wish to perform it would cause his entire nation to laugh.[3]

The son of the great Racine, in a poem entitled *Grace,* had this to say about England:

> England, formerly a source of great light,
> By accepting all religions today
> Has become nothing more than a sad heap of mad visions.

M. Racine is mistaken. England was plunged in ignorance and bad taste until the days of Chancellor Bacon. It is free thought that has sprouted so many excellent books in England. Men became bold only because they had been enlightened, and they reaped rewards for transporting their wheat over the seas only because they had become bold. It is this liberty that has made all the arts flourish and that has covered the ocean with vessels.

Regarding the mad visions with which the author of the poem *Grace* reproaches them, it is true that they have abandoned disputes over efficient and sufficient and concomitant grace, but in compensation, they have given us logarithms, the position of three thousand stars, the aberrations of light, as well as its physical properties, the mathematical entity known as *infinity* and the mathematical law per which all the globes of the universe gravitate toward one another. It must be admitted that the Sorbonne, although highly superior, has not yet made any such discoveries.

These little yearnings to make an impression by inveighing against our era, by leading men from issues of substance to food for squirrels and by incessantly repeating irrelevant and worn-out clichés, will no longer make a man's fortune.

It is ridiculous to think that an enlightened nation is no happier than an ignorant one. It is horrid to insinuate that tolerance is dangerous when we can see England and Holland at our doorstep, populated and enriched by this same tolerance, and other beautiful kingdoms, lying fallow and depopulated by the contrary opinion.

Men who think freely are not persecuted because they are thought dangerous, since assuredly nary a one of them has ever caused four rascals to mob Maubert Square or the king's reception hall. No philosopher has ever spoken to Jacques Clément, or to Barrière or Chastel, or to Ravaillac or Damiens.

No philosopher has ever prevented anyone from paying taxes necessary to the state's defense, nor ever disturbed the procession of the relics of St. Geneviève through the streets of Paris to bring us rain or sunshine. And when the convulsionaries sought heavenly intercession, no philosopher ever bludgeoned them with logs.

When the Jesuits used slander, the confessional, and secret warrants of arrests against all those they accused of being Jansenists, in other words a rival order, and when the Jansenists revenged themselves as well as they could against the insolent persecutions of the Jesuits, the philosophers took no part whatsoever in their quarrels. They made these quarrels look contemptible and rendered the nation an eternal service by doing so.

If a papal bull, written in bad Latin and sealed with the Fisherman's Ring, no longer decides the destiny of states; if a Papal Nuncio no longer gives orders to our kings or takes a tenth of our incomes, to whom are we obliged? To the maxims of the Hospital Knight, who was a philosopher; to the writings of Gerson who was also a philosopher; to the wisdom of Attorney General Cugnières, who passed for a philosopher; and especially to the solid writings of our day, which have so ridiculed the follies of our fathers that it has become impossible for their children to be as foolish as they were.

True men of letters and true philosophers deserve more esteem than a Hercules, an Orpheus, or a Theseus because it is finer and far more difficult to tear civilized men from their prejudices than to civilize crass men. It is rarer to correct than to establish.

Where then does the rage of a few bourgeois and a few inferior writers against these highly estimable and useful citizens come from? From the fact that these bourgeois and little writers, deep in their hearts, have felt themselves contemptible in the eyes of these men of genius and have been brazen enough to get jealous. A man accustomed to being praised in the obscurity of his little circle goes wild with rage when he finds himself despised in the world at large.

Haman wanted to have all the Jews hanged because Mordecai hadn't bowed down before him. Acanthos wanted to have all the sages burnt because one sage had said that one of Acanthos' discourses was worthless.

Oh Acanthos![4] Have Reverend Father Croiset's *Meditations* bound in Moroccan leather and, if it seems like a good book, run and denounce it to all those who won't read it anyway. But if you burn a useful book, the sparks will fly back in your face.

LETTER FROM CHARLES GOUJU TO HIS BROTHERS

1761

Inspired by the fraudulent bankruptcy of Jesuit colonial racketeer, Father Antoine La Valette, Voltaire invents an extra victim to pose some scathingly pertinent questions. This pamphlet was condemned by Rome on May 24, 1762, but the scandal contributed to the suppression of the Jesuit order in France in 1764, along with the Malagrida affair evoked in the *Sermon of Rabbi Akib*.

I beseech, not only my dear compatriots, but also my dear brothers the Germans, the English, and even the Italians to consider with me, for their edification, the events taking place these days regarding the reverend Jesuit fathers.

I am the cousin of Monsieur Cazotte and related by marriage to Monsieur Lioncy, who Father La Valette, Apostolic Prefect of Commerce, has driven to utter ruin. God have mercy on His prefect! Yet I ask any man who makes use of his reason whether it be possible that Reverend La Valette, having done two years of theology, having read the Gospel and taken the vow of poverty, could have believed in the Christian religion while dealing in commerce to the tune of six million francs? Is it in human nature for a theologian who believes in his religion to damn himself so light-heartedly in doing what his faith and his vows so adamantly forbid?

For a believer, carried off in a fit of violent passion, to commit a crime and then repent of it, is within human nature. But when God's servants rob us while preaching and confessing us, when they persist in these maneuvers year after year, I ask you dear brothers, is it possible to be true believers while being that deceitful? Can they truly believe they hold God in their hands at Mass when they pillage us upon leaving the altar?

It has been established by the depositions of the conspirators of Lisbon that their confessors, the Jesuits, assured them that they could assassinate the king in clear conscience. I do not examine what motives of vengeance inspired these conspirators. I simply ask whether it is possible that men who used a sacrament to incite a parricide could have believed in that sacrament?

I pass from these great crimes to iniquities of another sort. Do you think that the Jesuit Le Tellier believed in Jesus Christ? Do you think he believed in a just God who rewards and punishes when he took advantage of King Louis XIV's ignorance in theology to persecute the virtuous Cardinal de Noailles, and when he forged and showed letters to his penitent, the king, from several bishops, which these bishops had not written? Does such conduct, sustained over several years, not prove that this confessor believed nothing he made his penitent believe?

And the adversaries of the Jesuits, who invented convulsions and so many other miracles, who have been convicted of so many impostures—have they been truer believers than the Jesuit Le Tellier?[1]

I repeat, a man may believe in God yet kill his father; but it is not possible that he believe in God yet spend his life committing an uninterrupted series of premeditated crimes, frauds, and impostures. He would at least repent on his deathbed, but I defy you to find anywhere in history a single theologian who confessed his crimes upon his deathbed.

We see murderous, incestuous laymen and women do public penance every day, but I submit to offer the ten thousand ecus that remain of the entire fortune Father La Valette took from me if you can show me a single penitent theologian.

Would you like grander examples? You can find them among the first popes: Jules II, in armor and helmet; the voluptuous Leon X; Alexander VI, befouled in his incests and murders; so many popes, surrounded by mistresses and bastards, playing off human credulity in the midst of their debauchery, did they lift their blood-stained hands full of gold to God? Did a single one do penance in retirement? While we watch Charles Quint sing his De Profundis to Saint Just.

The greatest unbelievers of all time have thus been the theologians, great and small, shorn or mitered.

If I am not mistaken, this is how every one of them has reasoned: the Christian religion that I teach is clearly not that of the first centuries. The synaxes of the first Christians were not private masses. It is obvious that the images we invoke were forbidden for over two hundred years, that auricular confessions were unheard of for a very long time, that all of our practices have changed without a single exception. All of our dogmas have visibly changed as well. We know at what period the procession of the Holy Ghost was added to the Apostle's Creed. Of all the opinions that incited so many wars, not a single one of them has any clear relation to our Gospels. It is all our handiwork, and therefore, arbitrary. We cannot therefore believe what we teach, and we should therefore take advantage of human foolishness. We can therefore despoil them with nothing to fear, confess them, assassinate them and administer the last rites to them.

Not only have they reasoned this way, but it is impossible for them to have reasoned otherwise, for again, it is not in human nature to say: I firmly believe in all I teach and I shall do the exact opposite throughout my entire life and at my death.

Many secular persons, especially among the powerful, have imitated the theologians in all religions. Mustapha has said: "My mufti doesn't believe in Mahomet, so I needn't either. I can therefore have my brothers strangled without the slightest scruple." This abominable syllogism, "My religion is false, so there is no God" is the most common one that I know, and the most fertile source of all crimes.

What, my brothers! Because Father Malagrida is a murderer, Father Le Tellier a forger, Father La Valette a fraudulent bankrupt, and the mufti a knave, it follows that there is no Supreme Being, no creator, no guardian, no equitable judge who rewards and punishes? I once knew a Dominican Doctor of the Sorbonne who became an atheist because his prior obliged him to maintain in his cloister that the Virgin was conceived in sin, while at the Sorbonne he was obliged to maintain the contrary. He told me coldly, "My religion is false. And since my religion, which is indisputably the best, contains only elements of falsehood, there is no religion, and there is no God. I obviously committed a very great folly in becoming a Dominican at age fifteen."

I took pity on the poor man and said to him, "It's true that it was exceedingly daft of you to become a Dominican, but my friend, whether Mary was born maculate or immaculate, does God exist any less? Does that make God any less the father and judge of all men? Does he not command men equally, from the first colao in China to the lowest ranking Dominican, to be moderate, just, sincere, and to do unto others what every Dominican would like done unto himself? Dogmas change, my friend, but God does not. The Franciscan friar, Saint Bonaventure, and the Dominican, Saint Thomas, are almost never of the same opinion. Well then! Think like neither Thomas nor Bonaventure. Certain books have been falsified; others, alleged. This causes you grief. Console yourself. The great book of nature cannot be falsified, and in it is written: "Adore one God and be just." I saw with pleasure that my sermon had made a big impression on my Dominican.

My brothers, religion must be purified. All Europe cries out for it, and in order to purge it, it isn't by purifying theology that we must begin. It must be abolished entirely. It is altogether too shameful to have made a science of this grave folly, which has only capsized thousands of brains and overthrown one government after another. It alones creates atheists. The great number of little theologians, who are sensible enough to see the absurdity of this chimeric science, do not know enough to be able to replace it with a saner philosophy. They conclude, like the young Dominican, that the Divinity is a chimera, because theology is chimeric. That is precisely like saying that one shouldn't take quinine for a fever, or be bled for an apoplexy, or fast after an excess, because there are quacks in the world. It would be like denying the obvious effects of chemistry because a few charlatan chemists claimed to have made gold. And society people, even less knowledgeable than these little theologians, say, "Here are bachelors of science and university graduates who don't believe in God. Why should we believe?"

My brothers, a fake science creates atheists. A true science prostrates us before the Divinity and makes wise and just men of those theology had made vicious and senseless.

That, my dear brothers, is my profession of faith, and it should be yours, for it is the faith of all honest people. *Amen.*

THE SERMON OF RABBI AKIB

given in Smyrna, on November 20, 1761
(translated from Hebrew)

On receipt of information just in from Lisbon about the burning of thirty-two Jews, two Muslims, and three Jesuits by the Inquisition, Voltaire adopts the guise of a rabbi to deliver his most scathing attack on anti-Semitism. It turned out that the report was erroneous: only the Jesuit Malagrida had been burned this time. He had been involved in an attempted assassination of the king of Portugal, but Voltaire is correct in reporting that the clergy did not burn him for that reason, but for absurd "theological errors." Voltaire continued to reprint this biting defense of the Jews nonetheless. The assassination attempt, along with the racketeering of Father La Valette, the subject of the "Letter of Charles Gouju," contributed heavily to the suppression of Jesuits in France in 1764, joined by Portugal, Spain, Poland, Lithuania, and Russia. The Jesuit Order was restored by Pope Pius VII in 1815.

My Dear Brethren, We have learned of the human sacrifice of forty-two victims that the savages of Lisbon held in public in the month of *etanim* in the 1691th year[1] after the destruction of Jerusalem. These savages call such executions *acts of faith*. My brothers, these are not acts of charity. Raise our hearts to the Eternal!

In this horrifying ceremony, three of what the Europeans call *monks* and what we call kalenders, two Muslims, and thirty-seven of our condemned brothers were burned.

We have no authentic accounts as yet, apart from the *Accordao dos inquisidores contra o Padre Gabriel Malagrida jesuita*. The rest is only known to us through the pitiful letters of our Spanish brothers.

Alas! First see in this *Accordao* to what state of depravity God has abandoned so many of the peoples of Europe. The Jesuit Malagrida was accused of complicity in the assassination of the King of Portugal. The Council of Supreme Justice, established by the king, had this kalender declared demented and convicted him of having exhorted the assassins in God's name to revenge themselves of an undertaking against their honor by the murder of this prince; of having encouraged the guilty through his confessional, in accordance with a custom only too common in parts of Europe; and of having told them expressly that it would not even be a venial sin to kill their sovereign.

In what country on earth would a man accused of such a crime not have been solemnly judged by the civil courts of this prince, confronted with his accomplices and condemned to death, according to the laws?

Who would believe it, my brothers! The King of Portugal does not have the right to have a kalender accused of patricide judged! He has to ask permission from a Latin rabbi in Rome,[2] and this Latin rabbi refused it! This king was obliged to return the accused to the Portuguese kalenders who alone can judge crimes against God, they say, as if God had given them the sovereign right to decide what offends him, and as if there were any greater crime against God than to assassinate a sovereign we regard as his image on earth!

The kalenders did not even question Malagrida regarding his complicity in this parricide. It was a small worldly error, they said, absorbed in the immensity of the crimes committed against the divine majesty.[3]

Malagrida thus stands convicted of having said that "a woman named Annah[4] had been blessed in her mother's womb in the days of yore, that her daughter had spoken to her before being delivered into this world, that Mary had received several visions of the archangel Gabriel, that there will be three Antichrists, that the last one will be born of a kalender and a kalendress in Milano, and that Malagrida is his John the Baptist.

And that is why this poor Jesuit was burned in public in Lisbon at the age of seventy-five. Raise our hearts to the Eternal!

If the Jesuit Malagrida alone had been condemned to the flames, we wouldn't be talking about it in this holy synagogue. Little does it matter to us that the kalenders have burned a Jesuit kalender. We know only too well how often these European aesthetes[5] have deserved this fate. It is one of the woes attached to this sect of barbarians. Their histories are filled with the crimes of their dervishes and we know only too well to what extent their fanatic disputes have bloodied thrones. Every time we have seen a prince murdered in Europe, the superstitions of these people have always sharpened the dagger. The learned chaplain of the French Counselor to Smyrna counted ninety-four kings, emperors, and princes put to death by the quarrels of these wretches, either by the fakirs'[6] own hands or by the hands of their penitents. As to the number of lords or citizens these superstitions have massacred, it is immense, and in all these horrible murders, there is not one that was not meditated, encouraged, and blessed by this sacrament they call confession.

The first Christians, as you know my brothers, originally imitated our praiseworthy custom of accusing ourselves of our faults before God and of confessing ourselves sinners in our temples. Six centuries after the destruction of this holy temple, the archimandrites[7] of Europe thought up the idea of obliging their fakirs to confess to them in secret twice a year. A few centuries later, people of society were obliged to do the same. You may well imagine what dangerous authority this custom gave those who wished to abuse it. Family secrets were now in their hands. Husbands lost influence over their wives and fathers over their children. The flames of discord were ignited in civil wars by these confessors who took sides and refused what they call absolution to those on the opposite side.

At last, they persuaded their penitents that God commanded them to kill the princes who displeased their archimandrites. Yesterday, my brothers, the counselor's chaplain showed us, in the history of the little nation of Franks[8] who live on a patch of land at the edge of the Occident and who are not without merit, the story of a fakir named Clément who received explicit orders in confession from his prior, named Bourgoin, to go assassinate his legitimate king, named Henri, I think.[9] Quite frankly, in the little I've read myself regarding these neighboring nations, I felt as though I were reading the history of cannibals. Raise our hearts to the Eternal!

My brothers, besides the monk named Malagrida, the savages burned two other monks whose names and sins I do not know. May God take their souls.

And then two Muslims were burned. Charity demands that, seized with horror, we shrug our shoulders, and pray for them. You know that when the

Muslims conquered all Spain with their scimitars that they molested no one, forced no one to change their religion, and treated the vanquished with humanity, just as they did us Israelis. Your eyes have witnessed with what kindness the Turks have treated the Orthodox Christians, the Nestorian Christians, the papist Christians, the Disciples of John, the ancient ignicole Parsis[10] and ourselves, the humble servants of Moses. This example of humanity was unable to soften the hearts of these savages who inhabit the little tongue of land called Portugal. Two Muslims were delivered to the cruelest of tortures because their fathers and grandfathers had a little less foreskin than the Portuguese, because they wash three times a day instead of once a week like the Portuguese, because they call the Eternal Being *Allah* instead of *Dios* like the Portuguese, and because they put their thumbs by their ears while reciting their prayers. Ah, my brothers, what good reasons for burning a man!

The counselor's chaplain showed me a notice from a great rabbi in the land of the Franks, whose name ends in *ic* and who lives in a burg or town called *Soissons*.[11] This good rabbi says in his notice, entitled *Mandate,* that we must regard all men as brothers and that a Christian should love a Turk. Long life to the good rabbi!

May all of Adam's children, white, red, black, grey, tanned, bearded or beardless, castrated or whole, think like him forever! And may all fanatics, persecutors, and the superstitious become men! Raise our hearts to the Eternal!

My brothers, it is time to shed our tears over our thirty-seven Israelites burned in the act of faith. I do not say that they were all slowly burned to death. We are told that three were whipped to death and that two were sent to prison. That leaves us thirty-two consumed by flames in this savage sacrifice.

What was their crime? Only to have been born. Their fathers begot them in a religion that their forefathers have professed these past five thousand years. They were born Israelites. They celebrated Passover in their cellars. And that is the sole reason the Portuguese burned them. We haven't been told that all of our brothers were eaten after having been thrown in the flames, but we must presume it of two rather plump fourteen-year-old boys and a chubby little twelve-year-old girl who were very appetizing.[12]

Would you believe that while the flames were devouring these innocent victims, the inquisitors and the other barbarians were chanting our prayers? The

Grand Inquisitor himself was intoning the makib,[13] or psalm, of our good King David, which begins with these words: "Have pity on me, oh Lord, in accordance with your divine mercy!"

This is how these pitiless monsters invoke the God of clemency and goodness, the God of mercy, while committing the most atrocious and barbaric crimes, exercising cruelties that even raging demons would not wish to perform on their brother demons. This is how, in a contradiction as absurd as their furor is abominable, that they offer our makibs to God and borrow our religion itself while punishing us for having been raised in that same religion. Raise our hearts to the Eternal!

> (The preceding may be regarded as the first point of Rabbi Akib's sermon; the following, as his second point.)

Oh Pious tigers! Fanatic panthers! who have such contempt for your sect that you think you can only maintain it with the help of executioners! If you could reason, I would interrogate you. I would ask you why you immolate us, the fathers of your fathers?

What could you reply if I said to you that your God was of our religion? He was born a Jew and he was circumcised like all the other Jews. He received his baptism, as you admit, from John the Jew, which was an antique Jewish custom, an ablution done in those days, a ceremony we used on our neophytes. He fulfilled all the duties of our ancient laws. He lived a Jew, died a Jew, and you burn us because we are Jewish.

I call your own books to witness. Did Jesus say anywhere that the Mosaic Law was bad or false? Did he repeal it? Were his first disciples not circumcised? Did Peter not abstain from the meat forbidden by our law when he ate with the Israelites? And did Paul, become an apostle, not himself circumcise a few of his disciples? Did this same Paul not sacrifice in our temple, according to your own books? What were you to begin with but part of ourselves, who separated from us after a time?

Unnatural children, we are your fathers and the fathers of the Muslims. A misfortunate and respectable mother has had two daughters, and these two daughters have chased her from her house. And you reproach us for no longer inhabiting this demolished house! You make a crime of our misfortune and you punish us for it! But these Parsis, these sages, more ancient than us, the first Persians who were our conquerors and masters in the olden days and who taught us to read and write, are they not dispersed over this earth like us? Are not the Banians,[14] more ancient than the Parsis, also scattered all over the borders of India, Persia, and Tartary without ever mixing with other nations or marrying foreign women? What am I saying? Your Christians, who are living peacefully under the yoke of the great Padishah[15] of lands, do they ever wed Muslim girls, or girls of the Roman Church? Just what superiority do you claim over the fact that we never integrate ourselves in the nations we live in?

Your dementia goes so far as to say that we were dispersed because our fathers condemned the man you adore to agony. How ignorant you are! Can you not see that he was condemned only by the Romans? We had no right to swords. We were governed then by Quirinus, Varus, and Pilate since, God be praised, we have almost always been slaves. The torture of the cross was not a custom of our people. You will not find in our histories a single example of a man being crucified, nor the slightest reference to this chastisement. So cease persecuting an entire nation for an event for which it cannot be held responsible.

I need only your own books to confound you. You admit that Jesus called our Pharisees and priests "a race of vipers" and "hypocrites"[16] in public. If one of your own continually walked through the streets of Rome calling the pope and his cardinals vipers and hypocrites, would you suffer it? It is true that the Pharisees denounced Jesus to the Roman governor who made him perish by the usual Roman tortures. Is that a reason to burn Jewish merchants and their daughters in Lisbon?

I know that certain barbarians, to justify their cruelty, accuse us of having been able to recognize the divinity of Jesus Christ, and of not having done so. I appeal to the scholars of Europe, for there are some. In their Gospels, Jesus sometimes calls himself the son of God or the son of man, but never God. And Paul never gave him this title.

Son of man is a very common expression in our language. Son of God means a just man, just as Belial[17] means a wicked one. For three hundred years, the Christians considered Jesus a mediator sent by God, the most perfect of His creatures. It was only at the Council of Nicaea that the majority of bishops certified his divinity, despite the opposition of three-quarters of the empire. If the Christians themselves denied his divinity for that long and if there are still Christian societies today who deny it,[18] by what preposterous reversal of logic can we be punished for failing to recognize it? Raise our hearts to the Eternal!

We shall not recriminate herein the various sects of Christians. We leave them to the reproaches they make to each other for having falsified so many books and passages, for having forged oracles by the sibyls and so many miracles. Their various sects reproach each other's prevarications more than we could ever do.

I will confine myself to a single question I will ask them. If someone, just leaving his *auto-de-fé*, should tell me he is a Christian, I will ask him in what way he can be one. Jesus never practiced confession, nor had it practiced. His Easter, or Passover, was certainly not that of a Portuguese. Can religious orders or Extreme Unction be found in the Gospels? He instituted neither cardinals, popes, Dominicans, priests, or inquisitors. He had no one burned. He recommended only respect of the laws, love of God and our neighbors, following the example of our prophets. If he came back to earth today, would he recognize himself in a single one of those who call themselves Christians?

Our enemies today make a crime of the fact that we robbed the Egyptians and slit the throats of several small nations in the hamlets we seized long ago, that we sacrificed people and even ate a few, as Ezekiel says. I admit we were an ignorant, barbarous, superstitious, and absurd people. But would it be just today to go burn the pope and all the monsignori in Rome because the early Romans raped the Sabine women and despoiled the Samnites?

Let the prevaricators, who need so much indulgence regarding their own laws, therefore stop persecuting and exterminating those who, as men, are their brothers and who, as Jews, are their fathers.

Let each man serve God in the religion in which he was born, without wishing to tear his neighbor's heart out over disputes no one understands.

Let each man serve his prince and his country without ever claiming to obey God in order to disobey the laws. *Oh Adonaï*, who has created us all, who does not desire the woes of your creatures! God, the father of us all, God of mercy, grant that there be no more fanatics, no more persecutors on this tiny globe, the smallest of your worlds! Raise our hearts to the Eternal! *Amen.*

EXTRACT FROM THE *LONDON GAZETTE,* OF FEBRUARY 20, 1762

Still battling the Seven Years' War, the French navy is at this moment almost decimated and the country's debt is higher than ever. An article appears in the *Gazette de France* announcing that ships will be offered to the government by several cities, guilds, farmers-general, and banking groups. The clergy, always boasting of its "voluntary donations," is absent from the list. So Voltaire invents an article from a London paper applauding the patriotic zeal of the clergy who, it claims, will pitch in too—pseudo-innocently revealing the massive fortunes of these priestly lords.[1]

We learn that our neighbors the French are animated at least as much as us by the patriotic spirit. Several bodies of this kingdom have indicated their zeal for the king and for the fatherland. They give up necessities to furnish vessels, and we learn that the monks, who must also love the king and fatherland, will donate out of their surplus.

We are assured that the Benedictines, who possess an income of about nine million pounds[2] in the Kingdom of France, will furnish at least nine powerful vessels;

That the Abbot of Citeaux, a very important man in the State since he unquestionably possesses the best vineyards in Burgundy and the highest tonnage, will equip the navy with some of his barrels. He is currently building a palace whose estimated cost will be one million seven hundred thousand pounds, and he has already spent four hundred thousand francs on this house for the glory of God. He will have vessels built for the glory of the king.

We are assured that Clairvaux will follow this example, even though the vineyards of Clairvaux don't amount to much. But as the owner of just under forty thousand acres of woods, he is in the perfect situation to have some fine ships built.

He will be imitated by the Carthusian monks who wished even to precede him, considering that they eat the best seafood and that it is in their interest that the seas be free. They enjoy an income of three million in France with which to order turbots and soles. It is said that they will contribute fine flagships.

The Premonstratensian Order and the Carmelites, who are as necessary in a State as the Carthusians, propose to furnish the same quota. The other monks will donate in proportion. We have been so assured of this voluntary offering from all the monks that we would obviously have to consider them enemies of the fatherland if they defaulted on this duty.

The Jews of Bordeaux have contributed. Monks, who must be as good as Jews, will be enviously competitive no doubt to maintain the superiority of the new law over the old one.

As for the Jesuit brothers, we do not consider that they should be bled on this occasion, considering that France is soon to be purged of said brothers.

POST-SCRIPTUM

As France is a little short of sailors, the Prior of the Celestines has suggested to the regular abbots, priors, sub-priors, rectors, and superiors furnishing vessels that they send their novices to serve as cabin boys and their friars to serve as seamen. Said Prior has demonstrated in a fine speech how contrary to the spirit of charity it is to think only of one's salvation when one should be occupied with that of the State. This speech had a great effect and all the chapters were still deliberating when the postal service departed.

PRAYER TO GOD

1763

This famous deistic prayer constitutes the twenty-third chapter of Voltaire's *Treatise on Tolerance*.

It is thus no longer to men that I address myself; it is to thee, God of all beings, of all worlds and all times, if it is permitted of feeble creatures imperceptible to the rest of the universe and lost in its immensity to dare ask something of thee; of thee who has given all and whose decrees are as unchangeable as they are eternal. Deign to look upon the errors inherent in our nature with pity, and may these errors not prove our final downfall. Thou hast not given us hearts so that we should hate each other, nor hands to slit each other's throats. Make us help each other bear the burden of a fleeting life full of hardships and sorrow, so that these little differences between the clothes that cover our frail bodies, between all our inadequate languages, between all our ridiculous customs, our imperfect laws, our senseless opinions, and between all our conditions, so disproportionate in our eyes and so equal in your own; may these tiny nuances that distinguish these atoms called *men* from one another not become causes of hatred and persecution. May those who light candles at high noon to worship you tolerate those who content themselves with the light from your sun. May those who cover their robes with white linen to say you must be loved not detest those who say the same thing from beneath a coat of black wool. May it be equally good to adore you in a jargon drawn from ancient languages as in a newer jargon. May those whose garments are dyed in red or purple, who dominate a small parcel of some small mud pile of this world, and who possess a few round fragments of a certain metal enjoy what they call *grandeur* and *wealth* without pride; and may others see them without envy, for thou knowest that there is nothing to be proud of nor to envy in these vanities.

May all men remember that they are brothers! And hold all tyranny exerted over souls in horror, just as they hold in execration the brigands who take by force the fruit of honest and peaceful labor! If the scourge of war cannot be avoided, let us not hate or destroy each other in the bosom of peace and may we employ the moment of our existence to equally bless in a thousand different languages, from Siam to California, thy bounty, which has given us this moment.

CATECHISM OF THE HONEST MAN, OR DIALOGUE BETWEEN A CALOYER AND A MAN OF MEANS

Translated from the Common Greek by D.J.J.R.C.D.C.D.G.

1763

A caloyer is a monk of the Greek Orthodox Church. The long list of initials stands for Dom Jean-Jacques Rousseau, ci-devant citoyen de Genève (former citizen of Geneva). "Dom," a form of address for Benedictine monks, may be a wink at Rousseau's "The Savoyard Vicar's Profession of Faith" in *Emile* the previous year, which had greatly pleased Voltaire. *Catechism of the Honest Man* was hugely popular.[1] Thomas Jefferson echoes one of its closing statements while discussing the fiftieth Fourth of July celebration. The *Catechism* was condemned by Rome on July 8, 1765.

THE CALOYER

May I ask you, Sir, which religion you belong to in Aleppo, in the midst of all the sects that are received here and that all serve to make this great town flourish? Are you a Muslim who follows the rites of Omar or of Ali? Are you a follower of the dogmas of the ancient of Parsis or of the Sabaeans, so anterior to the Parsis, or of the Brahmins, who boast of even greater antiquity? Might you be Jewish? Are you a Christian of the Greek or the Armenian or Coptic or Latin Church?

THE HONEST MAN

I adore God, I try to be just and I seek to instruct myself.

THE CALOYER

But do you give no preference to the Jewish books over the Zend-Avesta, the Vedas, or the Koran?

THE HONEST MAN

I fear that I have not enough knowledge to judge books well, and I sense that I have enough to see, in the great book of nature, that one must worship and love one's master.

THE CALOYER

Is there something that bothers you about the Jewish books?

THE HONEST MAN

Yes, I admit I have trouble conceiving what they report. I see inconsistencies in them that surprise my feeble reason.

1. It seems difficult to me that Moses could have written the Pentateuch attributed to him in the desert. If his people came from Egypt, where the author says they lived for four hundred years (although he is mistaken by two hundred), the book would probably have been written in Egyptian, though we are told it is in Hebrew.

    It would have had to be engraved on stone or wood. There was no other way of writing in the time of Moses. It was an extremely difficult art, which required long preparations. The wood or stone had to be polished. It doesn't appear that this art could have been exercised in a desert where, according to the book itself, the Jewish horde did not even have what was needed to make clothes or shoes and where God was obliged to perform constant miracles for forty years to prevent their shoes and clothes from wearing out. It is so true that one only wrote on stone that the author of the Book of Joshua says that Deuteronomy was written on an altar of uncut stones[2] covered with mortar. Apparently, Joshua did not intend this book to last.

2. Men the most well-versed in antiquity think that these books were written more than seven hundred years after Moses. They found this on

what is said about kings, and there weren't any kings until a long time after Moses; on the position of the towns, which is false if the book were written in the desert but true if it was written in Jerusalem; and on the names of towns and villages that are mentioned, but that were not founded or called by those names till several centuries later, etc.

3. What may shock in the writings attributed to Moses is that the immortality of the soul and rewards and punishments after death are entirely absent from the setting forth of his laws. It is strange that he commands the manner in which one must make one's excrements, and speaks nowhere of the immortality of the soul. Is it possible that Moses, inspired by God, would have been more concerned with our bottoms than with our souls?[3] That he would have prescribed the manner in which we must go to the toilet in the Israeli camp and that he would not have breathed a single word about eternal life? Zoroaster, more ancient than the Jewish legislator, said: "Honor your parents if you wish to have eternal life."[4] And the Decalogue says "Honor your father and mother if you wish to have a long life on earth."[5] It seems to me that Zoroaster speaks as a holy man and Moses as a terrestrial one.

4. The events recounted in the Pentateuch surprise those unfortunate enough to judge only by their reason, and whose blind reason has not been enlightened by some special grace. The first chapter of Genesis is so beyond our conceptions that it was forbidden to read it among the Jews before the age of twenty-five.[6]

We see with some surprise that God came to stroll every day at noon in the Garden of Eden; that the sources of four great rivers, prodigiously far from each other, formed a fountain in this garden; that the serpent spoke to Eve, since he is the most subtle of animals, and that a she-ass, not half so subtle, also spoke a few centuries later;[7] that God separated the light from the darkness, as if darkness were something real;[8] that he created light, which comes from our sun, before the sun itself; that after having created man and woman, he then pulls woman from one of man's ribs and that he put flesh in the place of this rib; that he condemned Adam to death, and all his posterity to hell over an apple; that he put a mark on Cain, who had slain his brother, to save him and that Cain feared to be killed by the other men peopling the earth although, according to the text, the human race was limited to the family of Adam; that supposed cataracts in the sky inundated the earth and that all the animals came to enclose themselves in a box for a year.[9]

After this prodigious number of fables that all seem more absurd than Ovid's *Metamorphoses*, we are not less surprised to see that God delivers six hundred thousand combatants of his people from servitude in Egypt, not counting the old men, women or children, and that these six hundred thousand combatants, after the most astonishing miracles—equaled, however, by the magicians of Egypt—flee instead of combatting their enemies; and that in fleeing they do not take the road that leads to the land God is giving them; that they end up between Memphis and the Red Sea; that God parts this sea for them and lets them cross it on dry land, only to let them perish in a ghastly desert instead of bringing them into this promised land; that these people, taken in hand by God himself and before his eyes, ask Moses' brother for a golden calf to worship; that this golden calf was smelted in a single day; that Moses reduced this gold to impalpable powder and made the people swallow it; that twenty-three thousand men of this people allowed their throats to be slit by the Levites in punishment for having made this golden calf, but that Aaron, who had smelted it, was declared a great priest in reward;[10] that two hundred and fifty men were burned, and then another 14,700 for having wrangled over Aaron's incense censer,[11] and that on another occasion, Moses had another twenty-four thousand men of his people slain.

5. If one relies upon the simple laws of physics, and does not raise oneself to divine powers, it is difficult to imagine that there was a water that made adulterous women die but not faithful ones. One is even more surprised to find a true prophet among the idolaters in the person of Balaam.

6. More surprising yet is that in a village of the small land of Madiam, the Jewish people found 675,000 sheep, 72,000 steer, 61,000 donkeys, and 32,000 virgins; and one shivers with horror on reading that, by order of the Lord, the Jews massacred all the men and all the widows, wives, and mothers, and kept only the little girls.

7. The sun that stops at high noon to give more time to the Jews to slaughter the Amorites, already crushed by a rain of hailstones from heaven,[12] the Jordan opening its bed just like the Red Sea to let these Jews cross it, who could so easily have forded it, the walls of Jericho falling to the sound of trumpets; so many prodigies of every species demand, to be believed, the sacrifice of all reason and the liveliest faith. And finally, to what end do so many miracles performed by God himself for centuries in favor of his people obtain? To render them almost always the slaves of other nations.

8. The entire story of Samson and his loves, his hair, his lion, and his three hundred foxes seems to be written more to amuse the imagination than to edify the mind.[13] The stories of Joshua and Jephthah seem barbarous.

9. The story of Kings is a jumble of cruelties and assassinations that make your heart bleed. Nearly all the events are unbelievable. The first Jewish king, Saul, can only find two swords among his people, and his successor, David, leaves behind over twenty million in silver, cash. You say that these books are written by God himself, and you know that God cannot lie; therefore if a single fact is wrong, the entire book is an imposture.

10. The prophets are no less revolting for a man who does not have the gift of penetrating the hidden allegorical meanings of the prophecies. He is pained to see Jeremiah yoke himself and have himself tied with ropes; Hosea, formally ordered to do so by God, makes sons of whores with a public whore, then makes some with an adulteress; Isaiah, walking naked in a public place;[14] Ezekiel, who sleeps 390 days on his left side, then 40 days on his right, who eats a book of parchment, who covers his bread with the excrement of men, and then with cow dung; Oholah and Oholibah, who establish a bordello and of whom God says that they only like men hung like donkeys with the sperm of a horse.[15] Surely if a reader is not instructed in the customs of the country and in the manner of prophesizing, he is in danger of being scandalized; and when he sees Elisha have forty children devoured by a bear for having called him baldy,[16] a punishment so disproportionate to the offense may inspire him with more horror than respect.

So forgive me if the Jewish books have bothered me. I do not wish to revile the object of your veneration. I even confess that I may be mistaken on matters concerning propriety and justice, which are perhaps not the same in all eras. I tell myself that our customs are different from those of these remote times, but perhaps the preference you give to the New Testament over the Old can justify my scruples. The law of the Jews must not have seemed good to you, since you have abandoned it, for if it really was good, why would you not have always followed it? But if it was bad, how could it have been divine?

THE CALOYER
The Old Testament presents its difficulties. But you admit to me then, that the New Testament does not give rise to the same doubts and scruples as the Old?

THE HONEST MAN
I have read them both with attention, but suffer me to expose the anxieties into which my ignorance plunges me. You will take pity on them and relieve them.

I find myself here with Armenian Christians who tell me it is not permitted to eat rabbit, with the Greek Orthodox who assure me that the Holy Spirit does not proceed from the Son, with Nestorians who deny that Mary is the mother of God, and with a few of the Roman Church who boast that in the far reaches of the West, the Christians of Europe think entirely differently than those of Asia and Africa. I know that ten or twelve sects in Europe anathemize each other. The Muslims around me regard all these Christians with contempt, whom they tolerate nevertheless. The Jews hold in execration both the Christians and the Muslims, the Guebres[17] despise them all and what few remain of the Sabaeans would not like to dine with any of those I have named, nor can the Brahmins suffer the Sabaeans, the Guebres, the Christians, the Muslims, or the Jews.

I have wished a hundred times that Jesus Christ, by coming to incarnate himself in Judea had reunited all these sects under his laws. I have wondered why, being God, he didn't use the powers of his divinity; why, in coming to deliver us from sin, he left us in sin; why, in coming to enlighten all men, he left nearly all men in error?

I know that I am nothing. I know that in the depths of my nothingness I must not question the Being of all beings; but I am allowed, like Job, to raise my respectful complaints from the bosom of my misery.

What do you want me to think when I read two genealogies of Jesus, which directly contradict each other?[18] And that these genealogies, so different in the names and numbers of his ancestors, are not even his, but those of his father Joseph, who is not his father?

I torture my mind to understand how a God could die. I read the books both sacred and profane of his times. One of these sacred books tells me that a new star appeared in the East and led the Magi to the feet of God, who had just been born. No profane book speaks of this forever-memorable event, which sounds like it should've been perceived by the entire earth and noted in the annals of every state. One Gospel writer tells us that a king named Herod, to whom the Romans, masters of the whole known world, had given Judea, heard that a child just born in a stable would become King of the Jews, but how and from whom and on what foundation could he have heard this strange piece of news? Is it possible that a king who hadn't lost his mind could have imagined having all of the male babies in the country put to the sword just to include one obscure child in the massacre? Is there a single example on earth of a fury so abominable and so senseless?[19]

I see that the remaining Gospels contradict each other on nearly every page. I open the history of Josephus, an author who's nearly contemporary: Josephus, related to Miriam, who was sacrificed by Herod; Josephus, the natural enemy of this prince, doesn't say a word about this adventure. He's Jewish and he doesn't even speak of this Jesus, born among the Jews.

What uncertainties overwhelm me in the important search for what I must adore and what I must believe! I read the Scriptures and I see nowhere that Jesus, since recognized as God, ever called himself God. I even see the contrary. He says that the Father is greater than he and that the Father alone knows what the son does not.[20] And how should these words, father and son, be understood among a people who spoke of bad men as the sons of Belial, and of just men as the sons of God? I adopt some of the maxims of Jesus' morals, but what legislator ever taught bad morals? In which religion is adultery, larceny, murder, imposture not forbidden, and respect for one's parents, obedience to the laws, and the practice of all the virtues not expressly commanded?

The more I read, the more my pain redoubles. I seek prodigies worthy of a God, attested to by the universe. I dare say, with a painful naiveté that fears to blaspheme, that devils sent into the bodies of a herd of pigs, water changed into wine for people who were already drunk, a fig tree withered for not bearing figs before the season of figs, etc., do not fulfill the idea I had of the master of all nature, announcing and proving the truth by magnificent and useful miracles. Must I adore the master of nature in a Jew said to have been transported by the devil to the top of a mountain from which one could see all the kingdoms on earth?[21]

I read the words that have been reported of him. I see the imminent arrival of the kingdom of heaven represented by a mustard seed, by a fishing net, by money lent at interest, by a supper that the lame and the one-eyed are forced to attend. Jesus says that one does not put young wine into old kegs and that one prefers old wine to the new. Is this the way God speaks?

In short, how can I recognize God in a Jew of the rabble, condemned to death for having spoken badly of the government to this rabble and sweating blood in the anguish and fright that death inspires in him? Is that a Plato? A Socrates? An Antony, an Epictetus, a Zaleucus,[22] Solon, or Confucius? Who, of all these wise men, did not speak or write in a manner more fitting to the ideas we have of wisdom? And how else can we judge, if not by our ideas?

When I told you I had adopted some of Jesus' maxims, you must have sensed that I cannot adopt them all. I was afflicted to read, "I have come to bring the sword, not peace. I have come to divide son against father, daughter, mother and parents."[23] I confess that these words filled me with grief and terror, and if I considered these words a prophecy, I would believe I had seen its accomplishment in the quarrels that have divided Christians from the very beginning, in the civil wars that have put arms in their hands throughout so many centuries, in the assassinations of so many princes, in the horrible woes of so many families.

I confess further that feelings of indignation and pity seized my heart when I saw Peter make his followers bring their money to his feet. Ananias and Saphira kept something for themselves from the sale of their field. They didn't say so, and Peter punished them by making husband and wife drop dead on the spot.[24] Alas! That was not the sort of miracle I was expecting from those who say that they do not wish the death of a sinner, but his conversion. I dare to believe that if God worked miracles, it would be to cure men and not to kill them; that it would be to better them and not to destroy them; that He is a God of mercy and not a homicidal tyrant. What revolted me most in the story is that Peter, having made Ananias die, and seeing Sapphira come in turn, did not warn her, did not say to her, "Beware of keeping a few oboles for yourself. If you have some, admit it, give it all. Fear the fate of your husband." On the contrary, he entraps her. He seems to enjoy striking a second victim. I confess to you that this story has always made my hair stand on end, and I was consoled only when I saw how impossible and ridiculous it was.

Since you permit me to explain my thoughts, I continue and say that I have not found a single trace of Christianity in the story of Jesus. The four Gospels that remain to us are in opposition regarding several deeds, but they are unanimous in attesting that Jesus submitted to the Law of Moses from his birth unto his death. All of his disciples attended the synagogue. They preached reform, but they did not announce a new religion. The Christians were not completely separated from the Jews until much later. At what moment exactly did God then wish that we cease being Jews and become Christians? Who does not see that time accounts for everything and that all the dogmas came later, one after the other?

If Jesus had wanted to establish a Christian Church, would he not have taught its laws? Would he not have established all its rites himself? Would he not have heralded the seven sacraments, of which he does not speak? Would he not have said "I am God, begot but not created. The Holy Spirit proceeds from my Father without being begotten. I have two wills in one person and my mother is the mother of God? On the contrary, he says to his mother, "Woman, what is there between you and me?" He established no dogmas, no rites, no hierarchy. It was thus not he who created his religion.

When the first dogmas began to be established, I see the Christians supporting them by false books. They impute acrostic verses on Christianity to the Sibyls. They forge histories, prodigies, whose absurdity is palpable. Such is, for example, the story of the New Jerusalem, built in the air, whose walls were five hundred leagues in circumference and in height, which appears on the horizon throughout all the night and disappears at the break of day. Such is also the quarrel of Peter and Simon the Magician before Nero, and a hundred other fables no less absurd.[25]

What puerile miracles were invented! How many false martyrs and ridiculous legends! *Portenta judaica rides.*[26]

How did whoever wrote the legend of Luke, under the name of *glad tidings*, find the nerve to say, in chapter 21, that the generation he lived in would not pass away without seeing the heavenly bodies shaken, without there being signs in the sun, moon, and stars, and without seeing Jesus come in a cloud with great power and glory?[27] Clearly there have been no signs in the sun, moon, and stars, or heavenly bodies shaken, nor any Jesus arriving majestically in the clouds.

How could the fanatic who wrote the Epistles of Paul be bold enough to make him say, "I have learned from Jesus that those of us who live are reserved for his coming. As soon as the trumpets sound, those who died in Jesus will be resurrected first. Then those of us who are living will be carried away with them in the air to meet Jesus"?[28]

Was this lovely prophecy accomplished? Did Paul and the Christian Jews go to meet Jesus in the air to the sound of trumpets? And where, if you please, did Paul learn all these marvelous things from Jesus? Paul, who never saw him, who persecuted his disciples and who had joined in the stoning of Stephen? Had he spoken to Jesus when he was taken to the third heaven? And what exactly is the third heaven? Is it Mercury or Mars? In truth, if we read attentively, we would be seized with horror and pity on every page.[29]

THE CALOYER

But if this book has that effect on its readers, how could anyone have believed in it? How was it able to convert so many thousands?

THE HONEST MAN

It is because it wasn't read. Was it through reading that ten million peasants were convinced that three makes one, that God is in a wafer and that the wafer disappears, and is suddenly turned into God himself by some man? It was through conversations, preaching, cabals. It was through winning over women and children. It was through impostures and miraculous tales that they easily managed to establish a little flock. The books of the first Christians were extremely rare. It was forbidden to show them to catechists. People were initiated in secret into the Christian mysteries just like into the mysteries of Ceres. The underprivileged eagerly followed those who had convinced them that not only were all men equal, but that a Christian was far superior to a Roman emperor.

All the world was then divided into small societies: Egyptian, Greek, Syrian, Roman, Jewish, etc. The Christian sect had all the advantages among the rabble. Three or four hotheads like Paul were enough to draw a mob. Not long after, clever men arrived to take command. Nearly every sect was established in this manner except that of Mahomet, the most brilliant of all, since it alone among so many human institutions seemed to rise under the protection of God, owing its existence only to victories.

Moreover, the Muslim religion is still what it was under its founder, after twelve hundred years. Nothing has been changed. The laws, written by Mahomet himself, subsist in all their integrity. His Koran is as well respected in Persia as in Turkey, Africa, or India. It is observed everywhere to the letter. Their only division is over the right of succession between Ali and Omar. Christianity, on the contrary, differs on every count from the religion of Jesus. Jesus, son of a village carpenter, never wrote a word, and it is likely that he was unable to read or write. He was born, lived, and died a Jew, observing all the Jewish laws: circumcised, sacrificing according to Mosaic Law, eating Passover lamb with lettuce, abstaining from pork, ixion, and griffin, and also from hare, because it ruminates and does not have cleft feet, according to Mosaic Law.[30] You Christians, you think that it does have cleft feet and that it does not ruminate, and so you boldly eat it. You roast ixions and griffins whenever you find some. You are not circumcised and you do not practice sacrifice. Not a single one of your rites was instituted by Jesus. What can you have in common with him?

THE CALOYER

I confess that I would be a brazen impostor if I dared claim to you that the Christianity of today resembles that of the first centuries, or that that of the first centuries resembled the religion of Jesus. But you will also admit that God could have commanded all of these variations.

THE HONEST MAN

God vary! God change! The idea sounds like blasphemy. What! God's sun is always the same yet his religion would be a series of vicissitudes! What! You would make him resemble these miserable governments who issue new and contradictory edicts every day? He would have given one edict to Adam, another to Seth, a third to Noah, a fourth to Abraham, a fifth to Moses, a sixth to Jesus, and still more new edicts at every church council, and everything would have changed, from the prohibition of eating fruit from the tree of knowledge of right from wrong, to the papal bull Unigenitus of the Jesuit, Le Tellier! Believe me, you ought to tremble at outraging God in accusing Him of so much inconsistency, weakness, contradiction, absurdity, and even wickedness.

THE CALOYER

If all these variations are the work of men, acknowledge at least that the morals are from God, since they do not vary.

THE HONEST MAN

Let us consider then only these morals. But how the Christians have corrupted them! How cruelly have they violated the natural law taught by all lawmakers and engraved in the hearts of all men!

If Jesus spoke of this law as old as the world, this law established among the Hurons and the Chinese: *Love your neighbor as yourself*, the law of the Christians has been: *Hate your neighbor as yourself*. Athanasians, persecute the Eusebians,[31] and be persecuted yourselves. Cyrillians, crush the children of the Nestorians against the walls; Guelphs and Ghibellines, make civil war for five hundred years to determine whether Jesus ordered the supposed successor of Simon Barjona to dethrone emperors and kings and whether Constantine ceded the empire to Pope Silvester.[32] Papists, hang wretches from a gibbet thirty feet high, tear them, burn them if they don't believe that a piece of dough is changed into God at the voice of a Capuchin or Franciscan monk, to be nibbled by mice on the altar if the ciborium is left open. Poltrot, Balthasar Gérard, Jacques Clément, Châte, Guignard, Ravaillac, sharpen your holy daggers, charge your holy pistols. Europe, swim in blood, while the vicar of God, Pope Alexander VI, sullied by his murders and poisonings, sleeps in the arms of his daughter, Lucretia; while Leo X is awash in pleasures; while Paul III enriches his bastard sons with the spoils of nations; while Jules III makes his messenger monkey a cardinal (a dignity that suits the monkey better); while Pius IV has Cardinal

Caraffe strangled; while Pius V makes the Romans groan beneath the plunderings of his bastard son, Buon-Compagno; and while Clement VIII whips the great King Henry IV on the [surrogate] buttocks of Cardinals of Ossat and Duperron. Join the absurdity of your Italian farces to the horrors of your lootings everywhere, then send Brother Trigaut and Brother Bouvet to preach "the good tidings" in China.

THE CALOYER

I cannot condemn your zeal. The truth, against which one argues in vain, forces me to admit part of what you say, but you must admit too that amidst so many crimes, there were also great virtues. Must the abuses embitter you, and the good laws not move you at all? And join to these good laws the miracles that prove the divinity of Christ.

THE HONEST MAN

Miracles? Good heavens! And what religion does not have its miracles? Everything is a prodigy in antiquity. What? You don't believe the miracles reported by the Herodotuses and the Titus Livys, by a hundred authors respected by all nations, and you believe the adventures in Palestine recounted, they say, by John and Mark in books that were ignored by the Greeks and the Romans for three hundred years—books undoubtedly written long after the destruction of Jerusalem, as it is proven by the books themselves, that swarm with contradictions on each page! For example, it is said in the Gospel of Saint Matthew that the blood of Zacharias, son of Barachias, who was massacred between the temple and altar, will fall on the Jews.[33] Well we see in Flavius Joseph that this Zachariah was killed indeed between the temple and the altar during the siege of Jerusalem by Titus.[34] Therefore, this gospel was written after Titus. And why would the Lord God Jesus have performed these miracles? To be condemned to the gallows by the Jews! What? He resuscitated the dead and obtained nothing by it except to die himself by the cruelest of tortures?! If he had performed miracles, it would have been to make his divinity known. Think what it means to accuse God of having made himself into a man, quite uselessly, and to then have raised the dead only to be hanged himself? What? Thousands of miracles in favor of the Jews, only to make slaves of them, and miracles performed by Jesus, only to get

Jesus crucified! It's imbecilic to believe it and a criminal frenzy to teach it when one does not believe it.

THE CALOYER

I do not deny that your objections are founded and I can see that you are reasoning in good faith, but still, you must agree that men must have a religion.

THE HONEST MAN

No doubt, the soul must be nourished, but why turn it into poison? Why suffocate the simple truth beneath a mass of shocking lies? Why impose these lies by fire and the sword? What infernal horror! Ah! If your religion were from God, would you need henchmen to uphold it? Does a geometer need to say, "Believe or I will kill you?" The religion between men and God is adoration and virtue. Between a prince and his subjects, it is a matter for the police. And only too often between man and man, it is a commerce of swindling and deceit. Let us adore God sincerely, simply, and fool no one. Yes, there must be a religion, but it must be pure, reasonable, universal. It must be like the sun, which is the same for all men and not just for some little privileged province. It is absurd, odious, and abominable to imagine that God sheds light on all eyes but that he plunges nearly all souls into darkness. There is only one kind of integrity common to all; there is therefore only one religion. And what is this religion? You know well: to adore God and be just.

THE CALOYER

But then how do you imagine that my religion got established?

THE HONEST MAN

Like all the others. A man of great imagination finds followers among people of little imagination. The flock increases. Fanaticism begins, and deceit does the rest. A powerful man arrives. He sees a mob that has put a saddle on its back and a bit in its mouth. He climbs aboard and conducts it.[35] Once a new religion is adopted by the state, the government is henceforth only occupied in forbidding the means by which it established itself. It had begun with secret assemblies, so they are prohibited. The first apostles were sent out expressly to chase demons, so demons are forbidden. The apostles had proselytes bring them money, so whoever is found guilty of thus taking money is punished. They said it was better to obey God than men,[36] and on this pretext, they braved the laws. The government then maintains that to follow the laws is to obey God. In short, politicians struggle unceasingly to reconcile received errors with the public good.

THE CALOYER

But you are going to Europe. You will be obliged to conform to one of the received religions.

THE HONEST MAN

What? Will I not be able to do in Europe as I do here? To adore in peace the Creator of all the universe, the God of all men, who put the love of truth and justice in my heart?

THE CALOYER

No, it will be too risky. Europe is divided into factions, and you will have to choose one.

THE HONEST MAN

Factions? When we're speaking of universal truths? When it's about God!

THE CALOYER

Such is the misfortune of men. We are obliged to do as they do or flee them. I ask you to give preference to the Greek Church.

THE HONEST MAN

It is in slavery.

THE CALOYER

Would you prefer to submit to the Roman Church?

THE HONEST MAN

It is tyrannical. I want no more of a simoniac patriarch who buys his shameful dignity from a Grand Vizier than of a priest who believes he has been the master of kings these past seven hundred years.

THE CALOYER

It would not behoove a religious person such as myself to suggest the Protestant faith to you.

THE HONEST MAN

It is perhaps the one I would adopt the most willingly if I were reduced to the hardship of having to choose a party.

THE CALOYER

Why not prefer to it a more ancient religion?

THE HONEST MAN

It appears to me far more ancient than the Roman.

THE CALOYER

How can you imagine that Saint Peter is not more ancient than Luther, Zwingli, Calvin, and the reformers of England, Denmark, Sweden, etc.?

THE HONEST MAN

It seems to me that the Protestant religion was not invented by either Luther or Zwingli. It seems to me that it is closer to its sources than the Roman religion, and that it adopts only what it finds expressly written in the Gospels of the Christians, whereas the Romans have overladen the faith with new rites and dogmas. One only has to open one's eyes to see that the lawmaker of the Christians instituted no holy days, did not command that we worship images and the bones of the dead, did not sell indulgences or receive annuities, did not confer benefices, held no temporal dignities, did not establish an Inquisition to uphold his laws, and did not maintain his authority by the blades of executioners. The Protestants rejected all these scandalous and deadly novelties. They submit to the magistrates everywhere and the Roman Church has fought against the magistrates for eight hundred years. If the Protestants are mistaken like the others in principle, they have fewer errors in the results, and, since one must deal with men, I prefer to deal with those who mislead the least.

THE CALOYER

It sounds as though you choose a religion like one buys fabric in a shop. You go to the merchant who sells it the less dearly.

THE HONEST MAN

I told you what I would prefer if I had to make a choice, according to the rules of human prudence, but it is not to men that I should address myself. It is to God alone. He speaks to all hearts. We all have an equal right to hear him. The conscience that he gave all men is their universal law. Men from one pole to the other sense that we must be just, honor our fathers and mothers, help our fellow human beings, keep our promises. These laws are from God. The affectations are from mortals. All religions differ as do governments. God permits all of them. I thought that the outer manner in which one worships him can neither flatter nor offend him, so long as this worship is neither superstitious toward him, nor barbaric toward men.

For is it not, in fact, an offense to God to believe that he chose a small nation steeped in crimes as his favorite, in order to damn all the others? That the murderer of Uriah[37] be his beloved and that he holds the pious Antonine[38] in horror? Is it not the greatest absurdity to think that the Supreme Being would punish a caloyer for all eternity for eating rabbit or a Turk for having eaten some pork? There once were people who raised onions, they say, to the rank of gods.[39] There are others who have claimed that a piece of dough was changed into as many gods as there were crumbs. These two extremes of human dementia both rouse pity, but that those who adopt these reveries dare to persecute those who don't believe them, that is what is horrible. The ancient Parsis, the Sabaeans, the Egyptians, and the Greeks all believed in hell. This hell is on earth and it is persecutors who are the demons.

THE CALOYER

I detest persecution and constraint as much as you, and praise heaven the Turks under whose dominion I live in peace, as I've already told you, persecute no one.

THE HONEST MAN

Ah! May all the people of Europe follow the example of the Turks!

THE CALOYER
But I add that, as a caloyer, I cannot propose to you any religion other than the one I profess on Mont Athos.

THE HONEST MAN
And myself, I add that as a man I can only propose to you the religion that suits all men, all the patriarchs and all the wise men of antiquity: the worship of one God, justice, the love of one's fellow human beings, indulgence for all errors, and charity in all occasions that life gives. It is this religion, worthy of God, which God has engraved in all hearts. But he certainly did not engrave that three makes one,[40] that a piece of bread is the Eternal One, and that the she-ass of Balaam spoke.

THE CALOYER
Do not prevent me from being a caloyer.

THE HONEST MAN
Do not prevent me from being an honest man.

THE CALOYER
I serve God according to customs of my monastery.

THE HONEST MAN
And I, according to my conscience. It tells me to fear God, to love caloyers, dervishes, bonzes, and talapoins, and to regard all men as my brothers.

THE CALOYER
All right, all right, caloyer that I am, I think as you do.

THE HONEST MAN
Dear Lord, bless this good caloyer!

THE CALOYER
Dear Lord, bless this honest man!

OMER DE FLEURY, HAVING ENTERED, HAVE SAID

1763

At the bidding of Attorney General, Omer de Fleury, Paris *Parlement* had just ordered the Faculties of Theology and Medicine to give their opinion on smallpox vaccination and forbid its use in the meanwhile. "Having entered, have said" adopts the pompous language of these notices. Since a king referred to himself as *we*, Omer also refers to himself in the plural. As even the Royal family had lost innumerable members to smallpox (the present king, Louis XV, would die of it in 1774) and as Voltaire been arguing for the vaccination since his *Letters on England* in 1734, this piece ridicules the absurdity of leaving matters of health and science up to religious authorities.

Gentlemen,

As I am charged, *by my status* (page 3), with proposing theses on medicine to you, and as we are concerned with dissipating the clouds that weaken security and with desiring solutions to fears, the Wisdom that presides over your procedures will give new weight to what your authority can determine on inoculation, which presents itself under two aspects.

And as common smallpox (page 4) is usually left to the prudence of patients and doctors, you can well sense that inoculation, in which the mind is freer, must not be left to prudence of anyone.

But as what interests religion does not interest the public good in any manner (page 3) and as the public good does not interest religion, we must consult the Sorbonne which, *by its status*, is in charge of deciding whether a Christian should be bled or purged; and the Faculty of Medicine which, *by its status*, is in charge of determining whether inoculation is permitted by Canon Law.[1]

Thus, gentlemen, you who are the best physicians and the best theologians of Europe, must pronounce a decision on smallpox, just as you have done on the categories of Aristotle, on the circulation of the blood, on emetics, and on quinine.

It is known that you understand everything, *by status*, just as you do finance.[2]

Since inoculation, gentlemen, has succeeded in all the neighboring nations that have tried it; since it has saved the lives of foreigners who reason, it is just that you forbid this practice, given that it has not been registered, and to attain this goal, you will employ the decisions of the Sorbonne, who will tell you that St. Augustine did not know of inoculation, and of the Faculty of Paris, who is always of the opinion of foreign doctors.

Above all, gentlemen, do not give a time limit to the salutary and sacred Faculties for deciding, because the useful inserting of smallpox will be forbidden for as long as we wait.

As to syphilis, sister to smallpox, gentlemen of the inquiry are exhorted to scrupulously examine the pills of Keyser,[3] as much for the public good as for the particular good of those young gentlemen who have need of them, *by their status*; the Sorbonne having previously rendered its decree on this theological matter.

We hope that you order the pain of death (as Faculties of Medicine have sometimes done in slighter matters) against the children of our princes inoculated without your permission and against whoever may call into doubt your recognized wisdom and impartiality.

LETTER FROM MR. CLOCPICRE TO MR. ERATOU

Concerning the Question of Whether the Jews Ate Human Flesh and How They Prepared It

1764

Eratou is an anagram of Arouet—alias Voltaire, the pen name of François-Marie Arouet. In this imaginary comical debate between three scholars, Voltaire clarifies his reasons for thinking certain passages in the Bible indicate that human sacrifice was practiced by the ancient Jews, then shows that they would have hardly been unique in doing so.

My good Sir and dear friend, although there are many books, few people read, you may believe me, and among those who do, there are many who use only their eyes. Yesterday, I was conferring with Mr. Pfaff, the illustrious professor of Tübingen, so well known throughout the universe, and Mr. Crokius Dubius, one of the most knowledgeable men of our time. They had no idea that the Jews had often eaten human flesh. Even Dom Calmet himself, who copied the texts of so many ancient authors in his *Commentaries*, has never once mentioned this Jewish custom. I told Mr. Pfaff and Mr. Crokius that there were passages that proved that the Jews had appreciated human flesh and horse flesh very much in the olden days. Crokius said he doubted it, and Pfaff bluntly assured me I was mistaken.

I hunted up an Ezekiel at once and showed them these words in chapter 39: "Ye shall drink the blood of princes and fattened animals; ye shall eat fat flesh till ye be sated; ye shall eat your fill of the flesh of horses and their riders at table."

Mr. Pfaff said that this invitation was made only to the birds. Crokius Dubius, after a long examination, believed that it was also addressed to the

Jews since tables are mentioned, but he claimed it was only a figure of speech. I humbly begged them to consider the fact that Ezekiel lived in the days of Cambyses, and that King Cambyses had a lot of Scythes and Tartars in his army, who ate horses and men rather commonly, and that, even if this custom rather repulses our effeminate ways, it was very true to the male, heroic virtues of the illustrious Jewish people. I reminded them that in the Laws of Moses, among the threats of all the ordinary evils he frightens Jewish transgressors with, such as being reduced to no longer giving loans but having to borrow at usurious rates and getting ulcers in their legs, he adds that they will eat their children. "Well then," I said to them, "do you not see that it was as ordinary for the Jews to cook and eat their children as to get clipped, since their legislator threatens them with both these punishments?"

Several more reflections, which I supported by citations, finally shook up Mr. Pfaff and Crokius. "The most polished nations," I told them, "have always eaten men and especially little boys. Juvenal saw the Egyptians eat a man quite raw. He said that the Gascons had often had such meals. The two Arabian travelers, whose accounts were translated by Abbé Renaudot, said that they saw men eaten on the banks of China and the Indies.

"Homer, speaking of the Cyclops' meals, is only depicting the customs of his time. We know that Candide was nearly eaten by the Oreillons because they mistook him for a Jesuit and that, despite the bad joke that the Jesuits are no good, either roasted or boiled, the Oreillons are mad about Jesuit meat.[1]

"So you can plainly see, gentlemen," I told them, "that we mustn't judge the customs of antiquity by those of the University of Tubingen. You know that the ancient Jews sacrificed people. It so happens that sacrificed victims have always been eaten. In your opinion, when King Agag made himself Samuel's prisoner, and Samuel cut him into little pieces, was it not quite visibly for a stew? What would be the point of cutting a king into small pieces otherwise?

"The Jews did not eat stews," Crokius said. "I admit that their cooks were not as good as French cooks," I replied, "for I believe that it is impossible to cook good dishes without lard. Nevertheless, they did have a few stews. It is written that Rebecca prepared young goats for Isaac in the manner in which this fellow liked to eat them."

Pfaff was dissatisfied with my response. He claimed it was more likely that

Isaac liked his goats on spits and that Rebecca roasted them for him. I maintained that the goats were stewed, which was also Dom Calmet's opinion. He replied that that Benedictine did not even know what a spit was, that Benedictines don't know anything about them, and that Dom Calmet's opinion was erroneous. The discussion grew heated, and we lost sight of its principle object for quite some time, but just-minded people always come back to it in the end.

Pfaff was still entirely astonished by the horses and riders that the Jews ate and in the end, the dispute turned to the superiority that human flesh must have over all the others. "Man," said Mr. Crokius, "is the most perfect of all the animals. In consequence, he must be the best to eat."

"I do not agree with this conclusion," said Mr. Pfaff, "Many scholars claim that there is no analogy whatsoever between thought, which distinguishes men, and a good quivering piece of meat cooked just right. I am also well-founded in believing that we do not have short fibers and that they are not nearly so delicate as those of partridges and wild grouse."

"And that is with what I do not agree," said Mr. Crokius, "You have never partaken of wild grouse nor of little boys, and therefore you cannot judge."

This question left us in quite a predicament until a hussar arrived who certified that he had eaten a Cossack during the siege of Colberg, and that he had found him very hard to chew. Pfaff triumphed, but Crokius maintained that one must never generalize from a particular case. That there were Cossacks and Cossacks, and that tender ones could perhaps be found.

Nevertheless, we did feel some horror at the hussar's story and found him somewhat barbarous. "Really gentlemen, you're awfully delicate," he told us, "We kill two or three hundred thousand men, and everyone thinks it's fine. We eat one Cossack, and everybody screams."

ADAPT TO THE TIMES

1764

This recommendation is addressed to those who govern, we are told, and builds into a veritable mantra. André Magnan pointed out that the opening anecdote is also found in the letters of Mademoiselle Aîssé, a harem slave brought back to Paris by Charles de Ferriol, French ambassador to Constantinople, to be raised with his nephews, the Count of d'Argental and the Count de Pont de Veyle, Voltaire's lifelong friends.[1]

The late Monsieur de Montampui, my good friend, Rector of the University of Paris, wanted to go to a performance of *Zaïre*[2] one day, a very saintly play in which the only rendezvous the heroine gives is to have herself baptized.

The Rector had only to get in a fiacre to go from his college to the theater, dressed in his usual clothes, as all people of breeding do in Paris. But he believed, like Father Castel, that the universe had its eyes upon him, and believed it all the more because, being Rector of the University, he had, following the very meaning of the word, to inspect the universe, which, consequently, watched him continually. He felt that the universe would be surprised to learn that a certain Montampui had been to the theater, and that all future ages would be scandalized.

Montampui, not wishing to cause the universe this pain, nor to deprive himself of seeing the play, decided to disguise himself as a woman. He had in an old armoire some clothes that had belonged to his grandmother, who had died in the days of the Fronde.[3] So here he is, dressing up in a red woolen skirt and russet coat. He covers his aged Rector's head with a triple-tiered wig, topped with a big knot of dusty rose ribbons.

A pair of lacy cuffs, red and torn, disclose his brawny, hairy arms to their full advantage. Our rector, thus turned out, leaves by a secret door in the college and runs to the door of the theater.

This strange figure drew a crowd. Madame was shown little respect. She was tugged at, pegged as a dirty old man, and led to prison where she remained until she confessed that she was the Rector of the University of Paris. If Monsieur de Montampui had had this fine axiom in mind—*Adapt to the times*—he would not have given the universe this spectacle.

There is no need to teach this maxim to courtiers. They have always observed it faithfully with men in power: *serviebant tempori* (time served), as Tacitus said. Ladies and dandies have always revered fashion, and even outdone it. It is not to those who keep up with the times, it is to those that fate has placed at the head of governments that this little discourse is addressed.

Kings of England, you no longer pretend to cure scrofula now that your people have realized you are not doctors. The Royal Society of London has seen clearly that there is no physical nor metaphysical relation between the crown of England and phlegmatic humors. You have ceased this ceremony. You have adapted to the times.

I am certain that there were marvelous laws in Athens concerning the harvest of acorns before Triptolemus taught the Greeks how to sow grain. But when the Athenians began to eat bread and found this food better than the other, all the laws regarding acorns abolished themselves, and the archons were obliged to encourage agriculture.

Archbishops of Naples, the time will come when the blood of Monsieur St. Januarius, or Gennaro, will no longer boil when it is approached by his head.[4] The Neapolitan gentlemen and bourgeois will know enough in a few more centuries to conclude that this little conjuring trick isn't worth a ducat, that it is absolutely useless to the prosperity of the kingdom and to the well-being of its citizens, that God does not perform miracles on appointed days, and that he does not change the laws he imposed on nature. When these notions have descended from the nobles to the townsmen, and from these to that portion of the people who are able to reason, then we will see in Naples what was once seen in the little town of Egnatia where, in the days of Horace, incense lit itself without being approached by fire. Horace ridiculed the miracle, and it ceased to exist. This is how the holy navel of Jesus disappeared from the town of Châlons. This is how miracles have disappeared from half of Europe, along with relics. As soon as reason appears, miracles cease.

Ancient tribunals or new ones that lorded it over large towns erratically composed of palaces and thatched huts, disgusting and magnificent, inhabited in turn by savages, half-savages, Welches, Romans, Franks, and finally by the French, it's been a long time since you paraded the alleged carcass of the shepherd of Nanterre in the streets, and since Marcel and St. Geneviève met on the bridge of Notre-Dame to give us rain or sunshine.[5] You knew that the good bourgeois of Paris were beginning to suspect that it wasn't a little village girl who disposed of the seasons, but that God alone, who formed the elements and matter, was the sole master of the air and earth. And soon, Geneviève, humbly honored in her new church,[6] no longer shared the supreme domain of nature with God.

You will no longer pass decrees in favor of Aristotle, nor against vomiting. You will no longer be presented with indictments that prevent inoculation from saving the life of our princes and our citizens. You will adapt to the times.

The time approaches in which one will tire of sending money three hundred leagues away in order to possess in security a few meadows and vineyards in one's own country, accorded by the sovereign.

It will be seen that it is no more up to an Italian to meddle in what a Frenchman thinks than it is up to this Frenchman to prescribe to this Italian what he should think. People will sense how enormously ridiculous and dangerous it is to have a large body of citizens dependent on a foreign master in their state.[7] This body of citizens will itself understand that it will become more honored and more dear to its nation if, by reclaiming its natural independence, it ceases to enslave itself through a system of simony at its own expense. It will fortify itself in this wise and noble thought through the example of a neighboring island. You will then use your power and influence to break the chains that outrage the nation. You will adapt to the times.

It is finer yet, no doubt, to prepare them than to adapt, for there is little merit in feeding oneself from the fruits last year brought to bear. But it is greater to prepare the soil through wise cultivation, to bring to bear produce that one would not have enjoyed till late in life.

Opinion governs the world; but it is wise men who direct opinion in the long run.

When these wise men have enlightened men at last, they must not be treated as they were in the days of Pierre Lombard, Scotus, and of Gilbert de La Porée.[8]

An unsociable society, a stranger in its own country, composed of people of merit, fools, fanatics, and scoundrels, carried the banner of a man who pretended to rule the universe by divine rights from one end of the universe to the other. It manufactured in its patch of land, in the name of this man, a hundred arrows with which it devoutly pierced its enemies. It wished to persuade everyone that these arrows were made of gold, and that they had fallen from heaven.[9]

To support this tale, it used a sort of magic. The unbelievers who wished to prove that these arrows were only made of lead suddenly found themselves, without knowing how, some three to five hundred miles from their homes, or in a neighboring castle, dark and poorly furnished, from which they could not leave unless they signed papers swearing that the hundred and one arrows were of pure gold.

You have finally purged the country of these magicians.[10] You have finally seen the time approaching in which public execration would have exterminated them. You have not only adapted to the times, you have anticipated the times.

Do not spoil this charitable work by crushing fanaticism on the one hand, while prosecuting reason on the other.

When you see reason making such prodigious progress, consider it an ally that can come to your aid, and not as an enemy to be attacked. Believe that in the long run it will prove more powerful than you. Dare to cherish it, and not to fear it. Adapt to the times.

WIVES, SUBMIT TO YOUR HUSBANDS

1765

In a dig at Christian misogyny, we watch the wife of a highly distinguished French aristocrat and military commander discover Saint Paul in Ephesians 5:22 and/or Colossians 3:18. The abbé visiting her, Châteauneuf, was Voltaire's godfather.

Abbé de Châteauneuf told me one day that Madame the Maréchale de Grancey was highly imperious, but otherwise had a number of very great qualities. Her greatest pride consisted in respecting herself and in doing nothing she could blush at in secret. She never lowered herself to telling a lie. She preferred admitting a dangerous truth to employing useful dissimulations. She said that dissimulation was always a sign of cowardice. Her life was distinguished by a thousand generous actions, but she felt herself slighted if anyone praised her for them. She would say, "So you think that these actions cost me efforts?" Her lovers adored her, her friends cherished her, and her husband respected her.

She spent forty years in the types of dissipation and amusements that occupy women in all seriousness, having never read anything but the letters that were written to her, having never put anything into her head outside of the daily news, the absurdities of her fellow men, and the interests of her own heart. Then finally, when she had reached the age where it is said that beautiful women with intelligence pass from one throne to the other, she wished to read. She began with the tragedies of Racine and was surprised to feel even more pleasure in reading them than she had felt in watching them performed at the theater. Her good taste made her discern the fact that this man never said anything other than true and interesting things, all placed in the proper scheme of things; that he was simple and noble and never declaimed, never forced any point or sought to be witty, that all of his intrigues, just like all of his thoughts, were drawn from real life. She recognized in these readings the story of her own sentiments and the portrait of her life.

She was given Montaigne to read, and she was charmed by a man who conversed with her and who was riddled with doubts. Next she was given the *Lives of Great Men* by Plutarch. She asked why he had not written the history of great women.

Then one day, Abbé de Châteauneuf found her all flushed with anger. "What is the matter, Madame?" he said.

"I happened to open a book that was lying in my cabinet," she said, "Some collection of letters, I believe, where I saw these words: *Wives, submit to your husbands*. I threw the book away."

"What?! Madame, do you realize that those are the Epistles of Saint Paul?"

"I don't care who they are by. The author is highly impolite. My husband, the Maréchal has never written to me in this manner. I am persuaded that your Saint Paul was a very difficult man to live with. Was he married?"

"Yes, Madame."

"His wife must've been a very good creature. Had I been the wife of such a man, I would've shown him a thing or two. *Submit to your husbands!* Perhaps if he had contented himself with saying '*Be gentle, accommodating, attentive, or thrifty,*' I might have said here is a man who knows how to live. So why submissive, if you please? When I married Monsieur de Grancey, we promised to be faithful. I did not keep my word very well, nor he his, but neither he nor I promised to obey. Are we slaves? Is it not enough that a man, having married me, has the right to give me an illness that lasts nine months and that may prove fatal? Is it not enough that I give birth in atrocious suffering to a child who could plead against me in court when he reaches his majority? Is it not enough that I be subjected every month to incommodities very disagreeable to a woman of quality, and that the suppression of one of these twelve illnesses per year could cause my death without being told, on top of all that, *Obey?*

"Certainly nature has never said as much. She has given us organs different from those of men, but in making us necessary to each other, she has never claimed that our union is some form of slavery. I remember well that Molière said,

"Omnipotence goes with the beard."

But if that isn't a laughable reason for me to have a master! What? Because a man has his chin covered by crude nasty hairs that he is obliged to shave very closely and because my chin is born shaved, I am supposed to obey him very humbly? I know that as a rule, men have muscles that are stronger than ours, and that they can deliver a better punch, and I am very much afraid that this is not rather the origin of their 'superiority.'

"They pretend to have their heads better organized, and consequently boast of being better able to govern, but I can show them queens that are worth any number of kings. I was recently told of a German princess[1] who gets up at five in the morning to work at making her subjects happy, who directs all her affairs, answers all her letters, encourages all the arts, and who spreads as much good as she has wisdom. Her courage equals her learning, and I might add that she was not raised by imbeciles in a convent who teach us all the things we should ignore and leave us in ignorance of all that we should know. As to myself, if I had a state to govern, I feel myself quite capable of daring to follow her example."

Abbé de Châteauneuf, who was highly polite, took care not to contradict the Maréchale.

"By the way," she said, "is it true that Mahomet had such contempt for us that he claimed that we were not worthy of entering paradise and that we would only be allowed to remain near the entrance?"

"In that case," the Abbé said, "all the men would remain near the door. But console yourself, there is not one word of truth in all that is said of the Muslim religion. Our ignorant and wicked monks have greatly deceived us, as my brother, who was ambassador at the Porte[2] for twelve years, said."

"What? Is it not true, Monsieur, that Mahomet invented polygamy in order to rally the men to himself? Is it not true that we are slaves in Turkey and forbidden to pray to God in a mosque?"

"Not a word of it, Madame. Mahomet, far from having invented polygamy, repressed and restrained it. The wise Salomon possessed seven hundred wives. Mahomet reduced the number to only four. Ladies will go to paradise just like gentlemen and no doubt we will make love there, but in another manner than is done here; for you surely sense that in this world, we know love only very imperfectly."

"Alas! You are right," the Maréchale said, "man doesn't amount to much. But tell me, does your Mahomet order women to submit to their husbands?"

"No, Madame, that is nowhere in the Koran."

"Why then are women slaves in Turkey?"

"They are not slaves. They have their own possessions, can make testaments, and even ask for a divorce, if it suits them. They go to the mosque at their own hours, and have their rendezvous at others. They are seen in the streets with their faces veiled, just as you had your mask a few years back. It is true that they do not attend the opera or the theater, but it is because there isn't any. Can you doubt that if there were an opera in Constantinople, the country of Orpheus, that Turkish ladies would not fill the first row balcony seats?"

"*Wives, submit to your husbands!*" the Maréchale kept saying between clenched teeth. "That Paul was a brutal man."

"He was a bit harsh," the Abbé conceded, "and very fond of being the master. He treated St. Peter rather condescendingly, and he was a fairly good chap. Besides, one mustn't take literally everything he said. He is reproached with having had a great penchant for Jansenism."

"I might have suspected he was some sort of heretic," the Maréchale said, and she resumed her grooming.

REPUBLICAN IDEAS BY A MEMBER OF A CORPS

1765

As Peter Gay demonstrated, Voltaire had no penchant for despots of any kind, including the "enlightened" variety, but having lived under absolute monarchs in France and Prussia, a constitutional monarchy in England, the oligarchic republic of Geneva, and having been to Holland many times, what mattered to him were just laws applicable to everyone, including kings. Some strongly democratic thinking came to the forefront, however, during the uprising in Geneva of the citizens against the wealthy ruling classes. Voltaire espouses their cause in this piece, one of his most widely-quoted pamphlets. These extracts omit the articles concerning Rousseau's *Social Contract*, Montesquieu, or details pertaining to the conflict. Only general reflections on government and religion are retained.[1]

I

Pure despotism is the punishment of the bad conduct of humankind. If a community is submitted to the control of one person or of several, it is visibly because it has not had the courage or ability to govern itself.

II

A society governed arbitrarily perfectly resembles a herd of cows placed under a yoke for the service of a master. He only feeds them enough to put them in condition to serve. He only treats their illnesses insofar as their health can be useful to him. He only fattens them in order to feed off of them, and he uses the skin of some to harness others to the plough.

III

A nation is subdued this way either by a skillful compatriot who takes advantage of its imbecility and factions or by a thief called a conqueror who has come with other thieves to take over their lands, who has murdered those who resisted and made slaves of the cowards he let live.

IV

This thief, who deserves the rack, sometimes has altars raised to him. Those who are oppressed see in the children of this thief a race of gods. They see blasphemy in the examination of their authority, and sacrilege in the slightest effort made for freedom.

V

The most absurd of all despotisms, the most humiliating for human nature, the most contradictory and fatal is that of priests; and of all the priestly empires, the most criminal is unquestionably that of the priests of the Christian religion. It is an outrage made to our Gospels where Jesus Christ says in twenty places, "There will be no first or last among you; My kingdom is not of this world; The Son of man did not come to be served, but to serve," etc.[2]

VI

When our bishop, made to serve and not to be served, made to relieve the poor and not to devour their subsistence, made to catechize and not to dominate,

REPUBLICAN IDEAS   **155**

dared, in a time of anarchy, to have himself decreed prince of a town of which he was only the pastor, he was manifestly guilty of rebellion and tyranny.

VII

Thus the bishops of Rome, who were the first to give this fatal example, made both their domination and their sect odious throughout half of Europe; hence several bishops in Germany sometimes became the oppressors of the people they should have served as fathers to.

VIII

Why does human nature abhor those who have subjected us by dupery more than those who have subjected us with arms? It is because there is courage at least in tyrants who cow people, whereas there is only cowardice in those who deceive them. We hate the valor of conquerors, but we esteem it. We hate trickery, and we despise it. Hatred joined to contempt can shake off all the yokes.

IX

When we destroyed part of the papist superstitions in our town, such as the worship of cadavers, the tax on sin, the outrage made to God of buying off the punishments with which God threatens crimes, and so many other inventions that besotted human nature; when in shattering the servitude of these monstrous errors we expelled the papal bishop who dared declare himself our sovereign,[3] we did nothing more than to reinstate the rights of reason and liberty of which we had been despoiled.

X

We resumed a municipal government, more or less as it had been under the Romans, and it became illustrious and secured by the liberty bought with our blood. We did not experience that odious and humiliating distinction between nobles and commoners, which in its origins means only lords and slaves. Born equal, we remained so, and we only gave dignities, that is to say the burden of public responsibilities, to those we deemed most apt to uphold them.

XI

We instituted priests to be uniquely what they should be: teachers of morals for our children. These tutors should be paid and enjoy consideration, but they must not claim jurisdiction, authority, control, or honors. They must not under any circumstances equate themselves with the magistracy. An ecclesiastical assembly that would make a citizen kneel before it would be playing the role of a pedant punishing children or of a tyrant chastising slaves.

XII

It is an insult to reason and to the laws to say the words: civil and ecclesiastical government. One must say civil government and ecclesiastical rules, and not a single one of these rules should be made by any but the civil powers.

XIII

Civil government is the will of everyone, executed by one or several, in virtue of the laws made by all.

XIV

The laws that constitute government are all directed against ambition: people everywhere have thought to erect a dam against this torrent that would inundate the earth. This is why, in republics, the first laws regulate the rights of each body; it is why kings swear at their coronation to protect the privileges of their subjects. There is only the king of Denmark in all Europe who is, per the law itself, above the laws. The states, assembled in 1660, declared him the absolute arbitrator. It seems they were foreseeing that Denmark would have wise and just kings for over a century. Perhaps this law will have to be changed in ensuing centuries.

XV

Some theologians have claimed that popes had, by divine right, the same power over all the earth that Danish monarchs have over a small part of it. But they are theologians . . . the whole world booed them loudly, and the Capitoline rumbled at seeing the monk Hildebrand[4] speak as master in the sanctuary of laws where the Catos, the Scipios, and the Ciceros had spoken as citizens.

XVI

The laws that concern distributive justice, properly called jurisprudence, have been insufficient, equivocal, and uncertain everywhere, because men placed at the heads of state have always been busier with their own interests than with the public's interest. In the twelve grand tribunals in France, there are twelve different jurisprudences. What is true in Aragon [Spain] becomes false in Castile; what is just on the banks of the Danube is unjust on the banks of the Elbe. Even the Roman laws, demanded in all the tribunals today, are sometimes contradictory.

XVII

When a law is obscure, everyone must interpret it because everyone enacted it, unless some have been expressly entrusted with interpreting the laws.

XVIII

When times have changed appreciably, there are laws that should be changed. Accordingly, when Triptolemus brought the usage of plows to Athens, the policing of acorns was abolished. In the days when academies were composed only of priests, and they alone possessed the jargon of science, it was fitting that they choose all the professors: it was the policing of acorns. But now that the laity is enlightened, the civil power must resume its right to appoint all university chairs.

XIX

The law that would allow a citizen to be imprisoned on assumptions, before the facts, and without judicial formalities, would be tolerable in a time of disruption and war; but it is the work of torturers and tyrants in times of peace.

XL

A tribunal must have set laws, both criminal and civil. Nothing can be arbitrary, and even less so when it concerns one's honor and one's life than when one is pleading only over money.

XLI

A criminal code is absolutely necessary for citizens and for magistrates. Citizens then have no cause to complain of judgments and the magistrates will not have to fear incurring hatred, for it will not be their will that condemns, it will be the law. One power is needed to judge by this law alone, and another power to pardon.

XLIII

There has never been a perfect government because men are subject to passions, and if they had no passions there would be no need of government. The most tolerable of all is no doubt republican, because it is the one that brings people closest to natural equality. Every family's father should be master in his own house, but not in his neighbor's house. A society being composed of several houses and the land attached to them, it is contradictory that a single man should be the master of these houses and these lands, and it accords with nature that each master has a vote for the good of society.

XLIV

Should those who have neither land nor house in this society have their say? They have no more a right to it than a clerk paid by merchants would have to regulate their commerce, but they can be associated, either for services rendered or by paying for their association.

XLV

This land, governed in common, should be richer and more populated than if it were governed by a master because, in a true republic, each person, being secure in his or her possessions and of his person, works for him or herself with confidence and, by bettering his or her condition, betters that of the public. The opposite can happen under a master. A man can be quite astonished to hear that neither his person nor his goods belong to him.

XLVIII

Let us compare what we were under our bishop to what we are today. We slept in hovels, ate off wooden plates in our kitchens. Our bishop alone had silver-plated dishes and strolled with forty horses through his diocese, which he called his states. Today we have citizens who have three times his revenue and we possess, both in town and in the country, houses much finer than what he called his palaces, which we have made into prisons.

LV

"Lowly commerce was vile among the Greeks." I don't know what the author means by lowly commerce, but I do know that in Athens all citizens were engaged in trade.[5] Plato sold oil and the father of the demagogue, Demosthenes, was an iron merchant. Most of the workers were foreigners or slaves. It is important for us to note that trade was not incompatible with prestigious posts in the republics of Greece, except among the Spartans, who had no commerce.

LXII

Despite its faults, this volume should always be dear to men because the author has sincerely said what he thinks, whereas most writers of his country, beginning with the great Bossuet, have often said what they did not think. He has everywhere reminded men that they are free, he presents to human nature its titles that she has lost over the greater part of earth. He combats superstition and inspires morals.

LXIII

Will it be through books that destroy superstition and make virtue loveable that we will manage to make humanity better? Yes; if young people read these books with attention, they will be preserved from every species of fanaticism. They will sense that peace is the fruit of tolerance and the true goal of every society.

LXIV

Tolerance is as necessary to politics as to religion. It is pride alone that is intolerant. It is pride that revolts minds, in trying to force others to think like us. It is the secret source of all factions.

LXV

Politeness, circumspection, and indulgence strengthen the union between friends and families. They will have the same effect in a little state, which is one big family.

DIALOGUE BETWEEN A DOUBTER AND A VENERATOR BY ABBÉ TILLADET

1766

Thomas Jefferson wrote to Dr. Benjamin Rush on April 21, 1803, that although he was opposed to the corruptions of Christianity, he was not opposed "to the genuine precepts of Jesus himself. I am a Christian, in the only sense in which he wished any one to be; sincerely attached to his doctrines . . . and believing he never claimed any other." This statement echoes a similar line in the *Jefferson Bible*, from which he cut the fanatical or absurd sayings attributed to Jesus in the New Testament, perfectly reflects the theory presented here. This dialogue was in the Kehl edition of Voltaire's *Complete Works*, purchased by Jefferson during his stay in Paris.

THE DOUBTER

How will you prove the existence of God to me?

THE VENERATOR

Like the existence of the sun is proved, by opening your eyes.

THE DOUBTER

So you believe in final causes?

THE VENERATOR

I believe in admirable causes when I see admirable effects. God save me from resembling the lunatic who said that a watch doesn't prove a watchmaker, a house doesn't prove an architect, and that we can only prove God's existence by an equation of algebra, even though the equation was erroneous!

THE DOUBTER
What is your religion?

THE VENERATOR
It is not only the religion of Socrates, who made fun of the Greek fables, but that of Jesus, who confounded the Pharisees.

THE DOUBTER
If you are of Jesus' religion, why are you not of the religion of the Jesuits who own land three hundred leagues long and wide in Paraguay? Why do you not believe that of the Premonstratensians or of the Benedictines to whom Jesus gave so many prosperous abbeys?

THE VENERATOR
Jesus did not establish the Benedictines, the Premonstratensians, or the Jesuits.

THE DOUBTER
Do you think you can serve God while eating mutton on Friday and while never going to Mass?

THE VENERATOR
I believe so firmly, considering that Jesus never said Mass, that he ate meat on Friday and even on Saturday.

THE DOUBTER
So then you think that the simple, natural religion of Jesus has been corrupted, which was apparently the belief of all the wise men of antiquity?

THE VENERATOR
Nothing seems more evident. He must have been a wise man at heart, since he declaimed against priestly impostors and superstitions; but they impute things to him a wise man would never say or do. A wise man would never look for figs on a fig tree at the beginning of March, and then curse it because it didn't have any figs. A wise man would not change water into wine for people already drunk. A wise man would not send devils into the bodies of two thousand pigs,

in a country where there are no pigs. A wise man doesn't transfigure himself at night to have a white robe. A wise man is not transported by the devil. When a wise man says that God is his father, he surely means that God is the father of all men. The meaning people have wanted to see in it is impious and blasphemous.

It appears that the words and actions of this sage were very poorly understood, and that of the several stories of his life, written ninety years after he died, the most unlikely ones were chosen, because they were believed to be the most important ones to simpletons. Every writer prided himself on making the story wondrous. Every little Christian community had its own Gospel. It is the most obvious reason why these Gospels differ in almost everything. If you believe one Gospel, you have to renounce all the others. Perpetual contradiction is a laughable proof of truth. Follies battling each other is a ludicrous sort of wisdom.

It is therefore clear that fanatics first persuaded simple people, who then convinced others. The latter embellished even further on the first. The true story of Jesus was probably only that of a just man who rebuked the Pharisees for their vices and whom the Pharisees put to death. He was then made a prophet and, after three hundred years, a god. That is the march of the human spirit.

Fanatics, even the most stubborn ones, have acknowledged that the first Christians used the most shameful frauds to uphold their nascent sect. Everyone admits they made up false predictions, false stories, and false miracles. Fanaticism spread on all sides till finally, once it was dominant, it was only able to uphold with executioners what it had established through imposture and dementia. Every century has so corrupted the religion of Jesus that that of the first Christians is the exact opposite of it.

Though they have Jesus say that his kingdom is not of this earth, those who claim to be the successors of his first disciples have been, as far as they were able, the tyrants of this world, trampling on the heads of kings. Though Jesus lived a poor man, his strange successors have plundered our goods and the rewards of the sweat of our brows.

Consider the rituals that Jesus observed. They were all Jewish, and we burn those who practice Jewish rituals today. Did Jesus say there were two natures in him? No; and we have given him two natures. Did Jesus say that Mary was the mother of God? No; and we make her the mother of God. Did Jesus say that he was *trinus* and consubstantial? No; and we make him consubstantial and part of a trinity. Show me a single rite you have observed precisely as he did. Tell me of a single dogma that was exactly the same as his. I defy you.

THE DOUBTER
But Monsieur, in speaking this way, you are not a Christian.

THE VENERATOR
I am as Christian as Jesus was, whose heavenly doctrine was changed into an infernal one. Though he was content with being just, we have made a senseless man of him who wandered the fields of a little Jewish province comparing the heavens to a mustard seed.

THE DOUBTER
What do you think of St. Paul, murderer of Stephen, persecutor of the first Galileans, then Galilean and persecuted himself? Why did he break with his master, Gamaliel? Is it because, as certain Jews said, Gamaliel refused him his daughter's hand in marriage because he had crooked legs, was bald-headed, and his eyebrows joined, as it is reported in the Acts of St. Thecla, his favorite? In short, did he even write the Epistles released in his name?

THE VENERATOR
It is fairly widely admitted that Paul is not the author of the Epistle to the Hebrews in which it says, "Jesus became as much superior to the angels as the name he received is superior to theirs" (chap. 1, verse 4), while elsewhere it is said, "God made him for a time inferior to the angels" (chap. 2, verse 7). And in his other Epistles, he almost always speaks of Jesus as a simple man, cherished by God and raised to glory.

Sometimes he says that "women can pray, speak, preach, and prophesize, as long as they have their head covered, because a woman without a veil dishonors her head" (1 Cor. 11:5). And sometimes he says that "women should remain silent in churches" (1 Cor. 14:34).

He turned against Peter because Peter "didn't Judaize with foreigners, and then Judaized with Jews." But this same Paul Judaized himself for eight days in the Temple of Jerusalem and brought strangers to it, to make the Jews believe he was not a Christian. He is accused of having soiled the temple. The high priest slapped him. He is brought before the Roman Tribunal. How does he get out of it? He tells the tribunal and the Sanhedrin two impudent lies. He tells them, "I am a Pharisee and the son of a Pharisee," when he was Christian, then adds, "I am persecuted because I believe in the resurrection of the dead." This was not even in question and by this lie, which was besides all too easy to detect, he pretended to have compromised and divided the judges of the Sanhedrin, half of whom believed in resurrection while the other half did not.

Now there, I admit, is a singular apostle for you. This is nevertheless the same man who dared to say "that he was brought up to the third heaven and heard words it is not permitted to tell" (2 Cor. 12:2–4).

Astophe's voyage to the moon is more credible, since it's a shorter trip. But why would he want to make the imbeciles he is addressing believe he was taken to the third heaven? It is to establish his authority among them. It is to satisfy his ambition to be a party leader. It is to give weight to these insolent, tyrannical words: "If I come back among you, I will not pardon those who sinned nor any others" (2 Cor. 13:2).

It is easy to see in the gibberish of Paul that he kept his initial persecuting spirit, that horrid spirit that has made too many proselytes. I know that he was only commanding beggars, but it is the passion of men to wish to raise themselves above their fellow creatures and oppress them. It is the passion of tyrants. What! Paul, Jewish tent-maker, you dare write to the Corinthians that you will punish even those who have not sinned! Did Nero, Attila, or Pope Alexander VI ever utter such abominable words? If Paul wrote this way, he deserves an exemplary punishment. If falsifiers forged these Epistles, they deserve an even greater one.

Alas! This is how most popular sects begin. An impostor harangues the dregs of society in an attic, and the impostors who succeed him soon live in palaces.

THE DOUBTER

You are only too right. But after what you think of this fanatic, half Jewish and half Christian, named Paul, what do you think of the ancient Jews?

THE VENERATOR

What the sensible people of all nations think, and what reasonable Jews themselves think.

THE DOUBTER

So you do not believe that the God of all nature abandoned and condemned the rest of mankind in order to make himself king of a miserable little nation? You do not believe that a serpent spoke to a woman? That God planted a tree whose fruits gave knowledge of good and evil? And that God forbade man and woman to eat of this fruit—God who should rather have given them some so they would have this knowledge of good and evil, so absolutely necessary to the human race? You do not believe that he led his cherished people into the desert and that he was obliged to make their old sandals and old clothes last for forty years? You do not believe that he performed miracles, which were equaled by Pharaoh's magicians, that he had his cherished children cross the sea on dry land and as thieves and cowards, and all to pull them abjectly out of Egypt rather than give them the fertile land of Egypt?

You do not believe that he ordered his people to massacre everyone they met, only to make them almost always slaves of other nations? You do not believe that the she-ass of Balaam spoke? You do not believe that Samson tied three hundred foxes together by the tail? You do not believe that the inhabitants of Sodom wanted to rape two angels? You do not believe . . .

THE VENERATOR

No, without a doubt, I do not believe these impertinent horrors, the opprobrium of the human race. I believe that the Jews had fables, like all the other nations, but fables far more foolish and absurd because they were the coarsest of the Eastern peoples, just as the Thebans were the coarsest of the Greeks.

THE DOUBTER

I admit that the Jewish religion was absurd and abominable; but after all, Jesus, whom you love, was Jewish. He always observed Jewish law and all its rituals.

THE VENERATOR

That again is another great contradiction; that he was Jewish and that his followers are not. I adopt from him his morals only when they don't contradict each other. I cannot suffer the fact that he is made to say, "I did not come to bring peace, but the sword." These words are horrid. Once again, a wise man could not have said that the kingdom of heaven was like a mustard seed, like a wedding, like money we make grow through usury. These words are ridiculous. I adopt this sentence: "Love God and your neighbor." It is the eternal law of all men, and it is mine. It is in this way that I am the friend of Jesus; it is in this way that I am Christian. If he was a worshiper of God, an enemy to bad priests, persecuted by swindlers, I am with him. I am his brother.

THE DOUBTER

There has never been a religion that didn't say as much as Jesus, that did not commend virtue as he did.

THE VENERATOR

Well then! I am of the religion of all men, of that of Socrates, Plato, Aristides, Cicero, Cato, Titus, Trajan, Antonius, Marcus Aurelius, Epictetus, and Jesus.

I will say with Epictetus, "It is God who created me; God is within me, I carry him everywhere. Why would I soil him with obscene thoughts, base actions or odious desires? Every characteristic I have imposes a duty on me: man, citizen of the world, child of God, brother of all men, son, husband, father. All these names tell me, Do not dishonor a single one of us. My duty is to praise God for everything, to thank him for everything, to never cease blessing him till I cease to live."

A hundred maxims of this sort are well worth the Sermon on the Mount and this fine maxim: "Blessed are the poor in spirit."[1] In short I worship God, and not the deceits of men.

I serve God and not an ecclesiastical council in Chalcedon, or one *in trullo*.[2] I detest odious superstitions and will be sincerely attached to true religion till my last breath of my life.

LETTERS TO HIS HIGHNESS THE PRINCE OF ✶✶✶✶✶✶ ON RABELAIS

And Other Authors Accused of Having
Spoken Against the Christian Religion

1767

Almost a pastiche, on the one hand, of the many commentaries compiled by defenders of the faith on this same
subject, this text puts forth a powerful theme strangely overlooked till recently. Earlier compilations always began with
ancient Greek and Roman authors. Here, however, Voltaire
neglects them entirely to point out, for all his tongue-in-
cheek deploring of it, "the great work" begun 250 years
earlier by authors all across Europe—England, France,
Germany, Italy, the Jews included—to break the fetters of
superstition and banish ignorance through free-thinking
and the progressive discovery of the laws of nature. It also
debunks another myth constantly perpetuated by "the
faithful": most of these quiet seekers of the truth did not die
in terror and agonies of repentance as always claimed—
a lie later used more grotesquely on Voltaire himself than
perhaps ever before.

The asterisks masking the prince's name were common
usage, though Voltaire told an ally that the (purported)
addressee was Prince Charles-William Ferdinand of Bruns-
wick-Lüneburg, a nephew of King Frederick the Great of
Prussia who had visited the previous year. He was "lovable,
enlightened" and sick with anger and indignation over
the appalling condemnation of the Chevalier de La
Barre. These *Letters* received little notice at the time, over-
shadowed no doubt by several other potent pamphlets

released by Voltaire that year, such as *Zapata's Questions*, the *Important Study by Lord Bolingbroke*, and by the *Dinner at Count de Boulainvilliers'*.[1]

LETTER I

On François Rabelais

Milord,

As Your Highness wishes to fully acquaint himself with Rabelais, I will begin by telling you that his life story, as printed in the preface to his *Gargantua*, is as false and absurd as his story of Gargantua itself. We read that when Cardinal de Bellay brought him to Rome and kissed the right foot of the pope and then his mouth, Rabelais said that he would like to kiss his derrière, but that the Holy Father would have to wash it first. There are things that the respect of person, place, and propriety make impossible. This little story can only have been imagined by people from the dregs of society, in a cabaret.

His supposed request is in the same vein. He is supposed to have begged the pope to excommunicate him, so that he would not be burned—for, he said, his landlady, having wished to burn a stick, and not managing to do it, said that this stick had been excommunicated by the pope's big mouth.

The adventure attributed him in Lyon is just as false and implausible. It is claimed that, not having enough money to pay his innkeeper, nor to take the journey to Paris, he had her son label some small packets saying "Poison to kill the king," "Poison to kill the queen," etc., in order to be conducted to Paris and nourished at no cost to himself, and to give the king a laugh. They add that this was in 1536, which was the time at which the king and all of France were grieving the death of the king's son, François, who people believed had been poisoned, and when Montecucculli had just been drawn and quartered on suspicion of having poisoned him. The authors of this stale yarn did not consider the fact that Rabelais would've been thrown into a dungeon on such terrible evidence, enchained, that he would have probably undergone torture, and that, in such fatal circumstances and for an accusation as grave as this, a bad joke would not have served to justify him. Nearly all the *Lives* of famous men have been disfigured by tales that do not merit more belief.

His book, in truth, is a collection of the most impertinent and coarsest trash that a drunken monk could vomit forth; but one must also admit that it is a biting satire of the pope, the church, and of all the events of his time. He wished to protect himself behind a mask of folly, and implies it well enough himself in his prologue. "Consider," he says, "that in the literal sense, you will find matters jovial enough and corresponding to its title. Nevertheless just remain there one must not, as before the mermaid's song, but in its highest sense interpret what this adventure may mean in gaiety of heart. . . . Have you ever seen a dog encounter a marrowy bone? It is, as Plato said in Book II of *The Republic*, the most philosophic beast in the world. If seen it you have, you may have noted with what devotion he lies in wait for it, with what care he guards it, with what fervor he holds it, with what prudence he takes his first bite, with what affection he breaks it, and with what diligence he sucks on it. Who induces him to do this? What hope does he hold in his study? What good does he lay claim to? Nothing more than a bit of marrow."

But what happens? Very few readers resemble the dog that sucks the marrow. They are only attached to the bone, which is to say to the absurd buffooneries, to the ghastly obscenities that fill the book. If, unfortunately for Rabelais, the meaning of his book had been too well fathomed, if it had been taken seriously, it is likely that it would have cost him his life, as it did all others in his day who wrote against the Roman Church.

It is clear that Gargantua is [King] François I and Louis XII, the Grand Gousier, even though he was not the father of François, and that Henry II is Pantagruel. The education of Gargantua and the chapter on the *arse-wipers* are satires on the education then given princes. The colors blue and white obviously designate the livery of the kings of France.

The war over a wheelbarrow of cinder cakes is the war between [Emperor] Charles V and François I, which began with a frivolous quarrel between the House of Bouillon la Marck and that of Chimai. And this is so obviously true that Rabelais called Marckuet, who started the quarrel, the conductor of cinder cakes.

The monks of those days are portrayed very naively under the name of Friar John of the Chopping-Knives. It is impossible not to recognize Charles V in the portrayal of Picrochole.

As for the Church, he does not spare it. In chapter 39 of the first book, here is how he expresses himself: "How good is God to give us this good beverage! I confess to God, if I had lived in the days of Jesus Christ, I would have seen to it that the Jews didn't take him in the Garden of Olives. The devil take me if I would have failed to hamstring these gentlemen apostles who fled so cowardly after they had had a good meal and left their good master in the lurch. I detest worse than poison a man who flees when it's time to wield the knives. Oh, if only I were King of France for eighty or a hundred years! By God, I would leave you dogs who fled Pavia neutered, with clipped ears!"

Nor can one misinterpret the genealogy of Gargantua: it is a highly scandalous parody of the most respectable of genealogies. "And from them came the giants," he says, "and from them, Pantagruel, and the first was Chalbroth, who begat Sarabroth,

"Who begat Faribroth,

"Who begat Hurtaly, a great eater of soup who reigned at the time of the Deluge,

"Who begat Happe-Mousche (Fly-Snatcher), who first invented the smoking of ox-tongues,

"Who begat Fout asnon,

"Who begat Vit-de-Grain (Lives Off Grain),

"Who begat the Grand Gousier (Great Throat),

"Who begat Gargantua,

"Who begat the noble Pantagruel, my master."

All of our books on theology have never been more lampooned than in the catalogue of books Pantagruel finds in the library of Saint Victor: the *Bigua (biga) salutis*, *Bragueta juris* (The Codpiece of the Law), *Pantofla decretorum* (The Houseslipper of the Decretals), *The Elephantine Testicle of the Valiant*, *The Decree of the University of Paris on the Bosoms of Girls*, *The Apparition of St. Gertrude to a Nun in Labour*, *The Mustard Pot of Penitence*, *Tartaretus de modo cacandi* (Tartaret, On Methods of Shiting), *The Invention of the Holy Cross by the Clerks of Shrewdness*, *The Gropings Due Procurators*, *The Prelate's Bagpipe*, *The Cream Puff of Indulgences*, *Utrum chimaera in vacuo bombinans possit comedere secundas intentiones: questio debatuta par decem hebdomadas in concilio Constantiensi*,[2] *The Minor Mumblings of the Celestine Fathers*, *The Rat-Trap of Theologians*, *Chaut-couillonis de magistro*,[3] *The Comforts of*

Monastic Life, *The Paternoster of the Ape*, *The Shackles of Devotion*, *The Donkey-like Traits and Exhibitionism of Abbés*, etc.

When Panurge asks Friar John of the Chopping-Knives for his advice on whether he'll be cuckolded if he gets married, Friar John recites his litanies. These are not litanies of the Blessed Virgin. These are litanies of types of bottoms: cute b., stubby b., wide b., milky b., etc. These stale profanations would not have been pardonable from a layman, but from a priest!

After that, Panurge goes to consult the theologian, Hippothadeus, who tells him he will be cuckolded if it pleases God. Pantagruel goes to the Island of Lanternland. The Lanterners are the theological quibblers who began those horrible disputes in the reign of Henri II that gave birth to countless civil wars.

The Island of Tohu and Bohu, or Chaos Island, is England, which had changed religion four times since Henry VIII.

We can see that Popefig Island indicates the heretics. We meet the pope-maniacs, who give the name of God to the pope. Panurge is asked if he is happy for having seen the Holy Father. Panurge replies that he's seen three of them and didn't gain much from it. The Law of Moses is compared to the Law of Cybele, of Diane and Numa. The decretals are called *excretals*. Panurge claims that, having wiped himself with a page of one of the decretals called *clémentines* (deriving from St. Clément), he grew hemorrhoids a half a foot long.

Low masses are parodied with the term *dry masses*, and Panurge says he'd prefer a moistened one, provided that the wine was good. Confession is ridiculed. Pantagruel goes to consult the Oracle of the Holy Bottle to find out whether he should practice both forms of communion, and drink good wine after eating the blessed bread. Epistemon cries out on the way, *Vivat, fifat, pipat, bibat: oh apocalyptic secret!* Friar John of the Chopping-Knives asks for a cartload of girls to comfort him in case he's refused both types of communion. We meet the Gastrolacs, or possessed people. Gaster invents a way to not to be wounded by canon. It makes fun of all miracles.

Before reaching the island where the Oracle of the Holy Bottle is, they land on Ringing Island where they find shamjays, clerijays, monastjays, priestjays, abbejays, bishojays, capuchinjays, and, finally, the pope-in-jay, who is one of a kind. The shamjays, or bigots, had covered the entire island in excrements. The cardinjays were the birds the most foul-smelling and manic.

The fable of the Donkey and the Horse, the prohibition against donkeys coupling in the stables, and the liberty the donkeys give themselves of coupling at the fairgrounds symbolize fairly intelligibly the celibacy of priests and the debauchery attributed to them in those days.

The voyagers are admitted to the pope-in-jay's presence. Panurge wants to throw a stone at a bishop-jay who is snoring during High Mass.[4] Master Editus stops him, saying, "My good man, hit, smite, kill, or murder all the kings and princes in the world by treachery, poison, or otherwise, when you like. Unnest the angels from heaven. The pope-in-jay will grant you pardon. But never touch these sacred birds."

From Ringing Island, we go on to the Kingdom of Quintessence, or Entelechy. Now Entelechy is the soul. This unknown character, spoken of since men began to exist, is no less ridiculed than the pope, but doubts on the existence of the soul are more shrouded than the lampoons of the Court of Rome.

The beggar monks inhabit the Island of Humming Friars. They appear first in procession. One of them responds only in monosyllables to all the questions Panurge asks about their girls. "How many are there?" *Twenty.* "How many would you like?" *A hundred.*

"How is the wiggling of their bottoms?" *Well-supplied.*

"What do they say when you bang them?" *Nothing.*

"How are your tools?" *Big.*

"How many times day?" *Six.* "And a night?" *Ten.*

Finally, we reach the Oracle of the Holy Bottle. The custom in the church of those days was to give water to the secular communicants, to wash the host down. This is still the custom in Germany. The reformers insisted on wine, to symbolize the blood of Jesus Christ. The Roman Church insisted that the blood was in the bread together with the bones and flesh. However, the Catholic priests drank wine and didn't want the laymen and women to drink it. In the island of the Oracle of the Holy Bottle was a beautiful fountain of clear water. The great pontiff Bacbuc gave some to our pilgrims to drink, saying, "In days of yore, while a wise and brave Jewish captain was leading his people through the desert in utter famine, he obtained manna from the skies, which to their imagination tasted just like meat. Likewise, when you drink this fabulous liquor, you will taste whatever wine you may imagine. So *imagine and drink* is what we did, and Panurge cried out, 'By God, this is the wine of Beaulne, the best I've ever tasted, or I'll give myself to a hundred and six devils!'"

The famous dean of Ireland, Swift, copied this line in his *Tale of a Tub*, along with several others. Milord Peter gives his brothers, Martin and Jack, a piece of dry bread for their dinner and wants to make them believe that the bread contains excellent beef, partridges, and capons, as well as some excellent Burgundy wine.

You will notice that Rabelais dedicated the part of his book that contains this stinging satire of the Roman Church to Cardinal Odet de Châtillon, who had not yet dropped the mask and declared himself in favor of the Protestant religion. His book was printed with the *privilège* [the right to print], and the right to print this satire of the Catholic religion was accorded thanks to the obscenities that were more appreciated in those days than pope-in-jays and cardinjays. This book has never been prohibited in France, because everything is buried under a heap of extravagances that never leaves time free for disentangling the true goal of the author.

It is difficult to believe that the buffoon who laughed so openly at the *Old* and *New Testaments* was a priest. How did he die? In saying, *I go to seek a great perhaps.*

The illustrious Monsieur Le Duchat overburdened this strange work with pedantic notes and printed forty editions of it. Let us observe that Rabelais lived and died cherished, celebrated, and honored, and that those who preached the purest morals were put to death in the most horrendous tortures.

LETTER II

On the Predecessors of Rabelais in Germany and Italy, and First, on a Book Entitled *Epistolae Obscurorum Virorum*

Milord,

Your Highness asks me if books had been written with such license before Rabelais. We will reply that his model was probably the above-cited book, the *Collection of Letters of Obscure People*, which appeared in Germany at the beginning of the sixteenth century. This *Collection* is in Latin, but it is written with as much naiveté and boldness as Rabelais. Here is an old translation of a passage in the twenty-eighth letter:

> There is a concordance between the sacred notebooks and the poetic fables, as can be noted of the serpent Python slain by Apollo, called by the Psalmist: *This dragon formed to entertain you.* Saturn, the old father of the gods who eats his children, is in Ezekiel, who says: *Your fathers will eat their children.* Diane promenading with a large number of virgins is the blessed virgin Mary, according to the Psalmist who says: *Virgins will come after her.* Calisto, deflowered by Jupiter and returning to heaven, is in Matthew 12: *I will return to the house I left.* Aglaure transformed into stone is in Job 42: *Her heart will harden like stone.* Europa impregnated by Jupiter is in Salomon: *Listen, daughter, see, and incline thy ear, for the king has concupiscenced you.* Ezekiel prophesied of Actaeon, who saw Diane nude: *You were nude; I passed by there and I saw you.* The poets wrote that Bacchus was born twice, which signifies Christ, born *before time and in time.* Semele, who nourished Bacchus, is the prototype of the blessed Virgin, since it says in Exodus: *Take this child, feed him for me, and you will have a salary.*

These impieties are even less veiled than those of Rabelais.

It's already impressive that in the Germany of those days, people had begun to mock magic. One finds in a letter by Master Achatius Lampirius some fairly strong mockery of the formulas employed to make oneself loved by maidens. The secret consisted in taking a hair from the girl, and placing it first in her breeches. One had a general confession made and three masses said, during which one put the hair around one's neck. One lit a blessed candle at the last Gospel and pronounced this magic formula: "Oh candle! I conjure you by the virtue of God Almighty, by the nine choirs of angels, by the gosdrien virtue, bring me this girl in flesh and blood, so that I may manhandle her at my pleasure, etc."

The macaronic kitchen Latin in which these letters are written is so ridiculous that it is impossible to translate; especially a letter by Peter of the Charity, messenger of grammar to Ortuin, whose equivocal Latin cannot be rendered. Its point is to ask whether the pope can make a bastard child physically legitimate. There is another by Jean de Schwinfordt, Master of the Arts, where it is maintained that Jesus Christ was a monk, Saint Peter, a prior in a convent, Judas Iscariot, an innkeeper, and the apostle Phillip, a porter.

Jean Schluntzig relates, in a letter written under his name, that he had found Jacques de Hochstraten (Big street), a former Inquisitor, in Florence. "I bowed to him," he said, taking off my hat, and asked him, "Father, are you a reverend or aren't you?" He answered me, "I am he who is." I then said to him, "You are Master Jacques Big Street, sacred chariot of Elias. Why in the devil are you on foot? It's a scandal. *He who is* should not be walking about with his feet in mud and shit." He replied, "They came in chariots and on horses, but we come in the name of the Lord." I said to him, "By the Lord, it is highly rainy and cold." He raised his hands to heaven saying, "Dew of heaven, fall from above, and may the clouds of heaven mourn the just."

It must be admitted that this is precisely the style of Rabelais, and I doubt not that he had these *Letters of Obscure People* in front of him while he wrote his *Gargantua* and his *Pantagruel*.

The tale of the woman who, having heard that all bastards were great men, ran to ring the door of the Cordelier Friars to make herself a bastard child, is absolutely in the taste of our master François. The same obscenities and the same outrages abound in these two singular books.

On the Facetious Ancient Italian Tales that Preceded Rabelais

Italy, as early as the fourteenth century, had produced more than one example of such license. One only need look at Boccacio's *The Confession of Ser Ciapelletto* on the point of death. His confessor interrogates him and asks if he has never fallen into the sin of pride.

"Ah, Father!" says the rascal, "I'm very much afraid of having damned myself by a little self-indulgence, in realizing I have kept my virginity all my life!" "Have you been a glutton?" "Alas! Yes, my Father, because, outside the days ordained for fast, I have always fasted on bread and water three times a week, but I have sometimes eaten my bread with such appetite and delight that my gluttony no doubt displeased God." "And greed, my son?" "Alas, my Father, I am guilty of the sin of greed for having sometimes done a little commerce in order to give all my earnings to the poor." "And have you given in to anger?" "Oh, so often! When I see the divine service so neglected and sinners not observing the commandments of God, how angry I can be!"

Next, Sir Ciapelletto accuses himself of having had his room swept on a Sunday.

The confessor reassures him, and tells him God will pardon him. The penitent breaks down in tears, saying God will never forgive him, that he remembers that at the age of two, he had offended his mother, an unforgivable crime. "My poor mother," he says "who carried me nine months in her womb day and night, and who carried me in her arms when I was small. No, God will never forgive me for having been such a wicked child."

Finally, this confession, having become public, they make a saint of Ciapelletto, who had been the greatest rogue of his time.

The canon Luigi Pulci is far more licentious in his poem on *Morgante*. He begins this poem by daring to make a mockery of the Gospel of St. John.

> *In the beginning was the Word of God below,*
> *and was the Word, and God's Word Him:*
> *this was in the beginning, in my opinion, etc.*

I've no idea, after all, whether it was through naivety or impiety that Pulci, having put the Gospel at the head of his poem, finished it with the *Salve, Regina*; but whether puerility or audacity, such liberties would not be tolerated today. The reply Morgante makes to Margutte is even more condemned. This Margutte asks Morgante if he is Christian or Muslim:

> *Margutte then replied—— Briefly*
> *I believe no more in black than in blue,*
> *but in capon, roast or boiled.*
> . . . .
> *But above all in good wine I have faith.*
> . . . .
> *Now these are the three cardinal virtues:*
> *The throat, the nut, and the ass, as I have told you.*

One thing very strange is that almost all the Italian writers of the fourteenth, fifteenth, and sixteenth centuries had very little respect for this religion their country was the center of. The more closely they looked at the august ceremonies of this faith, and the first pontiffs, the more they abandoned themselves to a licentiousness that the court of Rome seemed to authorize by its example. These verses from *Pastor fido* could be applied to them:

> *Il lungo conver sar genero noia,*
> *E la noia dispresso, e odio al fine.*[5]

The liberties taken by Machiavelli, Ariosto, Aretino, the Archbishop Benevento la Casa, Cardinal Bembo, Pomponazzi, Cardano, and so many other scholars are known well enough. The popes paid no attention and, so long as indulgences were bought and people kept their noses out of government, it was permitted to say anything. The Italians in those days resembled the ancient Romans, who mocked their gods with impunity but never disturbed the state religion. There was only Giordano Bruno who, having braved the Inquisitor at Vienna and having made an irreconcilable enemy of a man so powerful and dangerous, was hunted for his book, *Della Bestia trionfante*. He perished in the flames, a torture invented among the Christians for the heretics. This very rare book is worse than heretical. The author only accepts the law of the patriarchs, natural law. It was composed and printed in London at Lord Philip Sidney's, one of the great men of England and a favorite of Queen Elisabeth.

All the princes and politicians of fourteenth, fifteenth, and sixteenth century Italy are commonly ranked among the unbelievers. It is claimed that if Pope Sixtus IV had had religion, he wouldn't have been involved in the conspiracy of the Pazzis, for which an archbishop of Florence was hanged in pontifical clothing from the windows of the town hall. The Medici assassins, who carried out their parricides in the cathedral at the moment the priest was showing the Eucharist to the people, could not, they say, have believed in the Eucharist. It seems impossible that there was the slightest religious instinct in the heart of Pope Alexander VI who brought about the deaths of all the princes he despoiled of their states by stiletto, rope, or poison, according them indulgences *in articulo mortis*[6] as they gave up their last breaths.

We shall not linger on these hideous examples. Alas! Milord, what do they prove? That the restraint of a pure religion, free of all superstitions that dishonor it, and which can make it unbelievable, was absolutely necessary for these grand criminals. If religion had been purified, there would've been less incredulity and less heinous crimes. Whoever firmly believes in a God who rewards virtue and avenges crime will tremble at killing an innocent man, and the dagger will fall from his hands. But the Italians of those days, knowing Christianity only through ridiculous legends, through the nonsense and shams of monks, imagined that there is no religion because a religion so dishonored seemed absurd to them. Because Savonarola had been a false prophet, they concluded that there was no God; which is very poor reasoning. The abominable politics of these dreadful times made them commit a thousand crimes. Their philosophy, no less frightful, smothered all remorse. They wished to annihilate the God who could punish them.

LETTER III

On Vanini

Milord,

You ask me for an account of Vanini. I can do no better than to direct you to the third section of the article entitled, "Atheism" in *The Philosophical Dictionary*. I will add to the wise reflections you'll find there that a *Life of Vanini* was printed in London in 1717. It was dedicated to a Milord *North and Grey*. It was a French refugee, his chaplain, who was the author. To introduce this character, it is enough to say that he bases his history on the testimony of the Jesuit Garasse the most absurd and insolent slanderer the Jesuits ever had, along with being their most ridiculous writer. Here are the words of Garasse, cited by the chaplain, and that are indeed in the *Doctrine Curieuse* of this Jesuit, on page 144:

> As for Lucile Vanin, he was a Neapolitan, a man of Nothingness, who had prowled throughout Italy and a good part of France in search of free banquets in his capacity as pedant. This nasty rascal, having come from Gascony in 1617, attempted to sow his chaff to his advantage and make a rich harvest of impieties, believing he had found brains susceptible to his propositions. He brazenly slipped in among the nobles and grabbed a stool as frankly as if he had been a servant of the house and had always been accustomed to the

temper of the country. But he met with stronger minds, more resolved to defend the truth, than he had imagined.

What can you suppose, Milord, from a life story based on such memoirs? What will surprise you even more is that when the unfortunate Vanini was condemned, none of his books were featured, which were supposed to contain the so-called atheism for which he was condemned. All the books of this poor Neapolitan were books of theology and philosophy, printed by the king's permission and approved by the doctors of the Faculty of Paris. Even his *Dialogues*, with which he is still reproached today and which one can scarcely condemn, except as a very boring work, was honored by the highest praise in French, in Latin, and even in Greek. Among these praises, we find everywhere repeated this verse by a famous doctor of philosophy in Paris:

> *Vaninus, vir mente potens, sophiaeque magister*
> *Maximus, Italiae decus, et nova gloria gentis.*

Since imitated as:

> *Honor of Italy, rival of Greece,*
> *Vanini spreads wisdom for all to embrace.*

But all this acclaim has been forgotten and it is only remembered that he was burnt alive. It must be admitted that people are sometimes burnt a little cavalierly, as Jan Hus, Jerome of Prague, Counselor Anne du Bourg, Servetus, Antoine, Urbain Grandier, the Marshal d'Ancre, Leonora Dori, Morin, and Jean Calas bear witness; as this incalculable throng of unfortunates that nearly ever Christian sect has made perish in the flames in turn also demonstrate; a horror unknown to the Persians, the Turks, the Tartars, the Indians, the Chinese, the Roman Republic, and to all the peoples of antiquity; a horror barely abolished among us, which will shame our children for having descended from such abominable ancestors.

LETTER IV

On the English Authors

Milord,

Your Highness asks who are those who have had the audacity to rise up, not only against the Roman Church, but against the Christian Church. The number is prodigious, especially in England. One of the first was Lord Herbert of Cherbury, who died in 1648, known for his treatises on the religion of laics and that of the Gentiles.

Hobbes recognized no other religion but that which the government sanctioned. He refused to have two masters: the real pontiff is the magistrate. This doctrine caused a revolt among the clergy. They screamed scandal and novelty. As for scandal, which means a cause for stumbling, there was one; but as to novelty, there was not, for in England the king had long been the head of the Church. The Empress of Russia heads hers in a country vaster than the Roman Empire. The Senate, in the republic, was the head of religion, and every Roman emperor was the sovereign pontiff.

Lord Shaftesbury surpassed Herbert and Hobbes by far, both in audacity and style. His scorn of the Christian religion shines forth too brightly.

Wollaston's *Natural Religion* is written with more caution but, lacking the charms of Milord Shaftesbury, this book has been little read except by philosophers.

On Toland

Toland delivered more violent blows. He was a proud and independent soul. Born in poverty, he could have acquired a fortune if he had been more moderate. Persecution irritated him. He wrote against the Christian religion in hatred and vengeance.

In his first book, entitled *Christianity Not Mysterious*, he wrote a bit mysteriously himself, and his boldness was veiled. It was condemned, and he was pursued in Ireland. The veil was soon torn. His *Judaic Origins*, his *Nazarenus*, his *Pantheisticon* were all battles he waged openly on Christianity. What is strange is that, having been oppressed in Ireland for the most moderate of his works, he was never bothered in England for the most audacious of his books.

He was accused of finishing his *Pantheisticon* with this blasphemous prayer, which can indeed be found in certain editions: "Omnipotens et sempiterne Bacche, qui hominum corda donis tuis recreas, concede propitius ut qui besternis poculis aegroti facti sunt, hodiernis curentur, per pocula poculorum. Amen!"[7]

But since this profanation was a parody of a prayer in the Roman Church, the English were not shocked. Moreover, it's been shown that this profane prayer is not by Toland. It had been invented two hundred years earlier in France by a club of drinkers. It can be found in the *Allegoric Lent*, printed in 1563. That crazy Jesuit, Garasse, speaks of it in his *Curious Doctrine*, book II, page 201.

Toland died with great courage in 1721. His last words were, "I'm going to sleep." Some verses were written to honor his memory. They were not written by priests of the Anglican Church.

On Locke

Erroneously, the great philosopher Locke has been counted among the enemies of the Christian religion. It's true that his book on *The Reasonableness of Christianity* differs a bit from ordinary faith, but the primitive religion called *Quakers*, so renowned in Pennsylvania, differs from ordinary Christianity even more, yet they are considered Christians.

He's been charged with not believing in the immortality of the soul because he is persuaded that God, absolute master of everything, could give (if he wished) feeling and thought to matter. Monsieur de Voltaire has vindicated him of this reproach.[8] He has proven that God could conserve the atom, or monad, eternally, which he might have deigned to favor with the gift of thought. This is the opinion of the famous and holy priest Gassendi, pious defender of what might be good in Epicurus' doctrine. Consider his famous letter to Descartes:

> From where does this notion come to you? If it proceeds from the body, then you must not be without extension. Teach us how it is possible that the species, or the idea of the body, which is extended, can be received in you, that is, in a substance not extended. . . . It is true that you know that you think, but you do not know what sort of substance you are, you who think,

although the operation of thought is known to you. The principle of your essence is hidden from you, and you do not know the nature of this substance, one of whose operations is to think, etc.

Locke died in peace, saying to Madame Masham and his friends who surrounded him, "Life is sheer vanity."

On Bishop Taylor and on Tindal

Taylor, Bishop of Connor, has been placed with perhaps as much injustice among the infidels because of his book, *A Guide for Doubters.*[9]

But as to Doctor Tindal, author of *Christianity as Old as the Creation*, he has constantly been the most intrepid mainstay of natural religion as well as of the Royal House of Hanover. He was one of the most learned men of England in history. He was honored till his death with a pension of two hundred pounds sterling. As he did not appreciate the books of Alexander Pope, whom he found absolutely devoid of genius and imagination, according him only a talent for versifying and for making use of other people's wit, Pope became his implacable enemy. Tindal was, what's more, an ardent Whig, and Pope a Jacobite. It is not surprising that Pope ripped him to shreds in his *Dunciade*, an imitation of Dryden, and too full of baseness and disgusting images.

On Collins

One of the most terrible enemies of the Christian religion was Anthony Collins, Grand Treasurer of the County of Essex, a good metaphysician and very erudite. It is sad that he used his profound dialectic gifts only against Christianity. Doctor Clarke, the famous Socinian, author of a very good book demonstrating the existence of God, was never able to respond to Collins' books in a satisfying way, and was reduced to insults.

His *Philosophical Researches* on the liberty of man, on the foundations of the Christian religion, on literal prophecies and on freedom of thought have, unfortunately, remained victorious.

On Woolston

The too-famous Thomas Woolston, Master of Arts at Cambridge, distinguished himself, in about 1726, by his discourses against the miracles of Jesus Christ and raised the banner so highly that he had the book sold in his own house in London. Three editions were printed, one after the other, of ten thousand copies each.

No one had yet pushed temerity and scandal quite so far. He called the miracles and the resurrection of Our Savior puerile tales and foolish talk. He said that when Jesus changed water into wine for guests already drunk, that he was apparently making punch. God being carried by the Devil to the pinnacle of the temple and to the top of a mountain from which one could see all the kingdoms of the world appeared to be a monstrous blasphemy to him. The devil sent into a troop of two thousand pigs, the fig tree withered for not bearing figs when it was not the season for figs, the transfiguration of Jesus with his clothes turning all white, his conversation with Moses and Elijah, in short, his entire sacred story is travestied into a ridiculous novel. Woolston is not sparing with the most injurious, despising terms. He often calls Our Savior, Jesus Christ, *the fellow*, the chap, the scamp, *a wanderer*, a vagabond, *a cabbage-cutting beggar friar*.

He saves himself, however, in favor of a mystical meaning, by saying that these miracles are pious allegories. All good Christians held his book no less in horror.

One day, a devout lady, seeing him pass in the street, spat in his face. He calmly wiped his face and said, "That is how the Jews treated your God." He died in peace, saying, "Tis a pass every man must come to." You will find in the *Dictionnaire portatif* of Abbé Ladvocat and in a *New Portable Dictionary*, which copies the same errors, that Woolston died in prison in 1733. Nothing is more false. Several of my friends saw him in his house. He died a free man, at home.

On Warburton

Warburton, Bishop of Gloucester, has been regarded as one the boldest infidels that ever wrote because, after having commentated Shakespeare, whose comedies, and even a few tragedies, teem with licentious taunts, he maintained in his

Divine Legation of Moses that God never taught his chosen people the immortality of the soul. It may be that this bishop has been judged too harshly, and that the pride and satirical spirit he has been reproached with upset the nation. Much has been written against him. The first two volumes of his work appeared to be only a vain jumble of erroneous erudition in which he doesn't even deal with his subject, and which is, moreover, contrary to his subject, since it only tends to prove that all legislators had established the immortality of the soul as the base of their religions; in which, Warburton is mistaken, since neither Sancho-niathon the Phoenician nor the Chinese book of *Five Kings* nor Confucius admits this principle.

But Warburton has never been able, in all his subterfuges, to respond to the leading personal arguments that have assailed him. You claim that all wise men have lain as the foundation of religion the immortality of the soul and rewards and punishments after death. Yet Moses does not speak of either in his *Decalogue* nor in a single one of his laws. So Moses, by your own admission, was not a wise man.

Either he knew of this great dogma, or else he did not. If he knew of it, he is guilty of not having taught it. If he did not know it, he was unworthy of being a legislator.

Either God inspired Moses, or he was only a charlatan. If God inspired Moses, he could not have hidden the immortality of the soul from him, and if God did not teach him what all the Egyptians knew, God deceived him and deceived his entire people. If Moses was only a charlatan, you destroy the entire Mosaic Law, and consequently, you sap the foundations of the Christian religion, built upon the Mosaic. Finally, if God did deceive Moses, you make the Infinitely Perfect Being an inveigler and a rascal. Whichever way you turn, you blaspheme.

You think you can get out of it by saying that God paid his people in cash, by punishing them temporarily for their transgressions, and by rewarding them with all the bounties of earth when they were faithful. This evasion is pitiful, for how many transgressors have spent their days in delight! Consider Solomon. Must one not have lost all common sense or decency to say that not a single Jewish villain escaped earthly punishment? Does Scripture not speak of the success of the wicked a hundred times?

We knew before you that neither the Decalogue nor Leviticus ever mentioned the immortality of the soul, nor its spirituality, nor rewards or punishments in the afterlife, but this was not for you to say. What may be pardonable from a layperson is not so from a priest. And you especially should not say it in four long boring volumes.

This is what has been objected to Warburton. He has responded with atrocious insults and believed himself right because his diocese brings him an income of two thousand five hundred guineas. All of England has come out against him despite his guineas. He has made himself odious by the virulence of his insolent character far more than by the absurdity of his system.

On Bolingbroke

Milord Bolingbroke was bolder than Warburton, and of better faith. He never ceases to say, in his *Philosophic Works*, that atheists are far less dangerous than theologians. He reasoned like a minister of state who knows how much blood theological quarrels have cost England, but he should be satisfied with proscribing theology, and not the Christian religion through which every statesman can draw very great advantages for the human race, by drawing it back within its limits whenever it has gone beyond them. After the death of Lord Bolingbroke, a few of his works still more violent than the *Philosophic Collection* were published.[10] He deploys a deadly eloquence in them. No one has ever written anything more severe. It is clear that he held the Christian religion in horror. It is sad that so sublime a genius wanted to uproot a tree he could have rendered useful by trimming the branches and cleaning off the moss.

Religion can be purified. This great work was begun some two hundred and fifty years ago, but men are only enlightened by degrees. Who would have foreseen then that sun rays would be analyzed, that we would electrify with lightning, or that the law of gravity that presides over the universe would be discovered? It is time, according to Bolingbroke, to banish theology, just as we have banished judicial astrology, witchcraft, possession by the devil, divining rods, a cure-all remedy, and the Jesuits. Theology has never served any purpose other than to overturn the laws and to corrupt hearts. It alone creates atheists, for the large number of theologians sensible enough to see the absurdity in this chimerical science don't know enough to replace it with a healthy philosophy. Theology, they say, means the science of God. And the scamps who have profaned this science have given us absurd ideas about God, and from that, they conclude that the Divinity is a chimera, because theology is chimerical. This is exactly like saying that one shouldn't take quinine for fever, nor fast when one has overeaten, nor be bled for apoplexy, because there have been bad doctors. It is like denying the course of the stars because we have had astrologers. It is like denying the obvious effects of chemistry because a few charlatan chemists claimed they could make gold. The people of this world, still less learned than these little theologians, say: Here are bachelors of science and men with diplomas who don't believe in God. Why should we believe? These are the fatal results of the theological spirit. A false science creates atheists. A true science prostrates men before the Divinity. It makes a man just and wise whom the abuses of theology had made iniquitous and irrational.

On Thomas Chubb

Thomas Chubb is a philosopher by nature. The subtlety of his genius, which he misused, made him embrace not only the viewpoint of the Socinians, who consider Jesus only a man, but also that of the most rigid theists who believe in God, but not in a single mystery. His misguided notions are methodical. He wished to unite all men in one religion he thought purified because it was simple. The word Christianity is on every page in his diverse writings, but the thing itself is not. He dares believe that Jesus Christ was of the religion of Thomas Chubb, but he is not of the religion of Jesus Christ. A perpetual abuse of language is at the core of his persuasion. Jesus Christ had said: Love thyself and thy neighbor; that is the only law, and all there is to man. Chubb abides by these words, and removes all the rest. Our Savior appears to him a philosopher likes Socrates, who was put to death like him for having fought the superstitions and the priests of his day. Moreover, he always wrote with restraint and covered his thoughts with a veil. The obscurity in which he envelopes himself has given him more fame than readers.

LETTER V

On Swift

It is true, Milord, that I have not spoken to you of Swift. He deserves a separate article. He is the only English writer of this sort who was amusing. It is very odd that the two men we should most reproach with having ridiculed the Christian religion were both priests in charge of souls. Rabelais was the parish priest of Meudon, and Swift was the dean of Dublin Cathedral. Both pelted Christianity with more sarcasm than Molière did doctors, and both lived and died in peace, while other men were persecuted, pursued, or put to death over a few ambiguous words.

> Sometimes one shatters where another is saved,
> And where one perishes, another is preserved.
> (*Cinna*, Act II, Scene 1, by Corneille)

The Tale of a Tub by Dean Swift is an imitation of *Three Rings*. The fable of these three rings is very ancient: it hails from the time of the crusades. In dying, an old man leaves a ring to each of his three children. They fight over who will have the most beautiful ring. In the end, after long disputes, we see at last that the rings were perfectly equivalent. The old man is theism, and the three children are the Jewish, Christian, and Muslim religions.

The author overlooked the religion of the Magi and the Brahmins and many others, but he was an Arab who only knew of these three sects. This fable leads to the indifference everyone so heatedly reproached Emperor Frederick II with, and his chancellor, De Vineis, who was accused of having written the book, *De tribus Impostoribus*,[11] which, as you know, never existed.

The fable of the *Three Rings* is found in a few ancient compendiums. Doctor Swift substituted three leotards for them. The introduction to this impious mockery is worthy of the book. It is an engraving showing three ways of speaking to the public: the first is the theater of Harlequin and Gilles, the second is a preacher whose pulpit consists of half a barrel, the third is a ladder from the top of which a man about to be hanged harangues the public.

A preacher placed between Harlequin and a hanged man doesn't cut a very impressive figure. The body of the work is an allegorical tale of the three main sects that divide Southern Europe: the Roman, Lutheran, and Calvinist sects, for he doesn't speak of the Greek Church, which possesses six times as much territory as any of the others, and drops Mohammedanism, far more widespread than the Greek Church.

The three brothers to whom their little old father leaves three plain leotards of the same color are Peter, Martin, and John, meaning the pope, Luther, and Calvin. The author has his three heroes commit more extravagances than Cervantes does his Don Quixote or Ariosto his Roland, but milord Peter is treated the worst of the three. The book is very badly translated in French. It was impossible to render all the comic touches it is seasoned with. The comedy often concerns the quarrels between the Anglican and the Presbyterian Churches, or common practices or adventures we know nothing of in France, and puns specific to the English language. For example, the word which means *une bulle de pape* in French also means a bull (*un boeuf*) in English. It's a source of ambiguity and jests entirely lost on a French reader.

Swift was much less of a scholar than Rabelais, but his wit was more astute and nimbler. He is the Rabelais of polite circles. Lords Oxford and Bolingbroke had the best benefice in Ireland, after the archbishopric of Dublin, bestowed on the man who had covered the Christian religion in ridicule, and Abbadie, who had written in favor of this religion a book given effusive praises, only received a poor little village benefice. But it is notable that both of them died insane.

LETTER VI

On the Germans

Milord,

Your Germany has also had many lords and philosophers accused of irreligion.

Your celebrated Corneille Agrippa in the sixteenth century was considered not only a sorcerer but a nonbeliever. That is contradictory, for a sorcerer believes in God since he dares to use the name of God in all his incantations. A sorcerer believes in the devil, since he gives himself to the devil. Accused of both these calumnies like Apuleius, Agrippa was lucky to have only been imprisoned and to only die in a hospital. It was he who first retailed the idea that the forbidden fruit Adam and Eve had eaten was a sexual orgasm to which they had abandoned themselves before receiving from God the nuptial blessing. It was he again who, after cultivating the sciences, first wrote against them. He condemned the milk with which he had been nourished, because he had digested it badly. He died in the hospital of Grenoble in 1535.

I know of your famous doctor Faustus only through the comedy of which he is the hero, which is played in all the provinces of your empire. In it, your Doctor Faustus is in steady traffic with the devil. He writes letters to him sent through the air by the means of a string, and he receives replies. We see miracles in each Act, and the devil carries Faustus off at the end of the play. It is said that he was born in Swabia and that he lived under the Holy Roman Emperor, Maximilian I. I don't think he made out any better with Maximilian than with the devil, his other master.

The famous Erasmus was also suspected of irreligion by the Catholics and the Protestants because he ridiculed the immoderation of both. When two parties are wrong, he who remains neutral and is consequently right is insulted by both sides. The statue raised to him in the square of Rotterdam, his home, avenged him both of Luther and of the Inquisition.

Melanchthon, black land, was more or less in the situation of Erasmus. It was claimed that he changed his opinion on original sin and predestination fourteen times. He was called the Proteus of Germany. He would have liked to be the Neptune who restrained the violence of the winds.

> *Jam caelum terramque meo sine numine, venti*
> *Miscere, et tantas audetis tollere moles !*
> Virgil, *Aeneid I, 133–34*[12]

He was moderate and tolerant. He came off as indifferent. Become a Protestant, he advised his mother to remain a Catholic. Based on that, he was judged to be neither one nor the other.

I will omit, if I may, the throng of sectarians who were accused of embracing factions rather than opinions and of having more faith in ambition or cupidity than in Luther or the pope. I will not speak of philosophers accused of having no Gospel other than Nature.

I come to your illustrious Leibniz. Fontenelle, delivering his eulogy in Paris to a full Academy, expresses himself on his religion in these terms: "He was accused of having only been a great and strict observer of natural law. His pastors rebuked him publically and pointlessly."

You will soon see, Milord, that Fontenelle, as he spoke, had suffered imputations just as grave.

Wolff, the disciple of Leibniz, was exposed to a greater danger: he taught mathematics in the University of Halle with prodigious success. The professor of theology Lange, who was freezing from the cold in the solitude of his school while Wolff had an audience of five hundred, took revenge by denouncing Wolff as an atheist. The late King Frederick William of Prussia, who better understood the drilling of troops than the disputes of scholars, believed Lange too readily. He gave Wolff a choice between leaving his states within twenty-four hours or being hanged. The philosopher resolved the problem at once by withdrawing to Marburg, where his students followed him and where his glory and fortune were increased. The town of Halle thus lost over four hundred thousand florins per year that the influx of Wolff's disciples had brought to it. The king's revenue suffered and the injustice done to the philosopher only fell back on the king. You know, Milord, with what equity and noble-mindedness the successor to this prince repaired the error his father had been led to make.[13]

It is said in an article on *Wolff* in a dictionary that Charles-Frederick, crowned philosopher and friend of Wolff, raised him to the dignity of Vice-Chancellor of the University of the Elector of Bavaria, and made him a baron of the empire. The king referred to in this article is indeed a philosopher, a scholar, a very great genius, as well as a very great captain on the throne. But his name isn't Charles. He does not have in his states any university belonging to the Elector of Bavaria, and the emperor alone makes barons of the empire. These little errors, far too frequent in our dictionaries, can be quite easily corrected.

Since this time, the freedom to think has made astonishing progress in all of northern Germany. This liberty has been carried to such extremes that in 1766, an eloquent preface was printed in an edition of Fleury's *Abrégé de l'histoire ecclésiastique* beginning with these words:

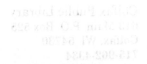

The establishment of the Christian religion had, like all the empires, feeble beginnings. A Jew from the dregs of society of dubious birth who combined the absurdity of ancient prophecies with moral precepts and to whom miracles were attributed is the hero of this sect. A dozen fanatics spread from the East to Italy, etc.

It is sad that the author of this piece, incidentally profound and sublime, let himself be carried away to an audacity so fatal to our holy religion. Nothing is more pernicious. Nevertheless, this prodigious license hardly raised a murmur. It is much to be wished that the spread of this book will remain very limited. Only a very few number of copies, I presume, were printed.

The discourse of Emperor Julian against Christianity, translated in Berlin by the Marquis d'Argens, Chamberlain to the King of Prussia, and dedicated to Prince Ferdinand of Brunswick, would be no less severe a blow to our religion if the author had not taken care to reassure alarmed spirits with learned remarks. The work is preceded by a wise and instructive preface in which he does justice (it is true) to the great qualities and virtues of Julian, but in which he admits the fateful errors of this emperor. I think, Milord, that this book is not unknown to you and that your Christianity has not been shaken by it.

LETTER VII

On the French

You have very well guessed, I believe, Milord, that there were more men accused of impiety in France than there were truly impious men, just as we see a lot more suspicions of poisoning than poisoners.

The disquietude, vivacity, glibness, and petulance of the French always supposed more crimes than were committed. This is why a prince rarely dies in Mézeray's histories without someone having poisoned him. The Jesuits Garasse and Hardouin found atheists everywhere. Numerous monks, or people worse than monks, fearing a waning of their credit, have been sentinels always crying out: Who goes there? The enemy's at the gates! Praise be to God that we have had far less people denying God than has been said.

On Bonaventure Despériers

One of the first examples in France of persecutions sparked by panicked terrors was the strange uproar that lasted so long over *Cymbalum mundi*, a little book of fifty pages at most. Its author, Bonaventure Despériers, lived at the beginning of the sixteenth century. He was a servant of Marguerite de Valois, the sister of King François I. Literature was beginning to revive. Despériers wanted to write a few dialogues in Latin in the style of Lucian. He composed four very insipid dialogues on predictions, on the Philosopher's Stone, on a talking horse, and on Actaeon's dogs. In all this motley mess by a dull schoolboy, there is assuredly not a single word that has the slightest or most distant bearing on anything we should regard as sacred.

Someone convinced a few doctors that they were designated by the dogs and the horses. As for horses, they weren't accustomed to this honor. The doctors barked. The book was immediately hunted up, translated into French, printed, and every loafer found allusions in it. The doctors screamed heresy, impiety, and atheism. The book was handed over to the magistrates, the printer Morin was put in prison and the author put in great anguish.

The injustice of the persecution was such a severe blow to Bonaventure's mind that he killed himself with his sword in Marguerite's palace. The tongues of all the preachers and the quills of all the theologians wagged over this dreadful death. He did himself in; therefore he was guilty; therefore he didn't believe in God; therefore his little book, that no one had nevertheless had the patience to read, was a catechism for atheists. Everyone said it, so everyone believed it. *Credidi propter quod locutus sum,* "I believed because I said it" is the motto of men. Something stupid is repeated and by dint of repeating it, we are persuaded of it.

The book became an extreme rarity: another reason to believe it diabolical. None of the authors of literary anecdotes and dictionaries failed to affirm that the *Cymbalum mundi* foreshadowed Spinoza.

We still have the work of a councilor of Bourges named Catherinot, very worthy of the coat of arms of Bourges.[14] This great judge says, "We have two impious books that I have never seen: *De tribus Impostoribus* and the *Cymbalum mundi.*" Well, my friend, if you have never seen them, why talk about them?

The Minim Friar, Mersenne, a messenger for Descartes and the same who attributed twelve apostles to Vanini, said of Bonaventure Despériers, "He's a monster and a rogue, utterly impious." You will notice that he hadn't read his book. There were only two copies left in Europe when Prosper Marchand reprinted it in Amsterdam in 1711. Then the curtain was drawn back: no one screamed impiety or atheism anymore. They screamed boredom and stopped talking about it.

On Théophile

It was the same for Théophile,[15] very famous in his day. He was a young man of good company who wrote mediocre verses with facility, but which enjoyed renown, highly instructed in literature, who wrote purely in Latin and spent as much time at suppers as in his study, welcomed by the young lords who prided themselves on wit, and above all, at the home of the illustrious and unfortunate Duke de Montmorency, who died on the scaffold after having won battles.

Finding himself with two Jesuits one day, and the conversation happening upon a few points of the ill-fated philosophy of his day, the dispute turned bitter. The Jesuits replaced reasons with insults. Théophile was poet and a Gascon, *genus irritabile vatum et Vasconum*.[16] He wrote a little piece in verse in which the Jesuits were not very well-treated. Here are three lines that ran through all France:

> This great and black machine
> Whose suppleness and great body
> Reaches as far as China

Théophile brings them back to mind himself in an epistle in verse written from his prison cell to King Louis XIII. All the Jesuits unleashed their fury on him. The two most enraged, Garasse and Guérin, dishonored the pulpit and violated the laws by naming him in their sermons and in calling him an atheist and an abominable man to excite the faithful against him.

A more dangerous Jesuit named Voisin, who neither wrote nor preached but whom Cardinal de La Rochefoucauld accorded great credit, brought a criminal suit against Théophile and suborned a young debauchee named Sajeot, who had been his pupil and who was said to have served his infamous pleasures, against him, which the defendant reproached him with at the confrontation. Finally, the Jesuit Voisin obtained an order of arrest for Théophile through the favor of the Jesuit Caussin, confessor to the king, on the accusation of impiety and atheism. The poor man fled. He was tried *in absentia* and burned in effigy in 1621. Who would believe that the rage of the Jesuits was still not appeased? Voisin paid a lieutenant of the constabulary named Le Blanc to arrest him in his retreat in Picardie. He was fettered with chains and locked in a dungeon to the cheers of the common folk while Le Blanc shouted "This is an atheist we are going to burn." From there, he was taken to Paris to the Conciergerie where he was put in Ravaillac's dungeon. He stayed there an entire year during which the Jesuits prolonged his trial to look for evidence against him.

While he was in chains, Garasse published his *Curious Doctrine*, in which he says that Pasquier, Cardinal Wolsey, Scaliger, Luther, Calvin, Bèze, the king of England, the Landgrave of Hesse, and Théophile were villainous atheists and carpocratians. This Garasse wrote in his time like the wretched Nonotte writes in his. The difference is that the insolence of Garasse was based on the prestige the Jesuits enjoyed in his time, and that the fury of the absurd Nonotte is the fruit of the horror and contempt into which the Jesuits have fallen in Europe. It is the serpent who still wants to bite after being sliced up. Théophile was interrogated above all over *Le Parnasse satirique*, a collection of impudences in the style of Petronius, Martial, Catullus, Ausonius, the Archbishop della Casa, the Bishop of Angouleme Octavien de Saint-Gelais and his son, Mellin de Saint-Gelais, Aretino, Nicholas Chorier, Marot, Verville, the epigrams of Rousseau,[17] and a hundred other licentious idiocies. This book was not by Théophile. The book's merchant had gathered everything he could from Maynard, Colletet, the magistrate, Frénicle, and from the Academy of Science and a few lords of the court. It was proven that Théophile had no part in this edition, against which he had petitioned himself. In the end, the Jesuits, powerful as they were at the time, could not obtain the consolation of seeing him burned and even had a great deal of difficulty in getting him banished from Paris. He came back despite them, under the protection of the Duke of Montmorency, who lodged him in his townhouse where he died in 1626 of the grief such a cruel persecution had plunged him into.

On Des Barreaux

The *Parlementary* counselor, Des Barreaux, who was a friend of Théophile's in his youth and who did not abandon him in his disgrace, was constantly taken for an atheist. And on what basis? On that of a tale told about him, regarding the adventure of a bacon omelet. A young man given to libertine sallies can very well eat meat in a tavern on a Saturday and throw the plate out the window during a thunderstorm saying, "That's a lot of noise over a bacon omelet" without deserving for all that the awful accusation of atheism. It is no doubt a great act of irreverence. It is an insult to the Church into which he was born. It mocks the institution of fast days. But it does not deny the existence of God.

What gave him this reputation was principally the indiscreet audacity of Boileau who, in his *Satire des femmes*, which was not his best, said he had seen more than one Capaneus

> Braving the vain tiles from the thunder above
> And speaking like Des Barreaux of God[18]

This magistrate never wrote anything against the Divinity. It is not permissible to call a worthy man an atheist to blacken his name without a shred of proof. It is despicable. The famous sonnet that ends this way was imputed to Des Barreaux:

> Tonne, frappe, il est temps; rends-moi guerre pour guerre.
> J'adore en périssant la raison qui t'aigrit;
> Mais dessus quel endroit tombera ton tonnerre
> Qui ne soit tout couvert du sang de Jésus-Christ?[19]

This sonnet is totally worthless. To use Jesus Christ in a verse is not tolerable; *rends-moi guerre* is incorrect French; *guerre pour guerre* falls flat, and *dessus quel endroit* is detestable. These verses are by Abbé de Lavau, and Des Barreaux was always very irritated to see them attributed to him. It is this same Abbé de Lavau who wrote the abominable epigram on the mausoleum raised in honor of Lulli in Saint-Eustache Cathedral:

. . . .

Laissez tomber, sans plus attendre,

Sur ce buste honteux votre fatal rideau;

Et ne montrez que le flambeau

Qui devrait avoir mis l'original en cendre.[20]

On La Mothe Le Vayer

The wise La Mothe Le Vayer, State Councilor, tutor to the brother of Louis XIV and even to Louis XIV for almost a year, suffered from just as much suspicion as the pleasure-loving Des Barreaux. There was still very little philosophy in France. His *Treatise on the Virtue of the Pagans* and *Dialogues of Orasius Tubero* made enemies for him. The Jansenists especially, who, in the footsteps of St. Augustine, considered the virtues of the great men of antiquity only as splendid sins, raged against him. It is the height of fanatical insolence to say, "No one has any virtue but us and our friends. Socrates, Confucius, Marcus Aurelius, and Epictetus were villains because they weren't of our faith." We have returned to this extravagance today, but at that time it dominated. It is reported in a curious book that one day one of these maniacs, seeing La Mothe Le Vayer pass through a gallery in the Louvre, said out loud, "There is a man without religion." Le Vayer, instead of having him punished, turned to this man said, "My friend, I have so much religion that I am not of your religion."

On Saint-Évremond

A few books against Christianity were given out under the name of Saint-Évremond, but none of them were by him. After his death, these dangerous books were passed off under the safety of his reputation because in his real works are found, in fact, some lines which indicate a mind freed from the prejudices of childhood. Moreover, his epicurean lifestyle and his highly philosophic death served as a pretext for all those who wished to accredit their particular views with his name.

We have above all an *Analysis of the Christian Religion* that is attributed to him. It is a work that tends to topple the entire chronology and almost all the facts of Scripture. No one has studied more deeply than its author the opinion of several theologians that the astronomer Phlegon had spoken of the darkness that covered the entire earth at the death of our savior, Jesus Christ. I admit that the author was completely right against those who wanted to rely on the remarks of this astronomer, but he was very much in the wrong to wish to combat the entire system of Christianity under the pretext that it was badly defended.

For the rest, Saint-Évremond was quite incapable of this learned research. His wit was a pleasant one and fairly just, but he had little learning, no genius, and his taste was somewhat iffy. His *Discourse on the Romans* won him a repute that he exploited to write some very tired comedies and the worst verses that have ever fatigued readers, and who are no longer fatigued since they don't read them. He can be ranked among the amiable, witty men who flourished during the brilliant epoch of Louis XIV, but not among its superior men. Furthermore, those who have called him an atheist are shameful slanderers.

On Fontenelle

Bernard de Fontenelle, later Secretary of the Academy of Science, had a worse shock to withstand. In 1686, he had a very ingenious *Relation of the Isle of Borneo* inserted into Bayle's *Republic of Letters*. It was an allegory on Rome and Geneva, designated under the names of two sisters, Mero and Eenegu. Mero was a tyrannical magician. She demanded that her subjects come tell her their most secret thoughts, and then bring her all their money. Before coming to kiss her feet, they had to worship the bones of the dead, and often, when they wanted to dine, she made the bread disappear. At last her spells and her fits of wrath raised a large faction against her, and her sister Eenegu deprived her of half of her kingdom.

Bayle didn't understand the joke at first. But once Abbé Terrasson did a commentary on it, it caused a furor. This was in the time of the Revocation of the Edict of Nantes. Fontenelle ran the risk of being locked up in the Bastille. He stooped to writing some pretty bad verses in honor of this revocation and of the Jesuits. They were inserted into a bad anthology entitled the *Triumph of Religion under Louis the Great*, printed in Paris by Langlois in 1687.

But having since then rewritten in French the learned *History of Oracles by Van Dale* with great success, the Jesuits persecuted him. Le Tellier, Confessor to Louis XIV, recalling the allegory of Mero and Eenegu, wanted to treat him like the Jesuit Voisin had treated Théophile. He solicited a *lettre de cachet* against him. The famous Keeper of the Seals, d'Argenson, police lieutenant at the time, saved Fontenelle from the wrath of Le Tellier. If one had to choose either Fontenelle or Le Tellier as an atheist, it was on the slanderer Le Tellier that the suspicion should fall.

This anecdote is more important than all the literary trifles with which Abbé Trublet compiled a huge volume on Fontenelle. It shows how dangerous philosophy is when a fanatic or a rogue, or a monk who is both, has the prince's ear. It is a danger, Milord, which one will never be exposed to with you.

On the Abbé de Saint-Pierre

The *Allegory of Mahometism* by the Abbé de Saint-Pierre was far more striking than that of Mero. All the writings of this abbé, several of which pass for reveries, are by a good man and a zealous citizen; but they all resonate with pure theism. Nevertheless, he was not persecuted. It's because he writes in a manner that makes no one jealous. His style has little charm. He isn't read much. He laid claim to nothing. Those who read him made fun of him and called him a little chap. If he had written like Fontenelle, it would have been fatal to him, especially while the Jesuits were still reigning.

On Bayle

And yet, the immortal Bayle arose during those years and even earlier, the foremost dialectician and skeptical philosopher. He had already given his *Thoughts on the Comet*, his *Responses to the Questions of a Provincial*, and finally his *Dictionnaire de raisonnement* (Critical Dictionary). His greatest enemies are forced to admit that there is not a single line in his works that is an obvious blasphemy against the Christian religion, but his greatest defenders admit that in the controversial subjects, there is not a single page that does not lead the reader to doubt, and often to incredulity. He cannot be convicted of impiety, but he creates unbelievers by putting the objections to our dogmas in such a luminous way that it is impossible for a mediocre faith to not be shaken; and unfortunately, the vast majority of readers have a rather mediocre faith.

It has been reported in one of these historical dictionaries, where the truth is so often mixed with lies, that Cardinal de Polignac, passing through Rotterdam, asked Bayle if he was Anglican, Lutheran, or Calvinist, and that he replied, "I am a Protestant, because I protest against all religions."

First of all, Cardinal de Polignac never went to Rotterdam, except when he went to finalize the Peace of Utrecht in 1713, after the death of Bayle.

Secondly, this learned prelate was not unaware that Bayle, born a Calvinist in Foix, and having never been in England or in Germany, was neither an Anglican nor a Lutheran.

Thirdly, he was too polite to go ask a man what his religion was. It is true that Bayle said some of the things they have him say. He said he was like Homer's cloud-gathering Jupiter. He was moreover a man of simple, well-ordered morals, a real philosopher in every sense of the word. He died suddenly after writing these words: Here is what the truth is.

He had searched for it all his life, and had found nothing but errors everywhere.

Things went much further after him. The Maillets, the Boulainvilliers, the Boulangers, the Mesliers, the learned Fréret, the dialectician Dumarsis, the intemperate La Mettrie, and many others have attacked the Christian religion as doggedly as the Porphyrys, the Celsuses, and the Julians.

I have often inquired what could determine so many modern writers to display such hatred against Christianity. A few have replied that the writings of the new apologists for our religion have outraged them; that if these apologists had written with the moderation with which their cause should inspire them, no one would have never thought to rise against them. But their bile provokes more bile. Their wrath gives birth to wrath. And the scorn they affect for philosophers arouses scorn; so that, in the end, what happens between the defenders and the enemies of Christianity is what we saw happen between all the sects. Writings fly with fury from all sides, and insults get mixed in with the arguments.

On Mademoiselle Huber

Mlle. Huber was a very intelligent woman and the sister of Abbé Huber, who was very well-known to milord, your father. She joined forces with a great metaphysician to write the book entitled *La Religion essentielle à l'homme* (The

Religion Essential for Mankind) around 1740. It must be admitted that this essential religion is, unfortunately, pure theism, much as the Noahides practiced it before God deigned to create a cherished people in the deserts of Sinaï and Horeb and give them particular laws. According to Mlle. Huber and her friend, the religion essential to mankind should apply in all times and all places to all minds. All mysteries are beyond man, and not made for him. The practice of virtue cannot have the slightest rapport with dogmas. The religion essential to man consists in what one should do, and not in what one cannot understand. Intolerance is to the essential religion what barbarity is to humanity and what cruelty is to kindness. That is the synopsis of the book. The author is very abstract: it is a series of lemmas and theorems that spread more obscurity at times than light. One struggles to follow along. It is surprising that a woman wrote like a geometer on such an interesting subject. Perhaps she wanted to put off readers who would have persecuted her had they understood it and had they had any pleasure in reading her. As she was a Protestant, she was hardly read except by Protestants. A preacher named Desroches refuted her, and even rather politely for a preacher. Protestant ministers should be, it seems to me, Milord, more moderate with theists than Catholic bishops and cardinals, for, supposing a moment, God forbid, that theism should prevail, that there would be only a simple religion subject to the authority of the laws and magistrates, that all of that would be reduced to the worship of the Supreme Being who rewards and punishes, the Protestant preachers wouldn't lose anything. They would still be in charge of presiding over public prayers to the Supreme Being and still be teachers of morals. Their pensions would be preserved, or if they lost them, the loss would be quite small. Their antagonists, however, have wealthy prelacies. They are dukes, counts, and princes. They have sovereignties, and although so much grandeur and wealth is perhaps unsuitable to the successors of the apostles, they will never suffer being despoiled of them. The temporal rights they have acquired are even so linked today to the constitution of Catholic states that they could not be deprived of them except by violence.

Theism, however, is a religion without zealots, which in itself will never cause a revolution. It is erroneous, but serene. All that can be feared is that theism, spread so universally, would gradually dispose all minds to despise the yoke of pontiffs and that the judicial authorities might reduce them to the function of praying for the people at the first occasion. But so long as they are moderate, they will be respected. Only the abuse of power has ever been able to anger power. Let us remark indeed, Milord, that two or three hundred volumes of theism have never diminished the revenue of Roman Catholic pontiffs by an écu, and that two or three writings by Luther and Calvin took about fifty million in income from them. A theological quarrel, two hundred years ago, could overturn Europe. Theism never herded together four people. One might even say that this religion, while deceiving minds, mellows them, and pacifies quarrels misunderstood truths give rise to. Whatever the case, I limit myself to conveying to Your Highness a faithful account. It's up to you to judge.

On Barbeyrac

Barbeyrac is the only commentator more esteemed than the author he critiqued. He translated and commentated the hodgepodge of Pufendorf, but enriched it with a preface that sells the book in its own right. He goes back to the origins of morals in this preface and has the bold sincerity of showing that the Church Fathers were not always familiar with these pure morals that they disfigured with strange allegories: like when they say that the scrap of red cloth shown at the window by the innkeeper Rahab is obviously the blood of Jesus Christ, that Moses raising his arms during the battle against the Amalekites is the cross on which Jesus expired, that the kisses of the Shunammite represent the marriage of Jesus Christ with his church; that the big door of Noah's ark represents the human body and the little door, the anus, etc., etc.

Barbeyrac cannot suffer, morally-speaking, that Augustine became a persecutor after having preached tolerance. He openly condemns the uncouth insults Jerome vomits against his adversaries, especially against Rufinus and Vigilantius. He points out the contradictions that he notices in the morals of the Church Fathers. He is incensed that they have sometimes inspired hatred for the homeland, like Tertullian, who strictly forbid Christians to carry arms to save the empire.

Barbeyrac had violent enemies who accused him of wanting to destroy the Christian religion by making those who had sustained it with indefatigable labor look ridiculous. He defended himself, but his defense betrays such a deep contempt for the Church Fathers, such disdain for their false eloquence and dialectics, and he so openly prefers Confucius, Socrates, Zaleucus, Cicero, the Emperor Antonius, Epictetus, that it is clear that Barbeyrac is rather a zealous partisan of the eternal justice and natural law given by God to men than of the holy mysteries of Christianity. If he was mistaken in believing that God is the father of all men and if he was unfortunate enough not to see that God can only love Christians submitted in their hearts and minds, his error is at least that of a beautiful soul. And since he loved mankind, it is not for men to insult him. It is up to God to judge him. He should certainly not be placed among the atheists.

On Fréret

The illustrious and profound Fréret was Perpetual Secretary of the Academy of Belle-Lettres of Paris.[21] He had made as much progress in the eastern languages and in the murkiness of antiquity as it is possible to make. In doing justice to his immense erudition, I do not intend to excuse his heterodoxy. Not only was he persuaded with St. Irenaeus that Jesus was over fifty years old when he died on the cross, but he believed with the Targum[22] that Jesus was not born in the time of Herod, but that his birth has to be carried to the time of the small king, Janneus, son of Hircan. The Jews are the only ones who have held this singular opinion. M. Fréret endeavored to support it, claiming that our Gospels were only written more than forty years after the year in which we place the death of Jesus; that they were only written in foreign languages and in towns very far from Jerusalem, like Alexandria, Corinth, Ephesus, Antioch, Ankara, and Thessalonica: all great trading towns, filled with faith healers, disciples of John, and with Jews and Galileans divided into several sects. This is why, he says, that there were a very great number of Gospels, all different from each other: every secret hidden society wished to have its own. Fréret claims that the four Gospels that have remained in the canon were the last to be written. He believes he brings incontestable evidence: it is that the first Church Fathers very often cite phrases that can only be found in The Gospel of the Egyptians, of the Nazarenes or of St. James, and that Justin is the first to explicitly cite the accepted Gospels.

If this dangerous system were accredited, it would obviously follow that the books entitled Matthew, Mark, Luke, and John were only written toward the time of the childhood of Justin, approximately a hundred years into our

Common Era. That in itself would cause a sweeping overhaul of our religion. The Mahometans who saw their false prophet reel off pages of his Koran, and who saw them solemnly written down after his death by the caliph, Abu Bakr, will triumph over us. They will say to us, "We only have one Koran, and you have fifty Gospels. We have preciously preserved the original, and you have chosen four after a few centuries, whose dates you have never known. You built your religion piece by piece. Ours was made in one fell swoop, like the creation. You have changed a hundred times, and we have never changed."

Thank heavens we are not reduced to these baneful terms. Where would we be if what Fréret said was true? We have enough proof of the antiquity of our four Gospels: St. Irenaeus said expressly that only four were needed.

I confess that Fréret pulverized the pitiful reasoning of Abbadie. This Abbadie claimed that the first Christians died for the Gospels, and that one only dies for the truth. But this Abbadie acknowledges that the first Christians had fabricated false Gospels; therefore, according to Abbadie himself, the first Christians died for lies. Abbadie should have considered two essential points: first of all, that it is nowhere written that the first martyrs were interrogated by the magistrates about the Gospels. Secondly, that there are martyrs in all communions. But if Fréret demolishes Abbadie, he is demolished himself by the miracles our four true Gospels have performed. He denies the miracles, but we oppose a crowd of witnesses. He denies there were any witnesses, so we can only pity him.

I agree with him that we have often made use of pious frauds. I agree that it is written in the Appendix to the first Council of Nicaea that, to distinguish the canonical books from the false, they were piled pell-mell upon a table, the Holy Spirit was asked in prayer to make all the apocryphal books fall off, and off they fell, leaving only the true ones. Lastly, I admit that the Church was flooded with false legends. But, because there were lies and bad faith, does it follow that there was no truth or candor? Certainly Fréret goes too far. He tears down the building instead of repairing it. He leads the reader, like so many others, to the worship of one God without the mediation of Christ. But at least his book breathes a moderation that would almost get his errors pardoned. He preaches only indulgence and tolerance. He does not cruelly insult the Christians like Milord Bolingbroke. He does not mock them like the priest Rabelais and the priest Swift. He is a philosopher all the more dangerous because he is highly instructed, highly logical, and very modest. It must be hoped that scholars will be found who can refute him better than has been done till now.

His deadliest argument is that if God had deigned to make himself a man and Jewish, to die by heinous tortures in Palestine in order to expiate the crimes of the human race and to banish sin from the earth, there should be no more crime or sin. And yet, says he, the Christians have been monsters a hundred times more abominable than the followers of all the other religions combined. He gives as obvious proof the massacres, the breaking of bodies on the wheel, the gallows and burnings at the stake in Cevennes, with almost a hundred thousand throats cut in this province before our eyes: the massacres in the valley of Piedmont; the massacres in the Valtellina in the time of Charles Borromeo; the Anabaptists massacred and massacring in Germany; the massacres of Lutherans and Papists from the Rhine to the farthest reaches of the North; the massacres in Ireland, England, and Scotland in the time of Charles I, himself massacred; the massacres ordered by Bloody Mary and her father, Henry VIII; the St. Bartholomew's Day Massacre in France; and forty other massacres from the time of François I to the arrival of Henry IV in Paris; the massacres of the Inquisition, perhaps the most abominable because they are enshrined in law; and lately, the massacres of twelve million inhabitants of the New World, carried out crucifix in hand, without counting all the previous massacres carried out in the name of Christ since Constantine, and still without counting over twenty schisms and twenty wars of popes against popes, bishops against bishops, the poisonings, the assassinations and plundering of Popes John XI, John XII, John XVIII, Gregory VII, Boniface VIII, Alexander XI, and a few other popes who far outdid the heinous crimes of the Neros and Caligulas. Lastly he notes that this horrendous, nearly unbroken chain of religious wars for fourteen hundred years has never persisted anywhere else but among the Christians, and that no people, apart from them, has spilled a drop of blood over theological arguments.

We are forced to grant M. Fréret that all that is true. But in enumerating all the violent crimes that have erupted, he forgets the virtues that were hidden. He forgets above all that all the hellish horrors he displays so prodigiously are the abuses of the Christian religion and not its spirit. If Jesus Christ did not destroy the sin on earth, what does that prove? We could, at the most, infer along with the Jansenists, that Jesus didn't come for everyone, but for several: *pro vobis et pro multis.*[23] But, without understanding the higher mysteries, let us content ourselves with adoring them, and above all, let us not accuse this illustrious man of having been an atheist.

On Boulanger

We will have more trouble justifying M. Boulanger, Director of Civil Engineering. His *Christianisme dévoilé* (Christianity Unveiled) was not written with the method, the depth of erudition and analysis that characterizes the scholarly Fréret. Boulanger is an audacious philosopher who goes back to the roots without bothering to probe the streams. This philosopher is as gloomy as he is fearless. The horrors with which so many Christian churches have sullied themselves since their origins, the cowardly barbarity of magistrates who have sacrificed so many honest citizens to the priests; princes, who, in order to please them, became odious persecutors; all the madness of the ecclesiastic quarrels, all the abominations in these quarrels, people slaughtered and ruined, the thrones of so many priests built on the cadavers of men and cemented with their blood; these horrifying religious wars with which Christianity alone has inundated the earth; this enormous chaos of absurdities and crimes stirs M. Boulanger's imagination so powerfully that in some sections of his book, he goes so far as to doubt the existence of Divine Providence. Fatal error that the burnings at the stake of the Inquisition and our religious wars would excuse, perhaps, if it were excusable, but no excuse can justify atheism. Even if all the Christians had cut each other's throats, even if they had devoured the entrails of their assassinated brothers over arguments, even if there did not remain a single Christian on earth, we would still be obliged in looking up at the sun to recognize and adore the Eternal One. He could say in his grief and sorrow: My fathers and brothers were monsters, but God is God.

On Montesquieu

The most moderate, most subtle and refined of the philosophers was the President de Montesquieu.[24] He was only amusing in his *Persian Letters*; he was astute and profound in his *Spirit of the Laws.* This work, full of excellent things, moreover, and mistakes, seems founded on natural law and on indifference toward religion. It is that, above all, that made him so many partisans and enemies. But the enemies, this time, were vanquished by the philosophers. A cry long maintained was heard on all sides. The progress of theism, which had been taking deep roots for some time, was seen exposed at last. The Sorbonne wanted to censure the *Spirit of the Laws*, but it sensed it would find itself censured by the public and kept silent. There were only a few wretched obscure writers, like the Abbé Guyon and a Jesuit who hurled insults at the Président de Montesquieu, and they became even more obscure because of it, despite the celebrity of the man they were attacking. They would have rendered better service to our religion had they fought back with reasons, but they were bad advocates of a good cause.

On La Mettrie

Since then, there has been a deluge of writings against Christianity. Doctor La Mettrie, the best commentator on Boerhaave, abandoned the medicine of the human body to provide, as he put it, medicine for the soul. But his *Homme machine* (Man the Machine) showed the theologians he was only distributing poison. He was Court Reader to the King of Prussia[25] and a member of his Academy in Berlin. The monarch, satisfied with his morals and his services, did not deign to wonder whether La Mettrie had erroneous opinions in theology. He thought only of the physician, of the academician and, in this quality, La Mettrie received the honor of having this philosophical hero write his funeral oration. This oration was read in the Academy by a secretary at his orders. A king governed by a Jesuit might have proscribed La Mettrie and his memory. A king governed only by reason disassociated the philosopher from the unbeliever and protected and praised his merit, leaving it up to God to punish the impiety.

On the Priest Meslier

The parish priest Meslier is the most singular phenomenon that's been seen among the all these meteors fatal to the Christian religion. He was the priest of the village of Etrepigny in Champagne, near Rocroi, and also served a little annex parish named But. His father was a worker in the serge manufactory of the village of Mazerny, a dependency of the Duchy of Rethel-Mazarin. This man of irreproachable morals, and diligent in all his duties, gave what remained of his revenue every year to the parish poor. He died in 1733 at the age of thirty-five. People were startled to find three big manuscripts of three hundred and sixty-six pages each in his home, entitled *My Testament*, all three written in his handwriting and signed by his hand. On a gray paper that enveloped one of the three copies, he had written these remarkable words to his parishioners:

> I have seen and recognized the errors, the abuses, the vanities, the follies and the wickedness of men. I hate and detest them. I did not dare to say it during my life, but at least I will say it at my death, and it is so that it will be known that I write this present memoir, so that it might serve as testimony to the truth for all those who see it, and who read it if they wish.

The body of the work is a naive and crude refutation of every one of our dogmas, without a sole exception. The style is rather off-putting, as would be expected from a village priest. He had no other help in composing this strange work against the Bible and the Church than the Bible itself and a few church fathers. Of the three copies, one was retained by the Vicar-General of Reims, another was sent to the Keeper of the Seals, Monsieur Chauvelin, and the third remained with the local court clerk. The Count of Caylus had one of the copies in his hands for a time, and soon afterward there were over three hundred copies in Paris being sold for ten louis each. Several inquisitive people still conserve this sad and dangerous memorial. A priest who indicts himself, on his deathbed, of the crime of having professed and taught the Christian religion made a bigger impression on all minds than Pascal's *Pensées* (Thoughts).

It seems to me we should rather reflect on the tortured mind of this melancholic priest who wished to deliver his parishioners from the yoke of a religion he had preached to them for twenty years himself. Why address this testament to rustic men who couldn't read? And if they could read, why remove a salutary yoke, a necessary fear that can alone prevent secret crimes? Belief in rewards and punishments after death is a curb the populace needs. A purified religion would be the chief bond of society.

This priest wanted to annihilate all religion, even the natural sort. If his book had been well done, the nature of the author's position would have imposed on its reader too much. Several abridgements were made, and a few were published.[26] They were thankfully purged of the poison of atheism.

What is even more surprising is that, during the same period, there was a priest from Bonne-Nouvelle, near Paris, who dared to write, during his lifetime, against the religion he was charged with teaching. He was quietly exiled by the government. His manuscript is of an extreme rarity.

Long before this time, Lavardin, Bishop of Mans, had given an example not less singular in his dying moments. Actually, he did not leave a testament against the religion that had provided him with a bishop's palace, but he declared that he detested it. He refused the sacraments of the church and swore that he had never consecrated the bread and wine in saying Mass, nor had any intention of baptizing children and bestowing orders when he had baptized Christians and ordained deacons and priests. This bishop gave himself the malignant pleasure of embarrassing all those who had received the sacraments of the church from him. He died laughing at the qualms they would have and enjoyed their dismay. It was decided that no one would be rebaptized nor reordained, but a few scrupulous priests had themselves ordained a second time. At least Bishop Lavardin left no memorials against the Christian religion behind him. He was a voluptuary who laughed at everything; but the priest Meslier was a somber impassioned man, of rigid virtue, it is true, but more dangerous thanks to this same virtue.

LETTER VIII

On the *Encyclopedia*

Milord,

Your Highness asks for some details on the *Encyclopedia*. I obey your orders. This immense project was conceived by Messieurs Diderot and d'Alembert, two philosophers who do honor to France. One was distinguished by the generosities of the Empress of Russia, and the other by the refusal of a dazzling fortune offered by this empress but which his very philosophy did not permit him to accept. Monsieur le Chevalier de Jaucourt, of an old aristocratic family he makes illustrious by his vast knowledge and by his virtues, joined these two learned men and distinguished himself by his indefatigable toil.

They were helped by Monsieur le Conte d'Hérouville, Lieutenant-General of the King's Army, profoundly instructed in all the arts pertaining to your great art of war; by the Count de Tressan, Lieutenant-General as well, whose various merits are recognized by all; by Monsieur de Saint-Lambert, a former officer who, in writing better verses than Chapelle, has no less increased our knowledge regarding weaponry. Several other general officers have written excellent accounts on tactics.

Skillful engineers have enriched this dictionary with everything that concerns the attack and defense of strongholds. Presidents and councilors of *parlements* have furnished several articles on jurisprudence. In short, there is not a science, art or profession whose greatest masters have not enriched this dictionary to our heart's desire. This is the first time on earth, and perhaps the last, that a throng of superior men hastened to create an immortal storehouse of human knowledge without self-interest or any particular goal, not even that of glory (since a few of them worked anonymously).

This great task was undertaken under the auspices and before the eyes of Count d'Argenson, a Minister of State capable of understanding it and worthy of protecting it. The entranceway to this great edifice was a preliminary discourse composed by M. d'Alembert. I dare to boldly state that this discourse, applauded by all Europe, was superior to Descartes' method and equal to all the best that the illustrious Chancellor Bacon had written. If there are frivolous articles within the course of the work, and others that smack of declamation rather than philosophy, this fault is more than made up for by the prodigious quantity of profound and useful articles. The editors were unable to refuse a few young contributors who wanted to see their essays in this collection beside the chefs-d'oeuvres of the masters. The great work was allowed to be marred by politeness. It is the salon of Apollo where a few mediocre painters mingled their pictures among the Van Loos and the Lemoines. But Your Highness certainly perceived in glancing through the *Encyclopedia* that it is precisely the contrary of other collections; that is to say, that the good far outweighs the bad.

No doubt you sense that in a town like Paris, more full of literary people than Athens or Rome ever were, those who were not admitted to this important enterprise inveighed against it. The Jesuits began to. They wanted to write the articles on theology and were refused. Nothing more was needed to accuse the *encyclopédistes* of irreligion. It's the usual course. The Jansenists, seeing their rivals sound the alarm, no longer kept quiet. They had to show more zeal than those they had so often accused of easy morals.

If the Jesuits shouted impiety, the Jansenists screamed it. There was a convulsionary or convulsionist named Abraham Chaumeix who presented the magistrates with a formal accusation entitled *Legitimate Prejudices Against the Encyclopedia*, whose first volume had just come out. It was a strange assemblage of the words prejudice, which properly means illusion, and legitimate, which only suits something which is reasonable. He pushed his very illegitimate prejudices to the point of saying that if the venom did not appear in the first volume, it would doubtlessly be perceived in the following volumes. He made the *Encyclopedia* contributors guilty, not of what they had said, but of what they would say.

As witnesses are needed in a criminal trial, he produced St. Augustine and Cicero. And these witnesses were all the more irreproachable in that Abraham Chaumeix could be not convicted of having had the slightest dealings with them. The cries of a few fanatics, joined to those of this madman, incited a fairly long persecution. But what happened? The same thing that happened to sane philosophy, emetics, the circulation of blood, and to inoculation: all of that was outlawed for a time, then triumphed at last over ignorance, humbug, and envy. The *Dictionnaire encyclopédique*, despite its faults, survived, and Abraham Chaumeix went to hide his shame in Moscow. They say that the Empress forced him to behave. It is one of the prodigies of her reign.

LETTER IX

On the Jews

Of all those who have attacked the Christian religion in their writings, the Jews would perhaps be the most to be feared and, if we did not confute them with the miracles of Our Lord Jesus Christ, it would be very difficult for a mediocre scholar to stand up to them. They consider themselves the eldest sons of the house who, in losing their inheritance, have retained their titles. They have employed a profound sagacity in explaining all the prophecies to their advantage. They claim that the Law of Moses given to them was meant to be eternal, that it is impossible for God to have changed or to have perjured himself, and that our Savior acknowledged as much himself. They object to us that, according to Jesus Christ, no point, no iota of the law should be transgressed, that Jesus came to fulfill the law, not to abolish it,[27] that he observed all the command-ments, that he was circumcised, that he kept the Sabbath, that he celebrated all the holidays, that he was born a Jew, lived as a Jew and died a Jew, that he never instituted a new religion, that we do not have a single line written by him, that the Christian religion was created by us, not him.

A Christian had best not attempt to argue with a Jew unless he knows the Hebrew language like his mother tongue, which alone can enable him to under-stand the prophecies and reply to the rabbis. Here is how Joseph Scaliger puts it in his *Excerpta*: "The Jews are subtle. How pathetic are Justin's writings against Tryphon! And Tertullian even worse! He who wants to refute the Jews must know Judaism thoroughly. The shame of it! Christians write against Christians, and dare not write against the Jews!"

The *Toledot Jeschu* is the oldest Jewish writing against our religion that has come down to us. It is a life of Jesus in total contradiction with our holy Gospels. It seems to date from the first century, written even before the Gospels because the author does not mention them and he would probably have tried to refute them if he had known of them. He portrays Jesus as born of the adultery between Miriah or Mariah and a Roman soldier named Joseph Panther. He says that he [Jesus] and Judas both wanted to become the head of a sect, and that both seemed to perform miracles by invoking the name of Jehovah, which they learned to pronounce in the way required to cast magic spells. It is a mishmash of rabbinical reveries that far outdo the *1001 Arabian Nights*. Origen refuted it, and he was the only one who could, because he was almost the only Greek Father well-versed in the Hebrew language.

The Jewish theologians didn't write much more reasonably than that until the eleventh century when, enlightened by the Arabs who had by then become the only learned nation, they used sounder judgment in their works. Those of Rabbi Ibn Ezra were highly esteemed. He was the founder of reason among the Jews, as far as we can call it that in disputes of this type. Spinoza used his works extensively.

Long after Ibn Ezra came Maimonides in the thirteenth century. He achieved even greater renown. From that time until the sixteenth century, the Jews had books that were intelligible, and consequently, dangerous. They printed a few as early as the end of the fifteenth century. The number of their manuscripts was considerable. The Christian theologians feared their appeal. They had all the Jewish books they could get their hands on burnt; but they could neither find all the books, nor convert a single man of this religion. It is true that a few Jews pretended to abjure at times, sometimes out of avarice, sometimes out of terror, but none ever embraced Christianity sincerely. A Carthaginian would have sided with Rome sooner than a Jew would have made himself a Christian. Orobio speaks of several Spanish and Arab rabbis who abjured and became bishops in Spain, but he takes good care not to say that they had renounced their religion in good faith.

The Jews have not written against Mohammedanism. They do not hold it in anywhere near the same horror as they do our doctrine. The reason is evident: the Muslims do not make a God of Jesus Christ.

By an ill-fate that cannot be sufficiently deplored, several learned Christians left their religion for Judaism. Rittangel, Professor of Eastern Languages at Konigsberg in the seventeenth century, embraced Mosaic Law. Antoine, Minister in Geneva, was burned for having abjured Christianity in favor of Judaism in 1632. The Jews count him among the martyrs who do them the most honor. His unfortunate persuasion must have been very strong to have preferred suffering the most horrid agonies to retracting.

We read in the *Nizzachon Vetus,* meaning the book of the ancient victory, some lines concerning the superiority of the Mosaic Law over the Christian law and the Persian that is very much in the Middle Eastern taste. A king orders a Jew, a Galilean, and a Muslim to leave their own religion, and he gives them the liberty of choosing one of the two other faiths; but if they don't change, the executioner is there to chop their heads off. The Christian says, "Since I have to change or die, I would rather be of the religion of Moses than that of Mahomet, because the Christians are more ancient than the Muslims, and the Jews are more ancient than Jesus. I shall therefore become a Jew." The Muslim says, "I cannot make myself a Christian dog. I would rather make myself a Jewish dog, because the Jews were the first born." "Sire," says the Jew, "Your Majesty can see that I cannot embrace the Christian law or the Muslim because they have both given preference to mine." The king, moved by this reason, sends the executioner away and becomes a Jew. All that can be deduced from this yarn is that princes should not have executioners for apostles.

Nevertheless, the Jews had strict and scrupulous doctors who feared that their compatriots might be vanquished by the Christians. There was, among others, a rabbi named Beccai who had this to say: "The rabbis forbid lending money to a Christian, for fear that the lender might be corrupted by the debtor. But a Jew can borrow from a Christian without fear of being won over by him, because a debtor always avoids his creditor."

Despite this fine piece of advice, the Jews have always lent to Christians at usurious rates, without being any the more converted by it.

After the famous *Nizzachon Vetus*, we have the account of a dispute between Rabbi Zechiel and the Dominican brother Paul, called Cyriac. It was in a meeting between these learned men in 1263, held in the presence of Don James, King of Aragon, and his wife, the queen.[28] This conference was highly memorable. Both athletes were learned in Hebrew and in antiquity. The Talmud, the Targum, and the archives of the Sanhedrin were on the table. The contested passages were explained in Spanish. Zechiel maintained that Jesus was condemned under the reign of King Alexander Janneus, and not under that of Herod the Tetrarch in accordance with what is written in the *Toledot Jeschu* and in the Talmud. Your Gospels, says he, were not written until the beginning of your second century, and are not authentic like our Talmud. We could not have crucified the one you speak of in the time of Herod the Tetrarch because we did not then have the right to condemn to death. We could not have crucified him since that form of execution was not practiced by us. Our Talmud relates that those condemned in the time of Janneus were stoned to death. We can no more believe your Gospels than the alleged letters of Pilate that you forged. It was easy to topple this vain rabbinical erudition. The queen ended the dispute by asking the Jews why they stank.

This same Zechiel had several other conferences, of which one of his disciples gives an account. Each side attributed the victory to itself, even though victory can only be on the side of the truth.

The Rampart of Faith, written by a Jew named Isaac and found in Africa, is much better than the relation of Zechiel which is very confused and full of puerilities. Isaac is methodical and a very good dialectician: error was perhaps never supported by better arguments. He gathered into a hundred propositions all the difficulties that the incredulous have spread ever since.

> It is there that we see the objections to the two genealogies of Jesus Christ, which are so different from each other;
>
> Objections to citations of the passages of the prophets, which are not in the Jewish books;
>
> Objections to the divinity of Jesus Christ, which is not expressly asserted in the Gospels, but which is nonetheless proven by the sacred councils;
>
> Objections to the opinion that Jesus had no brothers or sisters:
>
> Objections to the differing accounts of the gospel writers, which have nonetheless been reconciled;
>
> Objections to the story of Lazarus;
>
> Objections to the purported falsifications of the ancient books in the canon.

In short, the most determined unbelievers have hardly alleged anything that is not in this *Rampart of the Faith* of Rabbi Isaac. We cannot make it a crime for Jews to have tried to defend their ancient religion at the expense of our own. We can only pity them. But what reproaches should we not address to those who have taken advantage of these disputes between the Christians and the Jews to combat both religions! Let us pity those who, alarmed by seventeen centuries of contradictions and weary of so many disputes, have rushed headlong into theism, not wanting to accept anything but one God and pure morals. They may have preserved charity, but they have abandoned the faith. They wanted to be men instead of Christians. They should be submissive, and they only aspired to be wise! But as the apostle Paul says, how superior the foolishness of the cross is to this wisdom![29]

On Orobio

Orobio was a rabbi[30] so well-read he didn't fall into any of the delusions with which so many other rabbis have been reproached: profound without being obscure, well-versed in literature, a pleasant man of extreme good manners. Philippe [van] Limborch, theologian of the Arminian sect in Amsterdam, became acquainted with him in about 1685. They debated a long time together, but without bitterness, like two friends who want to enlighten themselves. Conversations rarely clarify the subjects treated. It is difficult to stay on subject and not stray. One question leads to another. A quarter of an hour later, we are amazed to find ourselves off track. They decided to write down their objections and responses, which they both had printed in 1687. It is perhaps the first dispute between two theologians in which they did not insult each other. On the contrary, both adversaries treat each other with respect.

Limborch refutes the opinions of the very learned and illustrious Jew, who refutes with the same polite phrases the very learned and illustrious Christian. Orobio never speaks even of Jesus Christ without the greatest circumspection. Here is a brief synopsis of the dispute:

> Orobio maintains first that the Jews were never ordered by their law to believe in a Messiah;
>
> That there is not a single passage in the Old Testament that makes the salvation of Israel depend on faith in a Messiah;
>
> That it is nowhere to be found that Israel is threatened with no longer being the chosen people if it does not believe in a future Messiah;
>
> That it is nowhere said that Judaic Law foreshadows and anticipates another law; that on the contrary, it says everywhere that the Law of Moses must be eternal;
>
> That any prophet, even one who performs miracles to change something in the Mosaic Law, must be put to death;[31]
>
> That in truth, a few prophets predicted to the Jews in the midst of their calamities that they would have a liberator one day, but that this liberator would be a supporter of the Mosaic Law, not its destroyer;
>
> That the Jews are still awaiting a Messiah, who will be a just and powerful king;
>
> That a proof of the eternal unchangeability of the Mosaic religion is that the Jews, dispersed all over the earth, have nevertheless never changed a single comma of their law, and that the Israelis of Rome, of England, of Holland, of Germany, of Poland, of Turkey, of Persia have consistently retained the same doctrine since the taking of Jerusalem by

Titus, without there ever being raised among them the slightest little sect that deviates from a single observance and a single opinion of the Israeli nation;

That, on the contrary, the Christians have been divided among themselves ever since the birth of their religion;

That they are still divided into many more sects than they have states, and that they have pursued each other with fire and bloodshed for more than twelve whole centuries; that if the apostle Paul found it good that the Jews should continue to observe all the precepts of their law,[32] today's Christians should not reproach them with doing what the apostle Paul permitted.

That it is not at all through hatred and malice that Israel did not accept Jesus; that it is not because of base and carnal views that the Jews are attached to their ancient law; that on the contrary, it is only in the hope of celestial rewards that they are faithful, despite the persecutions of the Babylonians, the Syrians, the Romans, despite their dispersion and their opprobrium, despite the hatred of so many nations; and that one should not call an entire people carnal who has been the martyr of God for almost forty centuries;

That it is the Christians who expected carnal goods, as witness almost all the first Fathers of the Church, who hoped to live a thousand years in a New Jerusalem amidst abundance and all the delights of the body;

That it is impossible for the Jews to have crucified the real Messiah, since the prophets say expressly that the Messiah will purge Israel of all sin, that he will not leave a single stain in Israel; that it would be the most horrible sin and the most abominable defilement, as well as the most palpable contradiction, that God would send his son to be crucified;

That the precepts of the Decalogue were perfect. Any new mission would be entirely useless;

That the Mosaic Law never had any mystical meaning;

That it would be deceiving men to tell them that things should be understood differently from the way in which they are stated;

That the Christian apostles never equaled the miracles of Moses;

That the gospel writers and the apostles were not simple men, since Luke was a doctor and Paul had studied under Gamaliel, whose writings the Jews have preserved;

That there was no simplicity or idiocy in having all their neophytes' money brought to them; that Paul, far from being a simple man, employed the greatest artifice in coming to sacrifice at the temple and in swearing to Festus Agrippa that he had done nothing against circumcision or the Jewish law;

And that, finally, all the contradictions found in the Gospels prove that these books could not have been inspired by God.

Limborch responded to all these assertions by the strongest arguments that can be used. He had so much faith in the goodness of his cause that he did not hesitate to print this famous dispute; but since he was a follower of Arminius, the Gomarists[33] persecuted him. He was reproached for having bared the truths of the Christian religion in a battle in which its enemies could triumph. Orobio was not persecuted in his synagogue.

On Uriel Da Costa

What happened to Uriel Da Costa in Amsterdam is pretty much the same thing that happened to Spinoza: he abandoned Judaism for philosophy. A Spaniard and an Englishman applied to him to become Jewish. He talked them out of it, and spoke against the religion of the Hebrews. He was condemned to receive thirty-nine lashings on the spinal column and to prostrate himself at the doorstep. All those present walked across his body.

He published this adventure in a little book we still have and it is there that he professes to be neither Jewish, Christian, nor Muslim, but a worshipper of one God. His little book is entitled *Exemplar Humanae Vitae* (Example of a Human Life). The same Limborch refuted Uriel Da Costa as he had Orobio, and the magistrate of Amsterdam did not get mixed up in these quarrels in any fashion.

LETTER X

On Spinoza

Milord,

It seems to me that the character of Spinoza has often been as poorly judged as have his works. Here is what is said of him in two historical dictionaries:

> Spinoza had such a strong desire to earn immortality that he would have gladly sacrificed his life for this glory, even had it meant being torn to shreds by a mutinous people. . . . The absurdities of Spinozism have been perfectly refuted . . . by Jean Bredembourg, a bourgeois of Rotterdam.

So many words, so many falsehoods. Spinoza was precisely the contrary of this depiction of him. His atheism should be detested, but his character should not be lied about. Never was a man more distant from vainglory in every sense, it must be admitted. Let us not slander him in condemning him. The minister Colerus who lived for a long time in the very room where Spinoza died, avowed, with all his contemporaries, that Spinoza always lived in deep retreat, shirking the world, a foe to all superfluity, humble in conversation, neglectful of his clothing, living off manual labor and never putting his name on any of his books. This is not the character of a man who thirsts for glory.

As to Bredembourg, far from refuting him perfectly, I dare think he refuted him perfectly badly. I have read this book and leave the judgment of it to whoever finds the patience to read it as I did. Bredembourg was so far from confounding Spinoza clearly, that he himself, affrighted by the weakness of his arguments, became despite himself the disciple of the man he had attacked: a fine example of the poverty and inconsistency of the human mind.

The life of Spinoza has been written in enough detail and is well enough known for me to add nothing to it here. May Your Highness permit me only to reflect with him on the manner in which this Jew, still young, was treated by the synagogue. Accused by two young people his age of not believing in Moses, the first attempt to set him on the right path was to stab him upon leaving the theater. Some say it was upon leaving the synagogue, which is more likely.

After having failed to kill his body, they did not want to miss his soul. He was conducted to the great excommunication, the great anathema, a writ of *cherem*. Spinoza claimed the Jews had no right to exercise this sort of jurisdiction in Amsterdam. The town council sent the decision to a consistory of pastors. It concluded that if the synagogue had this right, the consistory had it even more so: the consistory decided in favor of the synagogue.

Spinoza was therefore outlawed by the Jews with great ceremony. The Jewish cantor intoned the words of execration. A horn was blown and black candles were melted drop by drop into a basin full of blood. Baruch Spinoza was committed to Beelzebub, to Satan, and to Astaroth, and the entire synagogue cried, "Amen!"

It is strange that such an act of jurisdiction, which more resembled a witches' Sabbath than an honorable judgment, was permitted. It is possible that, without the stabbing attempt and the black candles extinguished in blood, Spinoza might never have written against Moses or God. Persecution chafes. It emboldens anyone who feels any genius. A person whom indulgence might have restrained becomes irreconcilable.

Spinoza renounced Judaism, but without ever becoming Christian. He did not publish his *Treatise on Superstitious Ceremonies*, otherwise known as the *Tractatus Theologico-Politicus* (Theologico-Political Treatise) till 1670, about eight years after his excommunication. People claimed to find the seeds of his atheism in this book, for the same reason the face of a man who has done something wicked is always found to be unattractive. This book is so far removed from atheism that he often speaks of Jesus Christ in it as a messenger from God. The book is very profound and the best one that he wrote. I condemn the sentiments, no doubt, but I cannot prevent myself from admiring the erudition. It is he, I believe, who first remarked that the Hebrew word *ru'ag*, which we translate as soul, meant the wind or breath to the Jews, in its natural sense, and that everything grand was called divine: the cedars of God, the winds of God, the melancholy of Saul a bad spirit of God, and virtuous men children of God.

It is he who first developed the dangerous theory of Ibn Ezra; that the Pentateuch was not written by Moses, nor was Joshua written by Joshua. It was only after him that [Jean] Leclerc,[34] several theologians of Holland, and the famous Newton adopted this opinion.

Newton differs from him only in attributing the books of Moses to Samuel, whereas Spinoza makes Ezra the author. All the reasons for his opinions can be found in chapters VIII, IX, and X. There is a great deal of exactitude in his chronology, thorough knowledge of the history, language and customs of his former homeland, and more method and reasoning than in all the rabbis put together. It seems to me that few writers before him had proven clearly that the Jews acknowledged the prophets of the Gentiles. In a word, he used his insights in a blamable way, but his insights were very great.

You have to hunt for atheism in the old philosophers. It can only be found unconcealed in the posthumous works of Spinoza. His treatise on atheism, not being under this title, and being written in an obscure Latin in a very dry style, the Count de Boulainvilliers shortened it in French under the title, *Réfutation de Spinoza*. We only have the poison; Boulainvilliers apparently did not have the time to administer the antidote.

Few have noticed that Spinoza, in his deadly book, always speaks of an infinite, Supreme Being: he announces God in wishing to destroy him. The arguments with which Bayle overwhelms him seem to me beyond reply, if indeed Spinoza admitted the existence of God, for if this God was only the immensity of everything, if this God was at once both matter and thought, it is absurd, as Bayle proved all too well, to suppose that God is both the agent and the patient, the cause and subject, creating evil and suffering from it, loving and hating himself, killing himself and eating himself. A healthy spirit, Bayle adds, would prefer to cultivate the earth with his teeth and nails than to develop a hypothesis as shocking and absurd as that, because, according to Spinoza, those who say, "The Germans killed ten thousand Turks," express themselves badly and falsely. They should say, "God, modified into ten thousand Germans, killed God, modified into ten thousand Turks."

Bayle is very much in the right, if Spinoza acknowledged God; but the fact is that he did not acknowledge one at all, and that he only used this sacred word to avoid overly shocking mankind.

Fixated on Descartes, he also abused this equally famous and senseless phrase of Descartes: Give me movement and matter, and I will create a world.

Fixated as well on the incomprehensible anti-physical notion that everything has substance, he imagined that there could only exist a single substance, a single power that reasons in men, that feels and remembers in animals, that sparks in fire, that runs in the rivers, that rolls in the winds, that rumbles in the thunder, that vegetates on earth, and that is spread throughout all space.

According to him, everything is necessary, eternal; creation is impossible. There is no design in the structure of the universe, in the permanence of species. or in the succession of individuals. Ears are no longer made to hear, eyes to see, the heart to receive and expel blood, the stomach to digest, the brain to think, the regenerative organs to give life. The divine designs are only the effects of a blind necessity.

That, in short, is the system of Spinoza. And that, I believe, is the side on which his citadel should be attacked: a citadel built, if I am not mistaken, upon ignorance of physics and upon a most monstrous misuse of metaphysics.

It seems, and we may flatter ourselves, that there are few atheists today. The author of the *Henriade*[35] said, "A catechist announces God to children, and Newton demonstrates him to the wise." The more we study nature, the more we worship its maker.

Atheism can do no good for morals, and can do them great harm. It is almost as dangerous as fanaticism. You, Milord, are as distant from one as from the other, and this is what justifies the liberty I have taken in putting the truth before your eyes undisguised. I have answered all your questions, regarding everyone from the learned buffoon, Rabelais, to the bold metaphysician, Spinoza.

I could have added to this list masses of little books that are hardly known to anyone but librarians, but I feared that by multiplying the number of the guilty, I might diminish the iniquity. I hope that the little I have said will strengthen Your Highness' feelings for our dogmas and for our Scriptures when he sees that they have only been combatted by stubborn stoics, by scholars inflated with their learning, by worldly people who only know their vain reason, by jesters who mistake their quips for arguments, and at last by theologians who, instead of walking in the ways of God, strayed upon their own paths.

Once again, what should console a soul as noble as yours is that theism, which loses so many souls today, cannot disturb either the tranquility of states or the pleasures of society. Controversies have spilled blood everywhere, and theism stanched the flow. It is a bad remedy, I admit, but it has cured the most grievous wounds. It is excellent for this life, even if it is detestable for the next. It surely damns its adherent, but it makes him peaceful.

Your country was formerly in flames over arguments. Theism brought concord. It is clear that if Poltrot, Jacques Clément, Jaurigny, Balthasar Gérard, Jean Chastel, Damiens, the Jesuit Malagrida, etc., etc., etc., had been theists,[36] there would have been fewer princes assassinated.

God forbid that I should prefer theism to the holy religion of the Ravaillacs, the Damiens, and the Malagridas, whose goodness they failed to understand and outraged! I am only saying that it is more agreeable to live with theists than with Ravaillacs and Brinvilliers who go to the confessional; and if Your Highness disagrees with me, then I am mistaken.

DINNER AT
COUNT DE BOULAINVILLIERS'

1767

Voltaire attributed this piece to Saint-Hyacinthe, a deceased writer and journalist who had criticized his epic poem, *La Henriade*. The people portrayed at this dinner were all well-known bygone personages he had known in his twenties. Count de Boulainvilliers (1658–1722) wrote on feudalism, on Mahomet, and is mentioned in *Letters . . . on Rabelais . . .*, as is his erudite friend, Fréret (1688–1749).[1] This *Dinner* was a huge success. The single copy that first appeared was passed around with startling rapidity, its sixty-page brochure copied out by hand by many, according to Grimm. Every anti-religious pamphlet out was now being attributed to Voltaire, and the *Parlementarian* Pasquier, who had just had the young Chevalier de La Barre beheaded and burned alongside Voltaire's *Philosophical Dictionary*, was threatening his arrest, even though Voltaire was outside his jurisdiction. Fearing the local authorities might be persuaded, Voltaire implored Grimm and others to stop attributing these texts to him. The entreaties were largely ignored, but so were the threats, since the "infernal factory at Ferney" continued churning out pamphlets.

FIRST CONVERSATION

Before dinner

ABBÉ COUET

What! Count de Boulainvilliers, you believe that philosophy is as useful to the human race as the Roman Catholic Apostolic religion?

COUNT DE BOULAINVILLIERS

Philosophy's empire is spread throughout the world, and your church only dominates a small part of Europe. And, even there, it has many enemies. But you should admit that philosophy is a thousand times more wholesome than your religion as it has long been practiced.

THE ABBÉ

You astonish me. What on earth then do you mean by philosophy?

THE COUNT

I mean love enlightened by wisdom, sustained by love of the Eternal Being, rewarder of virtue and avenger of crime.

THE ABBÉ

Well! Is that not what our religion teaches?

THE COUNT

If that is what you teach, then we are in agreement: I am a good Catholic, and you're a good philosopher. Let neither of us take it further then. Let us not dishonor our religious and holy philosophy with either sophisms or absurdities that outrage reason, or with unbridled greed for honors and for riches that corrupt every virtue. Let us only listen to the moderation and the truths of philosophy. Then philosophy will adopt religion as its daughter.

THE ABBÉ

With your permission, Sir, this kind of talk lights stakes.

THE COUNT

As long as you continue to talk of stakes and use them to burn people alive instead of using reasons, you will have only hypocrites and imbeciles for followers. The opinion of a single wise man undoubtedly prevails over the prestige of rogues and the enslavement of a thousand idiots. You asked me what I understood by philosophy. Now I ask what you understand by religion.

THE ABBÉ

I would need a good deal of time to explain all our dogmas to you.

THE COUNT

That is already one big bias against you. You need thick books, I only need four words: Serve God, be just.

THE ABBÉ

Our religion has never said the contrary.

THE COUNT

I would like to never find the contrary in your books. These cruel words: "Force them to enter," which have been abused with so much barbarity, or these: "I have come to bring the sword, not peace," or these: "Let he who does not listen to the Church be viewed as a pagan, or as a tax collector," and a hundred similar maxims that frighten common sense and humanity.

Is there anything harsher and more odious than these words? "I speak to them in parables, so that in seeing, they will not see, and in listening, they will not hear"?[2] Is that the way one explains wisdom and eternal goodness?

The God of all the universe, who became a man to enlighten and to save all men, could he have said, "I have only been sent for the children of Israel,"[3] which is to say, for a tiny country thirty leagues in size at most?

Is it possible that this God, who was made to pay the per capita tax, told his disciples that they should pay nothing, that kings "only receive taxes from foreigners, and that his children are exempt?"[4]

THE ABBÉ

Those lines, which shock everyone, are explained by other passages.

THE COUNT

Good heavens! What kind of God has need of a commentary, and is perpetually made to say everything and its contrary? What kind of legislator has never written anything? What are four divine books whose date is unknown and whose authors, no better known, contradict each other on each page?

THE ABBÉ

All that can be reconciled, I tell you. But you will at least admit that you are very pleased with the Sermon on the Mount.

THE COUNT

Yes. They claim that Jesus said those who call their brother Raca will be burned,[5] as your theologians do every day. He says that he came to accomplish the Law of Moses, which you loathe. He asks with what we will salt if the salt fades. He says, "Happy are the poor in spirit for theirs is the kingdom of heaven." I know too that they have him say that wheat rots and dies in the earth to germinate, that the kingdom of heaven is a mustard seed or that it is money lent at usurious rates, or that one must not give dinner to ones parents if they are rich. Perhaps these expressions had some respectable meaning in their original language. I adopt all those that can inspire virtue, but have the goodness to tell me what you think of another passage, which is this one:

> It is God who made me. God is everywhere, and in me. Will I dare soil him with lowly and criminal actions, with impure words, with vile desires?
>
> May I, at my last moments, say to God, Oh master! Oh father! You wanted me to suffer and I have suffered with resignation. You wanted me poor, and I embraced my poverty. You put me in servility, and I did not wish for grandeur. You wanted me to die, and I die adoring you. I leave this magnificent spectacle giving you thanks for admitting me and for having let me contemplate the splendid order with which you rule the universe."

THE ABBÉ

That is sublime. In which Church Father did you find this divine piece? In the writings of St. Cyprian? In St. Gregory of Nanzianzus, or in St. Cyril?

THE COUNT

No, they are the words of a pagan slave, named Epictetus, and the Emperor Marcus Aurelius never thought any differently than this slave.

THE ABBÉ

Yes, I remember having read in my youth moral precepts from the pagan authors that made a great impression on me. I will even admit to you that the laws of Zaleucus, of Charondas, the guidelines of Confucius, the moral commandments of Zoroaster, and the maxims of Pythagoras seemed dictated by wisdom for the happiness of the human race to me. It seemed to me that God had deigned honor these great men with a purer light than ordinary men, just as he gave greater harmony to Virgil, greater eloquence to Cicero, and greater wisdom to Archimedes than to their contemporaries. I was struck by these great lessons in virtue that antiquity had left us. However, none of those people knew theology. They did not know the difference between a cherub and a seraph, between efficient grace, which one cannot resist, and sufficient grace, which does not suffice. They did not know that God was dead, and that having been crucified for all, he had nevertheless only been crucified for some. Ah, Count! If the Scipios, the Ciceros, the Catos, the Epictetuses, the Antonines had known that "the Father engendered the Son, and did not make him, that the Spirit was neither engendered nor made, but proceeds by spiration sometimes from the Father and sometimes from the Son and that the Son has everything the Father does except paternity," if the ancients, our masters in everything, I say, could have known a hundred truths of this force and clarity, in short, if they had been theologians, what advantages would they not have brought to men! Consubstantiality, above all, Count, transubstantiation, are such beautiful things! If only Scipio, Cicero, and Marcus Aurelius had examined these truths! They could have been great vicars for the archbishop, or receivers at the Sorbonne.

THE COUNT

Tell me in all conscience, between us and before God, if you think the souls of these great men are on spits, being eternally roasted by devils until they have regained their bodies, which will then be eternally roasted with them, and all that for not having been receivers at the Sorbonne or great vicars for the archbishop?

THE ABBÉ

You embarrass me a great deal, because "Outside the Church, no salvation."

None shall please heaven but us and our friends.[6]

"Whoever hears not the Church, let him be to you like a pagan or tax collector."[7] Scipio and Marcus Aurelius did not hear the Church. They were not received at the Council of Trent. Their spiritual souls will be roasted forever, and when their bodies, dispersed to the four elements, are found, they will also be roasted forever with their souls. Nothing is clearer, or more just. That much is positive.

On the other hand, it's very hard to burn for eternity Socrates, Aristides, Pythagoras, Epictetus, the Antonines, and all those who led such pure and exemplary lives, while according eternal bliss to the soul and body of François Ravaillac, who died a good Christian, his confession heard, and armed with efficient or sufficient grace. I'm a little perplexed in this matter, because, after all, I am a judge of all men. Their eternal happiness or misery depends on me, and I do have some repugnance to save Ravaillac and damn Scipio.

There is one thing that consoles me, and that is that we theologians can pull anyone out of hell we want to. We read in the Acts of St. Thecla, a great theologian and disciple of St. Paul (she disguised herself as a man to follow him) that she delivered her friend Faconilla from hell, who had had the misfortune of dying a pagan.

The great saint, John of Damascus, reports that the great saint Macarius, the one who obtained the death of Arius from God by his ardent prayers, interrogated the skull of a pagan about his salvation one day in a cemetery. The skull told him that the prayers of theologians gave infinite relief to the damned.

Moreover we know from exact science that the great pope St. Gregory pulled from hell the soul of Emperor Trajan. Those are fine examples of the divine mercy of God.

THE COUNT

What a wag. Then pull Henri IV out of hell with your holy prayers, who died without the sacraments like a pagan, and put him in heaven with Ravaillac, the well-confessed. The difficulty I see is how they will get along together and their faces when they see each other.

THE COUNTESS DE BOULAINVILLIERS

Dinner is getting cold. Here is M. Fréret arriving. Let us sit down to eat. You can pull out of hell whoever you like afterwards.

SECOND CONVERSATION

During dinner

THE ABBÉ

Ah, Madame! You're eating meat on Friday without express permission from the archbishop or from me! Don't you know it is a sin against the Church? The Jews are not allowed to eat hare, because it ruminates and does not have cleft feet. And it is a horrible crime to eat ixion and griffin.[8]

THE COUNTESS

You are always joking, Abbé. For pity's sake, tell me what an ixion is.

THE ABBÉ

I have no idea, Madame, but I do know that whoever eats a chicken wing on a Friday without the permission of his bishop, instead of gorging himself on salmon and sturgeon, commits a mortal sin. And that his soul will be burned while awaiting his body, and that when his body joins it, they will both burn forever without ever being consumed, as I said earlier.

THE COUNTESS

Surely nothing is more judicious or fair. What a pleasure to spend ones days in such a wise religion. Would you care for a wing of this partridge?

THE COUNT

Take it, believe me. Jesus Christ said, "Eat what is given you." Eat, eat. Don't let shame prevent you.

THE ABBÉ

Ah! In front of your servants, on a Friday, which is the day after Thursday! They
will go tell it all over town.

THE COUNT

So you have more respect for my lackeys than for Jesus Christ.

THE ABBÉ

It is true enough that our Savior never knew distinctions between days with or
without meat. But we have changed his doctrines for the better. He gave us full
power over heaven and earth. Did you know that, in more than one province,
we condemned people who ate meat during Lent to death by hanging? I could
give you examples.

THE COUNTESS

Good Lord! How edifying! And how well we see that your religion is divine!

THE ABBÉ

So divine that, in the very regions where we had those who had eaten an omelet
with bacon hanged, we had those who had taken the lard off a larded chicken
burned, which the Church still does occasionally, so well does she know how to
be proportional to the various weaknesses of men! Wine please . . .

THE COUNT

Speaking of proportional, Grand Vicar, does your Church allow marrying two
sisters?

THE ABBÉ

Both at the same time, no. But one after the other, according to need, to circumstances, payment to Rome and protection . . . Mind you, everything changes all
the time, and everything depends on our Holy Church. The holy Jewish church,
our mother that we detest and always cite, found it quite good that the patriarch Jacob married two sisters at the same time. It forbid marrying the widow
of one's brother in Leviticus, and ordered it expressly in Deuteronomy. And the
custom in Jerusalem allowed marrying your own sister, since you know that

when Amnon, son of the chaste King David, raped his sister, Thamar, this chaste and prudent sister said to him, "My brother, don't do foolish things to me, but ask for me in marriage from the king and he won't refuse you."[9]

But to get back to our divine law about the approval of marrying two sisters or the wife of one's brother, it varies according to the times, as I told you. Our pope Clement VII did not dare to declare the marriage of the English king Henry VIII with the wife of his brother, Prince Arthur, invalid for fear that the Emperor Charles V would put him in prison a second time and have him declared a bastard, which he was. But you may be certain that, as far as marriages go, as in all the rest, the pope and the archbishop are the masters of everything, when they have the most power. Wine please . . .

THE COUNTESS

Come, M. Fréret, you don't respond to these fine speeches. You say nothing!

M. FRÉRET

I keep silent, Madame, because I would have too much to say.

THE ABBÉ

And what could you possibly say, Monsieur, that could weaken the authority, dim the splendor or invalidate the truth of our Holy Mother, the Apostolic Roman Catholic Church? Wine please . . .

M. FRÉRET

Good Lord! I would say that you are Jews and idolaters, that you play us for fools and stuff your pockets with our money.

THE ABBÉ

Jews and idolaters! Listen to you!

M. FRÉRET

Yes, Jews and idolaters, since you force my hand. Was your God not Jewish? Was he not circumcised like a Jew? Did he not perform all the Jewish rituals? Do you not have him say several times that the Law of Moses must be obeyed? Did he not sacrifice in the temple? Was your baptism not a Jewish custom taken from the Middle East? Does your French word for Easter, *pâques* not derive from the Jewish word *pesach* for Passover? Have you not been singing for over seventeen hundred years in diabolical music Jewish songs that you attribute to an adulterous, murdering Jewish bandit kingling, "the man after God's own heart"?[10] Do you not lend money on collateral in Rome in your Jewries you call pawnbroker shops? And do you not sell off the pawns of the poor without an ounce of pity when they don't pay on time?

THE COUNT

He's right. The only thing you haven't retained of the Jewish law is a good jubilee, a real one, in which the lords recover the lands they gave you like fools when you convinced them that Elijah and the Antichrist were on their way, that the world was going to end, and that it was necessary to give all one's goods to the church "to save one's soul and not be ranked among the goats." That jubilee would be better than the one in which you only give plenary indulgences. I would earn over a hundred thousand pounds of rent for my part.

THE ABBÉ

I would be happy to see it, as long as you accorded me a big pension from that hundred thousand. But why does M. Fréret call us idolaters?

M. FRÉRET

Why, Monsieur? Ask St. Christopher, the first thing we encounter upon entering your cathedral, as well as the ugliest monument to barbarity you have. Ask St. Claire, who you invoke for eye ailments and to whom you have built temples. Ask St. Genou[11] who cures gout. Or St. Januarius, whose blood liquefies so solemnly in Naples when you place it near his head. Ask St. Antoine, who sprinkles the horses in Rome with holy water.

Will you dare deny your idolatry when you offer dulia worship in a thousand churches to the Virgin's milk, to the foreskin and navel of her son, to thorns you say were in his crown, to rotting bits of wood on which you claim the Eternal Being died? You who offer latria worship to a piece of wafer that you enclose in a box to keep the mice away? Your Roman Catholics have pushed their catholic extravagance so far as to say they change this bit of dough into God by virtue of a few words in Latin, and that all the crumbs of this wafer become so many creator-of-the-universe gods. Some vagrant made into a priest, a monk leaving his prostitute, comes dressed up like an actor for a dozen coins, mumbles in a foreign language what you call a "mass," swings three fingers quartering the air, bows, straightens, turns right, then left, steps up, steps down, and makes as many gods as he wants, drinks them, eats them, and eliminates them later in his chamber pot! And you will not admit that that is the most monstrous, ridiculous idolatry that ever dishonored human nature? Would you not have to be transformed into some kind of stupid animal to imagine you are changing white bread and red wine into God? Later-day idolaters, you cannot compare to the ancients who worshipped Zeus, the Demiurge, the master of gods and men, and who rendered homage to the secondary gods. Ceres, Pomona, and Flora were better than your Ursula and her eleven thousand virgins, and the priests of Mary Magdalene should not be mocking the priests of Minerva.

THE COUNTESS

Oh, Father, you have a tough adversary in M. Fréret. Why did you want him to speak? It's your fault.

THE ABBÉ

Oh, Madame, I'm a seasoned warrior. I am not frightened by so little. I've been hearing all these arguments against our holy mother the church for some time now.

THE COUNTESS

By my faith, you sound like a certain duchess some ill-humored person called a strumpet. She replied, "I've been hearing that for thirty years now, and I hope to hear it for another thirty."

THE ABBÉ

Madame, Madame, a witticism proves nothing.

THE COUNT

That's true. But neither does a witticism prevent one from being right.

238 VOLTAIRE'S REVOLUTION

THE ABBÉ

And what reason can be opposed to the authenticity of the prophecies, to the miracles of Moses, the miracles of Jesus, or to the martyrs?

THE COUNT

Ah! I don't advise you to speak of the prophecies now that little boys and girls know what the prophet Ezekiel ate for lunch, and which would not be decent to name at dinner, or now that they know the adventures of Oholah and Oholibah, which are difficult to discuss in front of ladies, or that they know that the God of the Jews ordered Hosea to take a whore and make sons of a whore. Alas! Do you find much other than gibberish and obscenities among those wretches?

Have your poor theologians henceforward cease arguing with the Jews over the meaning of the passages of their prophets, over a few Hebraic lines by an Amos, a Joel, a Habacuc, a Jeremiah; over a few words concerning Elijah, transported into the eastern celestial regions in a chariot of fire, who, by the way, never existed.

Let them be ashamed, above all, of the prophecies inserted into their Gospels. Is it possible that there remain any men imbecilic and cowardly enough to not be seized with indignation when Jesus predicts in Luke, "There will be signs in the moon and in the stars; roaring from the sea and ocean waves. Men fainting from terror will await what must happen to the entire world. The heavenly bodies will be shaken and then they will see the Son of Man coming in a cloud with great power and glory. I tell you verily that the present generation will not pass away until all these things have happened."[12]

It is assuredly impossible to read a prediction more precise, more detailed, and more false. You would have to be insane to dare claim it was accomplished, and that the son of man came in a cloud of great power and glory. How is it that Paul, in his first Epistle to the Thessalonians (chapter 4, verse 17), confirmed this ridiculous prediction with another even more impertinent? "We who still live and speak to you will be carried off into clouds to meet the Lord in the air, etc."

For what little knowledge remains to us, we know that the dogma of the end of the world and the forming of a new one was a chimera believed by nearly every nation. You can find the idea in Lucretius, Book IV. You can find it in the first book of Ovid's *Metamorphoses*. Long before that, Heraclitus said this world would be consumed by fire. The Stoics adopted this fancy. The half-Jews, half-Christians, who wrote the Gospels, did not fail to adopt a dogma so widely believed and to make the most of it. But as the world kept on surviving for so long, and as Jesus didn't return in the clouds with great power and glory during the first century of the Church, they said it would happen in the second century, then promised it for the third, and from century to century, the extravagance was renewed. Theologians have behaved like a charlatan I saw at the tip of the Pont Neuf bridge, on the quay of l'Ecole. Every evening, he would show people a rooster and a few bottles of balm, saying, "Gentlemen, I am going to cut off the head of my rooster and bring it back to life the moment after in your presence. But first, you have to buy some of my bottles." He always found people naive enough to buy them. "So, I'm going to cut off my rooster's head," the charlatan would continue, "but as it is late and this show is worth seeing in broad daylight, we will do it tomorrow."

Two members of the Academy of Science had the curiosity and persistence to come back to see how the charlatan would get out of it. The farce continued for eight whole days. But the farce of awaiting the end of the world among the Christians has lasted for eight whole centuries. So after all that, Monsieur, continue citing your Jewish or Christian prophecies.

M. FRÉRET

I don't advise you to speak of the miracles of Moses to people who have hair on their chins.[13] If all these inconceivable prodigies had taken place, the Egyptians would have spoken of them in their histories. The record of so many prodigious facts that startle nature would have been conserved by every nation. The Greeks, who knew all the fables of Egypt and Syria, would have made the news of these unnatural acts ring out at the four corners of the earth. But not a single historian, whether Greek, Syrian or Egyptian, says a word on it. Flavius Josephus, such a good patriot and as taken with his Judaism as he was, Josephus who gathered so many testimonies to prove the antiquity of his nation, could not find a single testimony to the ten plagues of Egypt, the parting and passing of the sea on dry foot, etc.

You know that there is no certainty as to who the author of the Pentateuch is. What sensible man could believe, on the faith of I don't know which Jew, Ezra or another, such appalling marvels, unknown to the rest of the earth? Even if all your Jewish prophets repeated these strange events a thousand times, it would still be impossible to believe them. But there is not a single prophet who cites the words of the Pentateuch on this heap of miracles, not one who goes into the slightest detail on these adventures. Explain this silence as you can.

Consider the fact that highly serious motives are required to overthrow all the laws of nature. What motive, what reason could the God of the Jews have had? To favor his little tribe of people? To give them fertile land? Why didn't he give them Egypt instead of performing miracles, most of which you say, were equaled by the Pharaoh's magicians? Why have an exterminating angel slay all the firstborn of Egypt and make all the animals die so that the Israelis, to the number of six hundred thousand combatants, could flee like cowardly thieves? Why part the Red Sea for them, so that they could all go die of hunger in the desert? You sense the enormity of these absurd inanities. You have too much sense to accept, and to seriously believe in a Christian religion founded on Jewish impostures. You sense the ridiculousness of the trivial reply that one must not question God, that one must not probe the abyss of Providence. No, one must not ask God why lice and spiders exist because, though we are certain that lice and spiders exist, we cannot know why they exist. But we are not so certain that Moses changed his rod into a serpent and covered Egypt with lice, however familiar they were to his people. We do not interrogate God. We interrogate madmen who dare put words in God's mouth, and attribute the excess of their own extravagances to him.

THE COUNTESS

My faith, dear Abbé, I do not advise you to speak of Jesus' miracles either. Would the creator of the universe have made himself a Jew in order to change water into wine at a wedding where everyone was drunk already? Would he have been carried by the devil to a mountain top from which he could see all the kingdoms of the world? Would he have chased demons from the bodies of two thousand pigs in a country that has no pigs? Would he have withered a fig tree for not bearing figs "when it was not the season for figs"? Believe me, these miracles are just as absurd as those of Moses. Bravely admit what you really think in the bottom of your heart.

THE ABBÉ

Madame, a little deference for my robe, please. Let me practice my trade. I have been a little beaten perhaps on the prophecies and the miracles, but as to the martyrs, it is certain they existed. And Pascal, the patriarch of Port-Royal des Champs, said, "I willingly believe stories whose witnesses died for them."

M. FRÉRET

Ah, Monsieur, what dishonesty and ignorance we find in Pascal! One would think, listening to him, that he saw the interrogations of the apostles, and that he witnessed their tortures. But where did he see that they had been tortured? Who told him that Simon Barjona, nicknamed Peter,[14] had been crucified in Rome, upside down? Who told him that this Barjona, a poor fisherman in Galilee, had ever been to Rome and spoke Latin there? Alas! If he had been condemned in Rome and the Christians knew it, the first church they built there in honor of the saints would have been St. Peter's, instead of St. John Lateran's Basilica. The popes would not have missed this chance: their ambition would have found a perfect pretext. What are we reduced to when, to prove that this Peter Barjona lived in Rome, we have to say that a letter attributed to him, dated from Babylonia, was in reality written from Rome? On which subject a famous author wisely said that, to go by such explanations, a letter dated from Saint Petersburg must've been written in Constantinople.

You know very well which impostors spoke of this voyage of Peter. It was an Obadiah who first wrote that Peter came from Lake Gennesaret straight to the emperor in Rome to make an onslaught of miracles against Simon the Magician. It is he who weaves the fairy tale about a relative of the emperor, half brought back to life by Simon, then entirely by the other Simon Barjona; he who sets the two Simons dueling, with one flying through the air till he breaks both legs through the prayers of the other; he who invents the famous tale of two big dogs sent by Simon to eat Peter. The whole thing is repeated by a Marcellus, then by a Hegesippus.[15] So there are the foundations of Christianity. You see nothing but a tissue of the most insipid impostures ever invented by the dregs of society, who alone embraced Christianity for a hundred years.

It was an uninterrupted series of frauds. They forged letters from Jesus Christ, letters from Pilate, letters from Seneca, apostolic constitutions, acrostic verses from the Sibyls, over forty Gospels, the Acts of Barnaby, liturgies from

Peter, from James, from Matthew, Mark, etc., etc. You know it, Monsieur, you have undoubtedly read these infamous archives of lies that you call pious frauds, and you will not have the honesty to admit, at least in front of your friends, that the pope's throne was only established on abominable chimeras, to the dire misfortune of the human race?

THE ABBÉ

But how would the Christian religion have been elevated so high if it were only based on fanaticism and lies?

THE COUNT

And how would Mohammedanism have been elevated even higher? At least its lies were nobler and its fanaticism more generous. At least Mahomet wrote and fought battles. Jesus neither knew how to write nor how to defend himself. Mahomet had the courage of an Alexander with the spirit of Numa, and your Jesus sweat blood and water as soon as he was convicted by his judges. Mohammedanism has never changed, and you and yours have changed your entire religion twenty times. There is more difference between what it is today and what it was in the beginning than between your customs and those of King Dagobert.[16] Miserable Christians. No, you do not worship your Jesus, you insult him by substituting your new laws for his. You ridicule him more with your *mysteries*, your *agnus*,[17] your relics, your indulgences, your benefices, and your papacy than you do every year on January 5th with your degenerate Christmases in which you cover with ridicule the Virgin Mary, the angel who visits her, the pigeon who impregnates her, the carpenter who is jealous, and the infant king three kings come to compliment between an ox and a donkey, worthy company for such a family.

THE ABBÉ

It is nevertheless this ridiculousness that St. Augustine found divine. He said, "I believe it because it is absurd, and I believe it because it is impossible."

M. FRÉRET

So? What do we care about the reveries of an African who was sometimes a Manichean, sometimes a Christian, sometimes a debauchee, sometimes devout, sometimes tolerant, and sometimes a persecutor? What do we care about his theological twaddle? Would you like me to respect this senseless rhetorician when he says in his twenty-third sermon that an angel got Mary with child through her ear: *impraegnavit per aurem?*

THE COUNTESS

Indeed, I see the absurdity, but not the divine. I find it very easy to believe that Christianity took shape among the populace, just like the sects of the Anabaptists and the Quakers did, like the prophets of the Vivarais and the Cévennes began, or like the convulsionaries, already gaining strength.[18] Zeal begins it, trickery completes it. The same holds true for religion as for gambling:

We start out dupes, and end up knaves.

M. FRÉRET

That is only too true, Madame. The most likely truth in all the chaos of the stories about Jesus, written against him by the Jews and in his favor by the Christians, is that he was a Jew of good faith who wished to assert himself among the people like the founders of the Recabites,[19] the Essenes, the Sadducees, the Pharisees, the Judaites, the Herodians, the Joanistes, les Therapeutes and so many other little factions begun in Syria, which was the fatherland of factions. It is probable that he got some women to adhere to it, along with all those who wanted to head a sect, that several indiscreet speeches against the local officials escaped him, and that he was cruelly punished with an agonizing death. But whether he was condemned under the reign of Herod the Great, as the Talmudists say, or under Herod Archelaus, as some of the Gospels say, is immaterial. It is known that his disciples were quite unheard of until they met a few Platonists in Alexandria who buttressed the reveries of the Galileans with the reveries of Plato. People were full of demons, evil spirits, obsessions, possessions, and magic in those days, like the savages are today. Nearly every sickness was a possession with evil spirits. The Jews, from time immemorial, had boasted of chasing demons away with *barath* root,[20] held under the nose of the sick person, and a few words attributed to Solomon. Young Tobias chased the devil away with the smoke of a fish on the grill. That is the origin of the miracles the Galileans boasted of.

244 VOLTAIRE'S REVOLUTION

The Gentiles were fanatical enough to agree that the Galileans could perform these prodigies, because the Gentiles believed they could too. They believed in magic like the disciples of Jesus. If a few sick people improved through the force of nature, they did not fail to assure everyone that they had been delivered from their headaches through enchantments. They told the Christians, "You have superb secrets, and we do too. You cure through words, and so do we. You have no advantage over us."

But when the Galileans, having won over a good part of the populace, began to preach against the official religion; when, having asked for tolerance, they dared to be intolerant; when they wanted to elevate their new fanaticism on the ruins of the old fanaticism, they horrified the priests and Roman magistrates and their temerity was repressed. What did they do? They dreamt up a thousand works in their favor, as we have seen. From dupes, they became knaves, then forgers. They defended themselves by the most shameful frauds, unable to employ other weapons until the time when Constantine, become emperor with their money, put their religion on the throne. Then the knaves became bloodthirsty. I dare assure you that from the Council of Nicaea up through the seditions in Cevennes, not a single year has passed in which Christianity did not shed blood.

THE ABBÉ

Ah, Monsieur! That's going a bit far.

M. FRÉRET

No, it isn't going far enough. Read *Church History*[21] alone. See the Donatists and their adversaries clubbing each other, the Athanasians and the Arians filling the Roman Empire with carnage over a diphthong. Watch these barbaric Christians bitterly complain that the wise Emperor Julian is keeping them from slaughtering and destroying each other. Watch the horrific procession of massacres, so many citizens dying in tortures, so many princes assassinated, the many stakes lit by your councils, twelve million innocent inhabitants of a new hemisphere, slaughtered like wild beats in a park under the pretext that they didn't want to be Christians.

And in our hemisphere, Christians ceaselessly setting fire to each other:

old men, children, mothers, daughters, dying en masse in the Albigensian Crusades, the Hussite Wars, the wars of Lutherans, Calvinists, Anabaptists, the St. Bartholomew Massacre, and those of Ireland, Piedmont, the Cevennes, while a bishop in Rome, cushily lounging on a day bed, has his feet kissed while fifty castratos hum to relieve his tedium. God is my witness that this is a faithful portrayal, and you will not dare to contradict me.

THE ABBÉ

I admit that there is some truth in all that, but as I was telling the Bishop of Noyon, these are not subjects for dinner conversation. Suppers would be too morose if conversation turned too long on the horrors of the human race. The history of the Church troubles one's digestion.

THE COUNT

The facts have troubled it even more.

THE ABBÉ

That is not the fault of the Christian religion. It is the fault of abuses.

THE COUNT

It would be fine if there had only been a few abuses. But since priests have wanted to live at our expense ever since Paul, or the man who took that name, said, "Have I not the right to be fed and clothed by you? Myself, my wife, or my sister?" and if the Church has always wanted to invade everyone, employing every arm at its disposal to take our belongings and our lives ever since the alleged adventure of Ananias and Sapphira who, they say, had brought the money of all their inheritance to Simon Barjona's feet, but kept a few drachmas for their own subsistence; if it is obvious that the history of the Church has been a continual suite of quarrels, impostures, vexations, deceits, robberies and murders, then it is apparent that abuse is in the thing itself, just as it is observable that a wolf has always been a flesh-eating beast of prey, and that it is not due to a few fleeting moments of excess that he has drunk the blood of our sheep.

THE ABBÉ

You could say as much of any religion.

THE COUNT

Not at all. I defy you to show me a single war incited by dogma in a single religion in all antiquity. I defy you to show me a single man persecuted for his opinions from Romulus up to the time the Christians overturned everything. That absurd savagery was reserved to you. You blush and sense the truth pressing upon you, and you have nothing to say.

THE ABBÉ

And so I don't answer. I admit that theological disputes are absurd and disastrous.

M. FRÉRET

Then admit that we should uproot a tree that has always borne poisonous fruit.

THE ABBÉ

That is what I will not grant you, because this tree has also borne good fruit. If a republic were perpetually in dissension, I wouldn't want the republic destroyed. Laws can be reformed.

THE COUNT

States are not like religions. Venice reformed its laws and flourished. But when attempts were made to reform Catholicism, Europe swam in blood. And more recently, when the eminent Locke wrote his book, *The Reasonableness of Christianity*, seeking to conciliate the impostors of that religion with the rights of humanity, he didn't have four disciples—strong enough proof that Christianity and reason cannot subsist together. There only remains a single remedy in the present state of affairs, and even then, it is only a palliative, not a cure. It is to make religion absolutely dependent on the sovereign and the magistrates.

M. FRÉRET

Yes, provided that the sovereign and the magistrates are enlightened, that they know how to tolerate all religions equally, to regard all men as their brothers, to take no regard of what they think but a great deal of regard for what they do, that they leave them free in their dealings with God and fetter them only to the laws in everything they owe to men. For magistrates who uphold their religion with executioners should be treated like wild beasts.

THE ABBÉ

And if all religions are authorized and they battle each other? If Catholics, Protestants, Greeks, Turks, and Jews box each other's ears upon leaving Mass, the sermon, the mosque, or the synagogue?

M. FRÉRET

Then a dragoon regiment must go disperse them.

THE COUNT

Even better than sending in dragoons, I would like to see them get lessons in moderation. We need to start by instructing people before punishing them.

THE ABBÉ

Instructing the people! Are you serious, Count? Do you believe them worthy of it?

THE COUNT

Oh I see. You still think they must only be fooled. You are only half cured. Your old disease was only in remission.

THE COUNTESS

Speaking of which, I forgot to ask you your opinion on something I read yesterday on the history of the good Mahometans that made a striking impression on me. Assan, son of Ali, was in his bath when one of his slaves inadvertently threw a cauldron of boiling water on him. Assan's servants wanted to impale the culprit. Assan, instead of having him impaled, gave him twenty pieces of gold. "There is," he said, "a level of glory in paradise for those who pay for services, a higher one for those who pardon wrongs, and an even higher one for those who reward involuntary wrongs." What do you think of this deed and this discourse?

THE COUNT

I recognize in it one of my good Muslims from the first century.[22]

THE ABBÉ

And me, my good Christians.

M. FRÉRET

As for myself, I am vexed that the scalded Assan, son of Ali, gave twenty pieces of gold to have glory in paradise. I don't like good deeds to be self-serving. I would have liked Assan to be virtuous and humane enough to console the despair of the slave, without thinking of being ranked in the third level of paradise.

THE COUNTESS

Let us go have coffee. I imagine that if, at all the dinners of Paris, Vienna, Madrid, Lisbon, Rome, and Moscow, conversations as instructive were taking place, the world would get on better.

THIRD CONVERSATION

After dinner

THE ABBÉ

This is excellent coffee, Madame. It is pure mocha.

THE COUNTESS

Yes, it comes from the land of the Muslims. Isn't it a pity?

THE ABBÉ

All jesting aside, Madame, mankind must have a religion.

THE COUNT

Yes, no doubt. And God gave them a divine one, eternal, and engraved in every heart. The one that, according to you, Enoch, the Noahides, and Abraham all practiced. It is the one that learned Chinese have conserved for over four thousand years: the adoration of one God, love of justice, and horror of crime.

THE COUNTESS

Is it possible that a religion so pure and holy was abandoned for the abominable sects that have inundated the earth?

M. FRÉRET

In matters of religion, Madame, we have had a conduct in direct contrast with the one we have had in matters of clothing, housing and food. We began in caves, in huts, in animal skins, eating acorns. We then acquired bread, salutary dishes, clothes of woven wool and silk, and clean, comfortable houses. But in matters of religion, we have returned to acorns, animal skins, and caves.

THE ABBÉ

It will be very difficult to get you out of it. You see that the Christian religion, for example, is incorporated into the state everywhere, and that from the pope to the lowest Capuchin monk, each and every one of them bases his throne or his recipes upon it. I have already told you that men are not reasonable enough to content themselves with a pure religion, worthy of God.

THE COUNTESS

You don't believe that. You yourself admit that they followed this religion in the days of your Enoch, your Noah, and your Abraham. Why would people be less reasonable today than they were then?

THE ABBÉ

I suppose I have to say it. It is because then there were no clergymen living off stipends, no Abbé of Corbie with a million in revenue, or any popes with revenues of sixteen or eighteen million. To restore this wealth to human society, it might take wars as bloody as those that were needed to wrest it from them.

THE COUNT

Even though I was a military man, I have no desire to make war on priests and monks. I do not wish to establish the truth through murder, the way they established error. But I would like this truth to enlighten men a little at least, to make them gentler and happier, to make people cease being superstitious, and heads of state tremble at the thought of persecuting anyone.

THE ABBÉ

It is a very awkward difficulty (since I have to explain myself at last) to take the chains they revere away from foolish people. You may well get yourself stoned by the people of Paris if, at a time of too much rain, you prevent them from parading what is said to be the carcass of St. Genevieve throughout the streets to bring fine weather back.

M. FRÉRET

I don't believe what you say. Reason has already made so much progress that this supposed carcass and that of St. Marcel have not been paraded in Paris for over ten years. I think that it is very easy to gradually uproot all the superstitions that have besotted us. Witches are no longer believed in, devils are no longer exorcised, and even though it said that your Jesus sent his apostles out precisely to drive out devils, not a single priest among us is crazy or foolish enough to boast of chasing them away. The relics of St. Francis have become ridiculous, and those of St. Ignatius will perhaps one day be dragged through the mud with the Jesuits themselves. We leave the duchy of Ferrara to the pope, which, in truth, he usurped; the domains that Caesar Borgia stole through the sword and poison, and that were returned to the Church of Rome for whom he did not work. We leave Rome itself to the popes because we do not want the Emperor to seize it. We consent to continue to pay him annates, though it's a ridiculous custom and an obvious simony. No one wants to make a ruckus over such a minor subsidy. People, ruled by customs, don't break a bad bargain made almost three centuries ago all of a sudden. But if the popes had the insolence to send legates *a latere* like in the old days, to impose tithes on the people, to excommunicate kings, to ban their states, to give their crowns to others, you would see how that legate *a latere* would be received. I would not despair of seeing the *Parlement* of Aix or Paris have him hanged.

THE COUNT

You see how many shameful prejudices we have thrown off. Now cast your eyes on the most opulent part of Switzerland, the Seven United Netherlands, as powerful as Spain, on Great Britain, whose maritime forces would carry the day against those of all the other nations combined. Look at the entire north of

Germany, and Scandinavia, these inexhaustible nurseries of warriors. All these people have surpassed us by far in the progress of reason. The blood of every head of this hydra they have chopped off has fertilized their countrysides. The abolition of monks has populated and enriched their states. We can certainly do in France what has been done elsewhere. France will be wealthier and more populated.

THE ABBÉ

Well then! Once you have shaken the vermin from the monks in France, once we will no longer see ridiculous relics, once we will no longer pay a shameful tribute to the Bishop of Rome, even once we will scorn consubstantiality and the procession of the Holy Spirit from the Father and the Son and transubstantiation enough to no longer speak of it; once these mysteries remain buried in the Summa of St. Thomas and when contemptible theologians will be reduced to silence, you will still be Christians. You will want in vain to go farther. That is what you will never obtain. A religion of philosophers is not made for mankind.

M. FRÉRET

Est quodam prodire tenus, si non datur ultra.[23]

I say to you with Horace, your doctor will never give you the eye of a lynx, but allow him to take the nebula[24] from your eyes. We groan beneath the weight of a hundred pounds of chains. Permit us to be delivered of three-quarters of them. The word Christian has prevailed. It will stay. But, little by little, we will adore God without admixture, without giving him either a mother or a son, without giving him a putative father, without saying he died a villainous torturous death, without believing we make gods with flour, in short without this mass of superstitions that set civilized people so far beneath savages. The unadulterated worship of a Supreme Being is beginning to be the religion of all reasonable people today, and soon it will descend among the saner portion of the populace itself.

THE ABBÉ

Do you not fear that disbelief (whose immense progress I am seeing) might have dire consequences in descending among the populace, and lead it to crime?

Men are subject to cruel passions and horrible misfortunes. They need a serious brake to restrain them and an error to console them.

M. FRÉRET

The reasonable worship of a just God who rewards and punishes would no doubt make for the happiness of society, but when this salutary awareness of a just God is disfigured by lies and dangerous superstitions, the remedy becomes poison, and what should deter crime encourages it. A vicious person who only half-reasons (and there are a great many of these) is frequently so bold as to deny a God painted in revolting terms.

Another wicked person, one with great passions and a weak soul, is often brought to evil by the assurance of forgiveness that the priests offer him. "Whatever the enormous multitude of crimes that have soiled you, confess to me, and all will be forgiven you through the merits of a man who was hanged in Judea many centuries ago. Plunge yourself in new crimes after that, seven times sixty-seven times, and all will be forgiven once again."[25] Is that not truly leading him into temptation? Is that not smoothing all the roads to iniquity? Did La Brinvilliers not go to confession after every poisoning she committed? Did Louis XI not do likewise in the olden days?

The people of antiquity had confession and atonements like us, but you were not redeemed for a second crime. A second murder of a relative was not pardoned. We took everything from the Greeks and Romans, and we corroded everything.

Their inferno was impertinent, I admit, but our devils are more idiotic than their furies. The furies were not damned themselves. They were considered executioners, and not victims of divine vengeance. To be both executioner and executed, burned and burning, like our devils, is an absurd contradiction, worthy of us, and it is all the more ridiculous that this foundation of Christianity, the Fall of the Angels, is not found in either Genesis or the Gospels. It is an ancient fable of the Brahmins.

Anyway, Monsieur, everyone laughs at your hell today because it is ridiculous. But no one would laugh at a God who rewards and punishes, from whom we can hope a compensation for our virtue and fear a punishment for our crimes, not knowing what type of penalty or justice to expect, but persuaded there will be one because God is just.

THE COUNT

It seems to me that M. Fréret has shown well enough how religion could be a salutary curb. I would like to try to prove to you that a purified religion is infinitely more consoling than yours.

There are pleasures in the illusions of devout souls, you say, and I believe it. There are in madhouses too. But what torments when these souls become disillusioned! In what doubt and what despair certain nuns pass their sad lives! You have witnessed it, you told me yourself.

The cloisters are the abode of repentance, but among the men especially, a cloister is the breeding place of discord and envy. The monks are voluntary galley slaves who battle each other while rowing together. I except a very small number who are truly penitent or useful. But in truth, has God put man and woman on earth to potter their lives away in prison cells, separated from each other forever? Is that the goal of nature? Everyone cries out against the monks, but I feel sorry for them. Most of them sacrificed their liberty forever when barely out of childhood, and out of a hundred, at least eighty wither away in bitterness. Where then are these great consolations that your religion gives humankind? A clergyman in a wealthy benefice is consoled no doubt, but it is by his money, not his faith. If he enjoys some little pleasure, he only tastes it by violating the rules of his order. He is only happy as a man of this world, and not as a man of the church. The father of a family, prudent, resigned to God, fond of his country, surrounded by his children and friends, receives blessings from God a thousand times more appreciable.

Moreover, everything you can say in favor of the virtues of your monks, I can say even more so of dervishes, marabouts, fakirs, and bonzes. They do penances a hundred times more rigorous. They devote themselves to austerities more appalling. And these iron chains beneath which they bend, these arms outstretched always in the same position, these frightful macerations are nothing in comparison with the young women in India who burn themselves alive on the funeral pyres of their husbands, in the insane hope of being reborn with them.

So stop boasting of both the hardships and consolations the Christian religion provides. Admit frankly that it doesn't even approach a reasonable worship that an honest family can offer the Supreme Being without superstition. Forget your convent prison cells. Forget your contradictory and useless mysteries, an object of derision the world over. Preach God and morals, and I promise you that there will be more virtue and felicity on earth.

THE COUNTESS

I am strongly of this opinion.

M. FRÉRET

And me too, without a doubt.

THE ABBÉ

Ah well, since I must tell you my secret, I am too.

At that point, the Président de Maisons, the Abbé de Saint-Pierre, Monsieur Dufay, and Monsieur Dumarsais arrived,[26] and the Abbé de Saint-Pierre read out his thoughts of that morning, as was his custom, on each of which a fine book could be written.

THE MISCELLANEOUS THOUGHTS OF ABBÉ DE SAINT-PIERRE

Most princes, ministers and men raised to prestigious posts do not have the time to read. They despise books, and are governed by a big book, which is the tomb of common sense.

If they had known enough to read, they would have spared the world all the miseries that superstition and ignorance have caused. If Louis XIV had been a reader, he would not have revoked the Edict of Nantes.

Popes and their henchmen have been so convinced that their power relied on ignorance alone that they have always forbidden the reading of the only book that founds their religion. They have said: "Here is your law, and we forbid you to read it. You will only learn of it what we deign to teach you." This extravagant tyranny is incomprehensible. It exists, nonetheless, and the entire Bible in one's spoken language is prohibited in Rome. It is only allowed in a language that is no longer spoken.[27]

All papal usurpations use as pretext a wretched play on words, a misleading street ruse, a line they make God say for which a schoolboy would be whipped. "You are Peter and upon this rock I build my church."[28]

If people knew how to read, or read, it would be obvious to them that religion has done nothing but harm government. It still does a great deal in France, through its persecutions of the Protestants, through its discords over Lord-knows-what Papal Bull, more despicable than a street barker's song, through its ridiculous celibacy of priests, through the idleness of its monks, through the bad deals it makes with the Bishop of Rome, etc.

Spain and Portugal, much bigger dolts than France, experience almost all these evils, and have the Inquisition on top of it, which, supposed to be a hell, would be the most abominable thing that hell has produced.

In Germany, there are interminable quarrels between the three sects accepted by the Treaty of Westphalia.[29] The inhabitants of countries directly submitted to German priests are brutes that barely have enough to eat.

In Italy, this religion, which destroyed the Roman Empire, left nothing but misery and music, eunuchs, harlequins, and priests. Treasures are heaped upon a little black statue called the Madonna of Loreto. And the lands are left uncultivated.

Theology is to this religion what poison is to food.

Have temples where God is adored, his blessings sung, his justice heralded and virtue recommended. All the rest is nothing but party spirit, faction, imposture, pride, and greed, which must be outlawed forever.

Nothing is more useful to the public than a parish priest who keeps a record of births, who provides assistance for the poor, consoles the sick, buries the dead, makes peace between families, and who is a master only of morals. To put him in a condition to be useful, he must be above poverty himself and not be allowed to testify against his local lord or his parishioners as so many parish priests do. They should be paid according to the region they live in, according to the extent of their parish and have no other cares besides fulfilling their duties.

Nothing is less useful than a cardinal. What is a foreign dignity, conferred by a foreign priest, a dignity without function, which is almost always worth a hundred thousand écus in income when a parish priest does not have enough to assist the poor, nor even to take care of himself?

The best government is unquestionably the one that accredits only the number of priests necessary, because a surplus of them is a dangerous burden. The best government is one in which the priests are married, because they are better citizens. They give children to the state and raise them with integrity. It is one in which the priests dare only to preach morals, for when they stir up controversy, it is the bell toll of discord.

Decent people read the history of the wars of religion with horror. They laugh at theological disputes like at an Italian farce. Let us then have a religion that makes no one shudder or laugh.

Are there sincere theologians? Yes, just as there are people who believe themselves sorcerers.

M. Deslandes of the Academy of Sciences in Berlin, who just brought out a *History of Philosophy*, says in volume III, on page 299, "The Faculty of Theology appears to me to be the most despicable body in the kingdom." It would become one of the most respectable if it limited itself to only teaching about God and morals. It would be the only way to atone for its criminal decisions against Henri III and the great Henri IV.[30]

The miracles that the beggars perform at Faubourg St. Médard can go far if Cardinal Fleury doesn't restore order. Peace must be exhorted and miracles strictly forbidden.

The monstrous Papal Bull, *Unigenitus*, can yet disturb the kingdom. Every papal bull is an assault on the dignity of the crown and the liberty of the nation.

The rabble creates superstitions. Upright people destroy them.

We are trying to perfect the laws and the arts. Can we neglect religion?

Who will start to purify it? Thinking men will. The rest will follow.

Is it not disgraceful that fanatics have zeal and that wise men do not? One must be prudent but not faint-hearted.

THE EMPEROR OF CHINA AND FRIAR CHUCKLES

OR

THE STORY OF THE BANISHMENT OF THE JESUITS FROM CHINA

1768

Friar Chuckles ("Frère Rigolet," which evokes *rigoler*—to laugh or jest) may well be Voltaire's most burlesque creation, but this story is based in fact. This piece first appeared under the second title ("Relation du bannissement des Jésuites de la China, par l'auteur du Compère Mathieu") in 1768, humorously adopting the name of another underground work, *Le Compère Mathieu*, which had been wrongly attributed to Voltaire. The title was changed to *L'Empereur de la Chine et le frère Rigolet* in 1775. The facts behind this send-up are related in the first few paragraphs below. The Jesuit, Dominican, and other missionaries sent to China soon began battling among themselves. In 1705, Pope Clement XI sent a Legate with a decree telling the Kangxi Emperor what converts were allowed to believe. In 1721, the emperor banned Christian missions altogether. His degree states that they were a small bigoted sect, impossible to reason with, and that their remarks were often incredible and ridiculous.

China, once entirely unknown, then long disfigured to our eyes, and now better known to us than several provinces in Europe, is the most populated, most flourishing, and most ancient empire in the world. We know from the last headcount taken under Emperor K'ang-hsi,[1] in only the fifteen provinces themselves, that there were sixty million men capable of going to war, without counting either veterans over the age of sixty, nor young men under twenty, nor the mandarins, nor the lettered men, and, even less, the women. Going by this count, it seems unlikely that there could be less than a hundred and fifty million souls, or what we call souls, in China.

The ordinary revenues of the emperor are two hundred million ounces of fine silver, which amounts to twelve hundred and fifty million in French money, or a hundred and twenty-five million in gold ducats.

The armed forces of the state, we are told, consist of a militia of about 800,000 soldiers. The emperor has 570,000 horses available for either riding to war, court voyages, or for the public messengers.

We are further assured that this vast stretch of land is not governed despotically, but by six principle tribunals that serve as a curb to all the lower courts.

Religion there is simple, and this is an incontestable proof of its antiquity. The emperors of China have been the supreme pontiffs of the empire for over four thousand years. They adore a single God and offer him the first fruits of a field that they have cultivated with their own hands. Emperor K'ang-hsi wrote these very words, and had them engraved on the frontispiece of his temple: "Chang-ti (or Tiānzhǔ, "Lord of Heaven") is without beginning and without end. He has made everything. He governs everything. He is boundlessly good and boundlessly just."

Yong-ching, son and successor of K'ang-hsi, had an edict published throughout the empire that begins with these words: "There is between the Tiān (Heaven) and man a certain, infallible correspondence as to rewards and punishments."

This religion of the emperor, the colaos, and all the learned people, is all the more beautiful in that it isn't sullied by any superstitions.

All the wisdom of the government was not able to prevent bonzes from entering the empire, any more than all the diligence of a head butler can keep rats from slipping into the cellars and the attics.

The spirit of tolerance, which made up the character of all the Asiatic nations, let the bonzes beguile the populace; but though they captivated the rabble, they were prevented from governing. They were treated like charlatans are treated: they are allowed to retail their quackeries in public squares, but if they rabble-rouse, they are hanged. So the bonzes were both tolerated and repressed.

Emperor K'ang-hsi had welcomed with singular bounty the Jesuit bonzes, and they, with the help of armillary spheres, barometers, thermometers, and field glasses they had brought from Europe, obtained public tolerance for the Christian religion from K'ang-hsi.

It should be observed that this emperor was obliged to consult the tribunals, to solicit them himself and to draw up the petition of the Jesuit bonzes in his own hand to obtain permission for them to exercise their religion, which clearly proves that the emperor is by no means despotic as so many poorly informed authors have claimed, and that the laws had more clout than he did.

The quarrels stirred up between the missionaries soon made this new sect odious. The Chinese, who are sensible people, were astonished and indignant to find these European bonzes daring to institute opinions with which they themselves did not agree. The tribunals presented reports on all these Europeans bonzes to the emperor, and especially on the Jesuits, much as we have since seen the *Parlements* of France draw up requisitions against this society and finally order its abolition.

This court case had not yet been judged when Emperor K'ang-hsi died on December 20, 1722. One of his sons, Yinzhen, the Yongzheng Emperor, succeeded him, one of the best princes God has ever given men. He had all the goodness of his father with a firmer, sounder spirit. As soon as he was on the throne, he received requisitions against the Jesuits from all the towns in the empire. He was warned that these bonzes, under the pretext of religion, were conducting an immense commerce, that they were preaching an intolerant doctrine, that they had been the sole cause of a civil war in Japan in which four hundred thousand souls had perished, that they were the soldiers and the spies of a priest from the Occident, they call the sovereign of all the kingdoms of the earth, that this priest had divided the kingdom of China into dioceses, that he had delivered a sentence against the ancient rites of the nation in Rome, and that, ultimately, if these unprecedented enterprises were not suppressed at the earliest opportunity, a revolution was to be feared.

Before deciding, the Yongzheng Emperor wanted to investigate the strange religion of these bonzes himself. He knew that one of them, Friar Chuckles, had converted a few children of the picklocks and washerwomen of the palace. He gave orders for him to be brought before him.

This Friar Chuckles was not a man of the court like Brothers Parennin and Verbiest.[2] He had all the simplicity and enthusiasm of a devotee. There are people like that in every religious society; they are necessary to their order. One day, Oliva,[3] the Superior General of the Jesuits, was asked to explain how there could be so many nincompoops in a society that passed for being so learned. He replied, "We must have saints." And so it was that Friar Chuckles appeared before the emperor of China.

He was in his glory and had no doubt that he would have the honor of baptizing the emperor within two days at most. After he had performed the usual genuflections and struck his forehead on the ground nine times, the emperor had tea and biscuits brought to him and said, "Brother Chuckles, tell me, in all conscience, what this religion is that you are preaching to the washerwomen and picklocks of my palace?"

Friar Chuckles—August ruler of the fifteen ancient provinces of China and of the forty-two provinces of Tartary, my religion is the only true one, as my provost, Brother Bouvet told me, who got it from his nursemaid. The Chinese, the Japanese, the Koreans, the Tartars, the Indians, the Persians, the Turks, the Arabs, the Africans, and the Americans will all be damned. One can only please God in a part of Europe, and my sect is called the Catholic religion, which means universal.

The Emperor—Very good, Brother Chuckles. Your sect is limited to a small part of Europe, and you call it universal! Apparently you hope to extend it throughout the world?

Friar Chuckles—Sire, Your Majesty has hit the nail on the head. That's what we mean. As soon as we are sent into a country by the Reverend Brother General in the name of the pope, who is Vice-God on earth, we catechize minds that are not yet perverted by the dangerous habit of thinking. The children of the lowest classes being the most worthy of our doctrine, we begin with them. Then we go to the women and soon they send their husbands. And as soon as we have a sufficient number of proselytes, we become powerful enough to force the sovereign to win eternal life by becoming subject to the pope.

The Emperor—One couldn't do better, Brother Chuckles. Sovereigns are much obliged to you. Show me on this geographical map where your pope lives.

Friar Chuckles—Sacred Imperial Majesty, he lives at the end of the world on this little angle you see here, and it is from there that he damns or saves all the kings of the earth, according to his will. He is the Vice-God, the Vice-Chang-ti, the Vice-Tian. He must govern the entire earth in the name of God, and our Brother General must govern under him.

The Emperor—My compliments to the Vice-God and to the Brother General. But your God, who is he? Tell me a little something about him.

Friar Chuckles—Our God was born in a stable, seventeen hundred and twenty-three years ago, between an ox and a donkey, and three kings, apparently from your country, were guided by a new star to come to adore him in a manger.

The Emperor—Indeed, Brother Chuckles, if I had been there, I would not have failed to form a fourth.

Friar Chuckles—I believe you, Sire, but if you have the curiosity to take a little journey, you would be free to see his mother. She lives here in this little spot you see on the coast of the Adriatic Sea, in the same house where she gave birth to God. This house, to tell the truth, wasn't originally in this spot. This is where it was in a little Jewish village, on the map. But after thirteen hundred years, celestial spirits transported it to where you see. The mother of God isn't really there in flesh and blood, but in wood. It is a statue that some of our brothers think was made by God, her son; who was a very good carpenter.

The Emperor—A carpenter God! A God born of a woman! Everything you tell me is admirable.

Friar Chuckles—Oh, Sire! She was not a woman, she was a virgin maiden. It's true that she was married, and that she had two other children named James, as the old Gospels say. But she was no less of a virgin for it.

The Emperor—What! She was a virgin, and she had children!

Friar Chuckles—Really, truly. That's the best part of the story. It was God who got this girl with child.

The Emperor—I don't understand you at all. You said earlier she was the mother of God. So God slept with his mother to be born of her afterwards?

Friar Chuckles—You've got it, Sacred Majesty! Grace is operating already. That's it, I tell you. God changed into a pigeon to make a child with the wife of a carpenter, and this child was God himself.

The Emperor—But then there are two gods altogether, a carpenter and a pigeon?

Friar Chuckles—Undoubtedly, Sire. But there is also a third one, who is the father of those two and who we always paint with a majestic beard. It is that god who ordered the pigeon to make a child with the carpentress, from which was born the carpenter god. But in fact, these three gods make only one. The father engendered the son before he came into the world, the son was then engendered by the pigeon, and the pigeon proceeded from the father and the son. However, you can see that the pigeon who proceeded, the carpenter born of the pigeon, and the father who engendered the son of the pigeon can only be one sole God, and that any man who does not believe this story must be burned in this world and the next.

The Emperor—That is as clear as day. A god born in a stable, seventeen hundred and twenty-three years ago, between an ox and a donkey; another god in a dovecote; a third god from whom the other two came and who isn't older than them, despite his white beard; a virgin mother. Nothing is simpler and wiser. Uh, tell me, Friar Chuckles, if your god was born, then I suppose he died?

Friar Chuckles—If he died, Sacred Majesty! You can take my word for it, and to gratify us. He disguised his divinity so well that he let himself be whipped and hanged, despite his miracles. But he also resurrected two days later without anyone seeing him and went back to heaven, after solemnly promising that "he would soon come back on a cloud, with great glory and majesty," as Luke said in his twenty-first chapter, the most learned historian who ever was. The trouble is that he didn't come back.

The Emperor—Come here, Brother Chuckles, let me embrace you. Go, you will never cause a revolution in my empire. Your religion is charming. You will make all my subjects bust a gut. But you must tell me everything. Here is your god, born, spanked, hanged, and buried. Before him, had you no other?

Friar Chuckles—Yes, indeed, there was another in the same small country, just simply called the Lord. That one did not let himself get hanged like the other. He was a God you didn't mess around with. He took it into his head to take a horde of robbers and murderers under his protection in favor of which he slaughtered all the animals and all the eldest sons of Egypt one fine morning. After which, he expressly ordered his dear people to steal everything they could and to flee without fighting, given that he was the God of armies. Then he opened up the sea, suspending the waters on the right and left to let them pass on dry land, for lack of boats. Then he conducted them all into a desert where they all died; but he took great care of the second generation. It is for them that he made the walls of towns fall to the sound of a cornetto, and through the ministry of a lady tavern keeper. It was for his dear Jews that he stopped the sun and moon at high noon, to give them time to slaughter their enemies more at their ease. He loved this dear people so much that he made them slaves of the other peoples, which they still are today. But you see, all that was only a model, a shade, an image, a prophecy, that heralded the adventures of our Lord Jesus, Jewish God, son of God the Father, son of Mary, son of God the pigeon who proceeded from him, and who also had a putative father.

Admire, Sacred Majesty, the profundity of our divine religion. Our hanged God, being Jewish, was predicted by all the Jewish prophets.

Your Sacred Majesty should know that among this divine people there were divine men who knew the future better than you know what is happening in Peking. Those people only had to play the harp and, straight away, all future events presented themselves before their eyes. A prophet named Isaiah slept with a woman by order of the Lord. He had a son, and this son was our Lord Jesus Christ because his name was Maher-Shalal-Hash-Baz, *quickly share the spoils*.[4] Another prophet, named Ezekiel, slept on his left side three hundred and eighty-four days, and forty on his right side, which meant Jesus Christ. If Your Sacred Majesty permits me to say it, this Ezekiel ate excrement on his bread, as he says in his fourth chapter. And that meant Jesus Christ.

Another prophet, named Hosea, slept with a prostitute named Gomer, daughter of Diblaim, by God's command. And that meant, not only Jesus Christ but his two older brothers, James the Greater and James the Lesser, according to the interpretation of the most learned Fathers of our Holy Church.

Another prophet, named Jonah, was swallowed by a sea dog and lived three days and three nights in its belly. This is visibly Jesus Christ again, who was buried three days and three nights, in subtracting one night and two days to make the count fall right. The two sisters, Oholah and Oholibah, spread their thighs to every comer, have a *bordel* built and give the preference to those who have genitals like donkeys or horses, according to the very words used in Holy Scripture,[5] and that means the Church of Christ.

And that is how everything was predicted in the Jewish books. Your Sacred Majesty was predicted. Even I was predicted, for it is written, "I shall call them to the extremities of the Orient," and it is Friar Chuckles who comes to call you to give yourself to Jesus Christ, my Savior.

The Emperor—In what days were these fine predictions written?

Friar Chuckles—I don't know that precisely, but I do know that the prophecies proved the miracles of Jesus Christ, my Savior, and the miracles of Jesus Christ prove the prophecies in turn. No one's ever been able to answer that argument, and it will no doubt establish our sect all over the world, if we have a lot of believers, soldiers, and ready money.

The Emperor—I believe it, and I have already been forewarned. One goes far with money and prophecies. But you haven't yet told me about the miracles of your God. You only told me that he was spanked and hanged.

Friar Chuckles—Ah, Sire, is that not already a very great miracle? But there were many others. Firstly, the devil carried him off to the top of a mountain, from which you could see all the kingdoms of the world, and said to him, "I will give you all these kingdoms if you worship me." But God mocked the devil. Later, our Lord Jesus was invited to a village wedding and the boys being drunk but out of wine, our Lord Jesus changed the water to wine on the spot, after insulting his mother.[6] Some time later, finding himself near Gadara, or Gesara, along the little Lake of Gennesaret, he encountered demons in the bodies of two persons possessed. He chased them out without delay and sent them into a herd of two thousand pigs that went off grunting and threw themselves into the lake where they drowned.[7] And what proves even more the greatness of this miracle is that there were no pigs in that country.

The Emperor—I am annoyed, Brother Chuckles, that your god played a trick like that. The owner of the pigs must not have been very pleased. Have you any idea how much two thousand fat pigs are worth in money? I see a man ruined, with no means of support. I am no longer surprised they hanged your god. The pig owner must have presented a petition against him, and I can assure you that, in my country, a god like that, performing a miracle like that, would not carry things any further. You give me a great urge to read the books the Lord Jesus wrote to see how he justified such a strange sort of miracle.

Friar Chuckles—Sacred majesty, he never wrote any books. He didn't know how to read or write.

The Emperor—Ah! Ah! Here is something worth all the rest. A lawmaker who has never written any law!

Friar Chuckles—Fie, heavens, Sire! When a god comes to get himself hanged, he doesn't bother with such bagatelles! He has his secretaries write them. Some forty of them took the trouble to write down all these truths, a hundred years later. It's true that they all contradict each other, but it is in that very fact that the truth consists, and from these forty stories, we chose four in the end, which are precisely those that contradict themselves the most, so that the truth will show more clearly.

All his disciples performed even more miracles than he did, and we perform still more every day. We have among us the god St. Francis Xavier, who resuscitated nine dead people altogether in India. Truth be told, no one saw the resurrections, but we celebrated them from one end of the earth to the other, and were believed. Believe me, Sire, become a Jesuit, and I guarantee that we will publish a list of your miracles before two years are out. We will make you a saint, celebrate your Feast Day in Rome and call you Saint Yongzheng after your death.

The Emperor—I'm in no hurry, Brother Chuckles. That may come in time. All I ask is not to be hanged like your god was, because it seems a rather high price to pay for divinity.

Brother Chuckles—Ah, Sire! That's because you have no faith yet. But once you've been baptized, you will be enchanted to be hanged for the love of our Savior, Jesus Christ. What pleasure you will have to see him at Mass, to speak to him, and eat him!

The Emperor—What? Death of me! You people eat your god?

Friar Chuckles—Yes, Sire, I make him and I eat him. I prepared four dozen this
morning, and I will you get some later, if Your Sacred Majesty commands.

The Emperor—You will give me great pleasure, my friend. Go quickly, fetch
your gods.

I will order my cooks to stand ready meanwhile, to cook them. You will
tell them what sauce to add. I imagine that a dish of gods must be excellent,
and that I will have never eaten better.

Friar Chuckles—Sacred Majesty, I obey your supreme orders, and I'll be back
in a moment. God be praised! Here is an emperor I will make a Christian
of, upon my word!

While Friar Chuckles went to get his lunch, the Emperor remained with his
Secretary of State, Ouang-Tse. They were both in the grip of the greatest astonishment and the keenest indignation.

"The other Jesuits," said the Emperor, "like Parennin, Verbiest, Péreira,
Bouvet, and the others, never admitted a single one of these abominable extravagances to me. I see all too clearly that these missionaries are scoundrels that
have imbeciles for followers. The scoundrels succeeded with my father by performing experiments in physics that amused him, and the imbeciles succeeded
with the populace. They are convinced, and they convince others. That can
become highly pernicious. I see that the tribunals had every reason to present
petitions against these disturbers of the public peace. Tell me, I implore you, you
who have studied the history of Europe, how it is that a religion so absurd, so
blasphemous, was adopted by so many small nations?

The Secretary of State—Alas, Sire! Just like the sect of the god Fo was spread
throughout your empire, by charlatans who won over the common people.
Your Majesty would not believe what a prodigious effect the charlatans of
Europe have had in their land. The scallywag who just spoke to you admitted
himself that his accomplices, after having taught dogmas to the rabble made
for them, then make it rise against the government. They destroyed a great
empire called the Roman Empire, which was spread across Europe and
Asia, and blood was spilled for over fourteen centuries by the divisions
among these sycophants who wanted to make themselves the masters

of men's minds. First they made the princes believe they could not rule without the priests, and soon they rose up against the princes. I read that they dethroned an emperor named Debonaire, a Henri IV, a Frederick,[8] and over thirty kings, and that they assassinated more than twenty.

If the wisdom of the Chinese government has restrained the bonzes who dishonor your provinces until now, it can never avert the ills that the bonzes of Europe will cause. Those people have a spirit a hundred times more fervent, a zeal more violent, and a fury more reasoned in their dementia than the fanaticism of all the bonzes of Japan, Siam, and all those who are tolerated in China.

The idiots among them preach, and the scoundrels intrigue. They subjugate men through the women, and women through the confessional. Masters of all the family secrets, which they relate to their superiors, they are soon the masters of the state without yet even appearing to be so, that much surer of achieving their designs for not seeming to have any. They reach power through humility, wealth through poverty, and cruelty through mildness.

Do you remember, Sire, the fable of the dragons who turned themselves into sheep, in order to devour men more easily? That is their character. There have never been monsters more dangerous on earth, and God has never had enemies more sinister.

The Emperor—Hush. Here comes Friar Chuckles with his lunch. A little fun is in order.

Friar Chuckles arrived indeed holding a great tin box that resembled a tobacco tin in his hand. "Let us see your god who is in the box," the Emperor said. Friar Chuckles at once took out a dozen little pieces of wafer, round and flat as paper. "My word," said the Emperor, "my friend, if we have only that for our lunch, we're going to have a meager meal. A god, to my mind, should be somewhat plumper. What do you expect me to do with these pieces of paste?" "Sire," said Friar Chuckles, "may your Majesty just have a pint of red wine brought, and the rest will be easy."

The Emperor asked him why he wanted red instead of white wine, which was better at lunch. Chuckles replied that he was going to change the wine into blood, and that it was easier to make blood with red wine than with pale wine. His Majesty found the reason excellent and ordered that a bottle of red wine be brought. In the meanwhile, he amused himself with gazing at the gods that Friar Chuckles had brought in the pocket of his drawers. He was very surprised to see that the little pieces of paste were stamped with a gibbet and a poor devil attached to it. "Uh, Sire," Friar Chuckles said, "don't you remember that I told you that our god was hanged? We always engrave his gallows on these little wafers that we change into gods. We put those gallows everywhere in our temples, our houses, our crossroads, along our main roads, and we sing, "Good day, our only hope."We swallow God with his gallows. "That's all very well," the Emperor said, "All that I wish you, is not to end as he did."

Meanwhile, the bottle of red wine was brought. Friar Chuckles set it on a table beside his tin box and took a greasy book out of his pocket. He put it in his right hand, then, turning to the Emperor, said, "Sire, I have the honor of being gatekeeper, reader, conjurer, acolyte, subdeacon, deacon and priest. Our Holy Father, the pope, the Great Innocent III, decided in his first book, *Mysteries of the Mass*, that our god had been a *gatekeeper* when he chased good merchants out of the temple with whips, who had permission to sell turtledoves to those who came to sacrifice. He was a *reader* when, according to Luke, he took the book of the synagogue, even though he didn't know how to read or write. He was a *conjurer* when he drove all the devils into the pigs. He was an *acolyte* because the Jewish prophet Jeremiah said, "I am the light of the world," and because acolytes carry candles. He was a *subdeacon* when he changed the water into wine because the subdeacons serve at table. He was a *deacon* when he fed four thousand men, not counting the women and small children, with seven small loaves of bread and a few small fish in the land of Magadan, known the world over according to St. Matthew, or else when he fed five thousand men with five loaves and two small fish near Bethsaida, as St. Luke said.[9] Finally, he was a *priest* in the order of Melchizedek[10] when he said to his disciples that he was going to give them his body to eat. Being therefore a priest like him, I'm going to change this bread into gods. Every crumb of this bread will be a god in body and spirit. You will think you are seeing bread, eating bread, and you will be eating God.

"Then although the blood of this god will be in the body I have created with some words, I will change your red wine into the blood of this same god. For a plenitude of right, I will drink it. It is entirely up to Your Majesty to do as much. I have only to throw water on your face to make you gatekeeper, reader, conjurer, acolyte, subdeacon, deacon and priest. You will have a divine meal with me."

Friar Chuckles promptly pronounced some words in Latin, swallowed two dozen hosts, drank a pint, and said grace very devoutly.

"But my dear friend," said the Emperor, "you have eaten and drunk your god. What will become of him when you need a chamber pot?" "Sire," said Friar Chuckles, "he will become whatever he can. That is his affair. Some of our doctors of theology say we deliver him in our water-closets; others, that he escapes through our perspiration. Some claim he returns to heaven. As for myself, I have done my duty as a priest, and that is enough for me. And if I am given a good dinner after this lunch with a little money for my trouble, I am happy."

"That isn't all, however," said the Emperor to Friar Chuckles, "I know there are other missionaries in my empire that are not Jesuits, that are called Dominicans, Franciscans, and Capuchins. Tell me in conscience whether they eat God like you?"

"They eat him, Sire," said the good man, "but it only leads to their damnation. They are all scoundrels, and our greatest enemies. They want to pull the rug out from under our feet. They are constantly denouncing us to our Holy Father, the pope. Your Majesty would do very well to chase them all out and only keep the Jesuits. That would be one real way of earning eternal life, even if you don't become Christian."

The Emperor swore he would not fail to do so. He gave a few silver coins to Friar Chuckles, who immediately ran off to announce the good news to all his confreres.

The next day, the Emperor kept his word. He had all the missionaries assembled, whether those that are called seculars, or those that are very irregularly called regulars, or propaganda priests, or apostolic vicars, bishops *in partibus*,[11] foreign mission priests, Capuchins, Franciscans, Dominicans, Hieronymites,[12] and Jesuits. He spoke to them in these terms, in the presence of three hundred colaos:

> Tolerance has always seemed to me to be the primary bond between men, and the primary duty of sovereigns. If there were any religions in the world that could arrogate the title of being the only right one, it is most certainly ours. You all admit that we were paying homage to a Supreme Being in a pure unadulterated religion before any of the countries you come from were known even to its neighbors, before a single one of your occidental countries

had even acquired the use of the written word. You did not exist when we already had a powerful empire. Our ancient religion, unalterable in our tribunals but having been corrupted among the people, we tolerated the bonzes of Fo, the talapoins of Siam, the lamas of Tartary, the secretaries of Laokium, and, regarding all men as our brothers, we have never punished any of them for straying. Error is not a crime. God is not offended at being worshipped in a ridiculous manner. A father does not cast out one of his children for bowing or curtsying incorrectly in greeting him. He is satisfied, so long as he is loved and respected. The tribunals of my empire do not reproach you with your absurdities. They pity your infatuation with the most detestable collection of fables that human folly has ever accumulated. They bemoan even more the poor use you make of what little reason remains to you to justify these fables.

But what they do not forgive you is to have come from the ends of the earth to destroy our peace. You are the blind instruments of a little Italian lama who, after having deposed a few of his neighboring kinglings, wishes to absorb vaster empires in our Oriental regions.

We are all too familiar with the horrible mayhem you caused in Japan. Twelve religions flourished there with commerce, under the auspices of a wise and moderate government. A fraternal harmony reigned between these twelve religions. You appeared, and conflict overwhelmed Japan. Blood ran on all sides. You did the same in Siam and in Manila. I must preserve my empire from such a dangerous plague. I am tolerant, and I expulse you all because you are intolerant. I chase you out because, divided among yourselves and detesting each other, you are prepared to infect my people with the poison that devours you. I will not cast you into dungeons, where you make all those not of your opinion waste away in Europe. I am even further from condemning you to torture, as you do all those you call heretics in Europe. We do not uphold our religion with executioners here. We do not use such arguments in our disputes. Leave. Take your atrocious follies elsewhere, and may you learn wisdom! The wagons that will conduct you to Macao are ready. I give you clothing and money. Soldiers will see to your security en route. I do not want the people to insult you. Go and be witnesses to my justice and clemency in Europe.

They left. Christianity was abolished in China, as it was in Persia, Tartary, Japan, India, Turkey, and all Africa. It's a great shame, but that's what happens when you're infallible.

Appendix

AN ANONYMOUS
CHARACTER SKETCH
OF VOLTAIRE

1734 or 1735

It has not been sufficiently noted that the nasty character traits endlessly attributed to Voltaire—greedy, vain, superficial, friendless, inconstant, unpatriotic, etc.—actually had their origin in this corrosive little tract written simply in retaliation for perceived slights to France in Voltaire's *Letters on England* in 1734,[1] such as his praise of England's relative tolerance, and of Bacon, Locke, and Newton, to the detriment of Descartes. Strachey called this book a first seed of friendship between France and England, which soon flourished mightily, despite centuries of hostility, but the book was burned in France in 1734 and Voltaire had to flee arrest. It became an international bestseller, however, exciting curiosity far and wide about Voltaire. This acounts for the astonishing spread of this tract, reaching even to America. Its authoritative assessment, from a man who did not know him, has been widely echoed ever since.

Y ou ask me, Sir, for a portrait of M. de V . . . whom you know only by his works, you say. Knowing the author is already a lot, in my opinion. You wish to see the man. I will depict both for you.

M. de V . . . is a little below the height of tall men, which is to say, a little above average height. (I'm speaking to a natural scientist, so no chicanery over observations.) He is thin, with a dry disposition. Ebullient,[2] with a gaunt face, a witty, caustic air and shrewd, sparkling eyes. All the fire you find in his works, you find in the way he moves. Quick to the point of heedlessness, he's an ardent man who comes and goes, who dazzles you and sparkles. A man so constituted cannot fail to have health concerns. The sword blade wears out the sheath. Gay by temperament, serious in conduct by choice, open but not frank, calculating but unsubtle, sociable without friends, he knows society and ignores it. Aristippus by morning, Diogenes by night, he likes grandeur and despises grandees, is at ease with them, and is guarded among his equals. He starts out politely, grows cold, and ends in aversion. He loves the Court and is bored there. He holds to nothing by choice and to everything by inconstancy. Rational but unprincipled, his reason has its fits, as madness does in others. His mind is upright, his heart unjust, he thinks everything over, and mocks it all. Libertine but not immoderate, he can also moralize without morals. Excessively vain, but even more self-interested, he works less for reputation than for money. He hungers and thirsts for that. In short, he hurries himself through work, so that he can live hurriedly. He was made to enjoy, but wants to hoard. There is your man. Now here is your author.

Born a poet, verses come too easily to him. This effortlessness harms him. He abuses it, and gives almost nothing that is fully achieved: a facile writer, ingenious, elegant. After poetry, his stock in trade would be history, if he did less reasoning and drew no parallels, though he makes quite good ones at times.[3]

M. de V . . . in his last work wished to follow in Bayle's approach. He attempts to copy it while censuring it.[4] It has long been said that for a writer to be without passions or prejudice, he would need to have no fatherland or religion. On that basis, M. de V . . . takes great strides toward perfection. First, he cannot be accused of being a patriot of his nation.

On the contrary, we find he has a tic approaching the quirk of old people. The good people always praise the past and are unhappy with the present. M. de V . . . is always unhappy with his country and praises excessively what is a thousand leagues away. As to religion, he is clearly undecided in this matter. No doubt, he would be the impartial man one seeks, except for a slight leaven of anti-Jansenism, a bit too apparent in his works.

M. de V . . . knows a great deal of French and foreign literature, and possesses that mixed erudition so *à la mode* today. Politician, physicist, geometer, he is all he wishes to be, but always superficially, incapable of probing deeper. Nevertheless, one must possess a nimble mind to touch on every subject as he does. His taste is more delicate than sure, an ingenious satirist and a bad critic. He likes abstract sciences, and no one is surprised. Imagination is his element, but he has no inventiveness, and everyone is surprised. He is reproached with never being in a reasonable middle ground. Now a philanthropist, now an exaggerate satirist. To sum it up, M. de V . . . wishes to be an extraordinary man, and that he most certainly is.

Non vultus, non color unus.[5]

OLIVER GOLDSMITH ON VOLTAIRE

This text provides a very different assessment from one of those many admirers in the British Isles, the Irish author of *The Vicar of Wakefield*. Published in Goldsmith's *The Citizen of the World*, it was inspired by a false report of Voltaire's death in 1760—just before his "ecr-l'inf" campaign began in full force, so it is a revealing glimpse of how Voltaire was already perceived internationally after his world history, *Essai sur les mœurs*, his poems on Natural Law and on the Lisbon Disaster, and his novel, *Candide*, among numerous other works. The "agonies" and "unmerited reproach" mentioned probably refer to the fiasco in Berlin 1752–53 and its aftermath.

A curious pseudo "memoir" of Voltaire, which may date from earlier years, follows this piece.

We have just received accounts here that Voltaire, the poet and philosopher of Europe, is dead. He is now beyond the reach of the thousand enemies who, while living, degraded his writings and branded his character. Scarce a page of his later productions that does not betray the agonies of a heart bleeding under the scourge of unmerited reproach. Happy, therefore, at last in escaping from calumny! happy in leaving a world that was unworthy of him and his writings!

Let others bestrew the hearses of the great with panegyric; but such a loss as the world has now suffered affects me with stronger emotions. When a philosopher dies I consider myself as losing a patron, an instructor, and a friend. I consider the world as losing one who might serve to console her amidst the desolations of war and ambition. Nature every day produces in abundance men capable of filling all the requisite duties of authority; but she is niggard in the birth of an exalted mind, scarcely producing in a century a single genius to bless and enlighten a degenerate age. Prodigal in the production of kings, governors, mandarins, chams [khans], and courtiers, she seems to have forgotten, for more than three thousand years, the manner in which she once formed the brain of a Confucius; and well it is she has forgotten, when a bad world gave him so very bad a reception.

Whence, my friend, this malevolence, which has ever pursued the great, even to the tomb? whence this more than fiendlike disposition of embittering the lives of those who would make us more wise and more happy?

When I cast my eye over the fates of several philosophers, who have at different periods enlightened mankind, I must confess it inspires me with the most degrading reflections on humanity. When I read of the stripes of Mencius, the tortures of Tchin, the bowl of Socrates, and the bath of Seneca; when I hear of the persecutions of Dante, the imprisonment of Galileo, the indignities suffered by Montaigne, the banishment of Descartes, the infamy of Bacon, and that even Locke himself escaped not without reproach; when I think on such subjects, I hesitate whether most to blame the ignorance or the villainy of my fellow-creatures.

Should you look for the character of Voltaire among the journalists and illiterate writers of the age, you will there find him characterized as a monster, with a head turned to wisdom and a heart inclining to vice; the powers of his mind and the baseness of his principles forming a detestable contrast. But seek for his character among writers like himself, and you find him very differently described. You perceive him, in their accounts, possessed of good nature, humanity, greatness of soul, fortitude, and almost every virtue; in this description those who might be supposed best acquainted with his character are unanimous. The royal Prussian, d'Argens, Diderot, d'Alembert, and Fontenelle conspire in drawing the picture, in describing the friend of man, and the patron of every rising genius.

An inflexible perseverance in what he thought was right and a generous detestation of flattery formed the groundwork of this great man's character. From these principles many strong virtues and few faults arose; as he was warm in his friendship and severe in his resentment, all that mention him seem possessed of the same qualities, and speak of him with rapture or detestation. A person of his eminence can have few indifferent as to his character; every reader must be an enemy or an admirer.

This poet began the course of glory so early as the age of eighteen, and even then was author of a tragedy which deserves applause. Possessed of a small patrimony, he preserved his independence in an age of venality; and supported the dignity of learning by teaching his contemporary writers to live like him, above the favors of the great. He was banished from his native country for a satire upon the royal concubine. He had accepted the place of historian to the French king, but refused to keep it when he found it was presented only in order that he should be the first flatterer of the state.[1]

The great Prussian[2] received him as an ornament to his kingdom, and had sense enough to value his friendship and profit by his instructions. In this court he continued till an intrigue, with which the world seems hitherto unacquainted, obliged him to quit that country. His own happiness, the happiness of the monarch, of his sister, of a part of the court, rendered his departure necessary.

Tired at length of courts and all the follies of the great, he retired to Switzerland, a country of liberty, where he enjoyed tranquility and the muse. Here, though without any taste for magnificence himself, he usually entertained at his table the learned and polite of Europe, who were attracted by a desire of seeing a person from whom they had received so much satisfaction. The entertainment was conducted with the utmost elegance, and the conversation was that of philosophers. Every country that at once united liberty and science were his peculiar favourites. The being an Englishman was to him a character that claimed admiration and respect.

Between Voltaire and the disciples of Confucius there are many differences; however, being of a different opinion does not in the least diminish my esteem; I am not displeased with my brother because he happens to ask our Father for favors in a different manner from me. Let his errors rest in peace; his excellencies deserve admiration; let me with the wise admire his wisdom; let the envious and the ignorant ridicule his foibles; the folly of others is ever most ridiculous to those who are themselves most foolish. Adieu.

> The following curious "memoir" of Voltaire has puzzled for years because, though Goldsmith claims "the honour of having seen him in Paris" and gives a vivid firsthand description, it is full of anachronisms. Goldsmith may have met Fontenelle and Diderot during his trip to Paris in 1754,

but Voltaire was then living in Geneva, not to return till 1778. Fontenelle died in 1757, so he could not have been present in 1778, nor apparently was Goldsmith. However, Goldsmith may have gathered these impressions from his friend, the English poet, Edward Young, who met Voltaire when he was in England (1726–1729). Young made a quip on the occasion, which was widely cited.[3] Or perhaps Goldsmith was simply struggling to find a way to write a "memoir" about Voltaire gathered from all these firsthand sources, but he died at the age of forty-four, before this piece was finished.[4]

Some disappointments of this kind served to turn our poet from a passion which only tended to obstruct his advancement in more exalted pursuits. His mind, which at that time was pretty well balanced between pleasure and philosophy, quickly began to incline to the latter. He now thirsted after a more comprehensive knowledge of mankind than either books or his own country could possibly bestow.

England about this time was coming into repute throughout Europe as the land of philosophers. Newton, Locke, and others began to attract the attention of the curious, and drew hither a concourse of learned men from every part of Europe. Not our learning alone, but our politics also began to be regarded with admiration; a government in which subordination and liberty were blended in such just proportions was now generally studied as the finest model of civil society. This was an inducement sufficient to make Voltaire pay a visit to this land of philosophers and of liberty.

Accordingly, in the year 1726, he came over to England. A previous acquaintance with Atterbury, bishop of Rochester, and the Lord Bolingbroke, was sufficient to introduce him among the polite, and his fame as a poet got him the acquaintance of the learned in a country where foreigners generally find a cool reception. He only wanted introduction; his own merit was enough to procure the rest. As a companion, no man ever exceeded him when he pleased to lead the conversion; which, however, was not always the case. In company which he either disliked or despised, few could be more reserved than he; but when he was warmed in discourse and had got over a hesitating manner which he was sometimes subject to, it was rapture to hear him. His meagre visage seemed insensibly to gather beauty; every muscle in it had meaning, and his eye beamed with unusual brightness. The person who writes this memoir, who had the honor and the pleasure of being his acquaintance, remembers to have seen him in a select company of wits of both sexes at Paris, when the subject happened to turn upon English taste and learning. Fontenelle, who was of the party, and who, being unacquainted with the language or authors of the country he undertook to condemn, with a spirit truly vulgar began to revile both. Diderot, who liked the English and knew something of their literary pretensions, attempted to vindicate their poetry and learning, but with unequal abilities. The company quickly perceived that Fontenelle was superior in the dispute, and were surprised at the silence which Voltaire had preserved all the former part of the night, particularly as the conversation happened to turn upon one of his favourite topics. Fontenelle continued his triumph till about twelve o'clock, when Voltaire appeared at last roused from his reverie. His whole frame seemed animated. He began his defence with the utmost elegance mixed with spirit, and now and then let fall the finest strokes of raillery upon his antagonist; and his harangue lasted till three in the morning. I must confess, that, whether from national partiality, or from the elegant sensibility of his manner, I never was so charmed, nor did I ever remember so absolute a victory as he gained in this dispute.

CONDORCET'S ACCOUNT OF VOLTAIRE'S BATTLE

Condorcet, a well-known philosopher, mathematician and political scientist in his own right, visited Voltaire twice in his twenties, when Voltaire was in his seventies. He befriended Thomas Paine and Thomas Jefferson during their years in Paris, and wrote one of the first biographies of Voltaire, *Vie de Voltaire*, from which this is an extract. It contains a few factual errors but provides an eyewitness account of Voltaire's "écrasez-l'infâme" campaign and its effects, as well as some details on the persecutions of Jean Calas, the Count de Lally, and the young Chevalier de La Barre, whose cases Voltaire championed.

A great revolution was preparing itself in the minds of the times. Ever since the rebirth of philosophy, religion, established exclusively in all of Europe, had only been attacked in England. Leibnitz, Fontenelle, and other less-famous philosophers accused of being freethinkers, had all shown it respect in their writings. Bayle himself, using a precaution necessary to his safety while permitting himself all the objections, had seemed to only want to prove that revelation alone could resolve them and wrote as though he had formed the project of debasing reason to uplift faith. In England, the attacks had had little success and little consequence. The powers that be in that nation believed it was useful to leave the people in ignorance, apparently so that the habit of adoring the mysteries of the Bible would fortify their faith in those of the constitution. They made a sort of social propriety out of respect for the established religion. Besides, in a country where the Chamber of Commons alone can lead to fortune, and where its members are tumultuously elected by the people, apparent respect for its opinions must necessarily be erected as a virtue by all ambitious men.

A few bold works had appeared in France, but their attacks were only indirect. Even the book *Spirit* [*of the Laws*] was only aimed at religious principles in general. It attacked the bases of all religions and left to its readers the care of drawing their own conclusions and applying them. Rousseau's *Emile* appeared. "The Savoyard Vicar's Profession of Faith" it contained said nothing on the belief in God for moral purposes nor on the inutility of revelation that was not already in Voltaire's *Poem on Natural Law*; but those who were being attacked were warned that it was indeed of them that we were speaking. It was under their own names that they were being placed upon the stage, and not under the names of the priests of India or Tibet.[1] This boldness surprised Voltaire and excited his emulation.[2] The success of *Emile* encouraged him, and its persecution did not frighten him in the least. A warrant had been issued for Rousseau only for having put his name on the book. He had been persecuted in Geneva mainly for having said, in another section of *Emile*, that the people could not renounce the right to reform a vicious constitution. This doctrine authorized the citizens of this republic to destroy the aristocracy that its magistrates had established, and which concentrated hereditary authority in a few rich families.

Voltaire could imagine himself sure of avoiding persecution by hiding his name and, while taking care to treat governments with consideration, to direct all his blows against religion, and to even interest the civil powers in weakening its empire. A flood of works, in which he alternately employs eloquence, discussion, and above all pleasantries, spread across all Europe, in every form that the necessity of veiling the truth or making it sting could invent. His zeal against a religion that he considered the source of the fanaticism that had desolated Europe from its inception and of the superstition that had besotted it, and as the source of all the evils these enemies of humanity continued to exert, seemed to double his activity and his might. "I am weary," he said one day, "of hearing them repeat that a dozen men sufficed to establish Christianity, and I feel like proving to them that it would only take one to destroy it."

The critique of works that Christians consider inspired, the history of the dogmas that have succeeded each other since the beginning of this religion, the ridiculous and blood-drenched quarrels they have excited, the miracles, the prophecies, the fables spread throughout ecclesiastic and legendary histories, the religious wars, the massacres ordered in God's name, the scaffolds covering Europe at the cries of priests, the fanaticism depopulating the Americas, the blood of kings running from the swords of assassins; all of these subjects ceaselessly reappeared under a thousand guises in all his works. He excited indignation, made tears flow, and poured out torrents of ridicule. We shuddered at an atrocious act, we laughed at an absurdity. And he didn't worry about painting the pictures too often or repeating arguments. "I am told that I repeat myself," he wrote. "Oh well! Then I will repeat myself until it is corrected."

In any case, these works, severely forbidden in France, Italy, Vienna, Portugal, and Spain, only spread slowly.[3] Not all of them reached all readers, but there was not a single desolate corner of any province, nor any foreign nation crushed beneath the yoke of intolerance, that at least a few of them didn't reach.

The freethinkers, who only existed before in a few cities where the sciences were cultivated and only among men of letters, scientists, or men in high places, multiplied at his voice to all the classes of society, as well as in all nations. Soon, realizing their numbers and their force, they dared to show themselves, and Europe was astonished to discover itself a nonbeliever.

This same zeal, however, made enemies for Voltaire of all those who had obtained or expected to earn their existence and fortune from this religion. But their ranks no longer had a Bossuet, an Arnaud, or a Nicole.[4] Those who had replaced them through their talent, philosophy, or learning had passed into the opposition; and the members of the clergy who were among the least inferior, ceding to the interest of not losing face in the opinions of enlightened men, kept their distance, or limited themselves to upholding the political utility of a belief they would have been ashamed to share with the common people, and substituted a sort of religious Machiavellianism for the credulous superstitions of their predecessors.

Masses of libels and refutations came out; but Voltaire alone, in responding to them, could have retained the names of these works, read uniquely by those they were useless to and who could not or would not listen to the objections or responses.

To the shrieks of the fanatics, Voltaire opposed the benevolence of monarchs. The Empress of Russia, the King of Prussia, those of Poland, Denmark, and Sweden took interest in his endeavors, read his works, sought to merit his praise, and at times seconded his good works. In every country, the ministers and those in high positions who aspired to glory, who wanted their names known throughout Europe, courted the suffrage of the Philosopher of Ferney, confiding in him their hopes and fears for the progress of reason, their plans for the growth of enlightenment and for the destruction of fanaticism. He had formed a league throughout Europe of which he was the soul, whose rallying cry was *reason and tolerance*. When some great injustice took place in a nation, or some act of fanaticism was heard of, or some insult was made to humanity, a writing by Voltaire denounced the guilty to all Europe. And who knows how many times the fear of this terrible swift vengeance stilled the arms of the oppressors!

It was above all in France that he exercised this ministry of reason. From the Calas affair on,[5] every victim unjustly immolated or pursued by the steel of the laws found in him a supporter or avenger.

The torture of the Count de Lally aroused his indignation. Legal experts judging in Paris the conduct of a general in India; a death sentence pronounced without it being possible to cite a single clear-cut crime, and on top of that announcing only a suspicion of the gravest accusations; a judgment rendered on the testimony of his declared enemies, on the memoirs of a Jesuit who had composed two in contradiction with each other, uncertain of whether he should accuse the general or his enemies, not knowing whom he hated the most, or whom it would be of most use to him to condemn: such a sentence should have aroused the indignation of every friend of justice, despite the opprobrium poured on the poor general's head. And the horrible barbarity of dragging him off to the torture chamber, gagged, should have made the last fibers of every heart not hardened by the habit of disposing of men's lives shudder.

Nevertheless, Voltaire was long the only one to speak out. Most employees of the Compagnie des Indes, interested in throwing the consequences of their own fatal behavior on a man who no longer existed, the powerful tribunal that had condemned him, and all the men who had sold their voices to it, plus other bodies united to it by similar functions and interests, considered its cause as their own, along with the ministry, ashamed of having had the weakness or cruel policy of sacrificing the Count de Lally to the hope of hiding in his tomb all the errors that had caused the loss of India: everything seemed to oppose a belated justice. But Voltaire, in returning often to this subject, triumphed over the interests fighting to conserve themselves and snuff it out. Good people only needed to be informed of it, which drew others. And when the son of the Count de Lally, so famous for his eloquence and courage, reached the age where he could plead for justice, minds were prepared to applaud him and solicit for him. Voltaire was dying, twelve years later, when this unjust conviction was overturned. He heard the news, was revived, and wrote: "I die content for I see that the king loves justice." These were the last words written by the hand that had so long upheld the cause of humanity and of justice.

In the same year of 1766, another arrest surprised Europe, which, from reading the works of our philosophers, had believed that enlightenment had spread throughout France—at least in the classes of society where education is a duty and where, after fifteen years, the colleagues of Montesquieu had had the time to absorb its principles.

A wooden crucifix on the bridge of Abbeville was violated during the night. The scandalized townsfolk had their emotions enflamed and prolonged by the ridiculous ceremony of an *amende honorable*.[6] The Bishop of Amiens, governed in his old age by fanatics, and no longer in a condition to foresee the consequences of this religious farce, excited them further by his presence. During this time, the hatred of a bourgeois of Abbeville directed the suspicions of the people to the Chevalier de La Barre, a young soldier of a noble family with ties to the magistrate, who was living with his aunt, the Abbess of Villencourt, just outside of Abbeville. The trial began. The judges condemned the Chevalier de La Barre and his friend d'Etallonde, who had had the good sense to flee, to tortures that would terrify the imagination of a cannibal. The Chevalier de La Barre had put himself in the hands of justice. He had more to lose in leaving France and counted on the protection of his relations who held high posts in *Parlement* and in the Council. His hopes were deceived. His family feared drawing the attention of the public to this trial instead of seeking the support of public opinion, and at the age of about seventeen, he was condemned, by a majority of two votes, to having his head chopped off, after having his tongue torn out and submitting to the torments of the *question* [torture].

This horrible sentence was carried out, even though the accusations were as ridiculous as the tortures were atrocious. He was only *vehemently* suspected of having had some role in the affair of the crucifix. But he was declared guilty of having sung, in some wanton party, a few of those songs, half obscene and half religious that, despite their coarseness, amuse young boys of this age, due to their contrast with the respect and scruples education inspires on these subjects; of having recited an ode, whose well-known author was then collecting a pension from the king; of having genuflected passing before some libertine works in vogue at a time where men, lost in the austerity of religious morals, are no longer able to distinguish between pleasure and debauchery; and at last, of having spoken in a manner worthy of these songs and works.

All these accusations were upheld by the testimony of the type of people who had served these young men in their pleasure outings, or the gate-keepers of convents, so easily scandalized.

The arrest revolted every mind. No law pronounced the death penalty for the breaking of images nor for blasphemies of this nature,[7] and so the judges had even gone beyond the penalties imposed by the laws that all enlightened men see with horror still soiling our criminal code. There was no father of any family who must not have trembled, since there are few youths who escape similar indiscretions, and the judges condemned one to an atrocious death for words most of them had permitted themselves in their own youth, and perhaps still permit themselves, and whose children were as guilty as those they had condemned.

Voltaire was outraged and terrified at the same time. They had adroitly placed *The Philosophical Dictionary* among the number of books before which it was said the Chevalier de La Barre had bowed. It was meant to show that the reading of Voltaire's books had been the cause of all these foolish impieties. However, the danger to himself did not prevent him from taking up the defense of these victims of fanaticism. D'Etallonde, hiding in Wesel, obtained at his recommendation a post in a Prussian regiment. Several works informed all Europe of the details of this affair and the judges were terrified, in their very tribunes, of the appalling judgments that tore them from their obscurity to condemn them to an immortality of shame.

. . . Voltaire outlived this injustice for twelve years, and never lost sight of the hope of obtaining reparation for the boy; but he never had the consolation of succeeding.

MADAME SUARD'S VISIT TO FERNEY

in 1775

Amélie Suard and her journalist husband, Jean-Baptiste, were friends of Condorcet, Baron d'Holbach, Helvétius, and Thomas Jefferson. She made a special journey to Geneva to meet Voltaire, who was now eighty-one, and sent her impressions of him in these letters to her husband. These firsthand, detailed impressions of Voltaire were later published in *Lettres à son mari* (Letters to Her Husband) in 1802, then inserted into her husband's works, *Mélanges de littérature de J. B. A. Suard* in 1803. Mme. Suard also wrote novels and essays.

PREFACE

Y ou wish then, my friend, to publish these letters that were only written for you alone and that were never destined for the honors of the printing press? You know my enthusiasm for Voltaire. You know that I had been nourished, so to say, in admiration for this great man; that during a trip he had made to Flanders, he had gone to see my father who had a very fine physics laboratory. This visit left its traces. We often recalled it in my family, where his beautiful works were intensely appreciated and felt. Surrounded since my marriage by all the friends and admirers of M. de Voltaire, incessantly amused or enchanted by the charm of his writings, my enthusiasm for him could only increase. How can one not admire a man who employs his genius to defend the oppressed, who speaks of God as the father common to all men, and of tolerance as both the most sacred of rights and as the most cherished of duties? I have always been disposed to believe that virtue exists in proportion to the feelings of goodness and humanity that each man carries in his heart. Ah! In what man can one find this sentiment deeper or more active than in Voltaire? The generous interest he took in the oppressed accompanied him until his last breath; even in his death throes, his last thoughts were addressed to M. de Lally-Tolendal on the happy success of a cause that had to triumph, since it was defended by filial piety and the most noble, moving eloquence.

While adoring the genius and the passionate soul of Voltaire for the interests of his fellow creatures, I do not pretend to approve the excesses to which the violence of his passions often led him. I do not consider him a model of virtue in his life, though it was filled with noble and generous acts. I envision him even less as a model of wisdom in all his works. I reserve the worship we owe perfect virtue to the Antonines, the Marcus Aureliuses, and the Fénelons. But our gratitude and our admiration is still attached to those who, despite their errors and their faults, employed all the means of a beneficent and active genius to rid us of deadly and dangerous errors and who labored constantly to give birth to new virtues among their fellow men.

LETTER I

Geneva, June 1775

I have finally obtained the goal of my desires and of my voyage: I have seen M. de Voltaire. The transports of St. Theresa never surpassed those the sight of this great man gave me. I felt as though I were in the presence of a god, but of a god long worshipped and adored, to whom I had been finally given the power to show all my respect and recognition. If his genius had not brought this illusion, his face alone would have. It is impossible to describe the fire in his eyes, nor the graces of his features. What an enchanting smile! There is nary a wrinkle that isn't graceful. Ah! How surprised I was when in the place of this decrepit figure that I thought I saw, appeared this physiognomy full of fire and expression. When, instead of a stooped old man, I saw a man of upright bearing, lofty and noble though somewhat neglectful, with a gait firm and even nimble yet, and speaking in a tone with a courtesy that, like his genius, belongs to him alone! My heart beat with violence upon entering the courtyard of this castle consecrated by the presence of this great man for so many years. Having reached the moment so acutely desired, that I had come from so far to seek, and that I had obtained by so many sacrifices, I would have liked to delay the happiness that I had always expected from the sights dearest to my life; and I felt almost relieved when Madame Denis[1] told us that he had gone for a walk. Madame Cramer, who had accompanied us, went ahead to announce me and my brother, and to bring him the letters from my friends. He soon appeared, crying out, "Where is this lady? Where is she? It's a soul I've come to seek." And as I advanced, "The letter says, Madame, that you are pure soul." "This soul, Monsieur, is filled with you and has been sighing for the happiness of approaching yours for ever so long."

I spoke to him first of his health and of the concern it had given his friends. He told me what his fears make him say to everyone, that he was dying, and that I had reached a hospital because even Madame Denis herself was ill, and that he regretted not being able to offer me shelter.

At that moment, there were a dozen people in the salon. Our dear Audibert was among the number. I had been sorry not to find him in Marseilles; I was enchanted to find him at Ferney. M. Poissonnier had also just arrived. He had not yet seen M. de Voltaire. He went to stand by his side, and it was to speak to him incessantly of himself. M. de Voltaire told him that he had rendered a great service to humanity by finding the means to desalinate sea water. "Oh, Monsieur!" he said, "I have rendered it an even greater one since. I was made for discoveries. I have found the means of conserving meat for years on end without salting it." It would seem he had come to Ferney to get himself admired, and not to pay homage to M. de Voltaire. Oh! How petty he appeared to me! What a miserable thing is vain mediocrity beside a modest and indulgent genius! For M. de Voltaire seemed to listen with indulgence, while I was impatient to excess. I had pricked up my ears to miss not a word that came out of the mouth of this great man, who says a thousand witty and amiable things with that easy grace that charms in all his works; but whose rapidity is more striking yet in conversation. In no hurry to speak, he listens to everyone with more flattering attention than he has perhaps ever received himself. His niece said a few words. His eyes full of benevolence were fixed on her, with the most amiable smile on his lips. When M. Poissonnier had spoken enough of himself, he was willing to cede his place. Pressed by a lively desire, by some sort of passion which surmounted all my timidity, I seized the moment. I had been a bit encouraged by something kind he had said of me. His look, his glances, his civilities had banished all my agitations and left me wholly to my warm enthusiasm. I had never felt anything like it. It was a feeling that had been nourished, that had grown for fifteen years, which, for the first time, I could discuss with the man who was its object. I expressed it in all the disorder with which such great pleasure inspired me. M. de Voltaire seemed to enjoy it. He stopped the torrent from time to time with kind words: "You're spoiling me. You want to turn my head." And when he was able to speak to me of all his friends, it was with the greatest interest. He spoke to me a lot of you, of his gratitude for your kindnesses. That was the word he used.[2] And of Maréchal de Richelieu. "How his conduct surprised and grieved me!" he said. He spoke a lot of Monsieur Turgot. He has three terrible things against him, he said: the financiers, the scoundrels, and gout. I told him that his virtues, his courage, and the public's esteem could be used against them. "But Madame, I've had letters saying you are among our enemies." "Well, Monsieur, you mustn't believe what's been written to you, but you may believe me perhaps. I am the enemy of no one. I pay homage to the virtues and knowledge of Monsieur Turgot. But I am familiar with the great virtues and knowledge of Monsieur Necker as well, which I honor as much. Besides, I like him personally, and I owe him my gratitude." As I had pronounced these words in a serious, earnest tone, M. de Voltaire looked as though he feared he had caused me grief. "Come now, Madame," he said gently, "calm yourself. God will bless you. You know how to love your friends. I am not at all Monsieur Necker's enemy, but you will forgive me for preferring Monsieur Turgot.[3] Let's speak no more about it."

Leaving the salon, he asked me to consider his house as my own. Already he had forgotten that he had just told me he was very sorry not to be able to offer me shelter. . . . "I beg you to, Madame, while regretting not being able to do you the honors." I contented myself with asking his permission to come to Ferney for an hour or so at times, to enquire after his health and that of Madame Denis. I assured him (for I know he fears visits) that I would leave content if I only perceived him from afar, and, as he seemed fatigued, I entreated him, kissing his hands, to retire. He squeezed and kissed mine with feeling and went into his study. I think he finished reading the letters there in which my friends had spoken so well of me, for shortly after he came back to join me in his garden. I strolled alone with him for quite a while. You can imagine how happy I was to speak at liberty with this sublime genius, whose works had been the charm of my life, and in these splendid gardens, before these rich hillsides that he had sung of so well! I spoke to him only of what might console him for the injustice of men, whose bitterness I saw he still felt. Ah! I said to him, if you could only see the applause, the acclamations that rise in the public assemblies when your name is pronounced, how content you would be with our gratitude and love! How sweet it would be for me to see you witness your own glory! If only I had, alas! the power of a god to transport you there a moment! "I'm there! I'm there!" he cried. "I'm enjoying all of that with you. I no longer regret a thing."[4]

Throughout the conversation, I was as surprised as delighted to see him walking by my side with steps both firm and agile, to the point where I could not have outstripped him without tiring myself (he was then eighty-four years old);[5] me who, as you know, am quite a walker. My anxiety stopped me from time to time. "Monsieur, are you not tired? For mercy's sake, don't trouble yourself." "No, Madame, I still walk very well, despite my sufferings." The fear he has of *Parlement* makes him speak this way to all who come to Ferney. Ah! How could they even conceive of troubling the last days of this great man! No, his retreat, his genius, and our love will save my country from a crime so cowardly. Before leaving him, I thanked him for his reception, so full of kindness, that had paid me with usury for the two hundred leagues I had just traveled to come find him. He didn't want to believe that I had left you, as well as my friends, only to see him. I assured him that the letters of my friends had deceived him about everything, except that. In short, I left him so full of the happiness I had tasted, that this sharp impression deprived me of sleep for the entire night.

LETTER II

Geneva, June 1775

We went to dine today, my friend, at Monsieur and Madame Florian's, relatives of M. de Voltaire,[6] who have a very lovely house near Ferney. They are two people whose greatest merit lies in belonging to his family. M. de Voltaire, who surely knows it better than anyone, nevertheless treats them with extreme kindness. I was boiling with impatience to leave them after dinner to go see the great man. M. Hennin, our resident in Geneva,[7] took me by the hand.

After having chatted a moment with Madame Denis, we were very promptly admitted. We found him sitting by the fire, a book in hand. He looked demoralized. His eyes, which flashed last we met, were clouded. He said to me, in that tone of courtesy that distinguishes him as much by his manners as by his genius, "Ah! Madame, how good you are! You don't abandon an old man. You deign to visit him." Can you conceive of anything more adorable? So gracious to all those he consents to see, even to expressing gratitude! I spoke to him of his health. He had eaten strawberries, he said, that had given him indigestion. "In that case," I said, taking his hand and kissing it, "you won't eat any more of them, will you? You will take care of yourself for your friends and for the public whose delight you are." "I will do anything you like," he said, and as I continued my caresses, "Isn't she sweet!" he cried, "You bring me back to life! How fortunate I am to be so miserable! She wouldn't treat me so well if I were only twenty." I told him that I couldn't love him more than I do, and that I would be pitiable if I could not show him all the intensity of the feelings he inspires in me. Indeed, his eighty-four years put my passion at its ease without diminishing its strength. We spoke of Ferney, which he had filled with inhabitants, which owes its existence to him. He congratulated himself. I remembered this verse, which I recited to him: *J'ai fait un peu de bien; c'est mon plus bel ouvrage.* (I have done a little good; it's my finest work.)

Our resident told him that, if ever his works were lost, they could be recovered in their entirety in my head. "So they will be corrected," he said, "with this inimitable grace?" And as he had abandoned his hand to me, which I kissed, "See how I let myself go," he said, kissing mine; "It's just that it's so sweet!" I asked him what he thought of the *Barmécides*, that M. de la Harpe had encharged me with bringing him. He praised them with moderation, leaving me with the inkling that there were things to be desired about which he would write to M. de la Harpe. As to *In Praise of Pascal* by Monsieur de Condorcet, he told me he found it so beautiful that he was horrified. "How so, Monsieur?" "Yes, Madame. If that man was such a great man, then we are all great fools not to think like him. M.

de Condorcet will do us all a great wrong, if he prints this work as he has sent it. That Racine was a good Christian," he added, "is nothing extraordinary. He was a poet, a man of imagination. But Pascal was a reasoner. We mustn't set the reasoners against us. He was, besides, something of a sick fanatic, and perhaps as dishonest as some of his antagonists." I did not choose to prove to him that a great man can still be a Christian. I preferred to let him speak. He spoke to us of his Jansenist brother who had, he said, such zeal for martyrdom that he once told a friend who thought like him, but who did not wish to do anything that might expose them to persecution, "Parbleu, if you don't wish to be hanged, at least don't discourage the others!"

After having spent a delicious hour with him, I feared to abuse his kindness. All the happiness I enjoy in seeing him, in hearing him will always give way to the fear of wearing him out. When the interest he inspires me with does not commit me to watching over his every movement to spare him the slightest constraint, my self-interest commits me to it even more; because I've been forewarned that he has a way of expressing his fatigue that I always take care to forestall. He conducted me to the door of his study, despite all my entreaties. Once there, I said to him, "Monsieur, I am about to undertake a long journey. I beg you to give me your blessing. I will consider it as good a protection against all dangers as that of our Holy Father." He smiled with infinite grace, leaning against the door of his study, looking at me with a gentle refined air, apparently at a loss for what he should he do. Finally, he said, "But my fingers cannot bless you. I would rather put my arms around your neck," and he kissed me. I went back to Madame Denis who heaped courtesies upon me. Tomorrow, I am to return for dinner and to spend the night there. I gave in to the insistence of Madame Denis with all the less scruple because they say that M. de Voltaire is never more amiable nor in better humor than when he has taken his *café à la crème*. He no longer dines nor appears at table. He remains abed nearly the entire day and works there until eight o'clock. Then he asks for supper, which has been scrambled eggs these past three months, even though there is always a good chicken on hand, in case the fancy strikes him. All the villagers who pass through Ferney also find a dinner ready and a coin of twenty-four sous, to continue their journey. Adieu, my friend, I speak to you only of the great man. He alone can interest me here.

LETTER III

Ferney, Sunday, 1775

I have just spent two days with M. de Voltaire, so I have a lot to tell you. He spent nearly the entire first afternoon in the salon. We talked first about the grain riots, on which I informed him of a few details he didn't know. A merchant who happened to be at Ferney seized the occasion to deplore the dismissal of M. L. who liked him, who had been very helpful to him on several occasions, and who had been on the point of helping him even more when he was sacked. In short, he kept deploring this loss to himself even though M. de Voltaire repeated three times, "You sound like that woman of the populace who cursed Colbert every time she made an omelet because he had laid a tax on eggs." This merchant was also a friend of Linguet's, of whom he sang pompous praises, and M. de Voltaire, whether by complaisance or sensitivity to a suffrage he should have disdained, spoke of him as of a man full of taste and learning. As my ears were a bit offended by these words *taste and learning*, given by an oracle of taste to a man who had never shown the slightest trace of any, I took the liberty to oppose him. "It seems to me," I said to M. de Voltaire, that the essential basis of learning, and even taste, should be a good disposition, which I have never seen in Linguet. His dishonesty," I added, "is the final straw which makes him an intolerable writer for me." M. de Voltaire did not offer a single word to defend his opinion. "Why, Monsieur, do I adore your genius? It is not only because it is fine, universal and luminous. It is because it is always based in reason. It is also that honesty that lends all its force and warmth to genius. That is the reason its success has been so universal. It is because you truly love humanity that you detest fanaticism, that you have torn the dagger from its hands. You were worthy of such a victory. You have devoted your entire life to obtaining it. It is only to those who love mankind that the glory of being our benefactors belongs. Linguet is a writer whose morals are corrupt, as are his principles in politics. He spreads only falsehoods, or dangerous errors. He should reap nothing but scorn, and I confess that you have grieved me in honoring him with your suffrage." M. de Voltaire remained mute, but he never ceased watching me with those eyes whose finesse and kind attention it is impossible to paint. Nevertheless the merchant took up the defense of Linguet, praising him even further; which, adding to the scorn already animating me in recollection of his baseness, caused me to summarize them to M. de Voltaire. I described Linguet, in the midst of his colleagues, tearing his hair the day they were to decide his fate at the palace, screaming that he was surrounded by assassins. I showed him describing himself in his *Theory of the Libel*, comparing himself now to Curtius, now to Hector, and speaking of his conduct with the Duke d'Aiguillon as though of a model of generosity and magnificence, even though this impudence was given lie by his letters that the Duke held in his hands. To conclude, I spoke of the outrages he had heaped upon his most estimable colleagues, and M. de Voltaire raised his hands and eyes to heaven in the greatest astonishment.

He returned to the salon several times after dinner. My joy at these unexpected appearances carried me to him each time; and each time I took his hands and kissed them several times. "Give me your foot," he cried, "Give me your foot that I may kiss it." I presented my face. He reproached me with coming to Ferney only to spoil him, to corrupt him. "It is you," I told him "that spoil us a great deal, Monsieur, in giving us your company so long and so often." As I showed some concern over the fatigue it might cause him, he said with a gallant nod it is impossible to describe, "Madame, I have been listening to you. That is not possible."

This man laden with so many years and so much glory, who, while enlightening Europe is also the protective divinity of Ferney, who would be pardoned for thinking himself the center of all the movements around him, which would be, I think, my first thought or need if I were so fortunate as to enjoy some small part of his fate, receives the slightest consideration or mark of attention like others receive a royal favor or a boon. That same day, he wanted to take a snuffbox that was on the mantelpiece. I saw him reach for it, for he is never out of my sight, came and gave it to him. He nearly dropped to his knee to thank me, and you would have to see with what grace he performed this courtesy. This grace is in his bearing, his gestures, his every movement; it also tempers the fire in his gaze, whose light is still so bright it would be almost unbearable if not softened by great compassion. His eyes, as bright and piercing as those of an eagle, have something superhuman about them,[8] but seem only to express benevolence and indulgence when they alight on his niece, as they command the respect of all those who surround her! For it is almost always with this smile of approval that he listens to her. His goodness also accounts for the great heed paid to Monsieur and Madame de Florian, which they would not find anywhere else but in Ferney. Madame de Florian has a young girl with her who laughs at everything and all the time. M. de Voltaire calls her "Quinze ans" (Fifteen years old) and lends himself to her childish gaiety with charming kindness. Sometimes they go to kiss him goodnight in his bed. He complains gaily over the fact that they have left such a handsome young man to sleep alone. But farewell, my friend, I am going to find mine as well for I am tired and I need to get up early to not miss the opportunity of seeing our lovable patriarch at his best.

LETTER IV

Ferney, Monday

M. de Voltaire had the goodness to send for news of me as soon as he knew I was up, and the hope of seeing him had awakened me quite early. I had his permission requested, which he accorded immediately. As soon as I appeared, he said with his usual grace, "Ah, Madame, you are doing what I should do." "Monsieur, I would pay a part of my life for the happiness you grant me," and I was not exaggerating in the slightest. I sat beside his bed, which is of the greatest simplicity and cleanliness. He was sitting up, as straight and steady as a young man of twenty. He was wearing a vest of white satin and a nightcap attached with a tidy ribbon. He has no other writing table in this bed, where he always works, but a chessboard.

I was struck by the order that reigns in his study. It is not like yours, with books pell-mell and great piles of paper. Everything is in order and he knows so well where everything is that, at one point, when we were discussing the trial of Monsieur de Guines a moment, he wished to consult a memorandum. "Wagnières," he said to his secretary, "My dear Wagnières, please take this memorandum from the third shelf on the right." And that's exactly where it was. What most abounds on his writing desk is a great quantity of quills. I entreated him to let me take one to keep as the most precious of relics, and he helped me choose one himself that he had used the most. He has the portrait of Madame du Châtelet[9] beside his bed, of whom he conserves the tenderest memories. But within his bedposts, he has two engravings of the Calas family. I had not yet seen the one that portrays the wife and children of this victim to fanaticism, embracing their father as he is about to be led to the torture chamber. It made the most painful impression on me, and I reproached M. de Voltaire for having placed it in a spot that kept it continually before his eyes. "Ah, Madame, I attended to this unhappy family and that of the Sirvens incessantly for eleven years, and during that time, I reproached myself with the slightest smile that escaped me, as though it were a crime." He said that so movingly and with such a ring of truth that I was pierced. I took his hand, which I kissed, and full of veneration and tenderness I held his thoughts on all the good he had done to these two families and on all the great services he had done humanity; on the happiness he should feel at being the benefactor of so many men, the bene-factor of the entire world, which would perhaps owe no longer being soiled by the horrors of fanaticism to him.

He told me that the triumph of enlightenment was far from being assured. He spoke of the arbiters of men's destinies and of the prejudice that enfolds their childhoods. The nannies, he told me, leave traces like that—he showed me the length of his arm—while reason, when it follows, leaves only traces the length of my finger. No, Madame, we have everything to fear from a man raised by a fanatic. This subject led him to make merry on the life of Jesus and on his mira-cles. I didn't dare take up his sarcasms seriously and wished even less to seem to approve of them. I defended Jesus Christ as a philosopher after my own heart, whose doctrine was divine and whose morals were indulgent. "I admire," I told M. de Voltaire, "his love for the weak and oppressed, the words he addressed to women several times, of sublime philosophy, or of touching indulgence." "Oh, yes," he said with a look and a smile full of the most lovable mischief, "he treated you women so well that you owe it to him to always take his defense." We also chatted quite a lot about all our friends; d'Alembert, La Harpe, Saint-Lambert, and our good Condorcet. He spoke of M. de La Harpe as the most promising for our theater, of M. Condorcet as the worthiest apostle of philosophy, and he greatly esteems M. de Saint-Lambert, both personally and his talents.[10] I told him of the sweet days I had passed in the solitude of Eaubonne, of his garden so full of flowers and fruit, of his affability toward his guests, of the perfection and voluptuousness of the meals, under Sarah's direction, where reason, the heart and appetite were all satisfied. "That is where I would like to transport myself," he said, "rather than to the entertainments or suppers of great lords. I would dine next to you and be surrounded only by friends and by your husband, whom I wish to meet, now that I have seen you, and whose kindness will always be dear to me." The word kindness that he used, called to his mind Monsieur de Richelieu, who had wanted to keep two men so worthy of entering it out of the Academy; two good writers and two men free from prejudice. That is, I believe, the basis on which he forms his opinion of his fellows. I sensed just how flattering your association with Abbé Delille was for you. He spoke of the Maréchal (Richelieu) as of a man who, having made a long journey, had learned nothing from his travels and who had reached old age retaining all the frivolities of his youth. That gave me the occasion to cite these verses to him:

> He who has not the spirit of his age
> Has all the woes of aging.

"Alas! Madame, that is so true," he said. The most one can manage is to cite one of his verses to him. I have not yet been able to speak to him of his works. Far from resembling these men whose conversation, as Montesquieu put it, is like a mirror constantly reflecting their impertinent selves, I have never seen him call attention to himself. Genius is, I believe, above this miserable need to constantly interest others; a need that makes mediocrity so unbearable. Satisfied with himself, he relies on the noble confidence of his might. He enjoys his own thoughts too much to feel the constant neediness of puerile vanity. It is by being useful to men that he attaches them to his memory.

When M. de Voltaire enters his salon, after a long day's work, he joins the subject of conversation without seeking to direct it. If the young ladies are chatting, he relaxes with them, and adds to their gaiety with lively and amiable quips. He lends himself to you and to whatever with the greatest simplicity, but if news arrives from Paris, if he learns of an interesting event, his soul is at once absorbed by it entirely. Like the evening of my arrival, when M. Audibert informed him that Abbé du B** had just been imprisoned in the Bastille with all his papers seized. He shed tears over his misfortune and spoke with the greatest indignation of this act of despotism. It is this sensitivity so earnest that makes me adore him; this sacred fire that warms and enlightens everything he touches upon. It is this imagination, so lively, so easy to move, that instantly transforms him into the person being oppressed, lending them the support of all his genius, and which creates perhaps his genius. For I believe, with Vauvenargues, that genius is born of a concordance and harmony between the soul and mind. Who has ever taken up the cause of the oppressed with more ardor and pursued it more steadily through all the obstacles? And don't tell me it was glory he was seeking by saving them. No, it was the joy! The love of glory is discouraged by all those things where genius cannot display itself. It is only the love of mankind that submits itself to this multitude of details success necessitates, and which is in itself its greatest reward.

You tell me, my friend, to speak to him of M. d'Etallonde, for whom his zeal with the King of Prussia and our *Parlement* has worked without respite for the last year.[11] I have already done so. I didn't know he was here. I asked for news of him. "Did you not notice the first day I saw you," he said, "a young man with a gentle, honest face, of modest bearing?" "I beg your pardon, Monsieur, at that moment, I only had eyes for you." "Well then! Pay attention. His face reflects his soul." Indeed, I have since spoken a lot with M. d'Etallonde, who strikes me as worthy, both by his soul and by his woes, of all M. de Voltaire's interest. His admiration for this great man is, like his gratitude, boundless, and when he appears before his benefactor, the latter extends his hand. "Good day, my dear friend," he says with touching tenderness. He is, I believe, the best of all men. Oh, how I admire him, and how much more I love him now that I have seen him. With what regret shall I leave him, doubtless, alas! to never see him again! "What shall I say to your friends," I said to him, "who, upon my return, will all gather about me to speak of you?" "Tell them that you found me in my grave, and that you brought me back to life."

LETTER V

Geneva, Friday evening

We are just back from Ferney, where we dined. My admiration and enthusiasm for M. de Voltaire are so well established that, when I arrive, nothing else is spoken of. I had his permission asked to see him a moment before the walk we were to take in his woods together, and I was soon admitted. I entered, and stroked him, and spoke about him, because I can scarcely speak of anything else, for a good quarter of an hour. It's like a passion that can only relieve itself by its effusions. He gave me the most affectionate names, called me his dear child, his beautiful queen. He seemed as touched as convinced of my tender veneration for him. We then talked about our friends in common, of M. d'Alembert, La Harpe, Saint-Lambert, and Condorcet. This latter is the one for whom he seems to me to have the most esteem and affection. He is of all men, he said, the one who resembles him the most. He has the same hatred of oppression and fanaticism, the same zeal for humanity, and the best gifts for protecting and defending it. I felt a real pleasure in hearing this great man speak like this to me of the friend who brings such sweet charm to my life. I was touched by a piece of advice he added to his praises. "Preserve this friend, Madame. He is the one most worthy of your soul and reason." "Oh, Monsieur," I said, "the friendship of my dear Condorcet is for me a prize beyond all treasures, and I wouldn't sacrifice it to the mastery of the universe." He returned to your subject on his own, and repeated again that he wished to see you. I spoke to him from my soul of my heart's best friend. He asked me how long I had been married, and congratulated me on being united with the man I preferred, and that my reason would also have chosen. I showed him your portrait. He thought that you had a witty, gentle face. "There is only one other fate," I told him, as he was looking at your portrait, "that could have tipped the scales in my heart from being the wife of Monsieur Suard: that of being your niece and of devoting my whole life to you." "Ah, my dear child, I would have united you two. I would have given you my blessing!" He was superb today. When I arrived, Madame de Luchet said to me, "M. de Voltaire, Madame, who knows you find him handsome in his finery, put on his wig and his best dressing gown today. Do you see," she said as he came out, "do you see how nice he looks? You are the object of this coquetry." M. de Voltaire smiled good-naturedly with a bit of embarrassment. This graceful smile reminded me of Pigalle's statue, which caught some traces of it. I told him that I had rushed to see it, and that I had given it a kiss. "It gave you one back, I trust?" And as I only replied with a kiss of his hand, he insisted, "But tell me, it did kiss you back, didn't it?" "It seemed to want to." We climbed into the carriage to ride through his woods. I sat beside him in rapture. I held one of his hands that I kissed a dozen times. He lets me, because he can see what a joy and need it is. We had a Russian with us that congratulated him on being still so loved by a young and, you'll pardon the epithet, pretty woman. "Ah, Monsieur, I owe all that to my eighty-four years." He compared himself to old Titon,[12] whom I had brought back to life and rejuvenated. "I wish I could," I said, "for then you would never grow old." He talked with Monsieur Soltikof of the Russians and of Catherine. He said of all the sovereigns of Europe, she was the one who had the most energy and brains. I don't know if he's right, but his head seemed to me the loveliest phenomenon in nature.

His forests, which he planted and loves deeply, are very vast. He has cut several very pleasant passages through it. It was a pleasure to watch him ride through his whole domain, unstooped and steady, almost agile. He tossed sharp glances left and right, and walking through his barn, which is very long, he pointed out a repair to be made in the roof with the cane in his hand. His barnyard is just as clean. He has lots of fine cows, and he wanted me to drink their milk. He went and fetched it himself, and presented it most charmingly. You can imagine how touched I was by all his attentions and in what tone I thanked him. This little trip was quite a binge for him, who almost never leaves Ferney these days. Moreover he soon said he didn't feel well and wished to return, which I found natural enough. His study is what he loves the best. That's where he lives, because that's where he thinks and where he finds the rest old age often needs. Therefore, far from urging him to remain another moment, I begged him to quickly climb into his carriage and offered my arm, which he accepted, to take him to it. But as he was about to board, he insisted on escorting me to mine, which we had had follow us. "Why don't you stay at Ferney?" he said. "When will you come and see me?" "I will have this pleasure Sunday next." "Well, then I will live in that hope." And he kissed me.

I see with pain that the persons who surround him, even his niece, have no indulgence for his frailty and his age. They often consider him like a capricious child, as though at eighty-four, it is not permitted to feel a need for rest, after spending three hours in society. They almost never wish to believe that he is suffering; it's as though they wish to avoid feeling sorry for him. This air of unconcern, which struck me again today, shocked me and touched the bottom of my heart.

LETTER VI

Geneva

But let's return to the great man. I don't know how I found the strength to speak to you of other pleasures than those I owe him. I considered the days I spent without seeing him as lost, and never saw him without delight. I went to sup and spend the night at Ferney yesterday. He had been ill almost all day. He had taken medicine but still came into the salon when I was announced. I found him worn out, but he received all the proofs of my tender interest with much loveable sensitivity. His conversation showed the effects of his physical condition; it was melancholic. He spoke of the discomforts of his life, without bitterness but with sadness. I thought of all the sorrows his ungrateful country had given him, in the days that he was honoring it with so many masterpieces: the fierceness with which they contrasted him with Crébillon, who cannot be compared to him in all fairness, and who they affected to raise above him. I thought perhaps he was recalling our ingratitude, and I gently reproached him with not enjoying a unique destiny that filled all Europe. "I admit, Monsieur, that with a sensitivity as sharp as yours, you must have felt enormous chagrin. But admit as well that you have had tremendous joys." "Ah, scarcely, Madame, scarcely!" "None of us have lived without tears," I added. "Alas" he said, "that is quite true." But as I was still trying to bring him back to pleasant, agreeable thoughts, "Our ruling passion has been satisfied, Monsieur. Few men, as you know, can boast of this advantage. You loved glory. I could say to you, as Father Canaye did to Maréchal d'Hocquincourt, she loved you too a lot. She has showered you with honors." "Ah, Madame, I didn't know what I wanted. It was my plaything, my toy." "We are very fortunate that your plaything did not serve for your pleasures alone, as it does for most, but that it has been the delight of all those who know how to think and feel."

The next morning.

I was so afraid of not seeing M. de Voltaire after his breakfast that I got up at six o'clock. Everyone was still sleeping. I went into the salon his study opens onto. Everything was silent. I threw myself onto a couch where I fell asleep till eight, when M. de Voltaire sent for news of me. I asked permission to see him a moment, which was granted me at once. You can be jealous if you like, but it is certain that I have a veritable passion for him. My first need upon seeing him was to tell him of the happiness he had given me in allowing me to see him in all his natural goodness and kindness. He gave me a thousand caresses with his lovely hand while I was kissing it, and said the loveliest things. "Preserve your goodwill toward me." And then, "But you'll forget me when you are in Paris!" "Oh, Monsieur! You don't believe that. I would be wretched if you thought it. You know how engrossed I was in you before having the joy of seeing you. Your presence and your kindness have made this memory a thousand times dearer yet." He then spoke to me of you and of his desire to see you with all his friends. He was very well this morning. Sleep had restored him entirely. He was suffering less, he said. His eyes were full of fire and even gaiety. He was busy revising a new edition of his works; he didn't want them to include what he called his mumble-jumble. "You don't reach posterity," he said, "with that much baggage." Then he added gaily, "Yesterday I was a philosopher, today I'm Polichinelle."[13] I'll spare you my compliments on this change of roles. I did get a peek of the author a moment, however. He was holding in his hand from this new edition, a volume of his little encyclopedia. He said to my brother, who had just entered, this is a little work I think highly of. My brother spoke to him of *La Pucelle* (The Maid of Orleans), which he knew by heart. "It is of all my works," he said, "the one I love the best. I'm crazy about this Agnes who always wants to be so wise and who is always so weak." My brother recited a few passages to him. He listened to them with a gaiety born more of the subject than of an author's vanity. He interrupted my brother a few times to say, "But that's not how verses are recited," and gave him a tone that conveyed more cadence and harmony. When he heard this verse on Madame de Pompadour:

Et sur son rang son esprit s'est monté (And on her rank her spirit mounted)

he disavowed the phrase, and asked what the devil is a spirit mounted on a rank? I only spoke to him of what I knew and liked of his Pucelle; the beginning of several cantos where I find much gaiety, philosophy, and verve. We left him to his corrections of the new edition and went into the salon, where he only appeared near evening, when he was tired of his work. His strength corresponds to the inspiration of his genius, I think. His head seems as full of ideas, and his soul as ardent as in his prime. There is no emptiness in his life; his thoughts and his profound love of humanity and of the progress of reason fill his every moment. But what always astonishes me, moves me, and enraptures me almost, is that he seems to strip away what is powerful in his genius, to keep only what is graceful and pleasant. Whenever he joins society a moment, I have never seen him distracted nor preoccupied. It's as though his courtesy, which has something noble and scrupulous, had imposed the law of forgetting himself completely when with others. If your eyes seek it, you are sure to find in his that look of goodwill and a sort of gratitude for the feelings he inspires. I think he trusts in mine, and I confess a veneration for him so tender that I would be wretched if I didn't think him convinced of it. I'm sleeping at Ferney tonight, and it will be for the last time.

LETTER VII

Ferney

We have just bid our farewells to the great man, my friend. Alas! No doubt our farewells for eternity. I didn't wish to speak to him of my departure, but it was clear he knew of it by the things he said to me. He was kind enough to admit me to his study once again, and to display the most loveable, flattering sentiments for me, even though he's very busy correcting the faults of his new edition at the moment. There are things on *Parlement* in it that he wants to mitigate absolutely. I can see he's afraid of it, and it grieves me, for what could be more ghastly at his age than to live in alarm and terror? He told me that M. Séguier had come to see him in passing by Ferney, not long ago. "And there, Madame, in the seat you are sitting in (I was seated near his bed), this Séguier threatened to denounce me to his assembly that would have me burnt if they got a hold of me." "Monsieur, they wouldn't dare." "And who would stop them?" "Your genius, your age, the good you've done humanity, the cries of all of Europe. Believe that every honest thing that exists, everyone you've made tolerant and human would rise up in your favor." "Ah, Madame, they would come to see me burn, and say in the evening perhaps, 'Still, it's such a shame.'" "No, I should never suffer it," I said, horrified at the very idea, "I would stab the executioner if they could find one capable of executing such an abominable decree." He kissed my hand and said, "You're a loveable child. Yes, I'll count on you." "Oh! You won't need my help. For mercy's sake, Monsieur, dismiss such horrid thoughts, which, I protest, have no foundation."

The next day, my first need upon awakening was to see him. Alas! It was for the last time that I entered his study, that I saw him and received the marks of his friendship! I was terribly saddened. I had dressed early because we were going to dine in the neighborhood. I learned too late that he liked to see ladies dressed in their finery, for I confess I would have employed this means to please him. As soon as I appeared, "Who is this beautiful lady, so glittering at my door?" he cried. "It is I, Monsieur," and I ran to kiss his hands. "My God, how sweet you are! I have written to Monsieur Suard that I was in love with you." "Oh, Monsieur, of all the kind things you've said, this is the one that flatters me most, for it is the one that will most affect him!" "You slept above my study." "Yes, Monsieur. It made me both proud and happy and will leave me with wonderful memories."

As there were a lot of people in his study, he soon grew weary, and I saw his head turn on his pillow, eyes shut and breathing hard. I said at once that we had to let him get the rest he needs. These words seemed to bring him back to life. He gave me a glance full of tender gratitude. I hugged him against my breast. "You found me dying," he said, "but my heart will always live for you." My tears flowed in abundance on leaving his house where I will never see him again, although he urged me to return with you, dear Condorcet, and M. d'Alembert this fall.

LETTER VIII

Addressed to Voltaire on Leaving Ferney

Monsieur,

I did not want to bid you my farewells. It is horrid to part with a great man when one has little hope of seeing him again. Permit me to thank you for all the happiness I owe to your kindnesses. Ah! How the feelings I take with me add to the tender veneration I have had so long for you! How moved I was in approaching you, in finding you always as perfectly good as you are great; in seeing you do as much good around you as you would have liked to do for the whole of humanity! What delicious memories my heart will conserve of these hours in which you deigned to await me in your study and to chat with me with a kindness so gentle and informal! How tempted was I to run back again in leaving Ferney and after having received your embraces! I could hear the sound of your voice. I wanted to throw myself at your feet. No, I'm far from having seen you enough, from having told you enough how much I admire you and, allow me to say it, how much I love you. But you should have convinced me that I envy, Monsieur, the fate of those around you. How sweet it must be to devote oneself to the old age of a great man! But I would be no use for you, I would converse at least. The joy of having seen you will add new charms to those I tasted in reading your immortal works. I will speak often of you with all those we both love. Receive with your usual kindness the assurance of my most tender respect and veneration.

REPLY FROM M. DE VOLTAIRE

Madame,

I wrote to your husband that I was in love with you. My passion has greatly increased upon reading your letter. You will forget me in the world of Paris. And me in my desert, where we are about to put on the play of Orpheus, I will miss you like he longed for Eurydice, with this difference: that I will descend to Hades first, and you will never come there looking for me. Speak of me with your friends and preserve your goodwill toward me. This heart is too moved to tell you that it is your very humble servant.

THE COUNT DE SÉGUR ON VOLTAIRE'S RETURN TO PARIS IN 1778

Louis Philippe Ségur, 1753–1830, was a soldier, diplomat, and writer who served in the American Revolution and under Napoleon. This is an extract from his three-volume *Mémoires*, published in 1824. He was also the author of an eleven-volume *History of France* and other historical works.

While all these great events, precursors of so many storms, were occupying all the cabinet ministers and the journalists of all classes . . . a new spectacle took hold of Parisian curiosity and held it.

Voltaire, the Prince of Poets, the Patriarch of the Philosophers, the glory of his century and of France, had been exiled from his fatherland for a great number of years. All the French read his works with delight, and hardly any of them had ever seen him. His contemporaries had become for him, if one dare say so, almost his posterity.

Admiration for his universal genius was, in many minds, a sort of worship or cult; his writings adorned every library, his name was present in all thoughts, and his physical features were absent to all eyes. His spirit dominated, directed, and modified all the minds of his era; but, apart from a small number of men who had been admitted to his philosophical sanctuary in Ferney, he reigned over the rest of his fellow citizens like an invisible power.

Never perhaps has any mortal operated changes as great as he had in the opinions and morals of his century. Never has the head of any sect both fought and vanquished, without appearing in the skirmishes, more enemies who believed themselves invincible, more errors consecrated by time, more prejudices deeply rooted in old customs.

Nevertheless, without rank, birth, or authority, his forces only composed of the clarity of his reason, the varied eloquence of his style, and the charm of his grace; in short, to strike down the old, formidable colossuses against which he fought, instead of using a club he only used the light weapons of ridicule and irony most of the time. It's true that no one had ever handled it more adroitly than he, nor delivered deeper and more incurable wounds with it.

Capitalizing on a few inexcusable temerities, a few writings contrary to morals, a few spots that slightly tarnished the disk of this brilliant star of our literature, the clergy's influence, a few old *parlementarians* inclined to severity, a small number of old courtesans, partisans of the old abuses of power, had obtained against him not a condemnation, or even an official order of banishment, but merely insinuations efficient enough to force him to seek his peace and safety in exile.

His return, like his disgrace, was further proof of the weakness of the authorities. Philosophical opinions so prevailed in the public, and intimidated the powers to such a degree, that he was allowed to return without being given the permission. The court refused to receive him, and the entire city seemed to fly to greet him. They refused to accord him the slightest pardon, and he was left to enjoy a smashing triumph.

The queen, swept along by the storm, made vain attempts to obtain permission from the king to receive this famous man, the object of such universal admiration. Louis XVI, from scruples of conscience, believed that he must not let a writer approach him whose bold strokes, not stopping only at abuses, had often undermined even ancient beliefs and venerated doctrines. The enclosures of the throne remained thus closed to the man to whom the nation was rendering a sort of cult in transports of admiration.

The rivals of the great man were dismayed; the clergy, indignant but silent; the *parlements* maintained silence, and the power of the *philosophes* grew from the presence and triumph of their chief.

One would have to have seen the public joy at this moment, the impatient curiosity, the tumultuous eagerness of the admiring crowds, to hear, to see, to even glimpse the celebrated old man, contemporary to two centuries, who had inherited the glamour and brilliance of the first and become the glory of the second.[1] One would have to have witnessed it all, I say, to give oneself an accurate idea of it.

It was the apotheosis of a demigod, still living. He said to the people, with as much affection as reason, "Are you trying to make me die of pleasure?" Indeed, the enjoyment of so many and such touching homages was more than his strength could bear. He succumbed, and the altars raised to him promptly changed into a tomb.

Being just as avid to admire the illustrious man up close, but more fortunate than the others in not having to push through the crowd of all those who wanted a look, I had the joy of seeing him at my ease two or three times in my parents' home, as in his youth he had had fairly close relations with them.

My mother was then afflicted with a cruel disease that had been consuming her strength in unbearable suffering for the previous two years. She could no longer leave her bed. Her extreme weakness may be judged by the fact that she breathed her last only a month after the period to which I am referring.

She had always been considered one of the women the most distinguished by her fine intellect, the excellence of her taste and wit, the rectitude of her reason, and by the elegance of her language and manners in Paris. Remarkable in her youth for her attractive features, she was considered a model of good taste and of the most appealing urbanity.

Voltaire had not forgotten her. He requested pressingly to see her and, despite the fact that she was barely in condition to see, hear, or answer him, she received him.

We often imagine men, places, and things that we have never seen, but that have struck our imagination from afar, quite differently from the reality. I had experienced this many a time, but when I saw Voltaire, he appeared to me exactly as I had imagined him.

His thinness bespoke of his long, immense works; his singular, antique dress[2] recalled to mind the last witness of the age of Louis XIV, the historian of that age and the immortal portraitist of Henri IV. His penetrating eyes sparkled with genius and mischief. One saw in them the tragic poet, the author of *Oedipus* and *Mahomet*, the profound philosopher, the ingenious, cunning storyteller, and the witty, satirical observer of the human race. His lean, bent body was now only a light envelope, almost transparent, through which it seemed one could see his soul and genius.

I was seized with admiration and pleasure, like someone who was suddenly permitted to be transported to distant times to find himself face to face with Homer, Plato, Virgil, or Cicero. Perhaps it is difficult today to understand such an impression. We have seen so many men, events, and things that we have become blasé. To conceive what I felt just then, one would have to partake of the atmosphere I lived it in: it was one of exaltation.

We did not yet know the sad fruit of long storms, of political discord, of envy, egotism, the need for rest, the unconcern produced by weariness, the indifference that follows the sad awakening from deceived illusions. We were dazzled by prisms of new ideas and doctrines, radiating with hope, consumed with ardor for every glory, enthusiastic for all talents, and lulled by the seductive dreams of a philosophy that wished to assure the happiness of the human race by chasing with its lighted torch the long, sad darkness that had enchained it with superstition and despotism for so many centuries. Far from foreseeing the woes, the excesses, the crimes, the overthrowing of thrones and principles, we saw only all the good that would be assured humanity in the future by the reign of reason.

Judge, after these dispositions, what must have been the effect on our minds at the sight of the illustrious man that our greatest writers and most famous philosophers regarded as their model and their master.

I was all eyes and ears in approaching Voltaire, as if I was expecting some oracle to ring forth from his mouth at any minute. It was not, however, either the time or the place to pronounce one, had he been Apollo himself, for he was at the bedside of a dying woman, whose sight could but inspire sad thoughts. She no longer seemed capable of either admiration or even consolation. Nevertheless, she made a great effort to conquer nature; her eyes recaptured some of their shine and her voice some of its force.

Voltaire, tactfully seeking to distract her from the present by the remembrance of the past, asked few questions about her condition. He merely told her, in few words, that having been in such agonies several times and as exhausted, he had, through the same courage she was showing, triumphed over his sufferings and recovered his health. "The doctors," said he, "perform few miracles; but nature works many wonders, especially for those to whom she has given this vital element that still shines in your eyes."

He then recalled many anecdotes regarding the society they once lived in together, and he did it with a vivacity of wit, a freshness of memory, a variety in phrasing and sallies that would have made you forget his age if his features and voice did not remind us that he was an octogenarian.

He could not cure anyone as ill as the woman who was listening to him, but he brought her back to life. For a few moments, she seemed to no longer feel her weakness and her sufferings. She carried the conversation in a rather lively manner, alluded to myself and so gave me one last faint ray of hope.

A few days later, Voltaire came back to see her again. As, by a stroke of luck, she felt a bit more strength that day than usual, she took a more active part in the conversation and even reproached the old philosopher, gently but ener-getically, the stubbornness with which he strove, in his numerous writings, to strike, to ridicule the Church and all its members, even religion itself, under the pretext of combating old errors, absurd superstitions, and dangerous fanatics.

"Be generous and moderate after the victory," she told him, "What have you to fear from such adversaries at present? The fanatics are struck down. They can do no more harm. Their reign has passed." "You are mistaken," Voltaire replied intensely, "the fires are covered but smoldering. These fanatics, these Tartuffes,[3] are mad dogs. They've been muzzled, but they still have all their teeth. They are no longer biting, it's true, but on the first occasion, if we don't pull out their teeth, you will see if they know how to bite."

Anger sparkled in his eyes, and the passion that inflamed him momentarily made him lose the decency and measure of the expressions that both reason and good taste dictate, and of which he was usually the most inimitable of models.

The desire to see this extraordinary man had drawn fifty or sixty people into my mother's salon, crowding them in rows around her bed, all craning their necks, rising up on their toes and, without the slightest noise, lending an attentive ear to every word that left Voltaire's mouth, so avid they were to seize the least of them, as well as the slightest movement of his features.

There, I saw to what point bias and enthusiasm, even among the most enlightened, can resemble superstition and approach the absurd. My mother, questioned by Voltaire on the details of the state of her health, replied that the most painful of her suffering came from the destruction of her stomach and the difficulty of finding some sort of food it could bear.

Voltaire sympathized with her and, seeking to console her,[4] told her that he had been in the same languor for nearly a year, thought incurable, and that nevertheless a simple means had cured him: it consisted of eating only egg yolks mixed with potato flour and water.

Obviously, there could be no question of clever sallies or ingenious witticisms in such a subject of conversation, and yet scarcely had he pronounced the words *egg yolks and potato flour* than one of my neighbors, well-known, it is true, for his excessive disposition to infatuation and for the mediocrity of his wit, fixed an ardent eye upon me, hugged me in his arms and said, with a cry of admiration: "What a man! What a man! Not a word without a witticism!"

You will laugh at this absurdity, which seems beyond all probability; and yet to convince you that it is not rare, observe in any country, in any era, the eager multitude that surrounds not only the quarters of a man of genius, or the throne of a great king, but the pulpit of a firebrand preacher, even the armchair where a prince who has scarcely left his crib is playing, and you will see that among the numerous and servile homages dictated by flattery, there are many, and the most absurd, that are sincere and born of a sort of idolatry that any sort of elevation inspires in a crowd of people. For it is not always through fear, but foolishness, that so many demigods of so many kinds have been created, both literally and figuratively.

Until then, I had held myself modestly, as I should, in the last row of those contemplating Voltaire. But at the end of the second visit, as he left my mother's chamber and passed into another room, I was presented to him. Several of his friends, Count d'Argental, the Chevalier de Chastellux, the Duke of Nivernais, the Count of Guibert, the Chevalier de Boufflers, Marmontel, and d'Alembert, who no doubt judged me too favorably, had spoken to him of me with a great deal of praise.

I owed it certainly only to their great kindness, since I was then only known for a few slight productions: a few short stories, some fables, and a few romances, whose success in society depended on the caprices of fashion, and often do not outlast them.

At bottom, I had only made myself worthy of their affection by the eagerness with which I strove to perfect my taste and wit in my discussions with them, and to enlighten myself with their knowledge. Thus it was more the zeal of a disciple than the budding talent of a writer that they praised in me.

Whatever the case, Voltaire charmed my vanity in speaking to me with grace and finesse of my passion for literature and of my first attempts. He encouraged me with some advice: "Don't forget," he said, "that you have earned the good that is said of you by carefully mixing some realities into the images of lighter pieces of poetry, some morality into the sentiments, and a few grains of philosophy into the gaiety. But beware of your penchant for poetry. You may follow it, but do not let yourself be swept away by it. From what I've been told, and in your position, you are destined for far more serious occupations. You have done well to begin by exercising yourself in writing verses, because it is difficult for those who have never loved them, and who know neither their art nor their charm, to ever write very well in prose. Come, young man! Receive the warm wishes of an old man who predicts a happy destiny for you. But remember that poetry, divine as it is, is a seductress."

I thanked him for the literary benediction he had given me, "remembering," I told him on this occasion, with vivid pleasure that in olden days, the words meaning great poet and prophet (*vates*, in Latin) were synonyms.

After that moment, I did not see Voltaire again until the performance of *Irène* at the Théatre-Français, a day of triumph that proved, by the amount of applause given the most mediocre of tragedies, the excess of enthusiasm with which its author inspired the public.

It could be said that there were two courts in Paris during several weeks; that of the king at Versailles and that of Voltaire in Paris; the first where the good king, Louis XVI, lived in simplicity without pomp or display, dreaming only of the reform of abuses and of the happiness of a people too taken with glamour to appreciate his modest virtues. This first court, I say, seemed to be the peaceful refuge of a sage in comparison with this townhouse on the Quai des Théatins,[5] where the cries and acclamations of an immense and adoring throng, which eagerly came to give homage to the greatest genius in Europe, were heard the whole day long.

Up till then, we had seen triumphs justly awarded great men by the governments of their country. The triumph of Voltaire was of an entirely new type; it was awarded by public opinion that had braved, so to say, the power of magistrates, the thunderbolts of the Church, and the authority of the monarch.

The avenger of Calas, the apostle of liberty, the constant enemy and happy victor of prejudices and fanaticism, had returned triumphantly to Paris after sixty years of war.

At the Académie Française, which he went to visit, the members came out to lead him in; and after this public homage, which no prince had ever received, the Prince of Letters presided over the literary senate of France, and the reunion of all its diverse talents in each of which his genius had produced masterpieces.

Back in his house, which seemed transformed into a palace by his presence, and seated amidst a sort of council composed of philosophers, and the boldest, most celebrated writers of this century, his courtiers were the most outstanding men of all classes, and the most distinguished foreigners of every country.

The only thing lacking this royalty were guards, and he truly needed some to assure his safety in the midst of this eager throng, rushing to see him from all quarters, besieging his door, engulfing him as soon as he exited, and barely leaving his horses the possibility of finding a passage.

His coronation took place at the Palace of the Tuileries, on the stage of the Théatre-Français. One cannot depict the ecstasy with which this illustrious old man was received by a public that flowed in, filling every bench, every loge, every corridor and all the exits of the room. Never has the gratitude of a nation burst forth in such lively transports of joy.

I will never forget the scene, and cannot conceive how Voltaire still found enough force in himself to support it. As soon as he appeared, the actor Brizard came to place a crown of laurel leaves upon his head, which he promptly tried to take off, but which the shouts of the people begged him to keep. In the midst of all these lively acclamations, people shouted and repeated the titles of all his works.

Long after the curtain was raised, it was still impossible to begin the play. Everyone in the room was still too occupied with seeing and contemplating Voltaire, with noisily shouting his praise. They were all too busy acting themselves to listen to those on the stage.

When finally a sort of weariness allowed the actors to come out, they found themselves constantly interrupted by the tumultuous agitation of the audience. As M. Grimm rightly said of this performance of *Irène*, "Never was a play more badly performed, more applauded, and less listened to."

When it was over, a bust of Voltaire was placed before the stage and surrounded by all the actors of the tragedy still wearing their costumes, by the guards who had been in the play, by the throng of spectators who had managed to crowd into the theater; and what was most singular was that the actor who came to lay a crown on the bust of this obstinate enemy of superstition was still dressed as a monk, as Léonce, a character in the play.

This bust remained upon the stage during the whole time a second little play was performed: *Nanine*, which was no better listened to and no less applauded than *Irène*. To complete this glorious day, Voltaire saw the captain of the guards of one of our princes enter his loge. He had come to tell him with what joy the prince associated himself with the just homage being paid to his genius in France.

A few days earlier, an unexpected death almost deprived Voltaire of this stunning triumph. A violent hemorrhage had put him in grave danger.

The clergy, who no longer dared combat him, had hoped to convert him. At first, Voltaire gave in, received Abbé Gaultier, confessed, and wrote a profession of faith that did not fully satisfy the priests, and that displeased a number of philosophers.

But once out of harm's way, he forgot his fears and prudence.[6] A few weeks later, in a relapse more serious than the first, he refused to see a single priest and ended, with apparent indifference, a great long life, agitated by so many projects, by so many storms, and radiant with such glory.

Those who had not had the power to oppose his triumph refused him a tomb in the midst of the Parisians. One of his relatives, a councilor in *Parlement*, removed his body and quickly transported it to the Abbey of Scellières, where he was buried before the local pastor received notice forbidding him to provide a burial. It arrived three hours too late. Without the zeal of this friend, the mortal remains of one of our greatest men would not have obtained a few feet of dirt to cover them.

Despite the efforts of the clergy, the magistrates, and the authorities, who forbid the papers to speak of Voltaire's death and the theaters to perform his plays, Paris was flooded with a deluge of verses, pamphlets, and epigrams; the only weapons that remained to the public to avenge this outrage to the memory of a man who had rendered his country and century illustrious.

LA CORRESPONDANCE LITTÉRAIRE, PHILOSOPHIQUE, ET CRITIQUE ON VOLTAIRE'S DEATH

June 1778

The *Correspondance Littéraire*, an underground newsletter on the latest literary news and gossip in Paris, was written by Baron von Grimm and diffused throughout Europe. But Denis Diderot and Jacques-Henri Meister took over for him while he was in St. Petersburg, which covers the time this article appeared.

Diderot displayed emotions toward Voltaire, varying from hero-worship to envy to irritation, provoked by malicious tales he was at times too prompt to believe, the letters that passed between them were mostly cordial.[1] Though often qualified as more radical than Voltaire, Diderot was in fact at first alarmed by Voltaire's pamphlet war and resisted his exhortations to join in.[2] This notice displays real grief, however, if not despair, alongside a ferocious indictment of the Archbishop of Paris for denying Voltaire burial. It was not yet known that the body had been secretly driven to Scellières, where its Abbé, Voltaire's nephew, buried him. The French Revolutionaries brought the body back in 1791 to re-inter him in the Pantheon with something close to a million people celebrating it over the course of its journey.

T he fatal veil has fallen; the last rays of this divine clarity have just been extinguished, and the night that will follow this fine day will last perhaps for a long succession of centuries.

The greatest, most illustrious, perhaps, alas! the unique monument of this glorious era where all the talents, all the arts of the human mind seemed to have reached its highest degree of perfection; this superb monument has disappeared! Some unknown plot of earth has hidden its sad remains from our eyes.

He is no more, he who was both the Ariosto and the Virgil of France, he who brought back to life the masterpieces of Sophocles and Euripides for us; whose genius attained the heights of Corneille's thought, the sublime pathos of Racine, and, master of the empire these two rivals of the stage occupied, discovered yet another even worthier of his conquest in the great movements of nature, in the awful excesses of fanaticism, in the imposing contrasts between manners and opinions.

He is no more, he who, in his immense career, embraced the entire extent of all our knowledge and who left us masterpieces and models in nearly every genre; the first to make France aware of the philosophy of Newton, of the virtues of our best kings, and of the true value of liberty in commerce and in letters.

He is no more, he who, the first perhaps, wrote history as a philosopher, as a statesman, as a citizen, who relentlessly combated all the prejudices fatal to man's happiness and who, burying error and superstition beneath opprobrium and ridicule, was able to make himself equally heard by the ignorant and the wise; by the populace and by kings.

Fortified by the genius of the age that saw his birth, he alone maintained the declining age that saw him die; he alone delayed its fall. He is no more, and already ignorance and envy dare to insult his revered remains. He who deserved a temple and altars is refused the repose of a tomb, the simple honors that are not refused even the lowliest of mankind.

Fanaticism, whose startled spirit trembled before that of a great man, scarcely sees him expiring before it already flatters itself of recapturing its empire, and the first effort of its impotent rage is an excess of dementia and cowardice.

What do you hope from such barbarity? What will you teach the universe in exerting your fury and vengeance upon these mortal remains, if only the terror and fright with which he inspired you until the last moment of his life? Here then is what your power is today! A single man, with no other support than the ascendancy of talents and glory, resisted your persecutions for sixty years, braved your furies for sixty years, and death alone delivered your victim to you, a vain shadow, insensitive to your insults, but whose name alone is still the love of mankind and the terror of its tyrants.

What was your design in refusing a simple tomb to him upon whom the nation had just conferred the honors of a public triumph? Were you afraid that this tomb might become an altar, and the place that enclosed it a temple? Were you afraid to see a man who had had raised himself above all ranks by the brilliance and superiority of his genius confounded with the common lot? Did you think it was so much in your interest to announce to all of Europe that the greatest man of his age died as he had lived, without weakness or prejudice?

In wishing to hide in the deepest obscurity, had it been possible, the place where the remains of Voltaire lie, in seeking to shroud the moment of his death in darkness and mystery, did you not tremble lest the most ardent of his disciples not take advantage of such favorable circumstances to establish the proof of his immortality and resurrection? Ah! You knew all too well that, had they tried, the works of his that remain to us would not allow belief in miracles of this species.

Weak and cowardly enemies of the shadow of a great man! By tormenting all the powers of heaven and earth in order to rob him of the honors due him, what benefit do you expect from such vain efforts? Will you erase him from the memory of men? Will you annihilate this multitude of masterpieces, eternal monuments to his glory, consecrated in every part of the world for the instruction and admiration of future races? Is it by a few puerile prohibitions, by a few impotent anathemas that you think you will enchain these torrents of light, spread from one end of the universe to the other?

. . . Public opinion, the homage of all his talents from all the most distinguished men of all nations, and the trust and friendship of several sovereigns, had erected for him a sort of tribunal superior in some ways to all the tribunals of the world, since reason and humanity alone had dictated its laws, and genius had pronounced its decisions. It was at this respectable tribunal that we had seen the thunderbolts of injustice, slander and superstition vanish more than once. It was there that the innocence of the Calas, the Sirvens, and the de La Barres were avenged. The imminent hope of re-establishing the unfortunate Count de Lally's reputation was the center of his last endeavors; it was the last success over which his nearly extinguished life seemed to light up once again. Shortly before its end, plunged into a sort of lethargy, he emerged a few moments when he was told about the final judgment of this affair, and the last lines that he dictated were addressed to the son of this illustrious, unfortunate man. They were: "The moribund resuscitates in learning this great news. He embraces M. de Lally tenderly. He sees that the king is the defender of justice. He will die content." That was, so to speak, the last sigh of this famous man.

FREDERICK THE GREAT'S EULOGY OF VOLTAIRE

Delivered before the Academy of Berlin

Frederick II of Prussia first wrote to Voltaire the day after he attained some autonomy in a place of his own in 1736, begging Voltaire to be "his master in everything." Their ensuing friendship, despite its storms, lasted until Voltaire's death, and a more fascinating forty-three-year correspondence is hard to come by. As Frederick granted freedom of beliefs in 1740, immediately upon succeeding to the throne, he played no small role in demonstrating its feasibility to all of Europe as well as to the American colonies where references to English translations of this oration can be found. The vehemence of Frederick's approval of Voltaire's battle is made abundantly clear at the end of this speech, which also provides an account of Voltaire's life, as interesting in its minor errors and omissions as in other details.

Gentlemen,

In every age, particularly in the most ingenious, civilized nations, men of rare and high-minded genius have been honored in their lifetimes, and even more so after their deaths. They were considered a phenomenon which shed their radiance on their homeland. The first legislators who taught men how to live in society, the first heroes who defended their fellow citizens, the philosophers who explored the chasms of nature and uncovered a few truths, the poets who transmitted the glorious acts of their contemporaries to future generations; all these men were considered superior to the average run of humans. They were thought favored with special inspiration from the Divinity. It is for this reason that altars were raised to Socrates, that Hercules was thought a god, that Greece honored Orpheus, and that seven cities fought over the glory of having been the birthplace of Homer. The people of Athens, whose education was the most perfected, knew the *Iliad* by heart, and gave heartfelt celebration to the glories of its ancient heroes in the cantos of this poem. We also see that Sophocles, who won the trophy for theater, was held in great esteem for his talents and that, furthermore, the Republic of Athens adorned him with the highest offices. Everyone knows how much Aeschines, Pericles, Demosthenes were esteemed, and that Pericles twice saved the life of Diagoras; first from the fury of the Sophists, and the second time, while helping him in his good deeds. Whoever had talents in Greece was sure to find admirers and even enthusiasts. It is these powerful encouragements that develop genius, that help minds soar and that help them break through the limits of mediocrity. What spirit of competition must not have inspired the philosophers when they learned that Philip of Macedonia had chosen Aristotle as the sole tutor worthy of raising Alexander! In this glorious age, every merit had its reward, every talent its honors. Good authors were given distinctions; the works of Thucydides and Xenophon were in everyone's hands. Every citizen seemed to participate in the fame of these geniuses who raised the name of Greece above that of all the other peoples.

Soon afterward, Rome furnished a similar spectacle. We see Cicero who, by his philosophic spirit and his eloquence, was raised to the height of honors; Lucretius who didn't live long enough to enjoy his reputation. Virgil and Horace were honored by the approval of this sovereign people. They were admitted into the familiar circle of Augustus and received their share of the rewards that this clever tyrant showered on those who, by celebrating his virtues, veiled his vices.

During the renaissance of letters in our Occident, we recall with pleasure the eagerness with which the Medicis and several sovereign pontiffs welcomed writers. We know that Petrarch was crowned a poet, and that death stole from Tasso the honor of being crowned in this same Capitol where the conquerors of the universe had triumphed in the past. Louis XIV, avid for every sort of glory, did not neglect that of rewarding the extraordinary men that nature produced under his reign. He did not limit himself to showering benefits upon Bossuet, Fenelon, Racine, Despréaux; he spread his munificence over all the lettered people, whatever their country, whenever their reputation reached his ears.

Such is the veneration all eras have had for these privileged geniuses who seem to ennoble the human race, whose works entertain and console us over the miseries of life. It is thus more than just that we pay tribute to the great man whose loss Europe is deploring, to give him the praise and admiration he so well deserved.

We do not propose, gentlemen, to enter into the detail of the private life of Monsieur de Voltaire. The history of a king should consist in an enumeration of the benefits he bestowed upon his subjects; that of a warrior, on his campaigns; that of a man of letters, in the analysis of his works. But as it is impossible to examine in detail the multitude of works we owe to the fecundity of M. de Voltaire, I hope you will content yourselves, gentlemen, with the meager sketch I will present, confining myself besides to barely touching on the principle events of his life. It would be dishonoring M. de Voltaire to dwell on researches that concern only his family. Contrary to those who owe everything to their ancestors and nothing to themselves, he owed everything to nature. He was the sole instrument of his fortune and his glory. We should content ourselves with knowing that his parents, who held employment in the judiciary branches, gave him an honest education. He studied at the college of Louis le Grand under Fathers Porée and Tournemine,[1] who were the first to discover the sparks of the brilliant flames that filled his writings.

Though young, M. de Voltaire was not regarded as an ordinary child. His verve had already made itself known. This is what introduced him to the home of Madame de Rupelmonde. This lady, charmed by the vivacity and talents of the young poet, launched him in the best social circles of Paris.[2] The upper classes became for him a school where his taste acquired that subtle tact, politeness and urbanity never achieved by those erudite scholars and solitary persons who misjudge what pleases refined society, too remote from their view to become familiar with it. It is mainly due to this tone of gracious banter and polish spread throughout the works of M. de Voltaire that they enjoy the vogue they do.

His tragedy *Oedipus* and a few poems appreciated in society had already appeared in public, when an indecent satire in verse on the Duke of Orleans, then the Regent of France, was sold in Paris. A certain La Grange, author of this dark work, to avoid suspicions, found a way to pass it off as M. de Voltaire's work. The government acted precipitously. The young poet, innocent though he was, was arrested and conducted to the Bastille, where he remained several months.[3] But as the essence of truth is to shed its light sooner or later, the guilty was punished and M. de Voltaire vindicated and released. Would you believe it, gentlemen, that it was in this very Bastille that our young poet composed the first two cantos of his *Henriade*? It is true, nonetheless. His prison became a Parnassus for him, where the Muses inspired him. What is certain is that his first and second cantos remained as he first timed them. For want of paper and ink, he learned the verses by heart and retained them.

Soon after his release, revolted by the disgraceful treatment and opprobrium whose shame he had endured at home, he withdrew to England, where he experienced not only the most favorable welcome from the public, but where he soon found a number of enthusiasts. He put the last touches to his *Henriade* in England, which he then published under the title, *Poem of the League*. Our young poet, who knew how to make the most of everything, applied himself principally to the study of philosophy while in England. The wisest and the most profound philosophers were flourishing there at the time. He seized the thread with which the circumspect Locke led himself through the labyrinth of metaphysics and, holding in check his impetuous imagination, he subjected it to the laborious calculations of the immortal Newton. He appropriated so well the discoveries of this philosopher, and his progress was such, that he was able to expose the great man's system in an abridgement clear enough for everyone to understand.[4] Before him, M. de Fontenelle had been the only philosopher who, by strewing flowers over the aridity of astronomy, rendered it capable of amusing the fair sex in their pastimes. The English were flattered to find a Frenchman who, not just content to admire their philosophers, translated them into his language. All the most illustrious of London hastened to meet him. No foreigner had ever been received more favorably by this nation. But however flattering this triumph was to self-esteem, the love of his country won out in the heart of our poet and he returned to France.

The Parisians, enlightened by the suffrages a nation as learned as profound had given our young author, began to suspect that a great man had been born among them. His *Letters on the English* then appeared, where the author paints in strong, rapid strokes the customs, arts, religions, and the government of this nation. The tragedy of *Brutus*, made to please this free-spirited people, soon followed, as did *Mariamne*, and a host of other plays.

At that time there was in France a lady celebrated for her taste for the arts and for the sciences. You guess well, gentlemen, that it is of the illustrious Marquise du Châtelet that we wish to speak. She had read the philosophic works of our young author. Soon, she made his acquaintance. The desire to instruct herself and eagerness to fathom the few truths that the human mind is able to, strengthened the ties of this friendship and made it indissoluble. Madame du Châtelet abandoned at once the *Theodicy* of Leibniz and the ingenious romances of this philosopher to adopt instead the circumspect, prudent methods of Locke, less apt to satisfy avid curiosity than strict reason. She learned enough geometry to follow Newton in his abstract calculations. Her application even persevered to the point of composing an abstract of this system for her son.[5] Cirey soon became the philosophical retreat of these two friends, where each composed works of a different genre that they shared with each other, striving through each other's remarks to perfect their productions as far as they could. It was there that the plays *Zaïre*, *Alzire*, *Mérope*, *Sémiramis*, *Catilina*, *Electra or Oreste* were composed.

M. de Voltaire, who brought everything into the sphere of his activity, did not limit himself uniquely to the pleasure of enriching the theater with his tragedies. It was particularly for the use of the Marquise du Châtelet that he composed his *Essay on World History*. His *History of Louis XIV* and his *History of Charles XII* had already appeared.

An author of so much genius, as varied as correct, did not escape the Académie Française. She claimed him as a property that belonged to her. He became a member of this illustrious body, and one of its finest ornaments. Louis XV, to distinguish him, also honored him with the post of Gentleman of the Royal Bedchamber and Royal Historian of France, a role he had, so to speak, already fulfilled by writing the history of Louis XIV.

Although M. de Voltaire was grateful for such dazzling marks of approval, he was nevertheless more grateful for his friendships. Inseparably bound to Madame du Châtelet, the glitter of a brilliant court did not dim his vision to the point of making him prefer the splendor of Versailles to a stay in Lunéville, and even less to his country retreat in Cirey. The two friends peaceably enjoyed what portion of happiness humanity is susceptible to, until the death of the Marquise du Châtelet put an end to this beautiful union. It was a severe blow to the emotions of M. de Voltaire, who needed all of his philosophy to withstand it.

Precisely during the time he was using all his strength to quell his grief, he was called to the Court of Prussia. The king, who had seen him in the year 1740, wished to possess this genius as rare as he was eminent. It was in the year 1752 that he came to Berlin. His knowledge knew no bounds. His conversation was as instructive as it was agreeable, his imagination as brilliant as it was varied, his spirit as prompt as it was present. He compensated for the sterility of certain subjects by the graces of fiction. In a word, he was the delight of all societies. An unfortunate quarrel that arose between him and M. de Maupertuis caused a falling out between these two learned men who were made to like and not to hate each other, and the war that occurred in 1756 gave M. de Voltaire the desire to settle in Switzerland.[6] He went to Geneva, to Lausanne, then purchased Les Délices, and finally chose to live in Ferney. His free time was shared between study and building. He read and wrote and, by the fertility of his genius, kept all the publishers of the cantons busy.

The presence of M. de Voltaire, the effervescence of his genius, and the ease of his productions persuaded the whole vicinity that to become a *bel esprit*, it was enough to only want to. It became a sort of epidemic illness from which the Swiss, not said to be among the glibbest, all seemed to suffer. They no longer expressed even the most ordinary things except by antithesis or epigrams. The town of Geneva was the most sorely affected by this contagion. The bourgeois, who believed themselves Lycurguses at least, were all inclined to give new laws to their country; but nary a one wished to obey those that were extant. These movements, caused by a zeal for misunderstood liberties, led to a sort of revolt or war that was merely ridiculous. M. de Voltaire did not fail to immortalize the event by singing of this so-called war in the tone Homer used on that of the rats and frogs. At times his fertile pen brought forth works for the theater, at others, mixtures of philosophy and history, at others, moral and allegorical novels. But at the same time that he was thus enriching literature with his new productions, he was applying himself to rural economy. We see to what point a fine mind is open to all sorts of forms. Ferney was nearly a wasteland when our philosopher acquired it. He brought it under cultivation. Not only did he repopulate it, but he helped numerous manufacturers and artisans set up there.

Let us not recall too soon, Gentlemen, the causes of our grief. Let us leave M. de Voltaire in tranquility in Ferney and cast a more attentive, thoughtful look meanwhile at the multitude of his various productions. History reports that Virgil, dying, and little satisfied with his *Aeneid*, which he hadn't been able to perfect as much as he would have liked, wanted to burn it. The long life M. de Voltaire enjoyed enabled him to hone and correct his poem, *The League*, and to bring it to the perfection it has now reached under the name of the *Henriade*. Those envious of our author reproached him with only writing an imitation of the *Aeneid* in this poem, and it must be admitted that there are cantos whose subjects resemble each other. But these are not servile copies. If Virgil depicts the destruction of Troy, Voltaire displays the horrors of the St. Bartholomew's Day Massacre. The love of Dido and Aeneas is compared to the love of Henri IV and the beautiful Gabrielle d'Estrées. To the descent of Aeneas into the underworld, where Anchises reveals the posterity to whom he will give birth, is countered Henri IV's dream and the future that St. Louis reveals to him by announcing the destiny of the Bourbons. If I dared to venture my opinion, I would give the prize to the Frenchman for two of these cantos; namely, the one on St. Bartholomew's Day and on the dream of Henri IV. Only in the love of Dido does Virgil seem to win out over Voltaire, because the Latin author interests and speaks to our heart, whereas the French author uses only allegories. But if one wished to examine these two poems with an open mind, without prejudices for either the ancients or the moderns, we would admit that a lot of details in the *Aeneid* would not be tolerated today in the works of our contemporaries, like, for example, the funeral honors Aeneas gives his father, Anchises; the fable of the harpies and the prophecy they give the Trojans, that they will be reduced to eating their plates, which then comes true; the sow with her nine piglets, who indicates the place where Aeneas' labors must end; his ships turned into nymphs; a stag killed by Ascanius, which sparks the war between the Trojans and the Rutuli; the hatred the gods put into the hearts of Amate and Livinia for Aeneas, whom Lavinia marries in the end. These are perhaps the defects Virgil himself was unhappy with, that made him want to burn his work and that, according to judicious censors, should place the *Aeneid* above the *Henriade*. If vanquished difficulties prove the merit of an author, it is certain that Voltaire had more of them to surmount than Virgil. The subject of the *Henriade* is the surrender of Paris, thanks to the conversion of Henri IV.[7] The poet did not thus have the liberty of manipulating marvels as he pleased. He was reduced

328 VOLTAIRE'S REVOLUTION

to limiting himself to the mysteries of the Christians, far less fertile in pleasant and picturesque images than the mythology of the Gentiles. Nevertheless, it is impossible to read the tenth cantos of the *Henriade* without admitting that the charms of the poetry ennoble every subject it touches upon. M. de Voltaire was the only one discontent with his poem. He felt that his hero was not exposed to grave enough dangers and that, consequently, he must be less interesting than Aeneas, who never escapes one peril without falling into another. . . .[8] His universal genius embraced every genre. After having tested himself against Virgil, and having perhaps surpassed him, he wanted to measure himself against Ariosto. He composed *La Pucelle* in the taste of *Orlando Furioso*; but this poem is not an imitation of the other. The fable, the marvels, the episodes, everything is original in it and breathes the gaiety of a brilliant imagination.

His *vers de société*[9] were the delight of every person of taste. Only the author himself took no account of it, though neither Anacreon, Horace, Ovid, Tibullus, nor any of the great authors of antiquity left us any models in these genres that he did not equal. His mind produced these works with no effort. This did not satisfy him. He felt that to obtain a well-deserved reputation, it was necessary to acquire it in overcoming the greatest obstacles.

After having given you a brief review of the talents of the poet, let us pass to those of the historian. *The History of Charles XII* was the first he wrote. He became the Quintus Curtius of this Alexander. The flowers he strews over the subject do not alter the basic truths in it. He paints the brilliant valor of the Northern hero in the brightest colors; his resolve on certain occasions, his obstinacy on others, his good fortune and his woes. After having tested his skills on Charles XII, he tried his hand at the history of the age of Louis XIV. It is no longer the Romanesque style of Quintus Curtius that he employs. He substitutes that of Cicero who, while pleading for the Law of Manilius, praises Pompey. It is a French author who relates with enthusiasm the famous events of this great century; who sheds the brightest daylight on the advantages that gave such preponderance to his nation over other peoples, on the arts and sciences protected by a polished court, the progress of industry of every sort, and the intrinsic power of France that made its king the arbiter of Europe. This unique work deserves to bestow the affection and gratitude of the entire French nation on M. de Voltaire, who elevated her more than she had ever been by any of her other writers. It is yet another style that he employs in his *Essay on Universal History*: a strong and simple style. The character of his spirit shows itself more in the way he wrote this history than in all his other writings. We see the fiery spirit of a superior genius who sees the grander view of everything, who heeds only what is important, and who disregards all the minor details. This work is not composed to teach history to those who haven't studied it, but to recall the essential facts to the mind of those familiar with it. He holds to the first law of history, which is to tell the truth; and the reflections he sows it with are not superfluous, they are born of the very matter at hand.

There remain to us droves of other treatises by M. de Voltaire, which it is almost impossible to analyze. Some of them turn on subjects of literary critique, others on metaphysical matters he's clarifying, others yet on astronomy, history, physics, eloquence, poetics, or geometry. Even his novels carry original characteristics: *Zadig, Micromegas, Candide* are works that, while seeming to breathe frivolity, contain allegorical morals or critiques of certain modern systems, where the useful is inseparably tied to the agreeable.

So many talents, so much diverse knowledge united in a single person, throws readers into an astonishment mixed with surprise. Recapitulate, Gentlemen, the lives of the great men of antiquity whose names have come down to us and you will find that each of them was limited to a single talent. Aristotle and Plato were philosophers; Aeschines and Demosthenes, orators; Homer, epic poet; Sophocles, tragic poet; Anacreon, lyric poet; Thucydides and Xenophon, historians; just as, among the Romans, Virgil, Horace, Ovid, Lucretia were only poets; Titus Livius and Varro, historians; Crassus, Marcus Antonius, and Quintas Hortensius kept to their harangues. Cicero, this consul orator, defender and father of the nation, is the only one who united diverse types of talents and knowledge. He joined the great art of words, which made him superior to all his contemporaries, to a profound study of philosophy as it was known in his time. This is apparent in his *Tuscalan Disputations*, in his admirable treatise *On the Nature of the Gods*, in *On Duties*, which is perhaps the best work on morals that we have. Cicero was even a poet. He translated the verses of Aratus into Latin, and it is believed that his corrections perfected the poem of Lucretius.

We have therefore been obliged to travel seventeen centuries to find, in the multitude of men who make up the human race, only Cicero whose knowledge can be compared with that of our illustrious author. One might say, if I may be permitted to express it so, that M. de Voltaire was worth an entire academy by himself. There are writings in which we think we recognize Bayle, armed with all the arguments of his dialectic. Others where we imagine we're reading Thucydides. Here, we have a physicist, discovering the secrets of nature. There, a metaphysician, who, relying on analogy and experience, carefully follows in the footsteps of Locke. In other works, you will find the follower of Sophocles. Here, he strews some flowers on the path; there, he laces on his comic boots; but the elevation of his spirit does not seem content to simply equal Terence or Molière. Soon, you see him on Pegasus, who, spreading his wings, carries him to heights of Helicon where the god of the Muses awards him his place between Homer and Virgil.

So much variety in his works and so many great efforts from his genius produced a vivid sensation on all minds in the end, and all Europe applauded the superior talents of M. de Voltaire. Not that jealousy and envy spared him: they sharpened all their traits to overwhelm him. The spirit of independence innate in all men, which inspires aversion for the most legitimate authority, revolts them with even more bitterness against a superiority in talents their failings cannot attain. But the cries of envy were smothered by even louder applause. Men of letters prided themselves on their acquaintance with this great man. Whoever was philosophic enough to esteem only personal merit set Voltaire high above those whose ancestors, titles, pride, and riches constitute their only merit. M. de Voltaire was among the small number of philosophers who could say, *Omnia mecum porto.*[10] Princes, sovereigns, kings, empresses, showered him with marks of their esteem and admiration. It is not that we mean to imply that the rulers of the earth are the best assessors of merit, but it proves at least that the repute of our author was so generally established that the heads of nations, far from contradicting the voice of the public, felt obliged to conform to it.

Nonetheless, as the bad is found mixed with the good everywhere in this world, it happened that M. de Voltaire, while not insensitive to the universal applause he enjoyed, was no less insensitive to the sting of all these insects who stagnate in the mire of the Hippocrene. Far from punishing them, he immortalized them by putting their obscure names in his works. But from them he received only slight splatterings in comparison with the more violent persecutions he had to suffer from ecclesiastics who, by their status, being only of ministers of peace, should have practiced only charity and benevolence. As blinded by a false zeal as they were besotted by fanaticism, they hounded him, hoping to condemn him through calumny. Their ignorance foiled the project. Lacking any discernment, they befuddled the clearest ideas to the point where the passages in which our author implies tolerance are interpreted by them as containing the dogmas of atheism. And this same Voltaire, who had deployed all the resources of his genius to forcefully prove the existence of God, heard himself accused, to his great astonishment, of having denied his existence.

The venom these devout souls poured so clumsily over him found supporters among those of their kind, but not among those who had the slightest smattering of dialectic.[11] His real crime consisted in not being cowardly enough to hide the vices of so many pontiffs who have dishonored the Church in his history; in having said, like Fra Paolo, Fleury, and so many others that passions often influence the conduct of priests more than the inspiration of the Holy Spirit does; that in his works, he inspires a horror of these abominable massacres that zealotry incited; and lastly, that he treated with contempt all the unintelligible, frivolous quarrels theologians of every sect attach such importance to. Add to this, to complete the canvas, that all of M. de Voltaire's writings sold swiftly as soon as they left the presses, while the bishops watched the worms gnaw at their mandates in holy vexation, or saw them rot in the shops of their booksellers. This is how imbecilic priests reason. Their foolishness would be pardoned if their bad syllogisms did not disturb the peace of so many individuals. All that the truth obliges us to say is that such bad reasoning is enough to characterize these vile, despicable beings who, while professing to submit their reason, openly divorce all good sense.

Since the point here is to justify M. de Voltaire, we should not conceal any of the accusations that have been made against him. The hypocrites further charge him, then, with having exposed the views of Epicurus, Hobbes, Woolston, Lord Bolingbroke, and other philosophers. But is it not clear that, far from strengthening these opinions by what any other man might have added, he contents himself with being the reporter of a trial whose verdict he leaves to his readers? Moreover, if religion has the truth as its foundation, what has it to fear from anything falsehood can invent against it? M. de Voltaire was so convinced of it, that he did not believe that the doubts of a few philosophers could prevail over divine inspiration.

But let us go further. Let us compare the morals spread throughout his works to those of his persecutors. Men should love each other like brothers, says he. Their duty is to help each other bear the burden of life in which the sum total of pain and evil outweighs the good. Their opinions are as different as their appearances. Far from persecuting each other for thinking differently, they ought to limit themselves to rectifying the opinions of those who are in error, with reason, and without using the fire and sword in place of arguments. In a word, they should conduct themselves with others as they would wish to be treated themselves. Is this M. de Voltaire speaking, or is it the apostle, St. John, or is it the language of the Gospels? Oppose to this the moral practices of hypocrisy or zealotry. It expresses itself like this: Let us exterminate those who do not think what we want them to think, condemn those who reveal our ambition and our vices, let God be the shield for our iniquities, let men rip each other apart, let blood flow. What does it matter so long as our authority grows? Let us make God implacable and cruel, so that the earnings of the custom houses of purgatory and heaven increase our revenues. That is how religion often serves as a pretext for the passions of men and how, through their perversity, the purest source of good becomes one of evil.

M. de Voltaire's cause being as good as we have just shown it, won the approval of all the tribunes where reason is better heeded than mystical sophisms. Whichever persecution he was enduring from theological hatred, he always distinguished religion from those were dishonoring it. He did justice to the ecclesiastics whose virtues had been a veritable ornament for the Church. He never blamed any but those whose perverse morals had made them a public abomination.

M. de Voltaire thus spent his life between the persecutions of the envious and the admiration of his enthusiasts, without the sarcasms of the first humiliating him and without the applause of the second augmenting his opinion of himself. He contented himself with enlightening the world and with inspiring a love of literature and humanity through his works. Not content with giving moral precepts, he preached benevolence by his example. It was his courageous support that came to the assistance of the unfortunate Calas family. It was he who pleaded the cause of the Sirvens and who tore them from the hands of their barbarous judges; he who would have brought the Chevalier de La Barre back to life if he had had the gift of performing miracles. How noble for a philosopher to raise his voice from the depths of his refuge and for humanity, whose voice he is, to force judges to reform unjust rulings! If M. de Voltaire had only this one trait in his favor, he would deserve to be ranked among the very small number of humanity's true benefactors. Philosophy and religion then both teach in concert the path of virtue. Which is more Christian? The judge who cruelly forces a family to leave its country, or the philosopher who takes them in and defends them? The judge who serves as the sword of justice to kill a scatterbrain, or the wise man who wants to save the young man's life to mend his ways? The executioner of Calas or the protector of his afflicted family? That, Gentlemen, is what will make the memory of M. de Voltaire forever dear to those born with a heart and with feelings that can be moved. However precious the gifts of the mind, the imagination, the elevation of genius and vast knowledge, these gifts, which nature bestows only rarely, still never take precedence over acts of humanity and benevolence. We admire the first and we bless and venerate the second.

However painful it is for me, Gentlemen, to separate myself from M. de Voltaire forever, I nevertheless feel the moment approaching where I must renew the sorrow his loss causes you. We have left him in peace in Ferney. Affairs of private interest engaged him to travel to Paris where he hoped to still have time to save some vestiges of his fortune from a bankruptcy that had enfolded him. He did not want to reappear in his country empty-handed. His time, which he divided between philosophy and belles-lettres, furnished a number of works of which he always had a few in reserve. Having composed a new tragedy on the subject of Irene,[12] he wanted to produce it on the stage of Paris. His habit was to subject his plays to the severest critiques before exposing them in public. In accordance with his principles, he consulted everyone of good taste in Paris that he knew, sacrificing vain pride to the desire of making his works more worthy of posterity. Docile to the informed opinions he was given, he corrected this tragedy with a singular zeal and ardor. He spent entire nights reworking his play, and either to dispel sleep or to reanimate his senses, he used an immoderate amount of coffee. Fifty cups per day barely sufficed him. This drink, which put his blood into the most violent agitation, caused him such prodigious over-excitement that, to calm the sort of hot fever it caused, he took recourse in opiates, and took such strong doses that, instead of relieving his suffering, it accelerated his end. Soon after the taking of this remedy with so little restraint, a sort of paralysis overtook him, followed by an apoplexy that ended his days.

Even though M. de Voltaire had rather poor health; even though his sorrows, worries, and great application to his work had weakened his constitution, he nevertheless pursued his career into his eighty-fourth year. His existence was such that, in his case, the mind won over matter in everything. His was a strong soul that communicated its vigor to a body almost diaphanous. His memory was astonishing, and he conserved all his faculties of thought and imagination until his last breath. With what joy I will recall to you, Gentlemen, the transports of admiration and recognition the Parisians showed this great man during his last stay in his homeland! It is rare but also moving when the public is equitable, when it does justice in its lifetime to these extraordinary beings that nature only revels in producing every now and then; to see them garner even from their contemporaries the approval they are sure to obtain from posterity. It should be expected that a man who had employed all the wisdom of his genius to celebrate the glory of his nation would see a few rays reflect on himself. The French sensed it and, by their enthusiasm, made themselves worthy of sharing the luster their compatriot had shone on them and on the century. But will it be believed that Voltaire, to whom pagan Greece would have raised altars, of whom statues would have been made in Rome, to whom a great empress, protectress of sciences, wanted to erect a monument in St. Petersburg, who would believe, I say, that such a being would not find a little earth to cover his remains in his fatherland? What! In the eighteenth century, where knowledge has spread more than ever, where the philosophic spirit has made so much progress, there are hierophants more barbaric than the Heruli,[13] more worthy of living among the peoples of Taprobana than in the French nation, blinded by zealotry, intoxicated with fanaticism, who would prevent the final respects of humanity from being paid to one of the most celebrated men that France has ever brought to bear! Yet that is what Europe saw in grief mingled with indignation. But whatever the hatred of these frenzied lunatics or the cowardice of the vengeance they take out on cadavers, neither the shrieks of envy nor their savage howls will tarnish the memory of M. de Voltaire. The kindest destiny they can await is for them and their vile artifices to be buried forever in the darkness of oblivion; whereas the memory of M. de Voltaire will grow throughout the ages and transmit his name to immortality.

EDGAR QUINET ON THE EXTERMINATING ANGEL

1844

Edgar Quinet (1803–1875) was a French historian, writer, and statesman. This extract, based on a series of lectures undertaken with his friend, the famous historian Jules Michelet, gives his take on Voltaire's effect sixty-six years after his death. The notion that Voltaire had been sent by God to clean up his church had also been expressed in Voltaire's lifetime, even by churchmen, and would be taken up again in Victor Hugo's fiery speech for the centenary of Voltaire's death in the turmoil of 1878, at the dawn of a Third, and definitive, Republic in France.[1]

My eyes have been following, these last forty years, the reign of a man who, in himself alone, is the spiritual direction, not only of his country, but of his era. From the back of his chamber, he governs the Kingdom of Minds. Intellects adjust themselves each day to his. A word from his pen sails throughout Europe in a moment. Princes love him, kings fear him. They feel uncertain of their kingdoms if he is not on their side. The people, for their part, adopt without discussion and echo every syllable that falls from his pen with relish. Who exerts this incredible power, that had not been seen anywhere since the Middle Ages? Is it another Pope Gregory VII? Is it a pope? No, it's Voltaire.

How did the power of the former pass to the latter? Is it possible that the entire earth was duped by an evil genius, sent by hell? Why has this man been enthroned over Minds without contestation? First of all, it is because he has often done the work reserved to popes in the Middle Ages. Everywhere that violence, injustice occurs, I see him strike it with the anathema of the Spirit. What does it matter if the violence calls itself Inquisition, Saint Bartholomew's, or Holy War? He placed himself in a region above the papacy of the Middle Ages. Overriding all the sects and all the denominations, it was the first time ideal justice was seen to strike violence and lies wherever they occurred.

The Church, no one denies it, had committed grave faults. She had to be chastised sooner or later, and as these were crimes against the Spirit, she had to be punished by flagellations of the Spirit. Voltaire is the exterminating angel sent by God against his sinful Church.

He shatters, with his terrible laugh, the doors of the Church, which, set up by St. Peter, had opened for the Borgias. It is the laugh of the universal Spirit that disdains all particular forms as just that many deformities. It is the ideal mocking the real. In the name of mute generations the Church should have consoled, he arms himself with all the blood she spilled, all the burning stakes, all the scaffolds she raised that, sooner or later, had to turn against her. This irony mingled with wrath does not belong simply to one individual or to a generation. It is melded to the laughter of all the abused generations, all the tortured dead who, recalling that they found violence on earth instead of mildness, the wolf instead of the paschal lamb, are moved to mock in turn, from the bottom of their graves.

What makes Voltaire's wrath a grand act of Providence is that he strikes, he flouts and overwhelms the infidel Church with the arms of the Christian Spirit. Humanity, charity, fraternity—are these not the sentiments revealed by the Gospels? He turns them with irresistible force on the violence of the fake doctors of the Scriptures. The biblical angel of wrath pours both sulphur and bitumen over condemned cities, amidst great winds. Voltaire's spirit likewise wanders across the face of the divine city. He strikes it with lightning, the sword, and with sarcasm. He pours gall, irony, and ashes upon it. When he is weary, a voice awakes him and cries out, "Continue!" So he begins again, relentless. He digs up what he has already dug, unhinges what he has already unhinged, and shatters what he has already shattered! For a task that took so long, never interrupted and always successful, was not the affair of a single individual. It was the revenge of God cheated and wronged, who used man's irony as the instrument of his wrath.

No, this man was not his own man; he was conducted by a superior force. As he overthrows with one hand, he builds with the other; and that is the marvel

of his destiny. He employs all the derision of his faculties to overthrow the bar-
riers separate churches had erected, but there is another man inside him. Full of
fervor, he establishes upon the ruins of orthodoxy common sense.

He feels the frauds, the lies, the injustice in his very fibers, not only in a
given moment of time, but in every pulsation of the human race. The separate churches had founded Christian rights only for themselves. Voltaire made
Christian rights the common right of all humanity. Before he came, we called
ourselves universal, and this universality stopped at the threshold of a particular
church or communion. Whoever was not a part of it was outside evangelical
law. Voltaire enveloped the entire earth within its rights.

Where did this old man of eighty-four find the force, I ask you, to plead
until the last hour of his life for the families of the Calases', the Sirvens, the
La Barres, and so many people he did not know? Where did he learn to feel
like a contemporary to all ages, to feel wounded to the depths of his being by
a given case of violence committed fifteen hundred years ago? What does this
daily, worldwide protestation against the powers mean? This indignation that
neither the distance of space nor of centuries can appease? What does this old
man want, who, with only his inspiration, makes himself the fellow-citizen, the
attorney and journalist of every society, past and present?

He awakes each morning, obsessed with the cries of extinct generations
and civilizations! In the midst of the agitations and distractions of the eighteenth
century, a cry, a sigh from Thebes, from Athens, from ancient Rome, from the
Middle Ages busies, obsesses, and torments him, keeps him from sleep! On St.
Bartholomew's Day, the twenty-fourth of August, he gets a fever.[2] History is not
a science for him, it's a screaming reality. What is the strange instinct that forces
him to be sensitive to everything, and to be present in the past? Where does this
new charity come from that traverses time and space?

What is it, I beg you, if it is not the Christian spirit itself, the universal spirit
of solidarity, fraternity, of a vigilance that lives, feels, suffers, and remains in
close communion with all humanity, past and present. And this is why the earth
proclaimed this man the living word of humanity in the eighteenth century. We
were not deceived by appearances. He tore words asunder and made the universal spirit burst forth. That is why we still proclaim him.

In good faith, what opposed him? What adversary entered battle against him? In the camp of the past, where did he appear, this fighter who, to vanquish Voltaire, would have had to have been more vigilant, more fervent, more universal than he in the cause of justice against force and violence?

In the hurried movement of our century, the dust rose up to heaven, beneath the feet of new generations. A few cried out in joy: Voltaire has disappeared! He has perished in the abyss with all his fame. But that was just one of the artifices of true glory. The mediocre alone were duped. The dust falls, and the light we thought extinguished reappears. It laughs at the mistaken joy of darkness. Like something resurrected, it shines with a purer light. And the century that had begun by renouncing it with pursed lips, ends in confirming everything that's immortal about it.

ROBERT G. INGERSOLL ON
THE GREAT INFIDELS

Ingersoll's famous speech, *The Great Infidels*, was printed in
the *Chicago Tribune* of May 5, 1881. Over three thousand
people had attended it on May 1. The reporter included
the audience's reactions, which are retained. For Ingersoll,
the first great infidel was Jesus, who did what he could to
tear down the religion of his day and who was not Christian himself. Giordano Bruno, burned in 1600, came next.
This extract concerns the next two "great infidels" evoked in
his speech: Voltaire and his Scottish contemporary, David
Hume.

Voltaire was born in 1694. When he was born, the natural was about
the only thing that the Church did not believe in. Monks sold amulets
and the priests cured in the name of the Church. The worship of the Devil
was actually established, which today is the religion of China. They say, "God
is good; He won't bother you: Joss is the one." They offer him gifts, and try to
soften his heart; so in the Middle Ages the poor people tried to see if they could
not get a shortcut, and trade directly with the Devil, instead of going round-
about through the Church. In these days, witnesses were cross-examined with
instruments of torture. Voltaire did more for human liberty than any other man
who ever lived or died. He appealed to the common sense of mankind—he
held up the great contradictions of the sacred Scriptures in a way that no man
once having read him could forget. For one, I thank Voltaire for the liberty I am
enjoying this moment. How small a man a priest looked when he pointed his
finger at him; how contemptible a King. Toward the last of May, 1778, it was
whispered in Paris that Voltaire was dying. He expired with the most perfect
tranquility. There have been constructed more shameful lies about the death of
this great and wonderful man, compared with who all of his calumniators, living

or dead, were but dust and vermin. (Applause) From his throne at the foot of the Alps he pointed the finger of scorn at every hypocrite in Europe. He was the pioneer of his century.

In 1771, in Scotland, David Hume was born.[1] Scotch Presbyterianism is the worst form of religion that has ever been produced. (Laughter) The Scotch Kirk had all the faults of the Church of Rome, without a redeeming feature.

The Church hated music, despised painting, abhorred statuary, and held architecture in contempt. Anything touched with humanity, with the weakness of love, with the dimple of Joy, was detested by the Scotch Kirk. God was to be feared; God was infinitely practical, no nonsense about God. They used to preach four times a day. They preached on Friday before the Sunday upon which they partook of the sacrament, and then on Saturday; four sermons on Sunday, and two or three on Monday to sober up on. (Laughter) They were bigoted and heartless. One case will illustrate. In the beginning of this nineteenth century a boy seventeen years of age was indicted at Edinburg for blasphemy. He had given it as his opinion that Moses had learned magic in Egypt and had fooled the Jews. (Laughter) They proved that on two or three occasions, when he was real cold, he jocularly remarked that he wished he was in Hell, so that he could warm up. (Laughter) He was tried, convicted, and sentenced to be hanged. He recanted; he even wrote that he believed the whole business, and that he just said it for pure devilment. It made no difference. They hanged him, and his bruised and bleeding corpse was denied to his own mother, who came and besought them to let her take her boy home. That was Scotch Presbyterianism. If the Devil had been let loose in Scotland he would have improved that country at that time. (Laughter)

David Hume was one of the few Scotchmen who was not owned by the church. He had the courage to examine things for himself, and to give his conclusion to the world. His life was unstained by an unjust act. He did not, like Abraham, turn a woman from his door with his child in her arms. (Applause) He did not, like King David, murder a man that he might steal his wife. (Applause) He didn't believe in Scotch Presbyterians. I don't see how any good man ever did. Just think of going to the day of judgment, if there is one, and standing up before God and admitting without a blush that you have lived and died a Scotch Presbyterian. (Laughter) I would expect the next sentence would be "Depart ye, cursed in everlasting life." (Laughter) Hume took the ground that a miracle could not be used as evidence until you had proved the miracle. Of course that excited the Church. Why? Because they could not prove one of them. How are you going to prove a miracle? Who saw it, and who would know a devil if he did see him? (Laughter) Hume insisted that at the bottom of all good is something useful; that after all, human happiness was the great object, end, and aim of life; that virtue was not a termagant, with sunken cheeks and frightful eyes, but was the most beautiful thing in the world, and would strew your path with flowers from the cradle to the grave. When he died they gave an account of how he suffered. They knew that the horror of death would fall upon him, and God would get his revenge. But his attending physician said that his death was the most serenest and most perfectly tranquil of any he had ever seen. Adam Smith said he was as near to perfect as the frailty incident to humanity would allow a human being to be.

GLOSSARY

Abbé—Originally an abbot, elected by monks to direct their abbey, there were several types of abbés by the eighteenth century in France. The type encountered perhaps most frequently was a "secular cleric" who had received the minor orders; a sort of honorary title. This type of "abbé" has no equivalent in English.

Albigensian, or Cathar, Crusade (1209–1229)—The Cathar sect, based on gnostic teachings, had sprung up two centuries earlier in and around the town of Albi in the south of France. They claimed that their beliefs, which gave more importance to women and the role of Mary Magdalene as a spiritual leader, dated from the earliest Christian times, a view now regarded as substantially correct. They had been declared heretical several times, when Pope Innocent III offered all their lands to French nobles willing to lead a "crusade" against them in 1209. Tens of thousands were slaughtered, their towns burned to the ground. Spearheaded by St. Dominic and his Dominicans, this genocide is often considered the beginning of the Inquisition.

Ananias and Sapphira—A couple in Acts 5 of the Bible who sold their land to lay the money at Peter's feet but who lied to hold back a little for themselves. When Peter rebuked them, they both magically dropped dead, causing great fear all around, it is said.

Annates—The lands and its revenues accorded to an ecclesiastic are called a benefice and the whole of the first year's profits, called annates, were given to the papal treasury, also known as the "First Fruits" (Latin *primitiae*), a concept that dates back to earlier Greek, Roman, and Hebrew religions.

Antonines—Voltaire references to the *Antonins* seems to refer to what is now called the Nerva-Antonine dynasty of Roman Emperors who ruled from 96 to 192 CE: Nerva, Trajan, Hadrian, Antonius Pius, Marcus Aurelius, Lucius Verus, and Commodu. The first five are commonly referred to as "the Five Good Emperors" who ruled with wisdom and virtue.

Balthasar Gérard (1575–1584)—Assassinated the Dutch independence leader

William I of Orange after Philip II, the King of Spain, had offered a large reward for it. He was sentenced to be quartered and disemboweled alive following several days of equally hideously appalling tortures.

Bishop of Rome—The pope, who was originally a bishop like all the other bishops.

Bonze—A now-obsolete Western term for Bikkhu, a male Buddhist monk.

Canon Law—The body of laws determined by a given church authority (Roman Catholic, Eastern Orthodox, Anglican, etc.) to govern its members.

Carpocratians—An early Gnostic sect accused of libertinism by early Church fathers such as Irenaeus and Clement of Alexandria. None of their own writings subsist, however.

Charles XII—The subject of Voltaire's first history book, Charles XII was King of Sweden from 1697 to 1718. He defended the Swedish Empire from a triple alliance of Denmark-Norway, Saxony-Poland-Lithuania, and Russia, led by Peter the Great. Charles' death effectively put an end to the Swedish Empire.

Chevalier de La Barre—Jean-François de La Barre (1745–1766). An impoverished French nobleman condemned for not taking off his hat before a religious procession and possibly singing impious songs, tortured and beheaded at the age of nineteen. Voltaire tried to rehabilitate his memory in several writings, in vain. Condorcet relates the story near the end of his extract in the Appendix.

Colao—A title given ministers in the Chinese Empire, sometimes translated as a "mandarin."

Consubstantiality—Refers to the belief that the three persons of the Christian Trinity (God the Father, God the Son, and the Holy Ghost) are all one. The term was coined by Tertullian (160–225) and has the same meaning as the Greek term "homoousios" favored by Athanasius and ratified at the Nicene Council in the fourth century.

Convulsionaries—The *convulsionnaires* evolved from among the more fanatical members of the Jansenists who vied bitterly with the Jesuits in the seventeenth and eighteenth centuries. They tortured themselves, some to the point of having themselves crucified with nails, in the belief that their convulsions provoked "prophetic visions."

Dom Calmet—Benedictine monk and well-known Biblical scholar. His twenty-three-volume *Literal Commentary on all the Books of the Old Testament and the New Testament*, composed from 1706 to 1716, was often consulted by Voltaire and Madame du Châtelet who both knew the author personally.

The Decalogue—The Ten Commandments.

Damiens—Robert-François Damiens (1715–1757). A French servant who stabbed French King Louis XV, probably because of the Catholic clergy's refusal to grant the holy sacraments to Jansenists. Though he intentionally inflicted only a slight wound in warning, as he said, he was drawn and quartered in a highly public execution, the legal punishment for regicide.

Dervish—A member of a Muslim religious group, noted for a fast spinning dance done as a part of worship.

Écu—Can refer to one of several French coins, usually gold. The first écu was minted in 1266. They disappeared during the French Revolution, though the term was still employed by the people for the five-franc silver coins. Its purchasing power before the Revolution was roughly equivalent to twenty-five US dollars in 2006.

Edict of Nantes—An edict issued by King Henri IV of France in 1598 extending tolerance and civil rights to French Calvinist Protestants, known as Huguenots, to end the Catholic-Protestant religious wars that had afflicted France (and all Europe) for the previous half century. Louis XIV revoked it in 1685.

Esdras—An earlier form of "Ezra," the prophet, used in the Catholic and Hebrew Bibles.

François I—French king who ruled during the Renaissance from 1515 to 1547, contemporary to King Henry VIII of England.

Grimm—Friedrich Melchior, Baron von Grimm (1723–1807), Born in Germany, he moved to Paris at the age of twenty-five and became a journalist and critic of the arts, writing in French. A member of Baron d'Holbach and Diderot's atheistic inner circle, a contributor to the *Encyclopedia* but best-known for his bimonthly newsletter, the *Correspondance littéraire, philosophique et critique*, published from 1753 to 1790.

Guebres, Ghebers, Parsis—Fire worshippers; descendants and followers of the ancient Persian religion reformed by Zoroaster. The name Guebre was given them by the Arabian Muslim conquerors, according to *Brewer's Dictionary of Phrase and Fable* and is now applied to fire worshippers generally.

Henri II—King of France from 1547 till his death in 1559. Married to Catherine de Medici when both were fourteen, but famous for his twenty-five year liaison with Diane de Poitiers, his widowed mistress and former governess, twenty-one years his elder. Killed in a jousting tournament, he had struggled to suppress the ever-increasing Protestant Reformation in France.

Henri III—The last of the Valois kings of France who reigned during the Catholic-Protestant wars. He was murdered by Jacques Clément who opposed his religious tolerance.

Henri IV—Protestant cousin of Henri III, and the first of the Bourbon kings of France. He converted to Catholicism, the dominant religion in France, famously saying that Paris was "worth a mass" but issued the Edict of Nantes granting tolerance for Protestants. Though much beloved by the people for his compassion and good humor, there were several attempts on his life, both from Protestants who considered him a traitor and Catholics who considered him a usurper. He was murdered in the end by a Catholic zealot, François Ravaillac. Voltaire wrote an epic poem about him called *La Henriade*, which was highly popular for a century and widely translated.

Huguenot—A member of the Protestant Reformed Church of France, which was inspired by Calvin in the 1530s. Roughly half a million Huguenots fled from France to Protestant countries and colonies during the religious wars and persecutions.

Hussite, or Bohemian, Wars—Five crusades launched by the pope from 1420 to 1431 against the Hussites, followers of Jan Hus, who denounced the corruption of the Church and Papacy and promoted the reformist ideas of English theologian John Wycliffe. Centered in Prague, the conflicts soon engulfed Bohemia, Moravia, Poland, Lithuania, and most of central Europe. Most of Bohemia was ravaged, and Hus was burned at the stake for heresy.

Ixion—A king in Greek legend who engendered the Centaurs—called ixionadie, after him—with a cloud in the form of Hera. It is one of Voltaire's pet jokes that the Old Testament in his day listed ixion among the forbidden foods, along with griffin (or gryphon), another legendary creature.

Jansenism—A Calvinistic movement within the Catholic Church that emphasized original sin, human depravity, predestination, the necessity of divine grace, and the denial of free will. Its most famous adherent was Blaise

Pascal, and its theological center was the Port Royal convent in Paris. The Jesuits had Jansenist teachings condemned as heretical several times, and both groups battled each other incessantly throughout the seventeenth and eighteenth centuries.

Jacques Clément (1567–1589)—Dominican lay brother and member of the Catholic League who regarded Protestantism as heresy and who murdered French King Henri III. Though his body was quartered and burned, he was praised by Pope Sixtus V, who considered canonizing him.

La Brinvilliers—Marie Madeleine Dreux d'Aubry (1630–1676). A French marquise convicted of poisoning her own father, both brothers, for attempts on her husband and possibly her sister, and who very likely poisoned a number of inmates at a charity hospital she visited, presumably to perfect her art. She appeared so pious at her execution that the crowd wanted her sainted. Madame de Sévigny, Alexandre Dumas *père*, and A. Conan Doyle, among others, wrote about her.

Lama—A title similar to guru in Tibetan Buddhism, applied to the Dalai Lama, for example.

Laokium—Followers of Laokium, or the sect of Tao-se. More details on this and other Chinese sects can be found at: http://en.wikisource.org/wiki/A_Dictionary_of_All_Religions_and_Religious_Denominations/Chinese.

Lettre de Cachet—Letters with the royal seal, or cachet, were orders directly from the king that could not be appealed. Often used to order imprisonment or expulsion without trial in the Old Régime.

Louis (the coin)—In the preface to *Voltaire en son temps*, the Voltaire Foundation in Oxford estimated that one louis was roughly the equivalent of twenty-four pounds sterling in 1987. One franc and one pound were equivalent sums in the eighteenth century.

Louis IX (aka St. Louis)—French king who reigned from 1226 till his death in 1270. He led the seventh and eighth Crusades, had some twelve thousand copies of the Talmud and other Jewish books burned at the bidding of Pope Gregory IX and is the only French king who was canonized (in 1297). He is often considered the ideal Christian monarch, and countless cities around the world are named St. Louis or San Luis in his honor. His hair shirt and scourge are on display in the Treasures of Notre-Dame de Paris.

M.—The abbreviation for Monsieur in French.

Madame du Châtelet—Gabrielle Émilie le Tonnelier de Breteuil, marquise du Châtelet (1706–1749); a mathematician and physicist, she was best known for her translation and corrections of Newton's *Principia mathematica* (on gravity)—still the standard translation in French. She and Voltaire became romantically involved in 1733 and lived together till her death, with the assent of her good-natured husband, a military commander rarely home.

Marabout—A dervish in Muslim Africa, believed to have supernatural power.

Parlement—French Parliaments were the Appeal Courts, the highest of the judicial institutions, and not legislative bodies like in England. However, laws and edicts from the Crown did not become official till the *parlements* gave their assent by publishing them. Members bought or inherited their office and ruled primarily for the benefit of their own class. There were thirteen *parlements* in France in Voltaire's day, although references to just "*Parlement*" meant the Parlement of Paris, which was the oldest and had the largest jurisdiction.

Parsis—See Guebres.

Pentateuch—The first five books of the Bible, traditionally attributed to Moses: i.e., Genesis, Exodus, Leviticus, Numbers, and Deuteronomy.

Philosophes—The French word for philosophers, but used in English it has come to mean specifically the French Enlightenment writers.

Platonist—A follower or disciple of Plato.

St. Bartholomew's Day Massacre—August 24, 1572, was in fact only the starting date of a Catholic-Protestant butchery, which began in Paris, then spread to twenty other provinces in France. Estimations of the death toll range from five to thirty thousand.

St. Genevieve (423–512 CE)—The patron saint of Paris, said to have diverted Attila the Hun from attacking the city by leading a prayer marathon. When Childeric I besieged and conquered Paris in 464, she acted as intermediary, collecting food and getting prisoners released. Her relics were carried in procession yearly and in times of crisis.

Simon Barjona—The original name of Peter, Jesus' apostle. The popes claim to be his successors.

Simony—The buying or selling of church offices or powers. The name is taken from Simon Magus (Acts 8:18), who tried to buy the power of conferring the gifts of the Holy Spirit. Simony became widespread in the tenth and eleventh centuries.

Sophism—An argument apparently correct in form, but invalid; especially one used to deceive.

Sorbonne—The Sorbonne University or college, founded in 1257 by Robert de Sorbon, is one of the oldest universities in Europe. In the eighteenth century, and ever since Medieval times like most universities, it taught mainly theology. It provided the censors used by the Old Régime.

St. Medard—A church in the Latin Quarter in Paris where the Convulsionaries gathered to perform their "miracles" in its cemetery.

Talapoin—A name given the Buddhist monks of Burma and Thailand by the Europeans in the seventeenth and eighteenth centuries, according to the Larousse dictionary.

Thales (624–546 BCE)—A pre-Socratic Greek philosopher and one of the Seven Sages, author of Thales' Theorem. Bertrand Russell said Western philosophy began with Thales, who attempted to explain natural phenomenon without mythology and was hailed as the first true mathematician for using geometry to calculate the height of pyramids and the distance of ships. He was also the first known to use deductive reasoning, define principles, and set forth hypotheses.

Tobias—One of the five books of the Latin Vulgate Bible the Protestant Bibles did not retain.

Transubstantiation—The belief that the bread and wine given at Communion become the body and blood of Jesus Christ when blessed.

Treaty of Westphalia—A series of treaties signed in 1648 to put an end to the Thirty Years' War and to the Eighty Years' War between Spain and the Dutch Republic. Calvinism was given legal recognition and the right of princes to determine the religion of their states was recognized, the options being Catholicism, Lutheranism, and Calvinism.

Zend-Avesta—A slight misnomer for the Avesta due to some eighteenth-century accounts. The Avesta contains the sacred texts of the Zoroastrians, composed in the Avestan language.

NOTES

INTRODUCTION

1. *On a voulu l'enterrer* is the title of the last volume of the five-volume biography, *Voltaire en son temps* (René Pomeau and Christiane Mervaud, eds. [Oxford: Voltaire Foundation, 1985–1994]. Fifteen scholars collaborated on the enterprise. The phrase is borrowed from Voltaire himself, in a letter to his niece in 1746: "On m'a voulu enterer. Mais j'ai esquivé. Bonsoir." (They wanted to bury me. But I dodged it. Good evening.)

2. Refusing burial was a means of obtaining deathbed recantations. Your corpse was thrown in a ditch and covered with lime otherwise. But Voltaire dodged recanting, too.

3. Miguel Benitez, "Voltaire and Clandestine Manuscripts," chap. 4 in *The Cambridge Companion to Voltaire*, ed. Nicholas Cronk (Cambridge, UK: Cambridge University Press, 2009). Page 77 notes copies found in Krakow, Budapest, and Stockholm. The rest of Europe was flooded with them. Mary-Margaret Barr and Paul M. Spurlin, among others, have done studies we will return to on the diffusion of Voltaire in America.

4. These include several translations of the *Philosophical Dictionary*, *A Treatise on Toleration and Other Essays* (which include the "Poem on the Lisbon Disaster," "We Must Take Sides," "The Questions of Zapata," "Epistle to the Romans," "The Sermon of the Fifty," and most of the "Homilies Pronounced in London"), as well as *God and Human Beings* (Dieu et les hommes), the last two available through Prometheus Books. Voltaire's *Micromégas, and Other Short Fictions*, translated by Theo Cuffe (New York: Penguin Books, 2002) also contains some pertinent texts.

5. Robert G. Ingersoll, "The Great Infidels," in *Complete Lectures of Col. R. G. Ingersoll* (Whitefish, MT: Kessinger, 2010), p. 317: "Voltaire did more for human liberty than any man who ever lived or died. He appealed to the common sense of mankind—he held up the great contradictions of the sacred Scriptures in a way that no man once having read him could forget." For the full excerpt, see Ingersoll in the Appendix.

6. To consider only books about Voltaire and not more general histories, the last attempted update seems to be Mary-Margaret Barr and Frederick A. Spear's *Quarante années d'Etudes voltairiennes, Bibliographie analytique des livres et articles sur Voltaire, 1926–1965* (Paris: Librairie Armand Colin, 1968). From America to China, they brought the number found in 1965 to 3,679. But new editions of Voltaire's correspondence by Theodore Besterman

tripled the number of his published letters in the 1970s, spurring countless new studies. *Studies on Voltaire and the Eighteenth Century (SVEC)* at Oxford has alone published over five hundred new studies to date.

7. A few of the better-known American books dealing with this subject include: Adrienne Koch's classic *The American Enlightenment: The Shaping of the American Experiment and a Free Society* (New York: George Braziller, 1965); Henry F. May, *The Enlightenment in America* (New York: Oxford University Press, 1976); Robert A. Ferguson, *The American Enlightenment 1750–1820* (Cambridge, MA: Harvard University Press, 1997); and Paul Merrill Spurlin, *The French Enlightenment in America, Essays on the Times of the Founding Fathers* (Athens, GA: University of Georgia Press, 1984).

8. See, for example, the following *New York Times* articles: "Happy Talk History," by Timothy Egan, February 27, 2015; "Texas Conservatives Win Curriculum Change," by James C. McKinley, Jr., March 12, 2010; and "Using History to Mold Ideas on the Right," by Erik Echholm, May 4, 2011. Highly pertinent call-ins protesting the influence Texas wields on schoolbook content in forty-eight states can be found at http://www.npr.org/templates/story/story.php?storyId=124737756.

Citations gathered at http://adultthought.ucsd.edu/Culture_War/The_American_Taliban.html are also eye-opening. David L. Holmes, *The Faiths of the Founding Fathers* (Oxford: Oxford University Press, 2006) explores the topic in chapter 12; and James W. Loewen, *Lies My Teacher Told Me: Everything Your American History Textbook Got Wrong* (New York: Simon & Schuster, 1995, 2007) gives a highly readable account of the various agendas and how the process works.

9. Guillaume Bourel, Marielle Chevallier, et al., eds. *Histoire 2de* (Paris: Hatier, 2006), p. 170. The subject is first introduced to students in the eighth grade, in fact. See, for example, *Histoire Géographie 4e* (Paris: Hachette Livre, 2006), pp. 50–54, both on the Enlightenment and on "the first written Constitution in history" adopted by the new United States, "directly inspired by *les Lumières*" (the French term for Enlightenment writers, Voltaire, Montesquieu, Rousseau, and Diderot in particular).

10. Translated from: Jean Michel Alfred Vacant, J. E. Mangenat, Emile Amann, et al., eds., *Dictionnaire de Théologie Catholique*, vol. 15 (Paris: Librairie Letouzey et Ane, 1950), p. 3468.

11. There is no mention of it in four of seven leading American textbooks: *Flagship History of the United States: 1740–1919* (New York: Harper Collins, 2008); *College Outline United States History to 1877* (New York: Harper Collins, 1991); *American History the Easy Way—Guaranteed to Improve Your Grades*, 3rd edition (Hauppauge, NY: Barron's, 2003); Bryn O'Callaghan, *An Illustrated History of the United States* (London: Longman, 2005).

In *A People and a Nation*, brief 6th edition (Boston: Houghton Mifflin Company, 2003) and *Barron's United States History to 1877* (Nelson Klane and Robert F. Jones, eds. [New York:

Barron's, 1994]), an "English Enlightenment" is evoked, solely concerned with science. Of the seven, only *Liberty, Equality, Power—A History of the American People*, 5th edition (Boston: Thomson Wadsworth, 2008), pp. 145-147, speak of the "Enlightenment rebellion" against superstitions and Puritan fanaticism, but it evokes only John Locke and the Archbishop of Canterbury, John Tillotson, the most Bible-friendly "rebels" that can be found.

12. In *Faiths of the Founding Fathers*, David Holmes explores the question and defines the different varieties of deism that existed.

13. Howard Mumford Jones, *America and French Culture: 1750–1848* (Chapel Hill, NC: University of North Carolina, 1927), pp. 365, 351.

14. Thomas Jefferson, *Notes on the State of Virginia*, Query XVII. The Acts regarding punishments are detailed in *The Papers of Thomas Jefferson*, vol. 1, ed. Julian Boyd (Princeton, NJ: Princeton University Press, 1950), pp 541–43. The American history textbook *Liberty, Equality, Power* cited above also mentions four Quakers hanged by the Puritans (p. 75).

15. Thomas J. Wertenbaker, *The Golden Age of Colonial Culture* (New York: Cornell University Press, 1949), p.152.

16. Norman L. Torrey, *The Spirit of Voltaire* (New York: Columbia University Press, 1938), p. 277.

17. Theodore Besterman, *Voltaire* (New York: Harcourt, Brace & World, 1969), pp. 338–40

18. The same argument is found in the opening sermon of Voltaire's *Sermon of the Fifty*, which can be found in English in both *A Treatise on Toleration and Other Essays*, and in Peter Gay, *Deism, An Anthology* (Princeton, NJ: Van Nostrand Company, 1968), p. 146.

19. Voltaire, *God and Human Beings*, trans. Michael Shreve (Amherst, NY: Prometheus Books, 2010), chapter 38 and 43. Voltaire, "Just," *Philosophical Dictionary*, ed. and trans. by Theodore Besterman (New York: Penguin Books, 1972).

20. The original title, *Essai sur les moeurs et l'esprit des nations*, has been translated into a variety of titles in English, including *Essay on Universal History*, *Essay on the Manners and Spirit of Nations*, *Universal History*, and other variations.

21. Besterman, *Voltaire*, p. 527.

22. J.-B. Bossuet, *Discours sur l'Histoire universelle* (Paris: Furne et Cie, 1847). See, for example, chapter 31, "Suite de l'Eglise catholique, et sa victoire manifeste sur toutes les sectes" (More on the Catholic Church and its Manifest Victory over all the Sects).

23. Will Durant, *The Story of Philosophy, The Lives and Opinions of the Greater Philosophers* (New York: Simon and Schuster, 1953), p. 169. Durant's account of Voltaire's life and character is full of errors, but his rendering of Voltaire's works is fairly reliable, if limited.

24. W. D. Howarth, Henri M. Peyre, and John Cruickshank, *French Literature from 1600 to the Present* (London: Methuen & Co., 1974), p. 49. Jean Goulemot, *Inventaire Voltaire* (Paris: Editions Gallimard, 1995), pp. 501–503.

25. John M. Robertson, *A Short History of Freethought: Ancient and Modern*, vol. 2 (London: Watts & Co., 1915), p. 229.

26. Gay, *Deism*, p. 144; G. Lytton Strachey, *Books and Characters* (London: Echo Library, 2006), pp. 67–68. Strachey felt these "second-rate insignificant" deists had little to teach a disciple of Bayle and Fontenelle like Voltaire. This 1914 essay contains some interesting insights on "Voltaire and England."

27. Benitez, "Voltaire and Clandestine Manuscripts," in *Cambridge Companion to Voltaire*, p. 66, p. 75n3. For more information on *L'Epitre à Uranie*, see Miguel Benitez's article on it in "Approches voltairiennes des manuscrits clandestins," *Revue Voltaire* 8 (2008).

28. George R. Havens, "James Madison et la pensée française," *Revue de littérature comparée* 3 (1923): 612. Also cited by Paul Merril Spurlin, *The French Enlightenment in America— Essays on the Times of the Founding Fathers* (Athens: University of Georgia Press, 1984), p. 177n37. Saul K. Padover, *The Complete Madison—His Basic Writings* (New York: Harper & Brothers, 1953) gives several extracts from Madison, re-explaining the concept over the years (pp. 306–12).

29. Gay, *Deism*, p. 144. Besterman published the original writ in Voltaire's *Correspondence and related documents*, vol. 2 (Geneva: Institut et Musée Voltaire, 1969), p. 498–99.

30. Voltaire's *Letter 5* opens with, "This is the land of sects. An Englishman, as a free man, goes to heaven by whatever path he likes." This remark from Frederick is reported in Robert B Asprey, *Frederick the Great: The Magnificent Enigma* (New York: Ticknor and Fields, 1986), p. 145, and Peter Gay, *Voltaire's Politics: The Poet as Realist* (New Haven, CT: Yale University Press, 1988), p. 165.

31. Hamilton's comment, on p. 29 of *Letter from Alexander Hamilton Concerning the Public Conduct and Character of John Adams* (New York, 1800) is reproduced in Zoltan Haraszti's *John Adams and the Prophets of Progress* (New York: Grosset & Dunlap, 1964), p. 7. Adams recorded his surprise at Franklin's fame in Paris in his *Diary*, reproduced by Koch in *American Enlightenment*, p. 33. Mary-Margaret Barr's *Voltaire in America, 1744–1800* (Baltimore: Johns Hopkins Press, 1941), provides extracts from newspaper and magazine articles on Voltaire and Frederick and advertisements for collections of their letters for sale (pp. 28, 35, 48, 50, 60, 63, 66, 70, 81, 87n). A translation of *Frederick's Panegyric of Voltaire* is announced on page 28. This was no doubt the *Eulogy* included in our Appendix.

32. The Danish film *A Royal Affair*, starring Mads Mikkelsen and nominated for an Oscar and a Golden Globe award in 2013, tells the latter story more fully.

33. The expression used by Torrey in *Spirit of Voltaire*, pp. 82–83. See pp. 153–60 for more on Voltaire and Frederick.

34. Christiane Mervaud, "Voltaire et Frédéric II: une dramaturgie des lumières, 1736–1778," *Studies on Voltaire and the Eighteenth Century* (*SVEC* 234) (Oxford: Voltaire Foundation, 1985) was written in light of the tripling of Voltaire's correspondence by Besterman

in the mid-twentieth century and is light-years beyond anything else written on the subject. On pages 1 through 6, she analyzes two of the most frequently cited nineteenth-century sources: the "memoirs" of Samuel Formey and those of Dieudonné Thiébault. Formey had few links to the court and Thiébault was a librarian hired some twenty years after Voltaire had left Berlin. His fatuous portrayals of himself giving Frederick "lessons on life" should have destroyed all credibility to begin with, but Thomas Carlyle, Georges Sand, Lytton Strachey, and countless others perpetuated these inanities with an astonishing lack of penetration.

35. André Magnan, *Dossier en Prusse: SVEC 244* (Oxford: Voltaire Foundation, 1986). Georg Brandes tells the story of the *Memoirs* in his book, *Voltaire* (vol. 2 [New York: Albert & Charles Boni, 1930], pp. 351–53) with more detail than most biographies in English. Alfred Noyes' biography, *Voltaire* (London: Faber and Faber, 1936) contains one of the fullest accounts of what happened in Berlin, although his views in other regards are highly contestable and his views on Madame du Châtelet very strange at best.

36. "The worst thing you did to me," Voltaire wrote Frederick on April 21, 1760, "is to make all of philosophy's enemies all over Europe say, here is a king who doesn't believe in Christ who invites a man who doesn't either, and mistreats him. . . . There is no humanity in these so-called philosophers and God is punishing them through each other." Five days later, he wrote to French mathematician d'Alembert that if Frederick spent "on *ecraser l'inf* . . . one hundredth part of what it has cost him to butcher everybody, I feel I could forgive him," adding in his *Notebooks*, 324, "He has missed a fine vocation."

37. In October/ November 1752, in Berlin, Frederick sent him several notes applauding the dictionary entries ("Abraham," "âme" [soul], "baptême") and discussing the overall plan for what became the *Dictionnaire philosophique*. Voltaire's secretary, Côme Alexandre Collini, published memoirs in 1807, *Mon Séjour auprès de Voltaire*, describing how the project was conceived in Berlin to be written in concert with the king, the Marquis D'Argens, and other writers at his court (pp. 32–33). Frederick started talking of Voltaire's scratching, slapping *l'infâme* in his letters as of May 1759. After a few exchanges in this vein, Voltaire replied that he meant to crush it.

38. Though numerous examples could be given, Nancy Mitford, who wrote a popular biography on each of them, typifies this. Her published correspondence with her brother reveals that she disapproved of Voltaire's crusade against religion and she accordingly avoids referring to it in both books. Her gossipy *Voltaire in Love* (London: Hamish Hamilton, 1957) conveniently ends with the death of Madame du Châtelet, and, when one deletes Voltaire's crusade altogether, he becomes indeed "very hard to understand," as she says on page 183 of *Frederick the Great* (New York: E. P. Dutton, 1970). He is thus reduced to being "a maddening guest with a foolish love for grandees." Omitting crucial facts even leads to a claim that Voltaire's *Memoires* prove he really hated Frederick for forty years, which is totally unten-

able. But then she oddly refers us to Theodore Besterman on page 175, "who knows Voltaire better than anybody," and his biography, *Voltaire*, takes the extreme opposite view. "Frederick's spiritual heir" was Hitler, he says (p. 333). Both were misled by Voltaire's fictitious letters to his niece and by unawareness of certain behind-the-scenes machinations by Frederick and his court, not brought to light till 1986 in André Magnan's *Dossier Voltaire in Prusse*, but at least Besterman does not omit the religious issues.

39. Torrey, *Spirit*, reprints this letter in English (pp. 133–34).

40. Robertson, *Short History of Freethought*, pp. 289–91, extracts a list over two pages long from "Buckle's compendius account" of authors punished and books condemned over matters "so trifling" it would be ridiculous were it not for "the gravity of their . . . results." And this list does not even include the well-known cases of Voltaire, Diderot, Buffon, or Rousseau. In the note on page 229, he gives a partial list of Voltaire's condemned books and threats of arrest: *Letters on England* in 1734, *Le Mondain* in 1736, *Recueil des pieces fugitifs* in 1739, *La Voix du Sage et du people* in 1751, his *Poem on Natural Law* in 1758, *Candide* in Geneva in 1759, the *Dictionnaire philosophique* in both Paris and Geneva 1764–1765, and his complete works *en masse* in 1785. But there are a great many oversights in the list, including *Dieu et les hommes* in 1767 and many of the pieces in this book, as indicated in their introductions.

41. Roland Barthes, "Le dernier des écrivains heureux," in *Essais critiques* (Paris: Editions du Seuil, 1964). Noted Voltairian André Magnan also remarks that such views are "fantasies" and quite mistaken (Goulemot, *Inventaire Voltaire*, p. 1034).

42. For details from French police records, see Robert Anchel, *Crimes et Châtiments au XVIII siècle* (Paris: Archives Nationales, Librairie Académique Perrin, 1933). Robertson, *Short History of Freethought* tells of the eighteen-year-old hanged in Scotland for deism (p. 181–82). "Only wealthy men could dare openly to avow their deism," he says, noting that this execution brought no cry of horror from any Christian writer. The clergy were hounding the Privy Council to try witches as late as 1697.

43. Louis-Sébastien Mercier, "Bicêtre," *Le tableau de Paris* (Paris: La Découverte/Poche, 1998). On the charity hospitals, see pp. 214–19. Peter Gay also evokes the hospitals, "those cesspools of infection," in *Voltaire's Politics*, p. 297.

44. Anchel, *Crimes et Châtiments*, pp. 32, 207–209. Among the places one could be hanged or burned he includes place Saint-Michel, place Maubert, place Dauphine, portes Saint-Antoine and Saint-Martin, place Bastille, place du Tertre, and the cour de Bicêtre (pp. 150–52). The site was often determined by proximity to where the crime had taken place, so other options were not excluded. He adds on pages 217 through 218 that burning at the stake "pure and simple," without hanging or the torture of the wheel first, became less frequent after 1775 but that the stakes were still lit often enough on the eve of the Revolution.

45. *Diderot Correspondance* (Paris: Editions Robert Laffont, 1997). See the letter to Sophie Volland, October 8, 1768. Madame Suard's remarks are in our Appendix, Letter VII.

For an overview of these laws in France, see Raymond Trousson, *Voltaire et la réforme de la législation criminelle* (1993), available online at http://www.arllfb.be/ebibliotheque/communications/trousson091093.pdf (accessed November 13, 2014).

46. Goulemot, *Inventaire Voltaire,* cites Fréron, p. 1034.

47. An English translation of his *Commentary on Beccaria* is available in *Voltaire, Political Writings*, ed. David Williams (Cambridge, UK: Cambridge University Press, 1994). Further denunciations and insights into the penal conditions of the times can be found in Voltaire's *Prix de la justice et l'humanité*. For the priest-accompanied "death walk" (La Marche au supplice), see Anchel, *Crimes et Châtiments*, p. 150.

48. Besterman edition and translation.

49. Voltaire, *God and Human Beings*, pp. 150–51.

50. The attempted murder of the King of Portugal by a Jesuit is evoked in *The Sermon of Rabbi Akib* herein. Damiens' attack on the French king, Louis XV, can be found in the Glossary.

51. *Jefferson Papers*, vol. 1, ed. Julian Boyd, p. 525n. For an overview, see Bernard Bailyn, *The Ideological Origins of the American Revolution* (Cambridge, Massachusetts: Belknap Press of Harvard University Press, 1967), pp. 257–72.

52. Adams to Jefferson, May 18, 1817, *The Adams–Jefferson Letters: The Complete Correspondence Between Thomas Jefferson and Abigail and John Adams*, ed. Lester J. Cappon (University of North Carolina Press, 1959).

53. Franklin to Henry Bouquet, September 30, 1764, *The Papers of Benjamin Franklin*, vol. 11, ed. Leonard W. Labaree (Yale University Press: 1967), p. 367. The passage he cites from Voltaire occurs near the end of chapter 4 of the *Traité*, beginning, "Mais que dirons-nous de ces pacifiques primitifs que l'on a nommés Quakres . . ."

54. For Adams' remarks see Harry Hayden Clark, "Thomas Paine's Relation to Voltaire and Rousseau," *Revue Anglo-américain*, avril–juin 1932, p. 311; or Woodbridge Riley, *American Philosophy, The Early Schools* (New York: Odd, Mead & Company, 1907), p. 299.

55. Mumford Jones, *America and French Culture*, pp. 368, 378, 390–91. *The Journal of Rev. Francis Asbury, Bishop of the Methodist Episcopal Church, from August 7, 1771, to December 7, 1815*, vol. 1 (New York, 1821), pp. 179–88. Samuel Drew, *The Life of Rev. Thomas Coke, LL.D.* (New York, 1818), p. 94.

56. Lyman Beecher, *Autobiography, Correspondence, Etc.*, vol. 1, ed. Charles Beecher (New York, 1864), p. 43, cited by Mumford Jones, *America and French Culture*, p. 378, who also cites Dwight, p. 392–93, 512n. M.-M. Barr, *Voltaire in America*, also provides five pages of extracts by Dwight in this vein (pp. 108–22). Henry May tells us in *Enlightenment in America,* page 186, that "It has been clearly demonstrated that this picture is untrue." Though some of Yale's students "dabbled in dangerous thoughts" or adopted "foppish manners," he says, the atmosphere was one of religiosity. But the proof he offers in note 14, Edmond

Morgan, "Ezra Stiles and Timothy Dwight," Massachusetts Historical Society, *Proceedings*, 73 (1957–60), pp. 101–17, in fact confirms that there was a staggering rise of deism. "Anyone reading the Connecticut newspapers for the latter half of the eighteenth century cannot fail to observe the increasingly outspoken hostility to the clergy during the 1770s, '80s and '90s," wrote Morgan. What Morgan disproved is that Dwight, whom May considers a "moderate," full of hopes for America and its "pure religion" as the site of the Christian millennium, changed this situation, as Beecher and later admirers claimed. The effects of a few religious revivals, begun around 1802, generally wore off within four years.

57. Russell Shorto, "How Christian Were the Founders?" *New York Times,* February 14, 2010.

58. Jefferson details them more fully in Query XVII of his *Notes on the State of Virginia*.

59. See, for example, the *New York Times* articles "Texas Conservatives Win Curriculum Change," by James C. McKinley, Jr., March 12, 2010, and "Using History to Mold Ideas on the Right," by Erik Echholm, May 4, 2011, and related links.

60. *Autobiography of Thomas Jefferson, 1743–1790* (New York: Knickerbocker Press, 1914), p. 71. (Available at https://archive.org/details/autobiographyoft00jeff.)

61. Edmund S. Morgan, *The Birth of the Republic 1763–1789* (Chicago: University of Chicago Press, 1956), p. 94. Regarding the "failing" of the founders in giving voting rights only to the propertied, he notes, "it should be remembered that except in Virginia and perhaps South Carolina, where the number of tenant farmers was unusually high, the vast majority of white Americans could probably meet the property qualifications required" and in some states, like Pennsylvania, the right to vote was accorded to all taxpayers.

62. Bailyn, *Ideological Origins of the American Revolution*. This book is a partial synthesis of his parallel work in compiling *Pamphlets of the American Revolution, 1750–1776* (Cambridge, MA: Harvard University Press, 1965), as he explains in the Foreword.

63. Riley, *American Philosophy, Early Schools*, pp. 25–28, 193; Robert Darnton, *George Washington's False Teeth* (New York: W. W. Norton & Company, 2003), p. 104.

64. Riley, *American Philosophy, Early Schools*, pp. 26–28.

65. Ibid., p. 11.

66. John Adams speaks of the despotism of Cromwell in a letter of July 15, 1813, as does Thomas Paine at the end of his highly influential pamphlet, *Common Sense*. Churchill's comment can be found in his *History of the English-Speaking People—Volume Two: The New World* (New York: Bantam edition, 1963), pp. 240–42.

67. Bernard Glassman, *Protean Prejudice—Anti-Semitism in England's Age of Reason* (Atlanta, GA: Scholar's Press, 1998), provides, in chapter 2, the accusations they all made toward each other, as well as the persecutions and mob violence it inspired.

68. A succinct overview of religious persecution in America was written by Kenneth C. Davies for *Smithsonian Magazine*, October, 2010, entitled "America's True History of

Religious Tolerance," also available at http://www.smithsonianmag.com/historyarchae-ology/103060769.html#ixzz119eZC0F9.

69. Gay, *Voltaire's Politics*, p. 255, from volume 3 of Burton's *Anatomy of Melancholy*. The cure is partly medical, partly philosophical, Burton adds. "To purge the world of idolatry and superstition will require some monster-taming Hercules, a divine Aesculapius." Gay was struck by the resemblance of this text to Voltaire's dream of being a "Hercules-Aescula-pius." Aesculapius was the son of Apollo and the god of healing.

70. Susan Jacoby, *Freethinkers: A History of American Secularism* (New York: Henry Holt and Company, 2004), p. 1, 10, 151, citing Kenneth S. Latourette, *A History of the Expansion of Christianity*; and citing Samuel Mather, p. 15.

71. Mumford Jones, *America and French Culture*, pp. 377-8; Riley, *American Philosophy, Early Schools*, 11–12, 17 (and, citing Ezra Stiles, 215–16); Leonard Woolsey Bacon, *A History of American Christianity* (New York, 1897), pp. 230–31.

72. Jefferson to Roger C. Weightmen, June 24, 1826, ". . . our fellow citizens, after half a century of experience and prosperity continue to approve the choice we made. May it be to the world . . . the signal of arousing men to burst the chains [of] monkish igno-rance and superstition. . . . [W]e have substituted . . . the unbounded exercise of reason and freedom of opinion. All eyes are opened, or opening, to the rights of man." Koch, *American Enlightenment*, pages 371–72. The severest test had been his own election when "barbar-ians" felt sure they could put everything back in "the hands of power and priestcraft" but the country's "good sense" recovered "from delusion" he wrote to Priestley, March 21, 1801, auguring well "for the duration of our republic."

73. Glassman, *Protean Prejudice*, p. 64.

74. The "Prayer to God" constitutes chapter 23 of Voltaire's *Treatise* but has been omitted from Joseph McCabe's translation. The *Treatise* enjoyed considerable popularity in eighteenth-century America, and the "Prayer" was often reprinted in newspapers and maga-zines. See M.-M. Barr's, *Voltaire in America*, pp. 59, 119, and one translation reprinted in full, pp. 70–71. Paul Spurlin also mentions several listings of it in *The French Enlightenment in America*.

75. Compare Adams' letter of December 25, 1813, in Bruce Baden's *"Ye Will Say I am No Christian": The Thomas Jefferson / John Adams Correspondence on Religion, Morals and Values* (Amherst, NY: Prometheus Books, 2005), p. 124, to the same letter in Cappon's *Complete Correspondence* edition, p. 410. Other writers Adams cites in this vein are Priestley, Gibbon, Hume—"though a conceited Scotchman"—and Bolingbroke—"tho' a haughty arrogant supercilious Dogmatist." His marginal note explaining why he's "rejoicing in Voltaire, etc." is given in the footnote at the bottom of the page.

76. Barr, *Voltaire in America*, p. 14: "The printers of the colonies were comparatively few. . . . [T]heir efforts had to be expended primarily on government orders and local newspapers

rather than on books . . . easily imported from England or France." Spurlin also admits, "of course, most translations were published in England and exported to the colonies," on p. 63, but often concentrates on first American editions nonetheless.

77. Albert L. Rabinovitz and Nouvart Tashjian, *French Fiction—Index to Early American Periodical Literature, 1728–1870*, No. 5 (New York: William-Frederick Press, 1943). It also mentions two articles that compared *Candide* to Samuel Johnson's *Rasselas*.

78. Carl Becker, *The Declaration of Independence, A Study in the History of Political Ideas* (1922; repr., New York: Vintage Book, 1970), p. 27.

79. The "overlooked" references to Voltaire are on pp. 334, 340, 361, 408, 410, 438, 445, 454, 455, 464–65, 470–71, 473, and 541. Overlooked references to other French Enlightenment writers include Beaumarchais, 473; Buffon, 438, 445, 471, 473; Condillac, 561; Condorcet, 400, 429, 438, 444, 471, 473, 506, 518; D'Alembert, 455, 464, 467, 473, 486; D'Holbach, 468, 471, 592; Diderot, 400, 438, 445, 464, 471, 473, 592; d'Espinasse, 486; Frederick II, 184, 445, 454, 464, 485; Grimm, 468, 471, 486, 494–95, 507–508; Helvétius, 437, 473; La Harpe, 406, 439, 473, 503, 508; Marmontel, 473, 533; Montesquieu, 491, 501, 519; Rousseau, 400, 438, 445, 464, 473; and Turgot, 438, 518, 564. Frederick and Grimm, though German, wrote primarily in French. Another dozen or so references to non-French Enlightenment writers (Bolingbroke, Gibbon, Hume, Paine, Priestley, and Spinoza, notably) likewise go unlisted.

80. Adams to Jefferson, May 18, 1817, *The Adams-Jefferson Letters,* ed. Cappon, p. 515. In another unlisted mention, p. 405, Adams lumps biographies of Whitefield and Wesley together with those of St. Francis of Loyola: perfectly well-written and informative, but bigoted and superstitious throughout.

81. Bailyn, *Ideological Origins*, pp. 26–27.

82. May, *Enlightenment in America*, p. 118, versus page xvi where Voltaire was "grand master" of what May calls the skeptical Enlightenment, or page 59 where Voltaire, Hume, and Gibbon are "the leading infidels" the New Divinity men in New England have to counter. Though May avoids overt hostility, he regularly links Voltaire to the "bleak stoical resignation" deists are supposed to suffer (pp. 141–43) or the "spectacular" downfall of Aaron Burr, charged with treason (though acquitted), for example (p. 125).

83. Holmes, *Faiths of the Founding Fathers*, pp. 41–44.

84. Riley, *American Philosophy, Early Schools*, p. 299.

85. "The . . . total abolition . . . of everything appertaining to compulsive systems of religion, and . . . articles of faith has . . . rendered a work of this kind exceedingly necessary, lest, in the general wreck of superstition . . . and false theology, we lose sight of morality, of humanity, and of the theology that is true." Paine is speaking of France, where he had gone to join the Revolution after the one in America had been won, but where the battle was more violent, just as the oppression had been worse. Several writers say, like John Keane

in *Tom Paine, A Political Life* ([London: Bloomsbury Publishing, 1996], p. 391), that Paine "attempted something everyone thought impossible: attacking religion while defending a benevolent Creator," but this is precisely what Voltaire had done throughout his life, and especially during his pamphlet war in the 1760s and 1770s, much to the scorn of certain atheists who came to the fore later in France.

86. Besterman, *Voltaire*, p. 536.

87. Spurlin, *French Enlightenment in America*. Chapter 3 explores them case by case.

88. Tobias Smollett's translation of Voltaire's "complete works" (though somewhat incomplete) is one the most frequently listed in American library and bookseller catalogues, although they often do not mention which translation they have on hand.

89. Franklin to Noah Webster, December 26, 1789, and Franklin to Henry Bosquet, September 30, 1764, *Papers of Benjamin Franklin*.

90. Spurlin, *French Enlightenment in America*, pp. 7–8, 76.

91. Ibid., p. 71.

92. Ibid., pp. 58–59.

93. Barr, *Voltaire in America*, p. 19.

94. Again, under a variety of translated titles, including *Universal History*, *State of Europe*, *History of Europe*, and other variations on this theme. Barr, *Voltaire in America*, pp. 22–32.

95. Ibid., pp. 41–42, 77–78, 82; Spurlin, *French Enlightenment in America*, p. 104.

96. Barr, *Voltaire in America*, pp. 53–53.

97. Adrian H. Jaffe, "French Literature in American Periodicals of the Eighteenth Century," *Revue de Littérature Comparée* (Paris: Librairie Marcel Didier, 1943), pp. 51–60. Quotation found on pp. 53–54.

98. American history textbook, *A People and a Nation*, 6th edition (Boston: Houghton Mifflin, 2003) provides one on p. 25.

99. Wertenbaker, *Golden Age*, p. 40.

100. Benjamin Franklin, *Observations Concerning the Increase of Mankind*, cited in *A People and a Nation*, p. 74.

101. Mumford Jones, *America and French Culture*, pp. 22, 29, 525, and chapter 4 generally.

102. Thomas Paine, *Collected Writings* (New York: Library of America, 1995), p. 23.

103. Among others, Spurlin, *French Enlightenment in America*, advances this argument (pp. 14–15). William Howard Adams, *The Paris Years of Thomas Jefferson* (New Haven, CT: Yale University Press: 1997) qualifies it as a mere "backwoods reaction" (p. 29).

104. Mumford Jones, *America and French Culture*, pp. 351–61.

105. Barr calls it one of the most often quoted works in American newspapers and magazines (p. 119). Her other mentions include pp. 11, 24, 59, 70–71, and 101. Calas was

the most famous case because it was the first time a writer had actually shamed the authorities into reversing their decision by rousing public opinion, and in only four years at that. Several other less famous cases are detailed in chapter 10 of Gustave Lanson, *Voltaire* (New York: John Wiley & Sons, 1966).

106. "If the Protestants can get rid of twenty superstitions, they can get rid of thirty," he wrote in his *Notebooks* in Berlin, while circulating similar thoughts in his *Sermon of the Fifty*. This work contains some lines that shock many about the piece of dough that Catholics claim literally contains God at the bidding of a man "which we digest and eliminate with excrements." This was, however, an argument much repeated during the Protestant Reformation. The Eucharist subsequently became a symbolic rite in most Protestant sects.

107. Barr, *Voltaire in America*, pp. 107–108 for the Boston clergyman, and pp. 74–75 for the satire of Rousseau's "Eloisa," the name often used in translation.

108. "Narrative of the Prince de Broglie," trans. E. W. Balch (1782), *Magazine of American History*, 1 (1877): 378.

109. Spurlin, *French Enlightenment in America*, p. 15–16; Morgan, *Birth of the Republic*, p. 86.

110. Mumford-Jones, *America and French Culture*, pp. 519–20, 526. Henry May, *Enlightenment in America*, also provides a glimpse of this "hyperbolic" enthusiasm for the French (pp. 116–17), but only to assure us it was a "sudden and somewhat forced affection" that "proved brief and superficial," further bolstering the Anglo-Saxon/ Protestant view of American history that predominates in this book.

111. Franklin met with Voltaire a half dozen times in Paris. Stacy Schiff, *A Great Improvisation—Franklin, France and the Birth of America* (New York: Henry Holt and Company, 2005) covers most of their encounters (pp. 48, 81, 136–38, 192). Barr, *Voltaire in America*, reproduces John Adams' account (pp. 101–102).

112. Garry Wills, *Inventing America—Jefferson's Declaration of Independence* (New York: Doubleday, 1978), p. 10.

113. Mumford Jones, *America and French Culture*, provides several pages detailing these events (pp. 530–38).

114. Haydn Mason, *Voltaire, A Biography* (London: Granada Publishing, 1981), p. 153. Peter Gay says much the same in *Voltaire's Politics*, pp. 335–39, as does Lanson, *Voltaire*, pp. 156–60. A series of studies of French Revolutionary pamphlets by R. Galliani published in 1977–1978 also bears this out (*SVEC* 169 and 174).

115. Barr, *Voltaire in America*, pp. 54–56. The high-end estimate is found in S. G. Tallentyre, *The Life of Voltaire* (New York: Loring & Mussey, n.d.), p. 564. She said the procession itself consisted of one hundred thousand—"Six hundred thousand more witnessed it." As the procession took four days from its starting place in Romilly and was celebrated in every town along the way, she may have been including those turn-outs. Alfred Noyes, *Voltaire*,

claims that 250,000 paid homage at the sarcophagus' first night stop at the Bastille, where Voltaire had been imprisoned three-quarters of a century earlier, and that thousands of strangers flocked to the city for the event (p. 625).

116. Mumford Jones, *America and French Culture*, p. 537.

117. Ibid., pp. 539–41, 393. Riley, *American Philosophy, Early Schools*, pp. 311–13. Barr provides many rabid passages from Dwight (pp. 108–13), including the remarks on French soldiers cited.

118. Mumford Jones, *America and French Culture*, pp. 381, 397, 405–408.

119. Mumford Jones, *America and French Culture*, pp. 528–29, 539–41; Riley, *American Philosophy, Early Schools*, p. 294.

120. René Pomeau, *La Religion de Voltaire* (Paris: Librairie Nizet, 1974), p. 451–56. For accounts in English, see Noyes, *Voltaire*, pp. 609, 613–14, or Roger Pearson, *Voltaire Almighty—A Life in Pursuit of Freedom* (London: Bloomsbury, 2005), p. 390.

121. Riley, *American Philosophy, Early Schools*, p. 319–20.

122. J. N. D. Kelly, *The Oxford Dictionary of Popes* (Oxford: Oxford University Press, 1986), pp. 302, 306. Pomeau, *La Religion de Voltaire*, p. 462. The remark recalls Hugo's famous phrase in *Les Misérables*. When street urchin Gavroche is shot in battle, he feebly sings "Joie est mon caractère / C'est la faute à Voltaire." (I have a cheerful character / It's Voltaire's fault.)

123. The *Index Librorum Prohibitorum* is a list of books forbidden by the Catholic Church as heretical, anticlerical, or lascivious. It was formally abolished in 1966 but was declared still morally binding in 1985.

124. J. N. D. Kelly, *The Oxford Dictionary of Popes* (Oxford: Oxford University Press, 1986), pp. 302, 306.

125. Raymond Trousson, *Voltaire—Mémoire de la critique, 1778–1878* (Paris: Pups, 2008), pp. 21–24.

126. Robert Darnton, *The Forbidden Best-Sellers of Pre-Revolutionary France* (New York: W. W. Norton & Company, 1996). On page 65, Darnton lists Voltaire as the bestselling author from 1769 to 1789 at 3,545 book orders. But on pages 60–67, he explains that as these books were forbidden, the statistics, drawn from sources both limited and sketchy, are surely underestimates. Voltaire would have had a stronger showing, Darnton adds, if he had included the 1750s and 1760s in the survey, when Voltaire's campaign was at its peak. Customs seizures, police raids, "everything suggests they flooded the kingdom." The population of France was estimated at twenty-six million in Voltaire's day. Glassman, *Protean Prejudices*, reports the estimate of English literacy rates at the end of the eighteenth century (p. 165).

127. Lucien Bély, *Histoire de France* (Paris: Editions Jean-Paul Gisserot, 2003), p. 95. Privileged classes in the nineteenth century, which now included the bourgeoisie or upper

middle classes, frequently railed against people from the dregs of society learning to read or write at all. Darnton, *Forbidden Best-Sellers*, provides some examples on page 40.

128. John Remsburg collected a book full of such testimonies in *Abraham Lincoln: Was He a Christian?* See Preface and pp. 116–17, 135 especially. Robert Bray, *Reading with Lincoln* (Carbondale, IL: Southern Illinois University Press, 2010) provides a less sympathetic view (pp. 67–69).

129. Frances Trollope, *Domestic Manners of the Americans* (1832; repr., New York: Dover, 2003), chapters 11, 15, and pp. 90–91, 161, 168–69. Mrs. Trollope toured America for four years, beginning in 1827.

130. Jacoby, *Freethinkers,* Introduction, and pp. 1, 10.

131. *Benjamin Franklin—The Autobiography and Other Writings*, ed. L. Jesse Lemisch (New York: Signet Classic, 1961), pp. 69–70, 92–94, 102. In the famous letter to Reverend Ezra Stiles on March 9, 1790 (pp. 337–338), Franklin says "the present Dissenters in England," but the British colonists had called themselves "English" all their lives. Could he have meant "New England"?

132. *Benjamin Franklin—The Autobiography*, p. 111. A. O. Aldridge, "Benjamin Franklin and the *philosophes*," in *Studies on Voltaire and the Eighteenth Century* (*SVEC* 24) (Oxford: Voltaire Foundation, 1963) lists several references Franklin made to Voltaire in his gazette (pp. 43–44).

133. Charles Porset, *Voltaire humaniste* (Paris: Editions Maçonniques de France, 2003). Porset, a Mason himself, gives the fullest account of this much-debated question in chapter 6. Porset gives citations from Voltaire deriding these "extravagant ceremonies turned into sacred mysteries," which he attributes to a desire to distinguish and seclude oneself (p. 137–41). According to one Mason involved, Voltaire at first refused their invitation for fear of ridicule, till Franklin, Lalande, and other members insisted "with a vivacity that surprised him."

134. Jefferson to Adams, July 5, 1814.

135. Most famously in Jefferson's letter to Priestley of March 21, 1801, reprinted by Koch, *American Enlightenment*, pp. 341–42.

136. Jefferson to Adams, August 10 or 11, 1815.

137. Gilbert Chinard, *The Literary Bible of Thomas Jefferson, His Commonplace Book of Philosophers and Poets* (Baltimore: Johns Hopkins Press, 1928), p. 19. Spurlin, *French Enlightenment*, pp. 61, 131–32, 103–104.

138. *Jefferson Papers*, vol. 10, pp. 261–62; vol. 11, p. 460; vol. 12, p. 30 give several reports on these adventures.

139. Thomas Jefferson, *Notes on the State of Virginia*, Query VI. Aldridge, "Franklin and the philosophes" (*SVEC* 24), p. 64, relates the whale story.

140. The remark is in a letter to Charles Bellini, who became a professor of modern

languages at William and Mary at Jefferson's recommendation. It is cited by Page Smith, *Jefferson: A Revealing Biography* (New York: America Heritage Publishing, 1976), pp. 146, 181; and by Spurlin, *French Enlightenment*, p. 103.

141. Adams, *Paris Years of Jefferson*, pp. 71, 86. See also several listings at Monticello, including http://www.monticello.org/site/research-and-collections/houdon-bust-sculpture (accessed December 7, 2014).

142. William Short to Jefferson, July 20, 1791, *Jefferson Papers*, vol. 20, p. 654.

143. See *Jefferson Papers*, vol. 1, p. 32, for the famous Skipwith List; also cited by Adams, *Paris Years of Jefferson*, p. 30.

144. *Jefferson Papers*, vol. 16, p. 481, contains a list recommending Voltaire, addressed to John Garland. Vol. 8, p. 411, and vol. 12, p. 18 contains lists comprised entirely of books in French for Carr, the first sent to his tutor, Walker Maury. Koch, *American Enlightenment*, also reprints the letters cited to Peter Carr on August 19, 1785, and August 10, 1787 (pp. 310, 320).

145. A. S. W. Rosenbach, "The Libraries of the Presidents of the United States," reprinted from the *Proceedings of the American Antiquarian Society* for October, 1934, pp. 347–50. Spurlin also relates the Library of Congress incident here and adds, "The large amount of Voltaire of Voltaire material in the catalog of Jefferson's second library offers ample evidence of the Virginian's interest" (p. 103, and note 32).

146. For example, Jefferson's famous line, "It does me no injury for my neighbor to say there are twenty gods, or no god. It neither picks my pocket nor breaks my leg," resembles Voltaire's line, "Now, if in an impious act no handkerchief has been stolen, if no one has received the slightest injury . . . shall we punish this impiety as if it was a parricide?" in *Commentary on Beccaria*, article 6, among other lines not yet located in Voltaire's swarm of pamphlets. William Howard Adams also notes the paraphrasing of Voltaire in this Query on p. 141 of *The Paris Years of Jefferson*.

147. Barr, *Voltaire in America*, p. 116, cites pp. 48–49, 334–43, 389–91 of the 1926 edition by Chinard. Spurlin cites pp. 334–43 and the appendix in his *French Enlightenment in America*, p. 177n35. But see also note 36, below it.

148. Douglas L. Wilson, ed. *Jefferson's Literary Commonplace Book* (Princeton, NJ: Princeton University Press, 1989). It ends on page 153, well before the page numbers cited by both Barr and Spurlin.

149. D. H. Meyer, "The Uniqueness of the American Enlightenment," *American Quarterly*, Special Summer Edition, 1976.

150. Robert J. Buyck, "Chateaubriand juge de Voltaire" (*SVEC 114*, 1973), p. 270. Sainte-Beuve is cited on p. 234.

151. See, for example, Jefferson to Adams, July 5, 1814, and Adams' reply, July 16.

152. Haraszti, *John Adams & the Prophets of Progress*, Preface, p. v, and chapter 6, on Fred-

erick, Voltaire, and d'Alembert. The overview of Adams' personality in chapter 1 is excellent. Chinard's selections are in his "Notes de John Adams sur Voltaire et Rousseau," *Modern Language Notes*, vol. 46 (Baltimore: Johns Hopkins Press, 1931).

153. *Adams–Jefferson Letters*, ed. Cappon, pp. 466, 470, 410.

154. Ibid. Adams bewails his martyrdoms on July 12, 1813, p. 354, and regularly in less specific terms.

155. Adams to Jefferson, June 15, 1813. In direct citations, the original spelling and punctuation has been kept throughout.

156. Voltaire, *Political Writings*, ed. David Williams, pp. 216–17, xvi–xvii.

157. Voltaire, *Political Writings* (ed. David Williams) explores the subject thoroughly in the introduction, but still ends by debating Voltaire's "preference," even after more or less answering the question. For Voltaire's citation, see Torrey, *Spirit of Voltaire*, pp. 183–84.

158. Jean Sareil, *Voltaire et les grands* (Geneva: Librairie Droz, 1978), pp. 17–19.

159. Paine had proposed that King Louis XVI be exiled to America instead, in gratitude for his aid during the American Revolution.

160. Torrey, *Spirit of Voltaire*, p. 67.

161. Gay, *Voltaire's Politics*, pp. 166–69.

162. Adams to Jefferson, July 9 and December 25, 1813; Adams to John Quincy Adams, November 13, 1816.

163. Adams refers Jefferson to pages 247 through 249 of Condorcet's "Outlines of an Historical View of the Progress of Human Mind" without mentioning which translation he is reading.

164. The book is the *Acta Sanctorum* (Lives of the Saints), a work Adams has been trying to obtain or find out more about for months.

165. *Adams–Jefferson Letters*, p. 416.

166. For a few examples, in his *Correspondence littéraire* newsletter of June 1, 1766, Grimm calls Voltaire childish for saying "Every work of art attests to an artisan" in *The Ignorant Philosopher*, and retorts, "But who told you the universe is a work of art?" following it with long attack on deism to promote atheism. But this rather misses that the point of the work was to challenge common certitudes, as Pomeau noted in *Voltaire en son temps*, vol. 4, "Ecrasez l'infâme," pp. 245–46. In November 1767, Grimm also dismissed Voltaire's *Letters . . . on Rabelais* with "the patriarch is still sticking to his Rewarder."

167. Torrey, *Spirit*, explores these relationships on pp. 172–80. None of these men accepted the idea that there is a guiding intelligence in the universe, but no amount of disagreement kept Voltaire and Diderot from mutual admiration and respect, and D'Alembert was one of Voltaire's most loyal friends.

168. See Emile Lize's thorough study in "Voltaire et la Correspondance littéraire," *SVEC 180*, 1979.

169. *Adams-Jefferson Letters*, p. 471, "Digito comesce Labellum" (Cappon's translation). Their exchanges on Grimm occur between March 2 and August 1, 1816.

170. Adams to Jefferson, June 10, 1813. In Baden, *Ye Will Say*, pp. 236–39, we see Adams writing to Judge van der Kemp in 1809 that he'd been doing so "for sixty-five years at least." And in 1820, to Presbyterian minister Samuel Miller, that he "necessarily" became a reader of polemical writings on religion before he was twelve. This must refer to the earlier wave of writings by the English deists, which Voltaire powerfully revived in the 1760s.

171. Adams to Jefferson, February 10, 1812; Joseph Priestley to Dr. Benjamin Rush, August 8, 1799.

172. Jefferson to Adams, August 22, 1813; Adams to Jefferson, July 18, 1813, and Feb.–March 1814.

173. Torrey, *Spirit of Voltaire*, pp. 280–81; Pomeau, *Religion de Voltaire*, pp. 379–81.

174. Thomas Jefferson, *The Jefferson Bible—The Life and Morals of Jesus of Nazareth* (Boston: Beacon Press, 1989), p. 28. Forrest Church explores the evolution of this project in a well-documented introduction citing not only the letters exchanged with Adams but with Benjamin Rush, William Small, van der Kamp, and others.

175. Loewen, *Lies My Teacher Told Me*, pp. 314, 182.

176. Jefferson to Adams, June 15, 1813. On pp. 397–398n25, Loewen adds that right-wing critics, "rightly incensed" when religion is left out, nevertheless attacked another textbook for mentioning that Benjamin Franklin was a deist. "Unfortunately, [they] want only positive things said about religion, and mainly their religion, Christianity."

177. Adams to Jefferson, June 28, 1813.

178. Letter to Sophie Volland, October 11, 1767, *Diderot Correspondance*, ed. Laffont.

179. In Hugo's "Centenary Oration on Voltaire," delivered on May 30, 1878, found in *Voltaire—Studies by Oliver Goldsmith and Victor Hugo* (Emmaus, PA: Rodale Press, 1954), among other places. See also *Cambridge Companion to Voltaire*, chapter 14, "The Voltaire Effect," by Daniel Brewer, and the introduction by editor Nicholas Cronk, for more citations.

180. Cited more fully in the Appendix.

181. Bertrand Russell, "Voltaire's Influence on Me," *SVEC* 6, 1958.

182. Disraeli's lines are from *Contarini Fleming*, II, ii, cited in Besterman's, *Voltaire*, p. 11.

183. Michel W. Pharand, *Bernard Shaw and the French* (University of Florida Press, 2000), chapter 15. The extracts are just a few examples of Shaw's many references to Voltaire.

184. Or rather, "Au secours, Voltaire!" This incident concludes the five-volume biography of *Voltaire en son temps* under the direction of René Pomeau—though I saw it with my own eyes, too.

185. Lanson, *Voltaire*, pp. 170–71.

186. In Valéry's oration on the 250th anniversary of Voltaire's birth, just months before the Liberation of Paris in 1944, cited and translated by Haydn Mason in his biography, *Vol-*

taire, p. 155, and by Daniel Brewer, "The Voltaire Effect," *Cambridge Companion to Voltaire*, pp. 216–17.

187. Voltaire, "Religion—Seventh Question," *Philosophical Dictionary*, ed. Besterman, p. 359.

188. Trousson, "La Voltairiade, ou Aventures de Voltaire dans l'autre monde, occasionnées par un événement arrivé dans celui-ci," and "Les Soirées de Saint-Pétersbourg" by Joseph de Maistre, *Voltaire—Mémoire de la critique*, pp. 217–21, 323.

189. Torrey, *Spirit of Voltaire*, p. 78–80. See chapter 5 for the last citations and details regarding Voltaire's friendships.

190. Torrey qualified Grimm as possibly jealous, but certainly uncharitable in *Spirit*, p. 10.

191. Gay, *Voltaire's Politics*, p. 265.

192. Voltaire, letter to Damilaville, April 1, 1766, in Gay, *Voltaire's Politics*, pp. 265–66.

193. Sareil, *Voltaire et les grands*, p. 18.

194. This was said during an interview with Bernard Pivot on his cultural talk show *Bouillon de Culture*, which inspired James Lipton's famous questionnaire in *Inside the Actors Studio*.

195. Pomeau, *La Religion de Voltaire*, pp. 15, 475. Pomeau added a chapter in this edition to refute even Besterman, who tripled Voltaire's available correspondence in the 1970s. Besterman, an atheist, argues for atheism in his biography, *Voltaire*. Voltaire the Christian reformer was passionately argued by Alfred Noyes in 1936. The Holy See in Rome ordered his publisher to stop issuing the book, which they did in 1938, according to George Havens, chief editor of *A Critical Biography of French Literature* in 1951.

196. Gay, *Voltaire's Politics*, p. 363.

197. *Studies on Voltaire and the Eighteenth Century* (*SVEC*, for short) has alone published over four hundred volumes. An update and short history of the various editions of Voltaire's correspondence can be found in *The Cambridge Companion to Voltaire*, chapter 10.

198. Gay, *Voltaire's Politics*, Appendix 3. Bertram E. Schwarzbach, *Voltaire's Old Testament Criticism* (Paris: Librairie Droz, 1971) and his *Voltaire et les juifs: bilan et plaidoyer, SVEC* 358, 1997, the first, a very well-documented explorations of Voltaire's views, and the second also encompasses his real life dealings with Jewish people. Harvey Chisick lists a half dozen scholars who have argued in a similar vein in "Ethics and History in Voltaire's Attitudes Toward the Jews" (*Eighteenth-Century Studies*, vol. 35, 4 [2002]), opining that they have a strong case (p. 592n55).

199. The exchanges are in Abbé Guénée's *Lettres de quelques juifs portugais, allemands et polonais à M. de Voltaire* and Voltaire's *Un Chrétien contre six juifs*. Despite the title, Voltaire's opening lines show that he knew full well he was dealing with a Catholic priest and not "six Jews." Strachey, *Books and Characters* (p. 59), relates the first incident in London. When Vol-

taire left for England, he sent all of his money ahead in a bill of exchange. But, as he told a friend in somewhat faulty English, "On my coming to London, I found my damned Jew was broken," meaning broke. The Jewish banker he had sent it to had declared bankruptcy and disappeared with the money.

200. Pierre Aubery, "Voltaire et les Juifs: ironie et demystification," *SVEC* 24, 1963.

201. The *Philosophical Dictionary* was released as soon as he had obtained the rehabilitation of Jean Calas, a Protestant tortured to death after being falsely accused of murdering his son to stop him from converting to Catholicism. The even more scathing *Important Study by Lord Bolingbroke* came out in the wake of other similar instances and of the torture and execution of nineteen-year-old Chevalier de La Barre for blasphemy. Lanson lists more lesser-known cases in his *Voltaire,* chapter 10.

202. All of these extracts can be found in Isaac Kramnick, *The Portable Enlightenment Reader* (New York: Penguin Books, 1995), pp. 568–96. An English translation of *L'Education des filles* can be found in Voltaire's *Micromegas and Other Short Stories.* Voltaire praised Madame du Châtelet's genius publically in his *Eloge* to her and in his prefaces to *Elements of Newton* and *Alzire*. He praised her genius privately in countless letters.

203. Djavâd Hadidi explores Voltaire's views on this topic at length in *Voltaire et l'Islam* (Aurillac, France: Publications Orientalistes de France, 1974).

204. Darnton, *George Washington's False Teeth*, p. 14. Condorcet's *Réflexions sur l'esclavage des nègres* (Reflections on the Enslavement of Negros), 1781, seems to have been the first, or at least the best-known, denunciation of the practice, which, it might be added, was abolished in France during the Revolution. Though not exempt from prejudices himself, Condorcet was a leading Revolutionary.

205. Barr, *Voltaire in America*, p. 70. Barr does not appear to be aware of this earlier source herself, but comparisons between it and certain attacks she reprints from American gazettes are unmistakable.

206. Cronk, in "Voltaire and authorship," *Cambridge Companion*, shows how Voltaire's attempts to elude the censor was interpreted as a "swindle."

207. Pomeau, "D'Arouet à Voltaire," in *Voltaire en son temps*, vol. 1, chapter 20, reproduces the original text in French and devotes the chapter to it. Charost, the likely author, was a soldier and aspiring writer who died on the battlefield within the year.

208. Sareil, *Voltaire et les grands*, p. 2.

209. Graham Gargett, "Oliver Goldsmith et ses Mémoires de M. de Voltaire," in *Les Vies de Voltaire: discours et représentations biographiques, XVIIIe–XXXIe siècles*, ed. Christophe Cave and Simon Davies, *SVEC* 4, 2008, pp. 218–19; Peter Gay, *Voltaire's Politics*, pp. 4–5. André Magnan's *Dossier en Prusse* contains many previously unpublished items that reveal that Frederick maliciously fanned the flames over Voltaire's lawsuit with the Jewish trader Hirshell in Berlin, for reasons known only to himself. As Frederick had made Voltaire a chamber-

lain, Voltaire asked him to stop paying his pension several times while he was "in disgrace." Frederick refused because it would have changed Voltaire's status as his "servant," as Pomeau and Mervaud observed. But in light of these facts, Frederick's many allusions to Voltaire's "insatiable greed" or vanity become not only untenable but distasteful.

210. Sir Gavin de Beer and André-Michel Rousseau, "Voltaire's British Visitors," *SVEC* 49, 1967. The corroboration is not intentional.

211. Ibid., p. 61. Edward Gibbon, author of *The Decline and Fall of the Roman Empire*, also seems annoyed that no special notice was taken of him, although he does not report making any efforts to talk to Voltaire personally, nor had he yet written anything at this time.

212. Ibid., pp. 89–92. Boswell actually belongs to a third group, who came to gawk and to convert him. Sadly, he saves the details of their "honest, vehement dispute" for a later work he apparently never wrote, but he does report departing the next evening "thinking hard, and wondering if I could possibly . . . again feel my most childish prejudices."

213. Ibid., p. 160; Madame de Genlis, for example, who came in July 1772 to strut her disapproval. She expounds upon his "puerile vanity," "unaccustomed to being contradicted," which would make him "frown and change the subject." It never seems to occur to her how uncouth it is to beg invitations from people you despise in the first place.

214. Cronk, *Cambridge Companion to Voltaire*, p. 3. His article in chapter 3, with David Beeson, "Voltaire: Philosopher or *philosophe*," discusses Voltaire's contributions to science and philosophy. See also Diderot's account, summarized by Haydn Mason in *Voltaire*, p. 152.

215. Gay, *Voltaire's Politics*, p. 10.

216. Diderot, who calls Voltaire his master and frets over his safety, also reviles him a bit excessively at times, though he must have also been affected by Grimm and d'Holbach's constant aspersions of Voltaire. He relates bawling them out for it in a letter to Madame de Maux, summer of 1769, and bawls out Falconnet on May 15, 1767. For a brief overview, see "Etre Voltaire ou rien: réflexions sur la voltairianisme de Diderot," Jacques Chouillet, *SVEC* 185, 1980, or Torrey's *Spirit*, pp. 178–79, which also contains an excellent chapter on "Voltaire and Rousseau." Interesting insights can also be gleaned from J. Churton Collins, *Voltaire, Montesquieu and Rousseau in England* (London: Eveleigh Nash, 1908).

217. Sareil, *Voltaire et les grands*, pp. 14, 35. Marmontel recounts Voltaire's efforts to boost his career in his *Mémoires*. Voltaire's correspondence attests to innumerable others he helped, however many proved ungrateful.

218. Two were published together in *Mémoires sur Voltaire et sur ses ouvrages par Longchamps et Wagnière, ses sécretaires* (Paris: Aimée André, 1826), although they didn't know each other. Longchamps worked for Voltaire in his Cirey years, until he moved to Berlin, and Wagnière much later in Ferney. Côme-Alexandre Collini, who was hired in Berlin and stayed with him till well after he settled in Geneva, left separate memoirs already cited (*Mon Séjour auprès de Voltaire*).

219. Norman Torrey, *Voltaire and the English Deists* (Oxford: Marston Press, 1963), p. 142. For more examples, see Benitez, "Voltaire and clandestine manuscripts," *Cambridge Companion to Voltaire*, pp. 69, 73.

220. Lanson, *Voltaire*, pp. 169–70.

221. Didier Masseau, *Les ennemis des philosophes, L'antiphilosophie au temps des Lumières* (Paris: Bibliothèque Albin Michel, 2000), pp. 19–20.

222. Casanova wrote a rare and nearly verbatim rendering, he says, of three different conversations he had with Voltaire. The third contains this exchange. English translations of his "Memoirs on Voltaire" can be found at www.whitman.edu/VSA/visitors/Casanova.html.

223. Voltaire estimated the literacy rate at about five percent in his *Letters on England* in 1734, but there are many indications that it improved over his lifetime. Lanson, *Voltaire* (p. 204), cites a French study as saying that at the time of the Revolution, fifty-five years later, the literacy rate was at 25 percent for women and 50 percent for men.

224. Voltaire to Frederick, August 26, 1736. Frederick's response, November 4, wholeheartedly agrees: "They preach humility . . . with hearts full of hatred and ambition." "Their aim is always a despotic hold over consciences," etc. This, they never disagreed upon and discussed endlessly.

225. *Voltaire's Notebooks II,* ed. Theodore Besterman (Geneva: Institut et Musée de Genève, 1952), pp. 375–76, 380–81.

226. Letter of Voltaire to d'Alembert, April 5, 1762.

227. Christiane Mervaud, "Encyclopedia," *Inventaire Voltaire*. That the all-out war began with pamphlets directed at the enemies of the *Encyclopédie* is advanced by Diana Guiragossian, *Voltaire's Faceties*, chapter 3, although earlier pieces in this collection could arguably be included, along with his world history, *Essai sur les moeurs*, his *Poem on Natural Law*, and other works.

228. Gay, *Voltaire's Politics,* pp. 251, 254.

229. Torrey, *Spirit of Voltaire*, p. 7.

230. Ibid., pp. 277–78. Schwarzbach, *Voltaire et les Juifs*, p. 87: "la critique biblique de Voltaire constitue le début de l'exégèse moderne . . ." (Voltaire's biblical criticism constitutes the beginning of modern exegesis).

231. Schwarzbach, *Voltaire's Old Testament Criticism*, p. 101.

232. Adams to Jefferson, November 13, 1815. Michael Holroyd, *Lytton Strachey: The New Biography* (New York: W. W. Norton & Company, 2005), p. 397.

233. Voltaire, in the *Sermon de J. Rossette*; Thomas Jefferson, letter to Colonel Yancey, January 4, 1800; Thomas Paine, in the *Rights of Man*, p. 160.

234. Benitez, *Cambridge Companion to Voltaire*, p. 74, for the "Said to be by Voltaire" annotations. Gay, *Voltaire's Politics,* p. 239, for the Mr. Ecrlinf anecdote.

235. André Caquot and Philippe de Robert (*Les Livres de Samuel*, vol. 6 of *Commentaire de l'Ancien Testament* [Geneva: Labor et Fides, 1994], p. 489), discuss the fact that 2 Samuel

12:31 used to say that David sawed his Ammonite prisoners in half, rode over them with chariots armed with iron, and baked them in brick kilns, and the fact that this has been changed in most modern Bibles *since the Enlightenment* to "he consigned them to labor with saws and iron picks and made them work at brick-making."

GRATEFUL THANKS TO A CHARITABLE MAN

Original title: Remerciement sincère à un homme charitable.

    1. *Nouvelles écclésiastiques*, April 20, 1733.

    2. Robert Shackleton, "Allies and Enemies: Voltaire and Montesquieu," in *Essays by Divers Hands*, vol. 39, ed. John Press (New York: Oxford University Press, 1977), p.126–45, cited by Mark Waddicor in "Remerciement sincère à un homme charitable," *Les Œuvres Complètes de Voltaire*, vol. 32A (Oxford: Voltaire Foundation, 2006), p. 185n37. Hereafter referred to as the *OCV*.

    3. Alexander Pope.

    4. "Though willing and trying."

    5. Voltaire is being sarcastic, since it is well known that none of these philosophers had ever disturbed the peace. The St. Bartholomew's Day Massacre, however, was an infamous butchery of Protestants by Catholic mobs in 1572.

    6. A pejorative term coined by the clergy in France to pour scorn upon discussions of tolerance.

    7. *Le Formulaire* of 1661 had to be signed by all clergymen. It condemned the propositions of the Dutch theologian, Cornelius Jansen, who had inspired the Jansenist sect.

    8. A contract "à la grosse" or "grosse aventure" was a loan at high interest; but if the ship were to perish at sea, the debt would be cancelled.

    9. Pluche's highly popular *The Spectacle of Nature* ran into several editions.

    10. Son of Noah's son Cham in the Catholic Vulgate Bible, generally translated as Ham and Cush in Protestant Bibles.

    11. Balaam is the talking donkey of Num. 22:24 and 2 Pet. 2:16 in the Bible. The Prior and the Chevalier are two characters who converse in Pluche's *The Spectacle of Nature*.

EXTRACT FROM A DECREE

Original title: Extrait du décret de la Sacrée Congrégation de l'Inquisition de Rome, à l'encontre d'un libelle intitulé "Lettres sur le vingtième."

    For a fuller account of the context, see Waddicor's introduction in the *OCV*, vol. 32A, pp. 161–66, or Diana Guiragossian, *Voltaire's Facéties* (Geneva: Librairie Droz, 1963), pp. 66–67.

1. Guiragossian, *Voltaire's Facéties*, p. 67; Louis Moland, ed., *Oeuvres complètes de Voltaire*, vol. 23 (Paris: Garnier, 1877–1885), p. 463 (regarding the condemnation in Rome, January 25, 1751).

2. Minerva is the Roman goddess of wisdom.

3. The signature contains several quintessential Italian swear words. Coglionaccio, which literally means "small testicles," is commonly used to mean "a jerk," so an attempt at translation might give: Chief Cardinal Jerk, and Up Yours, Secretary of the Holy Office.

IN DEFENSE OF MILORD BOLINGBROKE

Original title: Défense de milord Bolingbroke par le docteur Goodnatur'd Wellwisher, chapelain du comte de Chesterfield.

1. René Pomeau and Christiane Mervaud, eds., *De la Cour au jardin*, vol. 3 of *Voltaire en son temps* (Oxford: Voltaire Foundation, 1991), p. 99.

2. An English version of this work can be found in *A Treatise on Toleration and Other Essays* (Amherst, NY: Prometheus Books, 1994), translated by Joseph McCabe.

3. Father Richard Simon, perhaps the most highly considered biblical scholar of the eighteenth century, attributed the writing of the Pentateuch to Ezra's scribes, as did Spinoza and many scholars since.

4. Voltaire's note: On page 94 of the first volume of his *Letters* in Miller's London edition.

5. Voltaire is referring to Samuel Formey, secretary of the king's Academy in Berlin, and to his article on Zimmermann in volume 11 of the *Nouvelle bibliothèque germanique*.

6. Frederick the Great, King of Prussia.

7. Voltaire and Frederick, both in regular contact with Formey, knew perfectly well who the author was.

8. True to his assumed identity, Voltaire continues speaking as a Protestant would speak.

9. One of Noah's sons.

10. This refers to the Protestant Reformation.

11. Pastor Pierre Jurieu and Pierre Bayle, famous philosopher and former Calvinist minister, both moved to Rotterdam in 1681, just four years before the Edict of Nantes, granting tolerance to Protestants in France, was revoked. It was well known in Voltaire's day that Jurieu's attacks on Bayle had made him lose his livelihood as a professor of history and philosophy in 1683.

DIALOGUE BETWEEN A BRAHMIN AND A JESUIT

Original title: Dialogue entre un brachmane et un jésuite sur la nécessité et l'enchaînement des choses.

1. A fuller discussion of this is provided by W. H. Barber and Robert L. Walters in *OCV*, vol. 32A, pp. 99–101.

2. See Ravaillac in the Glossary.

DIALOGUES BETWEEN LUCRETIUS AND POSIDONIUS

Original title: Dialogues entre Lucrèce et Posidonius.

1. Diderot's *Pensées philosophiques* of 1746 and *Letters on the Blind for the Use of Those Who See* in 1749 also contributed to these concerns.

2. Voltaire expresses these thoughts in the article, "Athéisme" in *Questions sur l'Encyclopédie*. Another text on the subject of atheism, *We Must Takes Sides* (Il faut prendre une partie) can be found in English in *A Treatise on Toleration and Other Essays*, translated by Joseph McCabe.

3. "For terror and fear make the stomach tremble, while joys soothe its pains," Epicurus.

4. Voltaire gives the reference here himself for the Latin lines he cites from Lucretius' *De Rerum Natura* (On the Nature of Things), which say what Voltaire has just essentially summed up in the preceding paragraph: "The soul, united to our senses, grows, forms with us. It feels the blows of the destiny that strikes us. In feeble childhood, a frail machine envelops a spirit weak and tender like itself and shares old age with it. Toddlers run about with tender, frail bodies, uncertain steps, just as their thoughts are without force. Then when strength grows with age, so do thoughts, and the power of the mind as well . . ." etc.

REFLECTIONS FOR FOOLS

Original title: Réflexions pour les sots.

1. Letter to Mme Roger de Genette, *Œuvres complètes*, ed. R. Descharmes, vol. 2 (1923), p. 410, cited and translated in Haydn Mason, *Voltaire: A Biography* (London: Granada Publishing, 1981), pp. 155–56.

2. Voltaire famously wrote a number of satirical pamphlets on newspaper editors, such as the Jesuit Berthier, the Academician Pompignan, and on others who had attacked the philosophers or tried to get them condemned.

3. This "holy service" consisted of applying a "royal touch" to people suffering from scrofula, an infection of the lymph nodes that provokes horribly disfiguring lesions and swelling on the face and neck, in order to cure them with the monarch's "divine powers." King Louis XV of France had only recently abandoned the ritual, which contributed greatly to a loss of popularity among his subjects. Queen Anne of England is said to have touched Samuel Johnson when he was a child. The practice only ceased in England under her successor, George I, who reigned from 1714 to 1727.

4. Diana Guiragossian wrote in *Voltaire's Facéties*, p. 56–57, and in the *Dictionnaire general de Voltaire* (Paris: Honoré Champion, 2003), pp. 1036–37, that "Acanthos" referred to Omer Joly de Fleury, the Attorney General of the *Parlement* of Paris, who contributed more than anyone to the condemnation of works of capital importance such as Diderot's *Encyclopedia*, Rousseau's *Emile*, and Voltaire's *Poème sur la loi naturelle*—a powerful and dangerous foe Voltaire referred to often and attacked by name in *Omer de Fleury, Having Entered, Have Said.*

LETTER FROM CHARLES GOUJU TO HIS BROTHERS

Original title: Lettre de Charles Gouju à ses frères.

1. The adversaries of the Jesuits refers to the Jansenists. Diderot reported that the Jansenists helped circulate this pamphlet, suppressing only this reference to themselves, so fueled by their hatred of Jesuits that they seemed oblivious to the harm they were doing their common religion. André Magnan, *Inventaire Voltaire* (Paris: Gallimard, 1995), p. 821; Guiragossian, *Voltaire's Facéties*, p. 71, 128.

THE SERMON OF RABBI AKIB

Original title: Sermon du Rabbin Akib, prononcé à Smryne le 20 novembre 1761 (traduit de l'hébreu).

1. September 1761, by the Jewish calendar.

2. The pope.

3. The Jesuit Malagrida was condemned, but not burned, for having incited the King of Portugal's assassination. He was burned instead for the crime for heresy, on September 21, 1761.

4. Annah's daughter Mary was the mother of Jesus.

5. *Thérapeutes*, in the original text, were a group of Jewish aesthetes who lived in communal fasting and abstinence in the first century, principally near Alexandria, Egypt, meditating on God and his laws. They were the models for the earliest Christian monasteries.

6. A fakir is a Moslem or Hindu beggar, often one claiming to perform miracles. The implication is that priests are no different.

7. The head of a monastery, or of several monasteries, in the Orthodox Eastern Church.

8. The French.

9. For Jacques Clément and Henri III, see the Glossary.

10. See the Glossary for Guebres and Parsis.

11. The land of the Franks is France, and the "great rabbi" is Berwick-FitzJames, Bishop of Soissons.

12. The key to this strange remark is to be found in the discussion of human sacrifices in the Bible, in the *Letter from Mr. Clocpicre to Mr. Eratou.*

13. The word *makib* or a source for it has not been found. The Hebrew term Voltaire apparently meant is *mizmor*, the equivalent of a poem, song, hymn, or psalm. My thanks to Bertram E. Schwarzbach for his help with this mystery.

14. Hindu traders.

15. A term applied to the kings of Persia and to the Sultan of the Ottoman Empire.

16. Matt. 3:7 and 23:27: *sépulcres blanchis*, or whitewashed tombs—beautiful on the outside and unclean on the inside.

17. Belial is variously interpreted as meaning worthless, lawless, an idolater, a personification of evil, or one of the fallen angels, like Satan.

18. Arians, Socinians, and Unitarians would be a few examples.

EXTRACT FROM THE *LONDON GAZETTE*

Original title: Extrait de la Gazette de Londres, du 20 février 1762.

1. Diana Guiragossian-Carr, *OCV*, vol. 56A, 2001, p. 249.

2. "Nine million *livres tournois*" in the original. *Livre*, the French word for *pound*, was equivalent to the English pound in those days, and one livre of the era has been estimated at the equivalent of four USD today.

CATECHISM OF THE HONEST MAN

Original title: Catéchisme de l'honnête homme ou Dialogue entre un caloyer et un homme de bien traduit du grec vulgaire par D.J.J.R.C.D.C.D.G.

1. Stéphane Pujol, *Inventaire Voltaire* (Paris: Gallimard, 1995), p. 214. It ran into six more editions and was included in two popular anthologies, *L'Evangile de la raison* (The Gospel of Reason) and the *Recueil nécéssaire* (Necessary Anthology).

2. Josh. 8:30–32.

3. Deut. 23:12–14. (*Voltaire's note.*)

4. See the Sadder. (*Voltaire's note.*)

5. Exod. 20:12.

6. Bertram Schwarzbach noted in "Voltaire et les Juifs: bilan et plaidoyer" (*SVEC*) that Voltaire had found this in the biblical exegeses of Dom Calmet, and that Calmet was mistaken.

7. Balaam's donkey speaks to him in Num. 22:28–30.

8. Voltaire means that darkness is only the absence of light; a point he made repeatedly in other texts.

9. Gen. 7.

10. Exod. 32:25–35, in the Vulgate. The NIV Bible reduces the number to three thousand slain. See Lev. 8 on the ordination of Aaron and his sons.

11. Num. 16:16–46.

12. Josh. 10:9–13.

13. Judg. 13–16.

14. Isa. 20.

15. The last two passages are in Ezekiel. In Ezek. 4:12, the Lord tells him to cover and bake his bread "with the dung that comes out of man" in the Vulgate and King James Bibles. The NIV has changed the passage to "using human excrement for fuel." Oholibah's preference for men hung like donkeys, etc., is in Ezek. 23:20.

16. 4 Kings 2:23–24 in Catholic Bibles. 2 Kings 2:23–24 in Protestant Bibles. The NIV somewhat softens the passage of the bears "tearing forty-two children" to "mauling" them.

17. See Guebres, Parsis, in the Glossary.

18. Matt.1 and Luke 3.

19. Matt. 2.

20. John 14:28, Matt.24:36, Mark 13:32, and Luke 18:19.

21. For the herd of pigs: Matt. 8 and Mark 5; the Cana wedding: John 2:1–11; the fig tree: Matt. 21:18–21, Mark 11; the devil tempting Jesus: Matt. 4:1–11.

22. Zaleucus is said to have devised the Locrian Code in the seventh century BCE, the first written Greek law code.

23. Matt.10:34–37; Luke 12:49–53 and 14:25–26.

24. Acts 5:1–11.

25. Voltaire went into more detail on most of these fables and forgeries in the *Collection des anciens évangiles*, *La Relation de Marcel*, the *Examen important de milord Bolingbroke*, the *Philosophical Dictionary*, and *God and Human Beings*, but *The Dinner at Count de Boulainvilliers'*, *Letters to His Highness . . . on Rabelais*, and other works herein also discuss them.

26. "Jewish wonders make you laugh," an adaptation of Horace's Epistle II, 209.

27. Also in Mark 13:30. Several recent translations have changed "this generation" to "this race."

28. 1 Thess. 4:15–17.

29. 2 Cor. 12:1–6: "I know a man in Christ who . . . was caught to the third heaven." The Vulgate Bible says that Paul was humbly speaking of himself in the third person.

30. Deut. 14:7.

31. Followers of Athanasius, Alexandrian bishop, 328–373 CE, and followers of Eusebius, Greek ecclesiastical historian, 264?–340 CE.

32. The Guelphs supported the authority of the pope against the Ghibellines in twelfth- to fourteenth-century Italy and Germany.

33. Matt. 23:35. The Vulgate and King James translations are used. The NIV translates their names as Zechariah and Berekiah.

34. Flavius Josephus, *The War of the Jews*, Book IV, chapter 19. Titus, son of Vespasian, was a Roman general and emperor from 79–81 CE.

35. This paragraph calls to mind to Thomas Jefferson's oft-cited remarks in a letter to Roger C. Weightman, June 24, 1826, regarding the upcoming fiftieth anniversary of American Independence: "May it be to the world, what I believe it will be (finally to all), the signal of arousing men to burst the chains under which monkish ignorance and superstition had persuaded them to bind themselves. . . . All eyes are . . . opening to . . . the palpable truth that the mass of mankind has not been born with saddles on their backs, nor a favored few booted and spurred, ready to ride them legitimately, by the grace of God."

36. Acts 5:29.

37. While committing adultery with Uriah's wife, Bathsheba, King David purposely sent Uriah into the front lines of a battle where he knew he would be killed. (2 Kings 11 in the Catholic Bibles; 2 Sam. 11 in the Protestant Bibles.)

38. Which Antonine emperor is meant is not clear, but it is probably Marcus Aurelius.

39. The Egyptians.

40. A reference to the Trinity.

OMER DE FLEURY, HAVING ENTERED, HAVE SAID

Original title: Omer de Fleury, étant entré, ont dit.

1. The Sorbonne University taught only theology at the time, so this is a dig at their ridiculous reversing of roles and competencies.

2. The kingdom's finances had of course been in a deplorable state for some time, as discussed in the tract of 1750, *Extract of a Decree by . . . the Inquisition of Rome.*

3. These were mercury- and vinegar-based pills, according to Diderot's *Encyclopedia*. They were much in vogue in the eighteenth century according to Moland's nineteenth-century notes to this text.

LETTER FROM MR. CLOCPICRE TO MR. ERATOU

Original title: Lettre de M. Clocpicre à M. Eratou sur la question: Si les Juifs ont mangé de la chair humaine, et comment ils l'apprêtaient?

1. This last detail is a comical interjection, since *Candide* is of course a novel by Voltaire. It is also an allusion to all the tales of cannibalism in the New World related by the early European explorers. Oreillons, or Orejones ("big ears"), was a name the Spaniards gave to Inca chiefs because the lobes of their ears had been artificially enlarged.

ADAPT TO THE TIMES

Original title: Conformez-vous aux temps.

1. André Magnan, *Inventaire Voltaire* (Paris: Gallimard, 1995), p. 304.

2. One of Voltaire's plays.

3. A series of civil wars in France, from 1648 to 1653. A *fronde* is a slingshot, which mobs were using to smash the windows of supporters of Cardinal Mazarin.

4. Thousands still gather in Naples three times a year to witness the "miraculous" liquefaction of his blood when brought close to his other relics.

5. "Ancient tribunals" refers to the *parlements* of Paris. Marcel seems to have been another saint or protector, sometimes paraded in wicker effigy with the relics of St. Geneviève. He is more difficult to identify, as there were a great many Marcels and Marcelluses.

6. King Louis XV had laid the foundation stone for the church that year, but Voltaire would have been amazed to learn that the French revolutionaries would convert the church into the Pantheon in April 1791 to contain the tombs of "the great men to whom the nation is grateful," and that he would be among the first to be reburied there that year.

7. A reference to the pope and all the priests, nuns, monks, etc. that he governed. Religious orders are estimated to have comprised close to a third of the population in Europe.

8. Reputed ninth- and twelfth-century theologians.

9. This metaphor would have been quite clear to contemporaries: the "unsociable society" is the Jesuits. The hundred and one arrows are the hundred and one proclamations in the papal bull *Unigenitus*. The "unbelievers" in the next paragraph are their rivals, the Jansenists, who were exiled or imprisoned in the Bastille, "a neighboring castle."

10. French *Parlement* had just abolished the Jesuit order in France. It was also formally abolished by the pope himself in 1773. In the backlash after the French Revolution and Napoleon, the Jesuits were reinstated to combat revolutions overthrowing traditional church and state systems in favor of republics.

WIVES, SUBMIT TO YOUR HUSBANDS

Original title: Femmes, soyez soumises à vos maris.
   1. Catherine the Great, Empress of Russia, who was born a German princess.
   2. Chief office of the Ottoman Empire in Turkey.

REPUBLICAN IDEAS BY A MEMBER OF A CORPS

Original title: Idées républicaines par un membre d'un corps.
   1. A complete translation can be found, however, in *Voltaire: Political Writings*, ed. David Williams (Cambridge University Press, 2003). Peter Gay's brilliant analysis in *Voltaire's Politics: The Poet as Realist* (Princeton: Princeton University Press, 1959) is used both for the comments and the dating, pp. 214–38 and Appendix II.
   2. Matt. 20:25–28; Mark 10:31; John 18:36.
   3. Pierre de La Baume, Bishop of Geneva, had been expulsed in 1534. Jacques Van Den Heuvel, *Voltaire: Mélanges* (Paris: Editions Gallimard, Bibliothèque de La Pléiade, 1961), p. 1462n505.
   4. Under the name of Pope Gregory VII.
   5. The author in question is Montesquieu. Voltaire's note references Book IV of *Spirit of the Laws*, chapter 8 here. He makes this remark because the nobility in France and other countries did not engage in commerce, considered lowly and beneath them. Voltaire had already contrasted England's attitudes (and wealth) to this in *Letters on England*, Letter 10.

DIALOGUE BETWEEN A DOUBTER AND A VENERATOR

Original title: Dialogue du douteur et de l'adorateur par M. l'abbé Tilladet. Abbé de Tilladet, author of several dissertations on the Romans, religion, and philology, had died in 1715.
   1. This line is interestingly translated in French as the "pauvres d'esprit" which also means the "empty-headed" or "madmen." Voltaire here and elsewhere questions its meaning.

2. Meaning "dome." Trullum was a room in the palace of the Byzantine emperors where two councils were held in the sixth century.

LETTERS TO HIS HIGHNESS THE PRINCE OF ****** ON RABELAIS

Original title: Lettres à S. A. Msg le Prince de ***** sur Rabelais et sur d'auteurs accusés d'avoir mal parlé de la religion chrétienne.

1. René Pomeau lists ten new works that year in *La Religion de Voltaire* (Paris: Librairie Nizet, 1974), p. 354. *Zapata* can be found in English in *A Treatise on Toleration and Other Essays*, trans. by Joseph McCabe (Amherst, NY: Prometheus Books, 1994), and by Kenneth W. Applegate in *Voltaire on Religion: Selected Writings* (New York: Frederick Ungar, 1974), which also contains the powerful piece attributed to Bolingbroke.

Most of the insights on this text come from the excellent *OCV* introduction to it by François Bessire, vol. 63B, pp. 357–69, and his article on the same subject in *Revue Voltaire* 8, both published in 2008.

2. "Whether a chimaera, bombinating in the Void, can feed on secondary intentions; subject debated for ten weeks before the Council of Constance."

3. Perhaps, "the hot gonads of the magistrate" or "gonaditis," although *couillon*, slang for testicles, is also used in French to mean a "putz" or simpleton.

4. Actually, while a pretty *abbegess* was singing to him in a park (Book 5, chapter 8). This seems to an error.

5. "Endless talking generated boredom. And boredom, in turn, generated contempt and, in the end, hatred."

6. At the point of death.

7. The *Pantheisticon, sive formula celebrandae sodalitatis socraticae* (Pantheisticon, or the Form of Celebrating the Socratic Society) imitates church liturgy with passages from or on the pagans, such as this one that begins, "Omnipotent and everlasting Bacchus, who foundest human society principally by drinking . . ." The rest of the phrase appears in several variations.

8. This probably refers to Voltaire's chapter on Locke in his *Letters on England*, an international bestseller in 1734, though banned. It is sometimes printed under the title, *Philosophical Letters*, or other variants of both titles.

9. *Guide des douteurs*, in Voltaire's original text, which is clearly a French translation, though of which book is difficult to ascertain; possibly of *Ductor Dunitantium, or the Rule of Conscience*.

10. The note to the Moland edition of *Voltaire's Works* says that he is here referring to his own *Examen important du milord Bolingbroke*, recently published under Bolingbroke's name.

11. *Treatise of the Three Imposters* (Moses, Christ, and Mohammed) is the name of an imaginary book attributed to various heretics and political enemies from the eleventh century through the eighteenth, when a couple of works under this title were produced.

12. Frederick Holland Dewey, in his *Students' Interlinear Translations* (New York: Translation Publishing Company, 1917) gives this line as "Do you now dare to mingle heaven and earth without my will, ye winds, and to raise such great masses?"

13. King Frederick William's son was Frederick the Great, the addressee's uncle, and a confidant of Voltaire for over forty years. His *Eulogy* of Voltaire can be found in the Appendix. The following paragraph seems to apply to Frederick II as well.

14. They depict a donkey, or a jackass, seated in an armchair, per Jacques Van Den Heuvel, *Voltaire: Mélanges* (Paris, Bibliothèque de la Pléiade, Editions Gallimard, 1961), p. 1517n1243.

15. Théophile de Viau (1590–1626).

16. "The irritable race of poets . . ." Horace, "of Vasco" adds Voltaire, referring to people known as the Vascones, a pre-Roman tribe near the Pyrenees from which the name "Gascon" derives.

17. Not Jean-Jacques, but Jean-Baptiste Rousseau (1671–1741), poet and dramatist, well-known for his satirical and sometimes licentious epigrams.

18. "Du tonnerre dans l'air bravant les vains carreaux/Et nous parlant de Dieu du ton de Des Barreaux."

Capaneus was a warrior in Greek mythology of immense size and strength who, while besieging Thebes, said Zeus himself could not stop him. In reply, Zeus struck him dead with a thunderbolt.

19. "Thunder, strike, it is time; render me war for war./ In dying I adore reason which embitters you/ But on top of which place will your thunder fall/ Which is not all covered with the blood of Jesus Christ?"

20. A straightforward unrhymed translation gives, "Let the fatal curtain fall, with no delay, on this shameful bust/ And show only the flaming torch which should have turned its inspirer to ashes." Giovanni Battista Lulli (1632–1687) was the French court's most famous composer and director of operas and ballets under the Sun King, Louis XIV. Some of his entertainments were orchestrated in collaboration with the famous playwright Molière.

21. A book entitled l'*Examen critique des apologists de la religion chrétienne* (Critical study of the Apologists of the Christian Religion) had appeared under Fréret's name the previous year. Voltaire mentions it in several letters, including one to d'Alembert on December 31, 1768, saying, "I know perfectly well who the author of the book attributed to Fréret is, and my loyalty to him is inviolable." Barbier attributed it to Lévesque de Burigny, according to the note in Moland.

22. A Targum is a translation made around the first century BCE and CE of Jewish

scripture from Hebrew into the common language of the listeners, mostly Aramaic, which was read alternately with the Torah.

23. "For you and for many"; taken from Jesus' words at the Last Supper, according to Matt. 26:28 and Mark 14:24.

24. Montesquieu was *Président à mortier* in Bordeaux. The *présidents* were chief magistrates in *parlement*, which was the Appeal Courts, the highest of the judicial institutions.

25. Frederick the Great of Prussia. Voltaire was living in Frederick's court at the time of La Mettrie's death in 1752.

26. Including one by Voltaire.

27. Matt. 5:17–18.

28. Although the names are different, this resembles the story of Nahmanides' disputation at Barcelona in 1263. Voltaire does not name his source here, so the error, if there is one, is difficult to pinpoint.

29. 1 Cor. 1:18.

30. Voltaire is speaking of Isaac Orobio de Castro, seventeenth-century Jewish philosopher and physician, often mistakenly represented as a rabbi in writings about him.

31. Deut. 13:1–5.

32. Rom. 2.

33. Franciscus Gomarus (1563–1641) and Jacobus Arminius (1560–1609) were Calvinist Dutch theologians who developed opposing views on predestination and other matters.

34. Leclerc published these views in *Sentiments de quelques théologiens de Hollande sur l'histoire critique du Vieux Testament compose par le P. Richard Simon*, 1685. (My thanks to Bertram E. Schwarzbach for this and other clarifications.)

35. Voltaire is the author of the *Henriade*, an epic poem on the French King Henri IV and the St. Bartholomew's Day Massacre that ran into sixty editions.

36. Jean de Poltrot (1573–1563) was a French Huguenot who murdered Francis, the Duke de Guise—one of the assassinations that led to the St. Bartholomew's Day Massacre. The Jesuit Malagrida is discussed in *The Sermon of Rabbi Akib*. Jaurigny, or Juan de Jàuregui, (1562–1582) shot Prince William I of Orange but only wounded him, two years before Balthazar Gérard managed to shoot him dead. Voltaire speaks of him further in his *Commentary on the Book on Crimes and Punishments* (by Beccaria), chapter 16. Jean Chastel (1708–1790) was a farmer-innkeeper, famed for killing, and possibly being, the Beast of Gévaudan in 1767. He was depicted in the 2001 French film, *Brotherhood of the Wolf* (Le pacte des loups). For the other men, please consult the Glossary.

DINNER AT COUNT DE BOULAINVILLIERS'

Original title: Le Dîner du Comte Boulainvilliers.

1. Boulainvilliers is mentioned in the article "On Spinoza," in *Letters . . . On Rabelais*. A richly researched analysis of this text can be found in *Oeuvres Complètes de Voltaire*, vol. 63A, 1990, by Ulla Kölving and José-Michel Moreaux, pp. 293–322, and in Patrick Nieirtz, "*Le Dîner du comte de Boulainvilliers*: un 'dialogue des morts' des auteurs clandestins," *Revue Voltaire* 8 (2008): 151–64.

2. Matt. 13:13, Mark 4:10–12.

3. Matt. 15:23–26.

4. Matt. 17:24–26.

5. Matt. 5:22. The Sermon of the Mount is in Matt. 5–7.

6. This echoes Molière's line, "None shall have wit but us and our friends," in *Les Femmes savants* (The Learned Ladies).

7. Matt. 18:17.

8. See Glossary for Ixion. Voltaire enjoys recalling that the Bible forbids the eating of certain mythological creatures that never existed. More amusing are clerical refutations, claiming that they did exist. Kölving's *OCV* intro, pp. 313–14.

9. 2 Sam. 13.

10. A reference to the biblical King David.

11. Literally, "St. Knee," or "St. Kneecap." A tenth-century French Benedictine monk wrote St. Genou's "Life," according to which St. Genou and his father, St. Genit, or Genitus, came to the region of Berry and Sologne in France and chased out all the demons it was infested with.

12. Luke 21: 25–32. Some twentieth-century revisions have changed *generation* to *race*.

13. The meaning seems to be similar to another line Voltaire used: "over the age of twelve."

14. Matt. 16:17, John 1:42, 21:15. Barjona has been changed to *son of Jonah* or *John* in some English-language Bibles.

15. These stories are also related in the apocryphal Acts of Peter and Paul—Gospels not retained by the Church.

16. Dagobert (603–639 CE) was a King of the Franks, who ruled what was then "France." He is also the subject of a famous French nursery rhyme that makes fun of him and his counselor, St. Eloi.

17. Agnus Dei, "Lamb of God." The Latin term, still the language used in Mass, referred to Jesus' role as a sacrifice, to atone for the sins of the world, as lambs were also used in Hebrew and other ritual sacrifices.

18. This last remark is anachronistic, since the sect began their "convulsions" on the tomb of Jansenist deacon, François de Pâris, who died in 1727, and Count de Boulainvilliers had died five years earlier. Voltaire's older brother was a convulsionary, so he is either taking artistic license or he is not sure what year Boulainvilliers died.

19. The Recabites are mentioned in Jer. 35 in the Bible.

20. Voltaire may be referencing Josephus here, who wrote of a root known as "baaras" (also sometimes written as "baraas" or "baras") used for driving out demons (*War of the Jews*, book 7, chapter 6). This root has been associated with mandrake, although some scholars argue they are different plants.

21. *Histoire ecclésiastique*, in the original text. Eusebius' perhaps.

22. Voltaire must have meant to say "from their first century" since Mahomet wasn't born until 570 CE.

23. "It is worthwhile to reach a certain point, even if we can't go further," Horace, Book I, epistle I, verse 32.

24. "Une taie" in the original; normally *a pillowcase* in French, but a rarer meaning is *nebula*, a medical term referring to "a slight cloudy opacity of the cornea," according to Merriam-Webster.

25. Citing Jesus in Matt. 18:22, himself perhaps citing Gen. 4:24.

26. Dufay was a chemist and the others were reputed freethinkers Voltaire had known. President (a high position in the French *parlements*) de Maisons had been a very dear friend. Voltaire caught smallpox with him during a visit to his chateau when they were in their twenties. Both survived, but de Maisons did not survive a second infection eight years later. There is an article on Abbé Pierre in *Letters . . . on Rabelais*.

27. i.e., Latin. The Latin Vulgate Bible, translated by St. Jerome, was the official Bible for over a thousand years (400–1530 CE) and the only Bible most Westerners ever encountered. Wycliffe made the first translation from it into English in 1382 and more Bibles, such as the King James Version, began appearing in translations into vernacular tongues in the late-fifteenth to early-sixteenth centuries. But Latin was used in Catholic masses until 1964.

28. Matt. 16:18. Peter, or Petros in Greek, from petra, meaning rock, Pierre in French.

29. The three sects accepted were Catholicism, Lutheranism, and Calvinism. This treaty recognized the prince's right to choose the religion of his own state.

30. See the Glossary on these two French kings. Voltaire is no doubt referring to the fact that Pope Sixtus considered canonizing Jacques Clément, the murderer of King Henri III. Sixtus also had medals struck and Te Deums sung over the assassination of Henri IV.

THE EMPEROR OF CHINA AND FRIAR CHUCKLES

1. An alternate spelling in English for the Kangxi Emperor, who ruled from 1661 to 1722.

2. Ferdinand Verbiest (1623–1688) was a Flemish Jesuit, mathematician, astronomer, diplomat, and cartographer, who had obtained the friendship of the K'ang-hsi Emperor. Voltaire's nineteenth-century editor Beuchot says that Parennin was another favorite of the emperor.

3. Giovanna Paolo Oliva (1600–1681) was an Italian Jesuit who was elected eleventh Superior General of the Society of Jesus and who extended the missions outside Europe, especially in Japan.

4. Isa. 8:3.

5. Ezek. 23:20.

6. Matt. 13:53, Mark 3:32, John 2:4-10, *Inebriati* (Voltaire's note).

7. Matt. 8:28, Mark 5, Luke 8:27.

8. Frederick II, Holy Roman Emperor (1194–1250) and probably, Louis the Debonaire, or the Pious (778–840), the only surviving adult son of Charlemagne and Hildegard, sole ruler of the Franks after Charlemagne's death in 814, except for a period in the 830s during which he was deposed.

9. The feeding of four thousand is reported in Mark 8 and Matt. 15. The feeding of five thousand is reported in Luke 9, John 6, Matt. 14 and Mark 6.

10. Melchizedek first appears in Gen. 14:18 as the King of Salem (i.e., Jerusalem) whom Abram encounters. He is mentioned again in Psalms 110:4 and in Hebrews several times.

11. Short for *in partibus infidelium*, meaning "in the land of unbelievers."

12. Hieronymites, or the Order of St. Jerome, is an order of hermit monks who live according to the Rule of St. Augustine following the example of St. Jerome. They date from the fourteenth century.

AN ANONYMOUS CHARACTER SKETCH OF VOLTAIRE

1. An excellent analysis of the text, its probable author, context, and repercussions can be found in *Voltaire en son temps*, vol. 1, ed. René Pomeau (Oxford: Voltaire Foundation, 1988). Chapter 20 is entirely devoted to the topic. Charost, the probable author, had no doubt observed Voltaire in cafés or the theater, but Voltaire never believed him guilty because they had never met.

2. He has "la bile brûlée" in the original text, which, despite Diderot's eighteenth-

century definition, remains difficult to interpret. Diderot's *Encyclopédie* calls "bile brûlée" the mildest form of the nefarious effects of bile, which itself comes from an "overly violent circulation of the blood," he says. "Ebullient" seemed closer to what this author intended, given what follows, than "bilious," which today means peevish or unpleasant to look at.

3. Voltaire had published only one history book per se at this point: a historical novel on Charles XII, King of Sweden. However, a number of his plays and his epic poem on Henri IV, *La Henriade*, were also based on history.

4. The "last work" is, of course, Voltaire's *Letters on England* or *Philosophical Letters*. (The title has had many variations in English translations.) England was France's traditional enemy, which helps explain the snide tone of this libel—although *Letters* also vastly inspired the next generation of writers such as Diderot and Rousseau. Rousseau evokes the thrill it gave him and much of his generation in Book 5 of his *Confessions*. Besides England's tolerance, Voltaire also praised its free commerce, its constitutional monarchy, and its adoption of the smallpox vaccination, hoping France would do the same. His praise of several English writers included Shakespeare, whose play on *Julius Caesar* he soon adapted to French tastes in *Brutus*.

René Pomeau explains in the analysis referenced above that the remark on Voltaire's "copying" Pierre Bayle refers to Bayle's writings in gazettes, which were in letter form, like Voltaire's *Letters on England*. Voltaire's "censor" of Bayle's more famous *Dictionary* is found in his poem, *Le Temple du goût* (The Temple of Taste). In it, Voltaire says that Bayle's voluminous *Dictionary* needed to be reduced to one volume to be admitted into "the temple." In England, Samuel Johnson, Joseph Addison, and others, commonly appraised their fellow writers. In France, however, "The Temple of Taste" started the legend of Voltaire's "vanity" with some, which this "portrait" echoes.

5. "Ever changing face and color": the phrase probably comes from Livy. Cf. Lewis & Short, *A Latin Dictionary* (Oxford, 1879), p. 371.

OLIVER GOLDSMITH ON VOLTAIRE

1. These last two statements are inspired to some degree by the journalistic nonsense referred to. Voltaire left the French court, but did not abandon his titles nor the work he had undertaken as Royal Historian, which he finished, with more liberty indeed, in Berlin, as *The Age of Louis XIV*. He was exiled in 1716, but only from Paris to Sully-sur-Loire, for *J'ai vu*, a poem he didn't write, although he did write one in Latin, *Regnante puero*, on the Regent, mentioning the Regent's incest with his own daughter. This incest inspired numerous pamphlets, unsurprisingly.

2. King Frederick the Great of Prussia.

3. After listening to Voltaire at a social gathering, he said, "You are so witty, profligate, and thin/ At once we think you Milton, Death, and Sin"—among other variations found.

4. I am deeply indebted to Graham Gargett's generous help and to his publication, "Oliver Goldsmith et ses Mémoires de M. de Voltaire," (*Les Vies de Voltaire: discours et representation biographiques, XVIIIe–XXIe siecles*, eds. Christophe Cave and Simon Davies [Oxford: Voltaire Foundation, 2008], pp. 203–222) for most of these insights. Any errors remaining are my own.

CONDORCET'S ACCOUNT OF VOLTAIRE'S BATTLE

1. As in Montesquieu's *Persian Letters* or many earlier plays and philosophical short stories by Voltaire.

2. Condorcet is oddly mistaken here, as Voltaire had published any number of "bold works" before *Emile* appeared in 1762. The publishing dates on the pamphlets herein bear witness; and they are only a selection. Did their anonymity work better than generally supposed? As Condorcet says, these pamphlets were all clandestine and "spread slowly," so his assumptions are interesting in themselves.

It is also fascinating to see that the idea, much put forward in recent years, that earlier writers, like Spinoza, had a greater effect on the issue of religion than Voltaire does not correspond to the impressions of the age, even from a man and writer so deeply involved in the approaching revolutions as Condorcet.

3. It is interesting to note that Condorcet, who knew Jefferson, Paine, and John Adams personally before this book came out, does not add America or Germany to the list of countries severely forbidding these works. Condorcet, among other French revolutionaries to-be, had sought their acquaintance and advice many a time after their arrival in Paris.

4. Bossuet (1627–1704), French bishop and strong advocate of the divine rights of kings, renowned for his sermons and his *Universal History*, is mentioned in this book's introduction. He was considered a brilliant orator and stylist, including by Voltaire. Antoine Arnaud (1612–1694), theologian, philosopher, and mathematician, was a leading Jansenist intellectual, who sometimes coauthored with distinguished Jansenist scholar, Pierre Nicole (1625–1695).

5. The story of Jean Calas, a French Protestant accused of murdering his son for wishing to convert to Catholicism, then tortured and burned for this far-from-proven crime, is exposed in Voltaire's *Treatise on Tolerance*, among other works.

6. "Honorable amends" were common penalties that consisted in forcing a convicted person to publically implore forgiveness of God—typically by being led barefoot to the door of the church with a noose around his or her neck, for example. In this case, it consisted in a procession of the entire town, since the guilty party had not yet been convicted.

7. Condorcet is again mistaken. The Ordinances of 1539 and 1670, still then in effect, prescribed the amputation of hands, death by fire, and the confiscation of goods for sacrilege, profanation, or the theft of sacred objects. These practices had all existed since medieval times, if only codified later. Condorcet had apparently not seen these laws applied, but several cases were found in the police archives of Paris of the eighteenth century by the National Archivist, Robert Anchel, as noted in our introduction.

MADAME SUARD'S VISIT TO FERNEY IN 1775

1. Marie-Louise Denis was Voltaire's niece, one of the two daughters of his beloved older sister who died while he was in England. Voltaire provided dowries for both girls and, though no clear mention was made of it at the time, he and Madame Denis became lovers after the death of her husband. Their love letters, discovered in the 1940s, came as a big surprise. She became his live-in companion and housekeeper in Geneva and Ferney. She proved not particularly faithful or disinterested, though she displayed a dutiful devotion to him. They never married, though it would have been possible under French law, possibly because she was already Voltaire's heir and, therefore, well provided for.

2. *Bontés*, in the original.

3. Anne-Robert-Jacques Turgot was Controller-General of Finances and an early advocate for economic liberalism. He was replaced by Jacques Necker in 1776, who remained in that post till the eve of the French Revolution in 1788.

4. After Voltaire's falling-out with Frederick the Great in Berlin over his mordant satire of Maupertuis and his persecutions of Konïg, Frederick wrote French King Louis XV that he would be obliged if Voltaire were not permitted to re-enter France. This is why Voltaire had been in exile since 1753, finally moving to Geneva, then to Ferney on the border of Switzerland and France.

5. This is an understandable error, as Voltaire later says that he is eighty-four, but he was, in fact, eighty-four when he died in 1778, three years later.

6. Madame Florian was the married name of Marie-Elisabeth Mignot, Voltaire's other niece.

7. Pierre Michel Hennin had been named French resident in Geneva in 1765, a diplomatic post similar to, but with less powers than, an ambassador. Pomeau, *Voltaire en son temps*, vol.4, p. 311.

8. These remarks on Voltaire's eyes, which sound so over the top, are in fact frequently paralleled by other observers, including hostile ones. Dozens of similar reactions can be found in *Voltaire's British Visitors*, ed. Gavin de Beer and André-Michel Rousseau (*SVEC* 49, 1967).

9. Voltaire and Madame du Châtelet—renowned for her work in science and mathematics and for her translation of Newton's *Principia*, the standard edition in French to this day—wrote, worked, and lived together as lovers from 1734 till her death in 1749.

10. This remark could scarcely be more magnanimous, for St. Lambert began a liaison with Voltaire's longtime lover, Mme. du Châtelet, two years before her death and was the inadvertent cause of it. She died as a consequence of delivering his child at the age of forty-two.

11. Jacques Marie Bertrand d'Etallonde was the Chevalier de La Barre's friend, condemned to torture and decapitation with him, although he managed to escape. Voltaire got his friend Frederick, King of Prussia, to give him a post in his army.

12. This may refer to *Titon et l'Aurore*, an opera by Jean-Joseph Mondonville, first performed in 1753.

13. Punch, of the Punch and Judy marionette shows.

THE COUNT DE SÉGUR ON VOLTAIRE'S RETURN TO PARIS IN 1778

1. Ségur is referring to the fact that Voltaire lived up to the age of twenty under Louis XIV, in *le Grand Siècle* (the Grand Century), an era considered the epitome of French culture and power, and then throughout the entire reign of Louis XV. But 1778 was in fact already three years into the new reign of Louis XVI. His eighty-four years thus spanned three reigns.

2. Voltaire continued to wear the long wigs in fashion under Louis XIV, for example, instead of the short ones that became fashionable under Louis XV.

3. A reference to Molière's protagonist in his famous play, *Tartuffe*, whose titular character feigns piety and divine authority to manipulate others for his sordid private ends.

4. Voltaire suffered from similar digestive problems on and off throughout his life, in fact, and is believed by some to have died of stomach cancer.

5. The Quai des Théatins in Paris, named after a monastery, was renamed Quai Voltaire during the French Revolution. It sits opposite the Louvre on the Left Bank of the Seine River.

6. By prudence, Ségur is referring to the fact that if the Church refused absolution, Voltaire could not be buried. This had happened to one of France's greatest actresses and Voltaire's dearest friends, Adrienne Lecouvreur, thrown into a ditch at her death and covered with lime, because actors were automatically excommunicated. He wrote a moving poem about it in shock and rage. Molière just barely avoided a similar fate the previous century for acting in his plays.

LA CORRESPONDANCE LITTÉRAIRE, PHILOSOPHIQUE, ET CRITIQUE ON VOLTAIRE'S DEATH

1. A concise, informed analysis of Diderot's references to Voltaire can be found in "Etre Voltaire ou rien: réflexions sur le voltairianisme de Diderot," by Jacques Chouillet, in *Studies on Voltaire and the Eighteenth Century* (SVEC 185, 1980).

2. D'Alembert, Diderot's co-editor on the *Encyclopédie*, responded to Voltaire's first invitations to do so on May 19, 1761, saying, ". . . écrasez-l'infâme! That's easily said when you live a hundred leagues away from the fanatics" (i.e., in Geneva, not Paris). Diderot expressed his amazement and concern to his mistress, Sophie Volland, on October 19, saying, "A man who prints works as bold or daring as the *Letter from Charles Gouju* and so many others has apparently put himself above all fears." On October 8 or 10, 1766, he wrote to Voltaire that he was "trembling" over Voltaire's *Important Study by Lord Bolingbroke*, and begged him to defer releasing it if possible. On October 8, 1768, he again wrote forebodingly to Sophie that, despite the esteem and fame Voltaire enjoyed, he might just get himself burned, not just his books: "Did you know they were deliberating over it three days ago?"

FREDERICK THE GREAT'S EULOGY OF VOLTAIRE

1. Lycée Louis le Grand was, and still is, one of the most rigorous and prestigious secondary schools in France. It was long run by the Jesuits. All schools were in fact run by one or another of the various religious orders or sects in the eighteenth century, in every country.

2. Actually, Voltaire was already well acquainted with such circles, through family ties and classmates at Louis le Grand, which consisted mostly of aristocrats and future ministers—including such lifelong friends as the Duke of Richelieu and Count d'Argental. Mme. de Rupelmonde was the inspiration for his earliest deistic work, "Epistle à Uranie," and this is likely the reason Frederick knew of her. See René Pomeau, *D'Arouet à Voltaire*, vol. 1 of *Voltaire en son temps* (Oxford: Voltaire Foundation, 1988), pp. 151–62.

3. Eleven months, in fact: almost a year.

4. Entitled *Elements of the Philosophy of Newton* in English, 1738, though it wasn't written when Voltaire was in England but in liaison with Mme Du Châtelet once he had returned to France.

5. *Institutions de physique*, 1740, which served as the basis for entries on physics in the *Encyclopedia* of Diderot and d'Alembert, who both admired her greatly. This portrayal of Emilie du Châtelet also omits her translation and commentary of Newton's entire *Principia*, including her corrections, still the standard text in French—as well as the fact that it

was Emilie who instructed Voltaire in math and science, as he repeatedly told Frederick in his letters.

6. These last few lines are a face-saving suite of misinformation. Voltaire arrived in Berlin in June of 1750 and left in March of 1753, after being held under house arrest by Frederick for three months, purportedly for a satire he had written on Maupertuis. Voltaire's eventual move to Geneva after a second arrest in Frankfurt ordered by Frederick likewise had nothing to do with the start of the Seven Year War in 1756. Frederick had done his best to blacken Voltaire, to justify his behavior, and Voltaire was ultimately refused permission to return to France. (Theodore Besterman, *Voltaire*, [New York: Harcourt, Brace, & World, 1969], pp. 327–36.)

7. More on Henri IV and the St. Bartholomew's Day Massacre can be found in the Glossary.

8. Roughly two pages of the eulogy have been cut here, in which Frederick similarly assesses five plays from among the fifty-nine that Voltaire wrote.

9. Witty and often ironic light verse, usually improvised for a given occasion.

10. "All that is mine, I carry with me" (i.e., My wisdom is my greatest wealth), Cicero.

11. Dialectic in philosophy as defined per Merriam-Webster as a method of examining and discussing opposing ideas in order to find the truth. In logic, it alludes to the Socratic techniques of exposing false beliefs to elicit the truth.

12. Irene, wife of Nikephoros, Emperor of Constantinople, per Voltaire's list of characters in the play. Possibly the Byzantine empress who ruled from 797–802 CE, although she doesn't seem to have married her brother-in-law, Nikephoros.

13. The Heruli were an East Germanic tribe who sacked Byzantium, Sparta, and Athens with the Goths in 267 CE.

EDGAR QUINET ON THE EXTERMINATING ANGEL

From *L'Ultramontanisme ou l'Eglise Romaine et la société moderne* (Paris: Hachette, 1844), pp. 186–93.

1. Pomeau, *La Religion de Voltaire*, p. 469.

2. A number of people had attested over the years to finding Voltaire in bed with a fever on that day, the date of the massacre of thousands of Protestants in France. The massacre was then still actively celebrated in Catholic countries as an official holy day.

ROBERT G. INGERSOLL ON *THE GREAT INFIDELS*

1. Whether the mistake was Ingersoll's or the reporter's, Hume was born in 1711. He died in 1776.

SELECTED BIBLIOGRAPHY

Adams, William Howard. *The Paris Years of Thomas Jefferson*. New Haven, CT: Yale University Press, 1997.

Anchel, Robert. *Crimes et châtiments au XVIII siècle*. Paris: Librairie Académique Perrin, 1933.

Bailyn, Bernard. *The Ideological Origins of the American Revolution*. Cambridge, MA: The Belknap Press of Harvard University Press, 1992.

Barr, Mary-Margaret. *Voltaire in America, 1744–1800*. Baltimore: Johns Hopkins Press, 1941.

Barr, Mary-Margaret, and Frederick A. Spear. *Quarante années d'Etudes voltairiennes, Bibliographie analytique des livres et articles sur Voltaire, 1926–1965*. Paris: Librairie Armand Colin, 1968.

Besterman, Theodore. *Voltaire*. New York: Harcourt, Brace & World, 1969.

———. *Correspondence and Related Documents, Œuvres Complètes de Voltaire* (OCV). vols. 85–135. Oxford: Voltaire Foundation, 1968–1977.

Boyd, Julian P. *The Papers of Thomas Jefferson*. New Jersey: Princeton University Press, 1950 – ongoing.

Braden, Bruce. *"Ye Will Say I am No Christian": The Thomas Jefferson / John Adams Correspondence on Religion, Morals, and Values*. Amherst, NY: Prometheus Books, 2006.

Brandes, Georg. *Voltaire*. 2 vols. Trans. Otto Kruger and Pierce Butler. New York: Albert & Charles Boni, 1930.

Cappon, Lester. *The Adams–Jefferson Letters: The Complete Correspondence between Thomas Jefferson and Abigail and John Adams*. Chapel Hill, NC: University of North Carolina Press, 1987.

Church, Forrest. *The Jefferson Bible: The Life and Morals of Jesus of Nazareth*. 1904. Reprint, Boston: Beacon Press, 1989.

Collins, J. Churton. *Voltaire, Montesquieu and Rousseau in England*. London: Eveleigh Nash, Fawside House, 1908.

Cronk, Nicholas. *The Cambridge Companion to Voltaire*. Cambridge, UK: Cambridge University Press, 2009.

Condorcet. *Vie de Voltaire*. Paris: Quai Voltaire, 1994.

Darnton, Robert. *The Forbidden Best-Sellers of Pre-Revolutionary France*. New York: W. W. Norton & Company, 1996.

———. *George Washington's False Teeth: An Unconventional Guide to the Eighteenth Century*. New York: W. W. Norton & Company, 2003.

De Beer, Gavin and André-Michel Rousseau. *Voltaire's British Visitors*. SVEC 49. Oxford: Voltaire Foundation, 1967.

Diderot. *Correspondance*. Vol. 5. Paris: Robert Laffont, 1997.

Durant, Will. *The Story of Philosophy: The Lives and Opinions of the Greater Philosophers.* New York: Simon and Schuster, 1953.

Ferguson, Robert A. *The American Enlightenment, 1750–1820.* Cambridge, MA: Harvard University Press, 1997.

Franklin, Benjamin. *The Autobiography and Other Writings.* New York: Signet Classic, 1961.

Frédéric II, roi de Prusse. *Œuvres philosophiques.* Paris: Librairie Arthème Fayard, 1985.

Gay, Peter. *Deism: An Anthology.* Princeton, NJ: Van Nostrand Company, 1968.

———. *The Enlightenment: An Interpretation, The Rise of Modern Paganism.* New York: W. W. Norton & Company, 1995.

———. *Voltaire's Politics: The Poet as Realist.* New Haven, CT: Yale University Press, 1988.

Glassman, Bernard. *Protean Prejudice: Anti-Semitism in England's Age of Reason.* Atlanta, GA: Scholars Press, 1998.

Goldsmith, Oliver. *Voltaire: Studies by Oliver Goldsmith and Victor Hugo.* Emmaus, PA: Rodale Press, 1954.

Goulemot, Jean. *Inventaire Voltaire.* Paris: Editions Gallimard, 1995.

Guiragossian, Diana. *Voltaire's Facéties.* Geneva: Librairie Droz, 1963.

Holmes, David L. *The Faiths of the Founding Fathers.* Oxford: Oxford University Press, 2006.

Howarth, W. D., Henri M. Peyre, and John Cruickshank. *French Literature from 1600 to the Present.* London: Methuen & Co., 1974.

Jacoby, Susan. *Freethinkers: A History of American Secularism.* New York: Henry Holt and Company, 2004.

Jones, Howard Mumford. *America and French Culture: 1750–1848.* Chapel Hill, NC: University of North Carolina Press, 1927.

Kelly, J. N. D. *The Oxford Dictionary of Popes.* Oxford: Oxford University Press, 1986.

Koch, Adrienne. *The American Enlightenment: The Shaping of the American Experiment and a Free Society.* New York: George Braziller, 1965.

Kramnick, Isaac. *The Portable Enlightenment Reader.* New York: Penguin Books, 1995.

Lanson, Gustave. *Voltaire.* Trans. by Robert A. Wagoner. New York: John Wiley & Sons, 1966.

Loewen, James W. *Lies My Teacher Told Me: Everything Your American History Textbook Got Wrong.* New York: Simon & Schuster, 2007.

Magnan, André. *Dossier Voltaire en Prusse 1750–1753. SVEC* 244. Oxford: Voltaire Foundation, 1986.

Mason, Haydn. *Voltaire, A Biography.* London: Granada Publishing, 1981.

Masseau, Didier. *Les ennemis des philosophes, L'antiphilosophie au temps des Lumières.* Paris: Bibliothèque Albin Michel, 2000.

May, Henry F. *The Enlightenment in America.* New York: Oxford University Press, 1976.

Mercier, Louis-Sébastien. *Le tableau de Paris.* Paris: La Découverte/Poche, 2006.

Mervaud, Christiane. *Voltaire et Frédéric II: une dramaturgie des lumières 1736–1778. SVEC* 234. Oxford, Voltaire Foundation, 1985.

Mitford, Nancy. *Frederick the Great*. New York: E. P. Dutton, 1970.

————. *Voltaire in Love*. London: Hamish Hamilton, 1957.

Morgan, Edmund S. *The Birth of the Republic 1763–1789*. Chicago: University of Chicago Press, 1956.

Noyes, Alfred. *Voltaire*. London: Faber and Faber, 1936.

Paine, Thomas. *Collected Writings*. New York: The Library of America, 1995.

Pearson, Roger. *Voltaire Almighty: A Life in Pursuit of Freedom*. London: Bloomsbury, 2005.

Pharand, Michel W. *Bernard Shaw and the French*. Gainesville, FL: University Press of Florida, 2000.

Pomeau, René. *La Religion de Voltaire*. Paris: Librairie Nizet, 1974.

Pomeau, René, and Christiane Mervaud, eds. *Voltaire en son temps*. 5 vols. Oxford: Voltaire Foundation, 1985–1994.

Porset, Charles. *Voltaire humaniste*. Paris: Editions Maçonniques de France, 2003.

Riley, Woodbridge. *American Philosophy, The Early Schools*. New York: Dodd, Mead & Company, 1907. Reprint, London: Forgotten Books, 2012.

Robertson, John M. *A Short History of Freethought: Ancient and Modern*. 2 vols. London: Watts & Co., 1915.

Sareil, Jean. *Voltaire et les grandes*. Geneva: Librairie Droz, 1978.

Schiff, Stacy. *A Great Improvisation: Franklin, France, and the Birth of America*. New York: Henry Holt and Company, 2005.

Schwarzbach, Bertram E. *Voltaire's Old Testament Criticism*. Paris: Librairie Droz, 1971.

————. *Voltaire et les juifs : bilan et plaidoyer. SVEC 358*, Oxford : Voltaire Foundation, 1997.

Simon, Edith. *The Making of Frederick the Great*. London: Cassell, 1963.

Smith, Preserved. *The Enlightenment 1687–1776*. New York: Collier Books, 1966.

Spurlin, Paul Merrill. *The French Enlightenment in America: Essays on the Times of the Founding Fathers*. Athens, GA: University of Georgia Press, 1984.

Studies on Voltaire and the Eighteenth Century (SVEC). Oxford: Voltaire Foundation, 1955–(ongoing).

Tallentyre, S. G. *The Life of Voltaire*. 1907. New York: Loring & Mussey, 1930.

Torrey, Norman L. *The Spirit of Voltaire*. New York: Columbia University Press, 1938.

Trollope, Frances. *Domestic Manners of the Americans*. London: Whittaker, Treacher, & Co., 1832. Reprint, New York: Dover, 2003.

Trousson, Raymond. *Voltaire: Mémoire de la critique, 1778–1878*. Paris: Pups, 2008.

————. *Visages de Voltaire (XVIII–XIX siècles)*. Paris: Honoré Champion, 2001.

Voltaire. *Essai sur les mœurs et l'esprit des nations et sur les principaux faits de l'histoire depuis Charlemagne jusqu'à Louis XIII*. 2 vols. Paris: Bordas, Classiques Garnier, 1990.

————. *God and Human Beings*. Trans. Michael Shreve. Amherst, NY: Prometheus Books, 2010.

————. *Micromégas, and Other Short Fictions*. Trans. Theo Cuffe. New York: Penguin Books, 2002.

————. *Philosophical Dictionary*. Ed. and trans. Theodore Besterman. New York: Penguin Books, 1972.

————. *A Treatise on Toleration, and Other Essays.* Trans. Joseph McCabe. Amherst, NY: Prometheus Books, 1994.

Wertenbaker, Thomas. *The Golden Age of Colonial Culture.* Ithaca, NY: Cornell University Press, 1975.

Williams, David, ed. *Voltaire, Political Writings.* Cambridge, UK: Cambridge University Press, 1994.

ABOUT THE TRANSLATOR
AND EDITOR

G. K. NOYER is a freelance writer and translator, born in Michigan, where she did copywriting and production work for the local PBS affiliate and radio before moving to France. She has written scripts in French for several television series, and translated others into English, along with translating plays, websites, and historical documents for museums. She is currently developing a feature-film script on Voltaire and his journey to the Enlightenment battle for freedom of beliefs, as well as a feature-length comedy inspired by one of his lesser-known works. Some of the findings in the introduction were previously presented at a Paris-Sorbonne University conference on Voltaire in 2014.